ESSAYS ON STRATEGY

ESSAYS
ON
STRATEGY

_____ XI _____

Edited by
JOHN N. PETRIE

1994
National Defense University Press
Washington, DC

National Defense University Press Publications

To increase general knowledge and inform discussion, NDU Press publishes monographs, proceedings of University-sponsored symposia, and books relating to US national security, especially to issues of joint, combined, or coalition warfare, peacekeeping operations, and national strategy. The Press occasionally publishes out-of-print defense classics, historical works, and other especially timely or distinguished writing on national security.

NDU Press publications are sold by the US Government Printing Office. For ordering information, call (202) 783-3238 or write to the Superintendent of Documents, US Government Printing Office, Washington, DC 20402.

First Printing, April 1994

CONTENTS

Part II:
External Strategic Challenges

FOREWORD

WITH THIS VOLUME, THE *ESSAYS ON STRATEGY* SERIES MOVES into its second decade of assessing major strategic issues. As always, the essays run the gamut from the classic strategic challenges confronting every generation of defense leaders, to the pressing problems of the moment.

The first essay, for example, returns to the structural issues that the Goldwater-Nichols Department of Defense reorganization legislation addressed, concluding that the momentum for change should be carried even further—toward the establishment of a General Staff. The next essay examines one of the most important problems of the moment—peacekeeping—and the UN Secretary-General's controversial proposals in this area. The third essay opens the history books on the American Civil War to shed light on another current topic, joint operations. The remaining eight essays address coalition warfare, strategic mobility, the conventional wisdom of attacking electrical power, the conflict in Bosnia, Islamic resurgence, regional stability, counterdrug operations, and the U.S. military space program—something for nearly everyone interested in the strategic issues for American defense policy in the mid-1990s.

Again, as in past volumes in this series, the essays are distinguished not merely by their variety, but by the cogent analysis, imagination, and sound judgment demanded of the students in our senior military colleges.

PAUL G. CERJAN
Lieutenant General, U.S. Army
President, National Defense
University

SUMMARY:
STRATEGIC CHALLENGES

WHEN PEN WENT TO PAPER FOR THE ESSAYS IN THIS VOLUME, THE world had become a new place for its authors. In 1986 the Goldwater-Nichols Act changed the organization and culture of the U.S. armed forces. The fall of the Berlin Wall, the international consensus that made the Gulf War's victorious coalition possible, the dismemberment of the Soviet Union, the ongoing "right-sizing" of the force, and the unprecedented influence of the United Nations changed almost every aspect of the strategic environment. U.S. policy, and the strategy to implement it, need to adjust to the emerging reality.

All of the assumptions that guided the professional careers of these writers during the Cold War need revalidation. Our success in that "war" created strategic challenges at least as imposing as the ones they replaced. The first post-Cold War Administration brought a new vision reflected in reordered national priorities and a reorganized Office of the Secretary of Defense.

The advice Alice got from the Cheshire Cat is still relevant. We must decide where we are going before we can choose the correct path. The questions asked in these pages are valid. The path we choose will determine which answers are correct and how they should be prioritized.

From the organization and structure of our forces to the influence of the demise of the Soviet Union on specific programs, strategic challenges are addressed by intellectually courageous and forward looking professionals in this volume. Each author engages an issue whose strategic aspects must be addressed now.

Strategic questions that must be answered inside the U.S. Government abound. Some also have important international implications. The command, organization, and composition of national and multinational forces; continuing shortfalls in strategic lift and tactical mobility; and some assumptions dispelled by in-depth analysis of Gulf War experience are addressed in the first part of this work. Part II deals with strategic problems presented by external forces that demand solutions. Many of these were unleashed as the international order began to lose its balance in December 1991. Others were already with us and passed into the new world order unsolved and inadequately addressed.

Today's security environment is full of similarities to that of the past. But today's environment is—at the same time—fundamentally different. What we once knew as the threat is now merely risk. Matters with global implications now compete for the same attention and resources as previously less significant regional issues. The United States must prioritize and meet these challenges or our superpower status will die the death of a thousand cuts.

The work begins with a review of the Joint Chiefs of Staff's composition and organization; and how that structure affects the credibility of their decisionmaking. Pete Chiarelli provides a thought-provoking and controversial look at the current arrangement. He argues that "dual hatting" our principal military advisors as Service Chiefs asks them to serve two masters. His conclusion is that Goldwater-Nichols didn't go far enough. A General Staff is the proposed solution. This debate is not new—nor, apparently, is it over.

Bill Hoffman takes a look at the pros and cons of Boutros-Ghali's Agenda for Peace—and its implications for the United States. He presents a broad range of issues that require thorough examination and will likely fuel debates among strategists and policymakers for the rest of the decade.

A fascinating examination of two joint campaigns conducted before the authors of the Goldwater-Nichols Act were born is presented by Scott Stucky. Looking at the War Between the States, he proves that some joint issues will not be solved by legislation. Only professionalism can keep them on track. Stucky shows how command structure, personalities, technology, and innovation all played key roles in our early joint campaigns.

Terry Pudas expands Stucky's theme into the multinational environment. Writing for the future U.S. Commander at any echelon of a multinational coalition, Pudas examines the types, characteristics, and requirements of coalition warfare, and offers some ideas on how to prepare to do it better.

Looking at our greatest coalition success since World War II, Scott Conrad and Thomas Griffith analyze force mobility and an aspect of targetting in *Desert Storm*. Conrad's ideas on the mobility of the force are insightful and should be read by every military strategist and campaign planner. The long-held assumption that the enemy's electrical supply and distribution systems are useful targets is dispelled by Thomas Griffith. He provides some compelling arguments to support his case.

Looking to external challenges, first Brett Barkey's timely examination of whether the United States should act in Bosnia raises important questions. Barkey provides us with a framework to bound the question and clarify decisionmaking. His analysis should not be ignored and his framework lends itself to broader use.

Comprehending security issues in the Middle East requires an understanding of Islam. Jon Ball explains that Islamic fundamentalism is not synonymous with terrorism. Fundamentalism is endemic to Muslim life. Ball describes the current environment in eminently logical fashion. He also analyzes the impact on incumbent governments of political activity across the spectrum of Islamic groups.

This essay lays out a plan for improving the ability of the United States to deal with Muslim states and factions in a more sensitive and useful manner.

Joe McBride does for counterinsurgency what Jon Ball did for Islam. McBride declares former policies "dead on arrival" in the new world order. He proposes an innovative strategic view based in more logical resource allocations and greater consistency in U.S. policy. Various models are examined and their usefulness explained. The essay identifies keys to victory and success; but major philosophical and bureaucratic changes will be required to take advantage of McBride's insights.

U.S. counterdrug policy is critiqued in William Dunn's contribution. Echoing McBride's call for reality testing of initiatives, his view of the future calls for better measures of effectiveness. By identifying the false assumptions of the current effort he builds a strong case for a new perspective and more balanced approach.

The final essay looks into the decisionmaking in past (Soviet) and present Russian space programs. Gregory Keethler argues that many of the right answers for our own program are counter-intuitive. The economies, or peace dividends, anticipated in the U.S. space program assume that the previous efforts were wholly anti-Soviet initiatives that we can scale back. The details of Keethler's analysis show that in many cases exactly the opposite is true.

The strategic imperatives we've understood—throughout our entire adult lives—directly engaged our "vital interests" with the threat of devastating military force of global reach. Will future imperatives be as clear? What questions must we ask ourselves in this new environment to act with confidence? The writers in this eleventh edition of *Essays on Strategy* begin to answer these questions. Before the United States can develop a useful strategy to take us into the future, we must find the best answers for these and many other questions.

JOHN N. PETRIE

ESSAYS ON STRATEGY

GOLDWATER-NICHOLS REVISITED:
Meaningful Defense Reorganization

PETER W. CHIARELLI

THE GOLDWATER-NICHOLS DEPARTMENT OF DEFENSE REORGanization Act of 1986 (Goldwater-Nichols) is frequently praised by civilian national security specialists and military leaders for correcting the organizational and structural deficiencies stemming from the National Security Act of 1947. Critics charge that prior to Goldwater-Nichols the Joint Chiefs of Staff (JCS) could not fulfill their responsibility to provide pragmatic and timely unified military advice to the "National Command Authorities" (the President, the National Security Council, and the Secretary of Defense). As a result, the NCA had to rely on civilian staffs for advice that professional military officers should have provided. Advocates of defense reform cited the conflict of

Lieutenant Colonel Peter W. Chiarelli, U.S. Army, was a student at the National War College when he wrote this essay, a Co-winner in the 1993 Chairman, Joint Chiefs of Staff, Strategy Essay Competition.

interest inherent in the dual responsibilities of the Service Chiefs. They also charged that the Service Chiefs did not have enough time to perform both roles, as head of their Service and member of the JCS.[1]

Goldwater-Nichols made the Chairman of the Joint Chiefs (CJCS) the principal military advisor to the NCA. No longer was the CJCS required to formally ask for, and receive, input from the Service Chiefs before answering a question from the NCA. Additionally, this major defense reorganization empowered the Commanders of Unified and Specified Commands (CINCs) and instituted a formalized joint officer personnel policy law (Title IV). The Joint Staff was enlarged and strengthened to support the expanded role of the Chairman and the CINCs. Incentives were legislated to force the Services to assign quality officers to joint duty assignments.

To the disappointment of supporters of radical reform, Goldwater-Nichols did not end dual-hatting, create a General Staff, and abolish the JCS. For traditionalists, reform cost the Service Chiefs and Staffs their preeminent role in defense policy formulation. They argue that Goldwater-Nichols reforms, and the leadership style and political power of General Colin Powell, "caused the Joint Chiefs of Staff as a corporate entity to be eclipsed by a new, all-powerful chairman."[2]

Both critics and supporters give Goldwater-Nichols credit for improving the operational synergy of the JCS and the NCA. The success of operations *Just Cause, Desert Shield*, and *Desert Storm* all support claims that the quality of joint operations has improved. Disagreement arises when the two sides review how the law has affected defense resourcing. The recent *Roles, Missions, and Functions of the Armed Forces of the United States* report (*R&M Report*)—required every 3 years by Goldwater-Nichols—is cited as corroborating the arguments of people who insist that the 1986 legislation did not improve the quality of NCA's resource advice.

The end of the Cold War and concern about the national debt support a significant downsizing of the military. Conversely, regional instability, prompted by heightened nationalism, an increase in nontraditional missions for the military, and the potential resurgence of communist factions in Russia argue for maintaining a mobile, lethal, well-trained force. This smaller military must be able to project power worldwide to protect vital U.S. interests or to participate in peacekeeping and peace-enforcement operations. Finally, the CJCS and JCS must maintain credibility with President Clinton, the first president since Franklin D. Roosevelt not to have served in the military, and with a Congress that includes over a hundred new members.

Widespread bipartisan criticism of the *R&M Report* focuses on several questions. First, is resource advice from the JCS discredited because of the perceived conflict of interests between Title X and joint responsibilities? Second, did Goldwater-Nichols succeed in creating a joint culture capable of competing with Services cultures that promote Service parochialism? And finally, can the Joint Staff take the lead from the Service Staffs in tackling difficult resource and force structure issues? If the answer to any of these questions is no, the NCA will question the credibility of JCS advice and rely on civilian experts for advice that should come from military leaders.[3]

The 1986 Defense Reorganization Act did not go far enough in its reform of the JCS and Joint Staff, according to the study. Indeed, the perception is growing that "the Joint Chiefs took a pass on their own opportunity to restructure the Services for a new era."[4] As long as the Service Chiefs wear two hats—no matter how valid their advice—JCS recommendations on resources issues will be characterized as being geared to the lowest common level of assent. This study argues that the JCS should be abolished and replaced by a council of military and civilian leaders similar to what General Edward C. Meyer proposed in 1982.[5] Further, this study takes exception to Goldwater-Nichols's attempt to legislate joint culture through Title IV Joint Officer management policies and contends that the only way to create a joint culture capable of competing with the individual Service cultures is by replacing the Joint Staff with a General Staff.

HISTORY OF THE JCS AND REFORM ATTEMPTS

One of the great lessons of World War II was that joint warfare had forever replaced single service operations. In 1942, President Roosevelt informally established the JCS. When the war ended, a debate ensued on how best to organize the postwar military. "The Army favored, but the Navy opposed, a highly integrated system."[6] Those who feared that formalizing the JCS organization would lead to service unification warned that placing a military officer and his staff atop this establishment would jeopardize civilian control.

The National Security Act of 1947 terminated reorganization proposals that had as their centerpiece Service unification and institutionalized Roosevelt's informal JCS organization—albeit in a weaker form. General Meyer summarized the 1947 legislation this way:

> The act formally established the JCS as a council of advisors to the President and Secretary of Defense on military policy, organization, strategy and plans. At the same time, members of that council, the Service Chiefs, were told to retain their departmental responsibilities to organize, equip, and train their forces.[7]

General Meyer is describing the congressionally mandated conflict of interest known as dual-hatting. This arrangement, along with a small, weak, and transient Joint Staff were the most often cited deficiencies targeted by successive reform efforts in the 35 years after its creation in 1947.

Civilian and military leaders that included President Dwight D. Eisenhower, General Omar Bradley, and General Maxwell Taylor quickly went on record with criticisms of the JCS. President Eisenhower appointed the Rockefeller Committee to study defense reorganization. In 1957, their report cited the "excessive workload . . . difficult mix of functions and loyalties" and blamed "the system and not the members" for the poor quality of advice they (the JCS) provided to the NCA.[8]

Not even Eisenhower, the quintessential military and civilian leader, could force reform. It took unsuccessful wars (Korea and Vietnam), an aborted hostage rescue attempt (*Desert I*), and criticism from a serving Chairman of the Joint Chiefs of Staff to prompt the first major defense reorganization since 1947. When the House began defense reorganization hearings in 1982, the United States was well into the largest and most expensive peacetime defense build-up in the history of the republic.

FROM JONES AND MEYER TO GOLDWATER-NICHOLS

General David C. Jones was chief of Staff of the Air Force for 4 years and Chairman of the Joint Chiefs of Staff another 4 years. Three months before retiring he published proposals for JCS reform in an article, "Why the Joint Chiefs of Staff Must Change." As a minimum, Jones called for strengthening the role of the Chairman, limiting Service Staff involvement in the joint process, and broadening the training, experience, and rewards for joint duty.[9] Jones's reorganization plan was moderate but significant, considering that he was still in uniform and serving as CJCS.

One month later, General Edward C. Meyer, Chief of Staff of the Army, supported and expanded Jones's call for reform. Meyer's more radical proposals included abolishing the JCS and replacing it with a National Military Advisory Council (NMAC). The NMAC would be composed of a senior flag officer from each Service and one civilian, and would be chaired by the CJCS. Members of this Council would be distinguished four-star flag officers, retired or active serving their terminal assignment.[10]

Meyer thought it imperative to end dual-hatting and to free the Service Chiefs to focus on their Title X responsibilities. The composition of the NMAC preserved the preeminent role of military leaders when formulating advice for the NCA. Members of NMAC were not dependent on, and would never return to, their service. This stipulation preserved military participation on the Council while eliminating—as much as possible—the perceived conflict of interest inherent in dual-hatting. Meyer wrote that "individual members would be sought who had particular expertise in areas of special importance to the joint arena; e.g., strategic nuclear policy; unconventional as well as conventional warfare; and command, control and communications."[11]

Under Meyer's proposal the Office of the Secretary of Defense (OSD) would relinquish the leading role in policy and program development, but would assume a major role in policy and program implementation, which is more consistent with its wartime role. Meyer explained:

> Based on guidance from the Secretary of Defense, this body of military advisors (the NMAC) would examine military alternatives and recommend strategic scenarios to govern how the military departments are to organize, equip, and prepare their forces for war.[12]

Service Secretaries would lose some voice in policy formulation but would have a stronger position in developing current and future force capabilities. CINCs would present the needs of their command in a continuous dialogue with the NMAC, which would be more capable of initiating change. Meyer also believed this arrangement would allow the CINCs to exercise considerable influence on near-term programs.[13]

Jones's and Meyer's proposals prompted the Investigations Subcommittee of the House Committee on Armed Services (HASC) to open hearings in April 1982, entitled "Reorganization Proposals for the Joint Chiefs of Staff." Countless civilian and military witnesses testified before the committee over four years and three Congresses (97th, 98th, and 99th). The Senate Armed Services Committee (SASC) began parallel hearings in 1985.

The testimony reveals that service affiliation was the most reliable predictor of support for reform. Not unlike the debate over unification after World War II, Army witnesses were more likely than Navy representatives to be advocates of reform. The testimony of former Chairman of the Joint Chiefs of Staff, Admiral Thomas H. Moorer—though extreme—is representative of the Navy's position:

> I cannot help but note that, just as surely as the swallows return to Capistrano, the studies and recommendations concerning the Joint Chiefs of Staff crop up at periodic intervals. . . . This makes about as much sense as reorganizing Congress or the Supreme Court to stop disagreements. . . . Everyone fancies himself a field marshal.[14]

The Reagan administration and Secretary of Defense Caspar Weinberger supported the status quo. Independent reports commissioned to study defense organization were almost unanimous in their call for JCS reform. The

Georgetown University Center for Strategic and International Studies (CSIS) published a report in February 1985 that nearly mirrored Jones's proposals.[15]

In addition to supporting JCS reform, the CSIS report specified that roles and missions among the Services were both underfunded (for example, strategic sealift and airlift) and inefficient (for example, close air support and tactical airlift). The working group avoided recommending shifts in roles and missions for two reasons. First, it was their judgment that roles and missions problems were the result of a weak JCS. They hoped that, if their recommendations on JCS organization were adopted, the Chairman, Joint Staff, and CINCs "would be in a position to review and act on the roles and missions issues." Second, the working group wanted to avoid the "intense political controversy that such proposals inevitably generate."[16]

Publication of the CSIS report and hearings in the Senate increased the momentum for reform in the face of continued administration opposition and Jones's and Meyer's retirement. In the House, Rep. Ike Skelton (D-MO) introduced H.R. 2314 which paralleled Meyer's proposal. Rep. Skelton's Senior Defense Staff Member and drafter of the legislation, Archie D. Barrett, stated:

> General Meyer's proposal for JCS reform was very similar to recommendations made by General Maxwell Taylor. In fact, Rep. Skelton sent me to Taylor's apartment to get his thoughts before drafting the legislation (H.R. 2314). Skelton believed in H.R. 2314. Its introduction was a clear signal to the military that Congress was serious about reform.[17]

In the SASC, a staff study published in October 1985 examined problems surrounding the Department of Defense (DOD) organizational structure and decision-making procedures. Directed by James R. Locher III, the group recommended reform similar in magnitude to that in the Skelton-sponsored bill.[18]

The introduction of H.R. 2314 and the SASC study signaled that some type of JCS reform was inevitable. The Services mobilized their considerable political power in an effort to minimize the change. Their strategy included restating an old and powerful argument from the postwar unification debates. Specifically, military witnesses testified that strengthening the position of the Chairman would somehow threaten civilian control of the military—the "man on a white horse" argument.

Most civilian witnesses discounted this concern. The argument of John Kester, former Special Assistant to the Secretary of Defense, is representative. He said:

> The idea of saying we have to play off the individual Services against each other to maintain civilian control . . . is not a good idea and, if it ever was a good idea, it certainly is an outdated one.[19]

Outdated or not, it proved an effective tactic for the Services to limit change.

The result of the debate was Public Law 99–433, the Goldwater-Nichols Department of Defense Reorganization Act of 1986. Its most important provisions for this study are:

• (Title I) Revises and clarifies DOD's operational chain of command and JCS functions and responsibilities . . . to provide for more efficient use of defense resources.

• (Title II) Assigns the Chairman of the JCS the role of chief military advisor, including responsibilities currently assigned to the JCS collectively, establishes the position of Vice Chairman, and revises Joint Staff duties and selection procedures.

• (Title IV) Establishes a joint officer specialty occupational category and personnel policies to provide incentives to attract officers to joint duty assignment.[20]

The legislation did not abolish the JCS, create a National Military Advisory Council or a General Staff, or end dual-hatting. Goldwater-Nichols did make the CJCS the principal military advisor to the Secretary of Defense and the President. Title I strengthened the CINCs and their role as commander of all the forces—regardless of the Service-assigned to their command. And finally, Title IV attempted to empower the Joint Staff and Headquarters Staffs of the Unified and Specified Commands through provisions intended to improve the quality of officers assigned to joint duty.

ENVIRONMENTS GENERATING DEFENSE REFORM

Of the several attempts to bring about defense reorganization since World War II, only two were successful. The political, economic, and military environments of the day supported defense reform.

1947 Army-Navy Compromise Plan

In January 1947, the Army-Navy Compromise Plan (Norstad-Sherman) fell short of the service integration predicted by many after World War II. The U.S. military mobilized from little more than a cadre force in the interwar years to the largest and most powerful military machine in history. It experienced operational success in every theater. However, many others argued that inter-theater, intra-theater, and intra-Service disputes had prolonged the war and cost lives (for example, Nimitz vs. MacArthur, Pacific vs. Europe, and Navy vs. Army). The most crucial military lesson learned concerned the prominence of joint operations. In the words of Eisenhower, "separate ground, sea, and air warfare is gone forever" and the Army–Navy Compromise Plan embodied "service systems of an era that is no more."[21]

After World War II, the United States was forced to abandon isolationism and assume a role as one of the world's two superpowers. Concurrently, the military "melted down" from wartime force structure levels, and conversion preoccupied most defense industries. Finally, there was considerable pressure to cut the defense budget to fund civilian programs neglected during the war. As a result, reliance on cheaper strategic nuclear weapons over conventional forces increased.

The 1947 Army–Navy Compromise Plan created little more than a loose confederation among the Services. Rather than integrate, the Air Force became a separate Service, which further complicated attempts to institutionalize joint warfare. The 1947 legislation was amended in 1949, 1953, and 1958 to strengthen the authority of the Secretary of Defense and increase the size of his staff. Between 1958 and Goldwater-Nichols in 1986, the only significant change was in 1978 when the Commandant of the Marine Corps was made a full member of the JCS. The pressure to preserve Service autonomy squelched all attempts at reform before Jones and Meyer published their proposals.[22]

Goldwater-Nichols

Throughout the 4 years of hearings leading to Goldwater-Nichols, operational failures in Vietnam, *Desert I*, and to some extent Grenada were seen as supporting reform. While the United States "won" in Grenada, the lack of progress in executing joint operations caused serious concern. Inadequate joint doctrine, equipment interface problems, and higher casualties than thought necessary led many within the military to question the effectiveness of joint operations.

The Services' added force structure—i.e., the 600-ship Navy—and their roles and missions became less clearly defined. The Marine Corps, for example, felt threatened when the Army added five light infantry divisions. The buildup and increased reliance on high-technology weaponry caused a boom in defense industries. However, a growing deficit and defense procurement scandals such as $640-toilet seats prompted warnings that the defense budget was out of control.

Listening to military leaders today, it is hard to believe they ever opposed JCS reorganization. Privately they might voice concern about certain specifics of the legislation, but publicly they proclaim Goldwater-Nichols a success. When the issue of further reform is raised, they point with pride at recent operational successes and state, "If it's not broken, don't fix it." Joint operational successes in Panama, the Persian Gulf (traditional), and initially in Somalia (nontraditional) support their argument that the U.S. military works and that jointness has improved.

Post–Cold War Period
With the disintegration of the Soviet Union and freedom for East European states, the Cold War ended. The post-Cold War world—void of bipolar competition—is initially more unstable. Nationalism and ethnic conflict is on the rise. Peacekeeping, peace-enforcement, and humanitarian relief are the most likely military missions in the post-Cold War world. In the 1993 *R&M Report*, the Chairman validated these missions by assigning an expanded U.S. Atlantic Command (USLANTCOM) the "principal responsibility for support to United Nations peacekeeping operations and training units for that purpose."[23]

All agree that the force must and should shrink. For over 2 years the services have been downsizing to meet "Base Force" levels by 1995—recommended by the CJCS and adopted by the Bush Administration. Reaching "Base Force" levels meant cutting 6 of 18 active Army Divisions.

Additional budget savings proposed by the Clinton administration will mean more trimming.

Recent reports indicate the Clinton budget will require $128 billion in cuts over the next five years. The administration is conducting a "bottom-up review" to identify specific force structure reductions to meet this target. The Defense Budget Project recently released a report recommending even greater reductions. This independent research organization proposes:

> Cutting the size of the armed forces to 1.2 million uniformed personnel by 1997, 200,000 fewer than Aspin's plan—and 400,000 fewer than what the Bush administration had planned. . . . This report was prepared under the supervision of Gordon Adams, who since has left this nonprofit organization to accept a top-level position in Clinton's OMB [Office of Management and Budget].[24]

Whether it is "Base Force," $128 billion over 5 years, or something in between, this downsizing promises to rival the defense reductions after World War II.

Many defense industries have begun the difficult and often impossible process of conversion to nondefense work. The Clinton administration recently proposed a $22 billion federal program to help individuals and locales make this transition. Communities and companies remaining in, or depending on, the defense business are experiencing severe cutbacks or uncertainty over the future.

Deficit reduction became a crusade when Ross Perot, entering the 1992 presidential campaign, made it the keystone of his economic program. According to recent studies, the American public is willing to pay higher taxes and slice spending to cut the budget deficit. Furthermore, national defense is seen as a nondomestic item that merits deep cuts. Polls indicate 63 percent of the public wants to cut the national defense budget by 17 percent.[25] Cuts of this magnitude are greater than even those proposed in President Clinton's budget.

TABLE 1: ENVIRONMENT FOR REFORM

Indicator	1947 (Norstad-Sherman)	1986 (Goldwater-Nichols)	1993 (Post-Cold War)
Defense budget	↓	↑	↓
Industrial base	↓	↑	↓
Force structure	↓	↑	↓
Operational success	↑	↓	↑
Operational advice	↓	↓	↑
Resource advice	↓	↓	↓

↑ = increasing/growing/considered adequate
↓ = decreasing/shrinking/considered inadequate

Thus, despite the military's operational successes since the 1986 JCS reorganization (not unlike 1947) other important indicators have created a difficult environment for defense planners. Table 1 compares the environment for reform in 1947, 1986, and 1993. Although it fell short of Service integration, the 1947 defense reorganization was radical compared to Goldwater-Nichols. The preceding discussion and table 1 demonstrate that the environment today more closely resembles 1947 than 1986. This kind of environment puts tremendous pressure on the military leadership to "address difficult questions being asked by

Congress and the American people about their Armed Forces."[26]   If the President, the Congress, and voters perceive that the CJCS cannot provide those explanations, they seek answers elsewhere.

Few, if any, senior military leaders advocate additional JCS reform because they think Goldwater-Nichols fixed what needed to be fixed. In a 1993 letter to the author, the CJCS stated: "I am confident that without the power of legislation (Goldwater-Nichols), we would not have seen the progress made over the last 6 years. Military advice is no longer discredited."[27]

Nevertheless, Goldwater-Nichols—like the 1947 legislation establishing the JCS—was a compromise. Both stopped short of instituting major proposals made by many military and civilian leaders.

WHAT GOLDWATER-NICHOLS CHANGED

Archie Barrett has been a House Armed Services Committee (HASC) Professional Staff Member for over a decade. He is recognized as one of a handful of principal architects of Goldwater-Nichols. Asked to rate the effectiveness of the 1986 law, he evaluates each title separately. He rated those changes directed at improving operational matters "most effective." Barrett stated, "the CINCs have been given command of all the forces, regardless of Service, assigned to their command. . . . The quality of operational plans is greatly improved."[28] Barrett is not alone in this appraisal. Commenting on the effectiveness of the 1986 reorganization, General Gordon R. Sullivan, emphasized successful operational employments of U.S. forces as proof that Goldwater-Nichols is a success.[29] It is hard not to argue that changes were for the better when comparing the performance of the U.S. forces in operations *Just Cause* and *Desert Storm* with operations *Provide Comfort* to Vietnam, Desert I, and Grenada.

The legislation prohibits the CJCS from exercising "military command over the Joint Chiefs of Staff or any of the armed forces."[30] That is, he was not inserted in the chain of command between the President and the CINCs. Nevertheless, two features of Goldwater-Nichols have enabled the Chairman to assert considerable authority in operational matters.

The law designates the CJCS as the principal military advisor to the NCA. He is encouraged—but not required—to seek the advice of the Service Chiefs and the CINCs. If the Chiefs are not unanimous in their opinion, "the Chairman shall, *as he considers appropriate*, inform the President, the National Security Council, or the Secretary of Defense, as the case may be, of the range of military advice and opinion with respect to that matter" [emphasis added].[31] Furthermore, the President may—as Reagan and Bush did—"direct that communications between the President or the Secretary of Defense and the commanders of the unified and specified combatant commands be transmitted through the Chairman of the Joint Chiefs of Staff."[32]

All the civilian experts and military leaders interviewed for this study were convinced that the position of the Chairman is strengthened by Goldwater-Nichols. None, however, could state with certainty whether the legislation has improved the quality of advice provided the NCA. The general consensus, however, is that it has. Barrett said he "would be surprised if advice is not better—at least in the area of operations." He was certain "Goldwater-Nichols accomplished the goal of ensuring advice is provided faster, quicker."[33]

Testifying before the HASC in 1982, John Kester pointed out that the JCS:

> Frequently arrive with their advice after the train has left the station. Events in the real world do not wait for the present

JCS system which is four layers of staffing to reach a compromise acceptable to each of the four Services.[34]

Barrett pointed out that because the Chairman has more autonomy, he no longer has to take the time to gather input from the Services and develop a corporate position.

Barrett credits defense reorganization and the Chairman for recent operational improvements but is unsure if structural changes or the persona of General Colin Powell accomplished these results. Barrett said that not since General Maxwell Taylor has there been a more powerful and highly regarded Chairman.[35]

The military leaders interviewed generally agreed with Barrett. They are justifiably proud of General Powell, the performance of the military since Goldwater-Nichols, and the progress their Services have made in developing and prosecuting joint doctrine and operations. Nevertheless, some voiced concern that power may have shifted too far in the direction of the Chairman and the Joint Staff.

Goldwater-Nichols increased the size of the Joint Staff, gave it much more autonomy, and enhanced responsibility. However, the legislation specifies that "the Joint Staff shall not operate or be organized as an overall Armed Forces General Staff and shall have no executive authority."[36] One senior officer complained about the "Imperial Joint Staff" and the direct access the CINCs have to the NCA, Congress, and the Chairman without going through Service leadership and the Service staffs. He sensed a growing resistance from Service Staffs to the extended power of the Joint Staff and the CINCs, yet he discounted it as a "natural resistance to change."[37]

Resource Advice
Barrett was much less sanguine about the portions of the legislation designed to improve resource allocation advice.

My biggest disappointment is the Chairman's failure to be more involved in resource allocation. Resource allocation is what the Services do 90 percent of the time. We expected the Joint Staff to put together resource requirements from the CINCs and compare that list against the Service POMs. The Chairman does not have the power to modify Service POMs, however, he can use his position to recommend changes to the Secretary of Defense. That has not happened. It is the name of the game in peacetime. I think it is time we went to a single Joint POM.[38]

General Meyer's 1982 reorganization proposal was based in part on the inability of the JCS to accomplish a horizontal, rather than vertical, examination of resource issues: "Simply put, the basic issue of aligning Service programming and expenditures to the requirements of unified command planning has been inadequately treated."[39]

In a recent interview, General Meyer used reports that the Air Force would recommend a delay in C-17 procurement to satisfy part of its most recent budget cut as proof that Goldwater-Nichols did not go far enough.[40] He believes a recommendation to delay or scale back this program should not be the Air Force's alone. Meyer points out that the C-17 project began over 10 years ago when he was Army Chief of Staff. "The C-17 is being developed by, not for, the Air Force."[41]

General McPeak supported and broadened General Meyer's point:

There may be a conflict in programmatic issues. Today the Services rely on each other. If the Navy cuts increased sealift out of their budget, I have a problem because I can't get everything the Air Force needs to the war. The Air Force relies on sealift to move much of its equipment. If I give up on the C-17, the Army has a problem. I could get along without the C-17, but the Army can't.[42]

Lieutenant General Ehlert, Deputy Chief of Staff for Plans, Policies, and Operations, U.S. Marine Corps, voiced concern about the expanded role the CINCs and their staffs play—contrasted to a reduced role for the Service staffs—in POM formulation. "I worry that when you serve on a CINC's staff you don't have a long-rang view—you are more concerned about short-term, day-to-day problems that can quickly become a crisis."[43] General McPeak voiced similar concerns when he said: "It is not clear that operational POM input from the CINCs is working . . . some joint headquarters are thinly veiled Service headquarters."[44]

Though central to the JCS reform argument in 1986, Goldwater-Nichols did not end dual-hatting. The Service Chiefs maintained Title X responsibility for organizing, training, and equipping their Service and their position as "military advisors to the President, the National Security Council, and the Secretary of Defense." As previously mentioned, the law specifies that the Chairman shall, as he considers it appropriate, consult with and seek the advice of the Service Chiefs and CINCs. It further specifies that Service Chiefs may submit to the Chairman "advice or an opinion in disagreement with, or advice or an opinion in addition to, the advice presented by the Chairman to" the NCA. Title II requires the Chiefs—individually or collectively—to provide advice "on a particular matter" when asked by the NCA.[45]

The Roles and Missions Review
Bipartisan criticism of recent *R&M Report* supports the concerns of Barrett and Meyer. This report met the Goldwater-Nichols requirement for a roles and missions review every three years, but Senator Nunn called for "a no-holds-barred, everything on the table review" to cut the "tremendous redundancy and duplication" in the military.[46] After being briefed on the *R&M Report*, Rep. Floyd D. Spence (R-SC), ranking Republican on the HASC, warned

that the Services "May have missed a chance to direct their own fate . . . efforts to further reduce defense spending may lead to a politically driven outcome that neither the military nor the nation can afford."[47] Even William J. Perry, Aspin's Deputy Secretary of Defense, said the report "was a good plan as far as it went, but it didn't go very far."[48]

If the Chairman, the CINCs, and the Joint Staff gained power as the result of Goldwater-Nichols, it came at the expense of the Service Chiefs and their staffs. The 1986 legislation redistributed a finite amount of power to influence defense policy decisions. The two Service Chiefs interviewed for this report were split over the question of their impact on defense policy since Goldwater-Nichols. General McPeak said, "The Service Chiefs are cut out of the process now. We are not present when the Chairman gives advice to the Secretary of Defense. General Powell asks us for our input and we give it to him—he looks for consensus."[49]

General Sullivan disagrees, saying the Chiefs are part of the process. "We meet and talk about the issues and provide our opinion to the Chairman." Sullivan specifically cited the 1993 *R&M Report* as proof that the system does not necessarily result in consensus on tough issues. "I think it is a good report. It asked the right question and I think the product is about right. Tough calls were made—especially for the Army."[50]

Testifying before the HASC, Robert W. Komer, former Under Secretary of Defense for Policy, characterized the JCS as a system with men of "high caliber" that works "poorly" because of systemic and institutional problems associated with dual-hatting. Komer provided the following specifics:

> The system is simply out of balance between service interests and joint interests. Because of the way it is set up there is a basic, built-in conflict of interest between the role of JCS members and the role of service chiefs. Indeed, it was

22

deliberately designed that way to protect parochial service interests even at the expense of the joint interests of the Nation, the President, the Congress, and the Department of Defense.

Komer went on to reinforce General Meyer's argument against dual-hatting:

The second major institutional failing is that no one man, I don't care how competent he is, can possibly perform adequately two full-time jobs. Naturally, as I believe most of the present Chiefs testified before you, the first role takes precedence. That means the second role, the role of providing joint advice, inevitably suffers.[51]

These arguments are central to critics of the 1993 *R&M Report* and provoke a similar reaction from military leaders today as in 1982. General Powell states in his memorandum forwarding the *R&M Report* to the Secretary of Defense: "Although I have consulted with the Joint Chiefs and combatant commanders in its development, this report presents my views and is not a consensus document."[52] He reiterated in a letter:

The Roles and Missions Report contains a number of recommendations that were not agreed upon by all the Services or by all the CINCs. I bear full responsibility for what is in the report and it is not intended to be a consensus document.[53]

Comments by General Sullivan support the Chairman. General Sullivan and LtGen Ehlert both cited the recommendation to designate U.S. Atlantic Command (USLANTCOM) the unified command and joint headquarters for CONUS-based forces as a decision that proves the report is not a consensus document. If implemented, Forces Command (FORSCOM), the specified command responsible for all Army forces stationed in the United

States, will relinquish its responsibilities to USLANTCOM. The report sums up this recommendation:

> While the Services would retain their Title X responsibilities, the training and deploying of CONUS-based forces as a joint team would be a new mission for this expanded CINC. Unification of the Armed Forces, which began in 1947, would at last be complete.[54]

Critics of the *R&M Report*, both before and after its release, use the question "Why four Air Forces?" as the centerpiece of their argument claiming inefficiencies and duplication in the military. Therefore, it is not surprising that the Chief of Staff of the Air Force has made the point that "aviation issues dominated the most recent roles and missions review" and "this caused him to be both more involved in the debate and more often in disagreement with the other Service Chiefs."[55]

General McPeak also insisted that "it is the Chairman's report—not anyone else's." Still, he seemed to break with the Chairman, General Sullivan, and other military leaders when he called it a "consensus report" and "at best tinkering at the margins." McPeak predicted that "since there is a new administration with a new set of assumptions, we—or someone—will soon be preparing a new report. I'm afraid the military may not take the lead in the next review," he warned.[56] The Air Force had more to win or lose than any of the other Services. The report looked at the possible consolidation of space and strategic commands, several air power issues (for example, continental air defense, theater air interdiction, and close air support), aircraft requirements, and theater air defense. All are Title X functions on which the Air Force would like to maintain, assume, or take the lead. Recommendations perceived as "consensus building" by General McPeak were undoubtedly viewed by the Chairman as what is needed "to maintain the maximum effectiveness of the Armed Forces."[57]

The issue is not whether there will be dissension when the JCS formulates resource advice; it is whether those disagreements translate into predictable advice owing to an inherent conflict of interest. Predictability—*or perceived predictability*—diminishes the utility of the advice to the civilian leadership in the NCA. Predictability was the issue in 1982 when Komer said, "The systemic inadequacies of the present system means [sic] that the civilian masters of the JCS are unable to get from it the kind of military inputs they really need and want."[58]

The current debate over the Chairman's *R&M Report* is proof that, at a minimum, Goldwater-Nichols did not erase the perception that the Chiefs cannot overcome parochialism when asked to provide resource advice. Now that the Chairman is the principal military advisor to the NCA, the issue of Service parochialism is important only if it causes the civilian leadership to question the Chairman's resource advice. Recently, when asked to evaluate whether General Powell's report should be interpreted as "stiffing" his call for a review of roles and missions, Nunn responded:

> No, I don't think the problem is Colin Powell. I think there are two Colin Powell reports. Phase one of the report really was what I think he believed and phase two *was what he compromised in order to get it through the chiefs.* So it's not a matter of one individual of Colin Powell [sic]. It's got to be every member of the chiefs [emphasis added].[59]

The Joint Staff

Prior to Goldwater-Nichols, the Joint Staff worked for both the Chairman and the Service Chiefs. The Services assigned some able officers and others less so. It was not an elite organization, and few officers wanted a single assignment on the Chairman's Staff—let alone more than one. The system was characterized as stifling initiative because Joint Staff officers were totally dependent on their own Services for assignment and promotion. Komer called the joint staff "a secretariat for reconciling Service views."[60]

Title IV instituted the "Joint Specialty Officer" (JSO) designation and several other provisions in an attempt to fix the Joint Staff and, over time, to create a joint culture. The prerequisites for JSO designation are graduation from a joint professional military education school (for example, the National War College) and completion of a full tour in a joint duty assignment.[61] Implementation legislation specified and approved a limited number of positions for designation as joint duty assignments. Goldwater-Nichols implemented two other provisions that supporters considered essential to improving the Joint Staff:

> 1.   . . . officers who are serving in, or have served in, joint duty assignment are expected as a group, to be promoted at a rate not less than the rate for all officers of the same armed force in the same grade and competitive category.

> 2.   An officer may not be selected for promotion to the grade of brigadier general or rear admiral (lower half) unless the officer has served in a joint duty assignment.[62]

General Powell gives Title IV credit for helping to make the Joint Staff "one of the best military staffs in the world." He considers joint education and assignment instrumental in improving the quality of officers assigned to the Joint Staff. Further, he states,

> The authority given to the Chairman to review promotion lists from a joint perspective has paid enormous dividends in enhancing jointness. I am confident that without the power of legislation, we would not have seen the progress made over the past 6 years.[63]

Everyone interviewed for this study agrees with General Powell on this issue and is convinced that Title IV provisions have improved the quality of the officers serving on the Joint Staff and their work. General Ehlert's comments were representative: "We [the Marine Corps] used to send officers who were retiring to work on the Joint Staff—not since Goldwater-Nichols. Now we send our sharpest folks and so do the other Services."[64] Nevertheless, the provision requiring completion of a joint duty assignment before promotion to flag officer will, if not amended, soon cause all the Services some potentially serious problems.

Congress enacted a number of temporary exemptions and waivers for use during the transition period to full implementation of Title IV. The two most important transitional waivers, "joint equivalency" and "serving-in," expire on 1 January 1994. Without these waivers "the current trend suggests that in 1994 nearly half the officers selected for brigadier general will not be qualified to serve in an Army position in their initial tour as a general officer. Instead, they must serve an initial two-year joint tour."[65] This is not just an Army problem. In fact, the Army is in the middle of the pack compared to the other Services. The only way to promote these officers will be to request a "Good of the Service" (GOS) waiver from the Secretary of Defense. If approved, the law requires that the officer's first assignment as a general be a two year joint tour. Unless Service cultures change, these officers will most likely fall behind joint qualified contemporaries who go to Service-specific operational assignments (for example, Assistant Division Commander).

This problem is exacerbated by the fact that the portion of the population given credit for JSO qualification includes officers exempt from joint duty based on "scientific/technical" waivers that do not expire (for example, civil engineers, chemical, military police, and public affairs officers). Therefore, a large majority of nominees needing a GOS waiver will be warfighters, for example, combat arms officers, pilots, and naval line offers.

In 1994, the Army projects 17 officers selected for general will require a GOS waiver with only 11 joint duty positions available for slating. This could mean in the worst case that the Army, and the other Services, will be forced to promote less qualified officers to flag rank. Thus, joint tour completion, not performance, could become the critical discriminator for promotion to flag officer. Army personnel managers predict that long-term solutions implemented in 1993 will not fix the problem until after the turn of the century.[66]

Until recently, the Services put this problem in the "too hard to solve box." Realization that the waivers would soon end prompted serious analysis to measure the full effect of Title IV provisions. This analysis showed that to reduce the number of GOS waivers requested in the out years, officers selected "below the zone" for major must be immediately slated into joint assignments. A finite number of joint positions and the reality that some young super-stars will fall from grace during follow-on Service staffs or in combat units make even this solution problematic. It is difficult, if not impossible, to predict which officers will be best qualified to be generals or admirals 10 years hence.

In addition, there are non-joint jobs—for example, operations billets within each Service culture that are considered *critical* assignments for any aspirant to flag officer. To date, the Services seem unwilling to fill these jobs with "second stringers" and force those with general officer potential into joint positions. Every military leader interviewed for this study complained that Title IV require-ments were particularly difficult for his Service.[67] All their arguments are convincing.

Supporters can claim that Title IV provisions have corrected serious defects in the Joint Staff system. All agree that high-quality officers are being assigned to joint billets and the quality of Joint Staff work has improved dramatically. If the intent of the legislation was to force officers to think joint duty important, Goldwater-Nichols is an unqualified success. For doubters of congressional intent, it will be made clear when transitional waivers expire. Many who thought they were competitive for promotion to flag rank may be passed over because they did not complete a joint assignment. When interviewed, Barrett left the impression that Congress would not be receptive to extending or renewing the transitional waivers.[68]

Nevertheless, there are concerns that Title IV may not be the best way to create a legitimate joint culture. Warfighters, the officers targeted by Title IV, have a natural aversion to serving on any staff. Nevertheless, a tour on a Service Staff is informally considered a prerequisite for anyone with high aspirations. Exposure to Service leadership can keep or help make these officers competitive for higher level command or selection to flag rank. The framers of Goldwater-Nichols were not willing to establish a General Staff with promotion authority; they chose instead to use Title IV incentives to stop high-quality pilots, combat arms, and line officers from avoiding joint duty. They wanted to create an environment where duty on the Joint Staff would be seen as analogous to duty on a Service Staff.

Title IV did not create a joint culture capable of attracting the military's best qualified officers to joint duty assignments. The finest officers do not compete for joint duty assignments; they go because the law requires them to. Once they finish their qualifying tour, they go back to their Service and the job that will keep them competitive for promotion. Furthermore, they generally believe their support for jointness to the detriment of their Service in a joint billet might cost them that all important, follow-on Service job.

During the Vietnam War, Congress accused the military of promoting "ticket punching." Officers were charged with managing their careers so as to serve only in assignments that supported promotion without regard to Service needs. Once assigned, they stayed only long enough to get their ticket punched before moving to the next carefully selected position. Congress cited Vietnam assignment policies as institutionalized "ticket punching."

Service in joint assignments should not be something officers are forced to do. If joint operations are indeed the future, joint duty should on its own merit attract the military's best and brightest. It is ironic that Congress has mandated "ticket punching" on the grounds that it is necessary to strengthen the Joint Staff.

Goldwater-Nichols is analogous to the Articles of the Confederation—each better than what it replaced but none that endowed the newly created organization with the authority needed to unify the parts. The Articles of the Confederation created a weak national government where citizens of individual states invested legitimacy in their state first and the confederation second. Goldwater-Nichols failed to go far enough in empowering the Chairman, the JCS, and the Joint Staff. The successor to Goldwater-Nichols must not legislate joint culture; it must ensure that jointness is legitimate.

The value of this analogy ends here. The sole purpose of the Services is to provide for the national defense of the United States, not constitutional protection to individuals or minorities. Funding, organization, and integration decisions must be made based on what is best for national defense, not on what is acceptable to each Service. Therefore, we must move beyond Goldwater-Nichols so that the critical defense decisions of the post–Cold War period support building the best military for the future.

MEANINGFUL JCS REFORM

The environment for reform today is similar to conditions after World War II (table 1). In 1947, the free world was challenged by a new threat; the United States was forced to choose between defense and spending cuts; the U.S. military was the best and largest in the world; and many communities were in the midst of shifting from a wartime to peacetime economy. Today, the world is increasingly unstable, the United States is struggling to cut a $4-trillion national debt; the U.S. military is the only force in the world capable of quickly projecting power; and communities are again trying to cope with the downsizing of many defense industries. Previous attempts to reform the defense establishment were designed to give credibility to the military advice produced by the system. Goldwater-Nichols states, "It is the intent of Congress . . . to improve the military advice provided to the President, the National Security Council, and the Secretary of Defense."[69] The 1986 legislation was intended to answer critics' charges that military advice, particularly when it involved allocation of resources, is ignored because it is thought to be the product of a committee. Making the Chairman the principal advisor to the NCA has not altered the perception that the "JCS system sacrifices the influences of the uniformed military as a whole in order to protect the interests of the separate military services."[70]

Meaningful reform must end dual-hatting. Asking a Service Chief who is required by law to organize, train, and equip his force to don his joint hat and to cut a program or personnel he deemed necessary when wearing his Service hat is unrealistic. Even when the Chiefs provide truly joint resource advice, the political leadership will often discount their recommendation. Dual-hatting is analogous to President Clinton's remaining Governor Clinton after moving into the oval office. If he continued to wear both hats,

Americans would undoubtedly question any of his decisions that seemed to favor interests in Arkansas.

National Military Advisory Council

General Meyer's proposal and bills introduced in the House and Senate in 1985 recommended abolishing the JCS and replacing it with a National Military Advisory Council (NMAC). Meyer believes Goldwater-Nichols did little to change the conditions that prompted his proposals. In fact, Meyer believes the creation of a NMAC is even more relevant today.

> In 1982 it was difficult for me to find the time to wear both hats. The Cold War and a bipolar world was less complicated than a world where the United States is the only superpower and there are many "hot spots." The bipolar world provided a framework with which to quickly and accurately evaluate conflicts and their impact on U.S. vital interests. Minus that framework, this process is much more complicated and time consuming for the JCS and the National Command Authority. This problem is exacerbated by the time and effort required to downsize the armed forces. Expert military advice is more critical because fewer members of Congress, the President and his advisors, served in the military.[71]

The Council would be made up of a distinguished four-star flag officer from each Service (not the current Service Chief), picked from the retired list or serving a final assignment before retirement. General Meyer did not discuss the specific qualifications for council membership. Possible prerequisites include Service as a CINC or on the Joint Staff. Former Service Chiefs also seem particularly well qualified for the Council. However, their membership could prompt accusations of parochialism—charges that the NMAC is nothing but a repackaged JCS.

In 1982 General Meyer included a civilian State Department representative as a full NMAC member. Today, he would expand what has become known as an interagency approach and add a second civilian, an economist. This emphasis on economics supports Secretary of Defense Aspin's view that the poor performance of the U.S. economy is one of the four principal threats facing the nation.[72] General Meyer is a trained economist, however, he feels few senior officers are schooled in economics to the degree required for high-level defense decisionmaking.[73] In addition, civilian representation facilitates the interagency perspective and coordination required for many of today's nontraditional missions. The NMAC would allow the Chiefs to focus totally on Title X responsibilities—organizing, training, and equipping their individual Services. They and their staffs could propose and lobby for initiatives designed to support the national military strategy. The NMAC, with input from the CINCs, would evaluate the proposal, prioritize it along with other defense initiatives, and formulate the final resource advice to the NCA. General Meyer added that "a recommendation from the NMAC would add credibility to the Chiefs' program or proposal."[74]

The major advantages of the NMAC over the current JCS system are threefold. First, the make-up of the Council is intended to end the perception that joint advice—especially resource advice—is invariably tempered by Service parochialism and ignores economic realities. Second, the NMAC maintains military expertise in the body charged with recommending cross-Service operational resource advice to the CJCS and civilian decisionmakers. And finally, the NMAC establishes a full-time Council whose members can focus on the formation, implementation, and resourcing of a viable national military strategy to protect U.S. interests in the post–Cold War world.

General Staff

Goldwater-Nichols establishes joint officer management policies designed to attract high-quality officers to the Joint Staff. Title IV was a compromise between the military and supporters of a General Staff. The principal argument against a General Staff has always been that it would threaten civilian control of the military. The German experience—especially Nazi Germany—was consistently raised as an example of a General Staff gone amuck. In the 4 years of Goldwater-Nichols hearings, successive historians pointed out that the Germans never had a General Staff. They emphasized that civilian control of the military is such a strong, consistent, and essential element of our culture, it would not be threatened if the United States moved to a General Staff.

Goldwater-Nichols attempts to create a joint culture capable of competing with established Service cultures without establishing a General Staff. There are indications that Title IV has failed in its attempt to legislate legitimacy.

First, the Services have had difficulty promoting JSOs "at a rate not less than the rate for all officers of the same armed force in the same rate and competitive category."[75] Furthermore, a more meaningful measure, given the intent of attracting the Services' best officers to joint duty, is what percentage of officers promoted below the zone (ahead of their contemporaries) are JSO qualified. In Army year-group 1971–76, 291 officers have been promoted below the zone. Of those officers, only 49 (17 percent) are joint qualified. In year-group 1971, the primary year-group for the 1995 Brigadier General board and the first to be constrained by the 1994 expiration of waivers, 20 officers have been promoted below the zone. Today, only 4 (20 percent) are joint qualified and would thus not require a GOS Waiver.[76] Table 2 shows how little progress the Services have made in getting officers joint qualified before their

*TABLE 2: OFFICERS REQUIRING JOINT DUTY WAIVERS,
ALL SERVICES, 1989–92*

Category/year	1989	1990	1991	1992
Promoted to 07, all services	131	120	107	114
Number requiring joint waiver[a]	62	57	57	54
Percentage requiring joint waiver[b]	47.3	47.5	53.2	47.3

Source: DCSPER Briefing Packet
a. Joint Equivalency Waiver + Currently Serving Waiver + GOS Waiver.
b. If Transitional Waivers did not exist, this is total percent requiring GOS Waiver.

promotion to flag rank. To date, experience indicates that Title IV without transitional waivers is unworkable. Second, Title IV did nothing to change the *perception* that officers serving on the Joint Staff who put jointness ahead of Service interests run the risk of Service retribution. Senior leaders have denied this is the case, but as long as this perception is widely held there will be an inherent bias in Joint Staff products. This is analogous to members of the President's staff who were born and live in Virginia feeling "we are first Virginians, and second, citizens of the republic."

Third, requiring JSO qualification before promotion to flag rank smacks of "ticket punching." If many more officers are competing for promotion to general officer than there are joint billets, competition for those slots, once transitional waivers expire, could create a new generation of sycophants like the fictitious Courtney Massingale.[77] This

TABLE 3: INSTITUTIONAL ROLES AND RELATIONSHIPS —TWO OPTIONS

Institution	*Goldwater-Nichols*	*NMAC/General Staff*
NCA (President and NSC)	■ Expect credible joint operational advice. ■ Rely on other than military advice when making resource decisions.	■ Expect credible military operational and resource advice. ■ Perception of Service conflict of interest diminished.
Secretary of Defense	■ Receives military advice from many sources. ■ Growing reliance on OSD for policy and program initiatives.	■ Confident that CJCS/NMAC will provide credible resource advice. ■ Relies on CJCS/NMAC for policy and program initiatives; relies on OSD for program implementation.
OSD	■ If JCS resource advice discredited, assumes preeminent roll in policy formulation, program initiatives and implementation.	■ Relinquishes leading role in policy and program development, assumes major role in policy and program implementation.
Service Secretaries	■ Influence policy/strategy.	■ Civilian oversight of Service Headquarters focused on Title X responsibilities.

Institution	Goldwater-Nichols	NMAC/General Staff
Chairman, Joint Chiefs of Staff	▪ Principal advisor to the NCA, quality staff provided by the Services.	▪ Supported fully to perform role as trusted military advisor to the NCA. ▪ Plays major roleshaping DOD and national debate over policy and program initiative. ▪ Influence national strategy debate, drive military strategy formulation.
National Military Advisory Council	—	▪ Gives credible,uninhibited joint advice to CJCS. ▪ Time to evaluate threats to U.S. interests and efficacy of "non-traditional" missions. ▪ Civilians provide balanced advice.
Joint/ General Staff	▪ Quality staff, dependent on parent Service for promotion and career enhancing jobs.	▪ Separate/parallel career path, personnel and promotion system. ▪ Prior Service experience. ▪ Separate and legitimate joint culture.

Institution	*Goldwater-Nichols*	*NMAC/General Staff*
Service Chiefs	▪ Dual-Hatted. ▪ Can make end run to Congress if in disagreement with CJCS.	▪ Single focus on Title X requirements. ▪ No longer dualhatted . . . no conflict of interests when advocating Service programs.
Service Staffs	▪ Preeminent staff for Service resource issues.	▪ Advocate for Service interests in keeping with Title X.
CINCs	▪ Major voice in recommending resources to support operational plans.	▪ Continual dialogue with NMAC operational and resource maters. ▪ Supported by staff empowered by separate and legitimate joint culture.

Source: Adapted from "Institutional Roles Under Three Options," in Gen. Edward C. Meyer, "The JCS—How Much Reform Is Needed?" *Armed Forces Journal International*, April 1982, 87.

prerequisite has improved the quality of officers serving on the Joint Staff, but these same officers must return to their Service for the jobs and exposure to stay competitive for senior leadership roles. You cannot move to the top of the Joint Staff—or any Service—by remaining on the Joint Staff.

The NMAC should be supported by a General Staff that is independent of all the services. It must be responsible for managing personnel and assignments and must be given the authority to evaluate performance and promote General Staff officers. This would allow the General Staff to attract the best officers from all the Services to a career path offering upward mobility (for example, promotions) and positions of responsibility comparable to those of the Services.

General Meyer did not propose the creation of a General Staff then, and he is unsure whether he would support it today. In 1982, he feared it would be viewed as creating a more powerful Chairman than politically acceptable. Today, he agrees that Title IV is not working as intended. Nevertheless, he is concerned that a General Staff would be manned by officers who, over time, would lose their warfighting skills.[78] This same objection was voiced during the Goldwater-Nichols hearings. Table 3 shows the changes in institutional roles if the NMAC and General Staff replaced the JCS and the Joint Staff.

The process the Services used to establish the Acquisition Corps is a good, albeit incomplete, model for creating a General Staff. Officers could volunteer or be requisitioned at different stages in their career. Some after successful lieutenant colonel/commander-level command, others after colonel/captain-level command, and a few after selection to flag rank. There would be two separate tracks: a Service track and a General Staff track. General Staff officers would be sent back to the field periodically for a Service sabbatical to cure the ivory tower syndrome and to regain operational currency. Further, Service officers could be sent to the

General Staff to provide field perspective and to receive a General Staff orientation.

CINCs and Deputy CINCs could be a mixture of Service and General Staff flag officers. If the CINC is a General Staff officer, his deputy would come from the Service track. A portion of the unified commands would be designated as General Staff commands, with the others remaining as Service command billets. The command of Army divisions and corps—and comparable commands in the Navy, Marines, and Air Force—would be filled by flag officers from the Service track. However, General Staff flag officers could be kept Service current, by assigning them as deputy or assistant commanders (for example, Assistant Division Commander Maneuver or Support). Service chiefs would be chosen from officers who remained in the Service track, the CJCS (a former CINC) from the General Staff.

Because the General Staff would take the lead in resource issues, it would most likely be larger than the Joint Staff.[79] If the joint career track does not attract the number and quality of officers required, the General Staff must have access to personnel records and the authority to requisition qualified candidates from the Services.

WHY THE MILITARY MUST LEAD THIS REFORM

Congress has been and will remain a major obstacle to JCS reform since it may have the most to lose. Testifying before the HASC in 1982, John Kester said:

> The attitude of the Congress towards the JCS has been essentially opportunistic. When it had appeared that there might be profit in it, members of Congress occasionally have tried to play off the Chiefs against their civilian superiors, though usually without much success. As a whole, the Congress has appeared happy to have the JCS remain a weak, compromise organization.[80]

Kester's observations are still valid. Goldwater-Nichols strengthened the Chairman and the Joint Staff but weakened the JCS. Therefore, will the pressure to reduce the deficit and maintain an adequate defense allow the Congress to support the kind of defense reorganization proposed by this study?

Congress set a recent precedent for relinquishing power to an institution like the NMAC when it created the Defense Base Closure and Realignment Commission (P.L. 01–510). To depoliticize the base-closing process, an essential element of downsizing and cutting the defense budget, Congress ceded authority to the commission to "shield members from the anguish—and the political hazards—of picking which bases to close."[81] Though lacking the autonomy of the Base Closing Commission, the NMAC Council would consist of distinguished military and civilian leaders whose advice would be hard to discredit. The politics of individual resource issues could require that a select group of members criticize advice formulated by the NMAC. However, for any single issue a majority of Congress could hide behind the prestige of the Council when making difficult resource decisions.

Conceivably, the most prominent hurdle to meaningful reform for the next 4 years, is Secretary of Defense Les Aspin. Investigative reporter Bob Woodward said this about Aspin:

> For years, Aspin has said it is necessary to ask three questions about any major political fight in Washington, no matter how important or fleeting. Those three questions are, according to Aspin: one, what is the fight really about? Two, who will win and who will lose? Three, what are the true implications?[82]

If the JCS were abolished and the advice provided by the NMAC gained credibility, OSD would be the biggest loser.

Aspin came to the Pentagon under Secretary of Defense Robert S. McNamara, "the father of the Pentagon systems analysis process that has already played a significant role in Aspin's development and is likely to play a large and controversial role in his time as Pentagon chief."[83] If a General Staff were established, it would take the lead in defense policy and program development, and OSD would be relegated to a major role in implementation. It is doubtful that Aspin will instigate any reform that would cause this kind of realignment. If defense reorganization is going to happen today, the leadership of the active duty military, like Jones and Meyer in 1982, will have to take the lead.

CONCLUSION

Goldwater-Nichols made the Chairman the principal advisor to the NCA and strengthened the Joint Staff. Nevertheless, the negative reaction to the Chairman's *R&M Report* indicates that his advice is being discredited by the perception that the JCS is incapable of making difficult resource choices.

The challenges of the post–Cold War period require replacing the JCS with an independent NMAC and the Joint Staff with a General Staff. Ending dual-hatting would allow the Service Chiefs to focus on their Title X responsibilities where they *should* be parochial. As a full time Council, the NMAC would be capable of evaluating nontraditional threats to U.S. interests and providing credible, uninhibited joint advice to the CJCS. Title IV provisions have improved both the quality of the officers and the product associated with the Joint Staff. Nevertheless, they have failed to create a joint culture capable of competing with the predominant Service cultures. Establishing a General Staff would create a separate career path and credible joint culture.

Neither Congress nor the civilian leadership in the Department of Defense is likely to initiate reform. Instead, they have announced that they will conduct their own examination of roles and missions. Secretary of Defense Aspin will direct a "bottom up review"[84] and Senator Nunn indicated that "It's going to be the Congress and the President that are going to have to take a look at" roles and missions. If the Armed Forces are to serve the nation effectively in confronting the challenges ahead, the military must take the lead in advocating reforms that eliminate the perception that no ideas get far without the backing of each of the military Services. The world continues to change. It is time the U.S. military did too.

NOTES

1. Congress, Senate, *Defense Organization: The Need for Change,* Staff Report to the Committee on Armed Services Washington, DC, 1985, 240.

2. Christopher Allan Yuknis, "The Goldwater-Nichols Department of Defense Reorganization Act of 1986: An Interim Assessment" (Carlisle Barracks, PA: US Army War College, 1992), 28.

3. Many say this was the case when the "whiz kids"—Les Aspin was one of them—ran the Pentagon under Robert S. McNamara.

4. "The Pentagon Balks," *San Francisco Chronicle,* 28 February 1993, 1.

5. Gen. Edward C. Meyer, USA, "The JCS-How Much Reform Is Needed?," *Armed Forces Journal International* (April 1982), 82–90.

6. Gen. David C. Jones, USAF, "Why the Joint Chiefs of Staff Must Change," *Armed Forces Journal International* (March 1982), 64.

7. Meyer, "How Much Reform," 84.

8. Meyer, "How Much Reform," 83.

9. Jones, "JCS Must Change," 62–72.

10. Meyer, "How Much Reform," 89.

11. Ibid.

12. Ibid.

13. Meyer, "How Much Reform," 87.

14. Congress, *Hearings Before the Investigations Subcommittee of the Committee on Armed Services,* House of Representatives, "Reorganizational Proposals for the Joint Chiefs of Staff." Washington, DC, 1982, 156, 161.

15. Rep. Les Aspin (D-WI.), Sen. Sam Nunn (D-GA.) Alice Rivlin, William Perry, and R. James Woolsey—all prominent in the Clinton administration—were members of the CSIS study group that wrote the report.

16. The Center for Strategic and International Studies, *Toward a More Effective Defense: The Final Report of the CSIS Defense Organization Project* (Washington, DC: Georgetown University, 1985), 165.

17. Archie D. Barrett, personal interview, 25 February 1993.

18. Locher is currently the Assistant Secretary for Special Operations for Secretary of Defense Les Aspin.

19. HASC Hearings 1982, 541.

20. *Goldwater-Nichols Department of Defense Reorganization Act of 1986,* Public Law 99–433, 99th U.S. Cong., 1 October 1986.

21. HASC Hearings 1982, 538.

22. Jones, "JCS Must Change," 64–65.

23. Chairman, Joint Chiefs of Staff, *1993 Report on the Roles, Missions and Functions of the Armed Services* (Washington, DC: JCS, 10 February 1993), pp.

24. John Lancaster, "Pentagon, OMB May Battle in Wake of New Budget Plan," *Washington Post,* 23 February 1993, A2.

25. Alan F. Kay, "What the American People Want in the Federal Budget," *American Talk Issues: Survey #18,* 12 November 1992, i.

26. *1993 Roles, Missions, and Functions,* x.

27. Gen. Colin L. Powell, USA, letter to author, 10 March 1993.

28. Barrett, personal interview, 25 February 1993.

29. Gen. Gordon R. Sullivan, USA, personal interview, 12 March 1993 and Gen. Merrill A. McPeak, USAF, personal interview, 8 March 1993.

30. Goldwater-Nichols, Title II, Sec. 152, para. (c).

31. Goldwater-Nichols, Title II, Sec. 151, para. (d).

32. Goldwater-Nichols, Title II, Sec. 163, para. (c).

33. Barrett, personal interview, 25 February 1993.

34. HASC Hearings 1982, 508.

35. Barrett, personal interview, 25 February 1993.

36. Goldwater-Nichols, Title II, Sec. 155, para. (e).

37. LtGen. E. Ehlert, USMC, personal interview, 16 March 1993.

38. Barrett, personal interview, 25 February 1993.

39. Meyer, "How Much Reform," 86.

40. David Evans, "Troubled Air Force Transport Investigated: C-17 Program May be Cut or Canceled," *Chicago Tribune*, 19 February 1993, 7.

41. Meyer, personal interview, 22 February 1993.

42. McPeak, personal interview, 8 March 1993.

43. Ehlert, personal interview, 16 March 1993.

44. McPeak, personal interview, 8 March 1993.

45. Goldwater-Nichols, Title II, Sec. 151, para. (a)-(e).

46. Barton Gellman, "Services Moving to Protect Turf: Powell to Rebuff Call to Streamline," *Washington Post*, 28 January 1993, A4.

47. "Dellums Wants Broader Pentagon Study of Roles and Missions," *Aerospace Daily*, 25 February 1993, 309.

48. William Matthews, "Nominee Perry Warns There's No Turning Back on Drawdown," *Air Force Times*, 8 March 1993, 4.

49. McPeak personal interview, 8 March 1993.

50. Sullivan, personal interview, 12 March 1993.

51. HASC Hearings 1982, 548.

52. Chairman, Joint Chiefs of Staff, Memorandum for the Secretary of Defense, Subj: "1993 Report on the Roles, Missions, and Functions of the Armed Forces," 10 February 1993.

53. Powell, letter to the author, 10 March 1993.

54. Besides FORSCOM, the Navy's Atlantic Fleet, the Air Force's Air Combat Command, and the Marine Corps' Marine Forces Atlantic will merge under this single CINC. Gen. Powell was FORSCOM Commander before becoming CJCS. CJCS, *1993 Roles, Missions and Functions*, xii.

55. Ibid.

56. McPeak, personal interview, 8 March 1993.

57. Chairman, Joint Chiefs of Staff, Memorandum, 10 February 1993.

58. HASC Hearings 1982, 549.

59. Interview with Sen. Sam Nunn, *Meet the Press*, 21 March 1993.

60. HASC Hearings 1982, 552.

61. Goldwater-Nichols, Title IV, Sec. 661, para. (c).

62. Goldwater-Nichols, Title IV, Sec. 662, para. (a), (3) and Sec. 404, para. (e).

63. Powell, letter to the author, 10 March 1993.

64. Ehlert, personal interview, 16 March 1993.

65. Deputy Chief of Staff of the Army for Personnel (DCSPER), Briefing Packet, Subj: "General Officer Joint Duty Qualification," n.d.

66. DCSPER Briefing Packet, n.d.

67. Vice Admiral Leighton Smith, USN, Deputy Chief of Naval Operations (Plans, Policy, and Operations) said the Navy would ask that the "Nuclear exemption" be continued. Gen. McPeak thought there were conflicts between keeping pilots operationally proficient and meeting Title IV requirements. Finally, Gen. Sullivan hinted that he would ask Congress to extend the deadline for existing waivers. Personal interviews.

68. Barrett, personal interview, 25 February 1993.

69. Goldwater-Nichols, Title IV, Sec. 3, Policy.

70. HASC Hearings 1982, p. 500.

71. Meyer, personal interview, 22 February 1993.

72. Les Aspin, address, National Defense University, Washington DC, 25 March 1993.

73. Meyer, personal interview, 22 February 1993.

74. Ibid.

75. Goldwater-Nichols, Title IV, Sec. 662, para. (a), (3).

76. DCSPER Briefing Packet, n.d.

77. Courtney Massingale is the Army careerist in Anton Meyer's great novel *Once An Eagle*.

78. Meyer, personal interview, 22 February 1993.

79. HASC Hearings 1982, p. 523.

80. Elizabeth A. Palmer, "Commission Comes to Life, Vowing a Fresh Look," *Congressional Quarterly's Washington Alert*, 20 April 1991, 994.

81. Bob Woodward, "What Les Aspin Really Believes," *Washington Post Magazine,* 21 February 1993, 29.

82. Woodward, "What Les Aspin Really Believes," 20.

83. Aspin address, 25 March 1993.

84. Nunn, *Meet the Press,* 21 March 1993.

2

THE UN SECRETARY-GENERAL'S PEACEKEEPING PROPOSALS

C. W. HOFFMAN, JR.

INTRODUCTION

IN JANUARY 1992, THE UNITED NATIONS (UN) SECURITY COUNCIL held the first summit meeting in its 46-year history. Basking in the relative warmth of the end of the Cold War, the Council re-acknowledged its responsibility for international peacekeeping and pledged to improve that capability.[1]   The Security Council invited the new UN Secretary-General, Boutros Boutros-Ghali, to analyze and recommend ways to improve the effectiveness of UN preventive diplomacy, peace enforcement, and peacekeeping activity.

Lieutenant Colonel C. W. "Bill" Hoffman, U.S. Marine Corps, is a 1993 graduate of the National War College and is the Judge Advocate General, Marine Corps Air Ground Combat Center, Twenty-nine Palms, CA.   This essay won the *Rich Higgins Memorial Award*; Colonel Higgins, an alumnus of the National War College, was assassinated by terrorists while assigned as a UN Peacekeeper in Lebanon.

Boutros-Ghali answered in June 1992 with an "Agenda for Peace," outlining a plan to improve UN ability to be a guarantor of international security. Among other things, he advocated enhanced peacekeeping capability by improving the availability of military personnel (staff support as well as troops), strengthening training, creating a pool of equipment and supplies for peacekeeping operations, and financial management of peacekeeping.[2]

In response to the "Agenda for Peace," President Bush, in a September 1992 address to the UN General Assembly, pledged to enhance U.S. participation in peacekeeping activities by providing military planning expertise and facilities for peacekeeping force training. He pledged to strengthen the U.S. ability to undertake joint peacekeeping missions, and to establish a permanent peacekeeping curriculum in U.S. military schools. Significantly, Bush also directed the Secretary of Defense to place new emphasis on peacekeeping.[3]

Over the last few years, peacekeeping has been a growth industry. UN peacekeepers have earned the respect of the international community: 500,000 peacekeepers from more than 50 countries won the 1988 Nobel Peace Prize for 40 years of important service to the world.[4] Why the recent rise in world interest in peacekeeping? Since 1945, over 100 major conflicts have left 20 million dead. Virtually every dispute during the Cold War was related to the U.S.-Soviet confrontation or exploited by one side or the other. Because of such bipolar politics, UN peacekeeping was largely ineffective: 279 vetoes had been cast in the Security Council which blocked a potential UN response. From 31 May 1990 until late 1993, there have been no such vetoes.[5]

The trend is clear: from 1945 to 1978, 13 peacekeeping operations were undertaken under UN auspices. For the next 10 years, there were no new operations. Since April 1988, 13 new operations[6] have been undertaken, with 13 more being discussed by the Security Council for 1993.[7]

Most recently, Operation *Restore Hope* in Somalia demonstrated the trend of international consensus beyond peacekeeping into humanitarian intervention, an unprecedented expansion of UN activism.[8]

The opportunities for U.S. participation in UN military operations are greater than ever before. The U.S. Congress has watched these developments with great interest, recently making a legislative finding that peacekeeping activities contribute to U.S. national interests, and authorizing and appropriating funds for the Secretary of Defense to support peacekeeping activities. Congress also requested that the President analyze Boutros-Ghali's "Agenda for Peace" proposals regarding a standing UN peacekeeping force, funding, and logistical support.[9] In effect, Congress asked for a U.S. policy on peacekeeping.

PROPOSAL: PARTICIPATION IN A STANDING ARMY

That the United States and other member states of the UN negotiate special agreements under Article 43 of the UN Charter to provide for those states to make armed forces, assistance, and facilities available to the Security Council of the UN for the purposes stated in Article 42 of that Charter, not only on an ad hoc basis, but on a permanent on-call basis for rapid deployment under Security Council authorization.[10]

Charter Authority

When "international peace and security" are threatened, Chapter VI, entitled "Pacific Settlement of Disputes," calls on parties to pursue peaceful settlement of the dispute, and authorizes Security Council participation in encouraging resolution through diplomatic means.

If these efforts fail, Chapter VII, entitled "Action with Respect to Threats to the Peace, Breaches of the Peace, and Acts of Aggression," envisions a stepped process of dispute resolution, first to impose measures not involving the use of armed force, such as interruption of economic and diplomatic relations.[11] If these means would be inadequate, or prove to be inadequate, then the Security Council may authorize "such action by air, sea, or land forces as may be necessary to maintain or restore international peace and security."[12]

In his "Agenda for Peace," the Secretary-General admits that the United Nations itself had never used force under this authority.[13] During the recent dispute between Iraq and Kuwait, the Council authorized member states to take action *on its behalf.* One obvious reason the United Nations did not take military action is that it lacked a military force.

The drafters of the UN Charter did envision such a force. Under Article 43, by joining the United Nations, member states have undertaken to make available to the Security Council, on its call, ". . . armed forces, assistance and facilities, and rights of passage, necessary for the purpose of maintaining international peace and security."[14] This undertaking is subject to "ratification by the signatory states in accordance with their respective constitutional processes."[15]

Employed under the authority of the Security Council, and under the command of the Secretary-General,[16] the Article 43 force would respond to outright aggression, imminent or actual, to restore or enforce international peace and security. Or, it could be used to deal with any situation which the Security Council decided, by a qualified majority, to address with force.[17]

Peacekeepers Distinguished

"Peacekeeping" is not specifically discussed in the Charter. The Secretary-General defines it, at least as a matter of past practice, as the deployment of a UN presence in the field, with the consent of the parties, normally involving UN military and/or police personnel and civilians to facilitate the peacemaking process.[18] Peacekeeping forces are voluntarily provided by member states in response to ad hoc requests from the Secretary-General.[19] In the past, the United States has not provided combat forces for UN peacekeeping duty.

Historically, UN peacekeepers have attempted to be neutral, served in support of peace negotiations, and used force only in self-defense. Recently, after lauding international peacekeeping as being in the national interests of the United States in maintaining global stability and order,[20] Congress characterized peacekeeping in such non-coercive terms as observer missions, monitoring of cease-fires, monitoring of police in the demobilization of former combatants, human rights and refugee monitoring, humanitarian assistance, conducting elections, and reforming judicial and other civil and administrative systems of government.[21] These are the traditional roles of peacekeeping. The distinguishing factor between peacekeeping and enforcement action by the Article 43 force is the implied or active use of military force to ensure or achieve objectives, respectively.

Why the revitalization of the standing (or "on call") army concept? The Secretary-General views the ability to act, if peaceful means fail, as the essence of the concept of international collective security. Taken as a last resort, he argues it is ". . . essential to the credibility of the United Nations as a guarantor of international security."[22] He believes that changed political circumstances—the end of the Cold War—make explicit and permanent Article 43 agreements more feasible, and that they will serve the important international interest of deterrence of those who might breach or threaten international peace.[23]

U.S. Law

Authority for U.S. military support to the United Nations is contained in the UN Participation Act of 1945,[24] which implements the UN Charter. It authorizes the President to negotiate Article 43 agreements (subject to Congressional approval) to support UN enforcement actions, and also authorizes additional troops to support "such activities of the United Nations as are specifically directed to the peaceful settlement of disputes and not involving the employment of armed forces contemplated by Chapter VII of the United Nations Charter."[25] Up to 1,000 such noncombat forces may be provided, along with the use of facilities, and the provision of services, supplies and equipment.[26]

Effect of a UN Decision to Employ Armed Forces

War is politics. "War is merely the continuation of politics by other means."[27] Whether a perceived threat to its existence, economic pressure, political differences, or simply an imperialistic desire for expansion, each disputant takes the decision that achieving its national interests outweighs the practical disadvantages of war. Those disadvantages are substantial. Massive use of conventional force and weapons of mass destruction not only destroys property and kill people, it also destroys entire societies, economies and ecosystems.[28] Strong convictions to support armed conflict are held as well by those involved in civil wars and internal strife, which frequently result in regional instability, refugees, and human rights abuses. These sorts of conflict are appropriate for UN intervention since they threaten international peace and security.

Armed conflict ends when one side is overwhelmed militarily and therefore cannot fight, or when both sides agree to stop fighting and negotiate a peace agreement. Belligerent sides will not agree, without some incentive, to negotiate away an interest that was originally important enough to take them to war. Tragically, in some cases the death and destruction caused by armed conflict and military stalemate will be the best incentive to reach a political settlement.

A premature UN Security Council decision to intervene forcefully in a burgeoning conflict before its consequences are translated into political decision by the participants may prolong the conflict. Although it may be able to stop the fighting, the United Nations cannot give effect to a political settlement of the conflict.[29] A standing army can do nothing to resolve the underlying causes for war.

Historically, UN forces have been used primarily to assist diplomatic efforts at peacemaking. There is general agreement that the United Nations provides its most important contribution to world peace by acting as a facilitator, providing the setting for complex negotiations.[30]

The strength of the United Nations in this capacity is that it has generally been perceived as neutral. An Article 43 force used to stop an on-going (or threatened) conflict could well alienate parties to the conflict and place the UN in an adversarial position, thereby damaging its ability to broker (as opposed to dictate) a peaceful resolution of the dispute.

Complications of force in an insurgency. Since the resounding international condemnation of Iraq's annexation of Kuwait, most UN peacekeeping operations have been directed at resolving internal conflicts.[31] "Ethnic strife, civil wars, separatist movements, religious strife—all threatening or undermining civil authority—will become the prevalent pattern."[32] The media account the variety and complexity of such wars; conflicts in Cambodia and Yugoslavia are stark examples.

In spite of the Charter restraints on interfering in essentially domestic matters, the Security Council has judged many internal conflicts as having an international character or threatening the international peace.[33] Insurgency generally does not respect borders. Refugees, arms trading, and military operations staged from neighboring countries threaten international security. And, today the international community is less tolerant of sovereign governments mistreating their citizens.[34] Intervention may also occur when the incumbent sovereign is dysfunctional and could not reasonably be expected to act to correct the problem, as in the December 1992 humanitarian intervention in Somalia.

China appears to be the only permanent Security Council member with significant and consistent reservations regarding intervention.[35]

Involvement in a civil war or insurgency will lead to significant complications. First, the incumbent government views insurgents as domestic criminals and terrorists rather than combatants entitled to the protection of the law of war. UN intervention legitimizes the insurgent, and by implication his political agenda and its methods, in the international community. Second, as indicated above, the use of force undercuts the UN claim to neutrality and its ability to mediate the resolution of strongly held interests. Third, if the incumbent government is dissolved, then the United Nations could become responsible, with Security Council concurrence, as a trustee for the people of the country.

In issues this complex, the primary emphasis in resolving the dispute should be diplomatic, not military. Successful conflict resolution efforts must be comprehensive, and may need to include international mediation, arbitration, the Secretary General's good offices (or those of another mutually trusted third party), negotiation, adjudication, inquiry and investigation, diplomacy, establishing a cease-fire, including separation of forces, border delimitation or demarcation, economic reconstruction, political reform, and humanitarian assistance. *The usefulness of an Article 43 force in internal conflicts, the most likely future conflict requiring UN participation, is doubtful.* They would, however, rapidly take up positions following a seriously taken cease-fire to avoid unnecessary or accidental breaches.

What is the character of the UN political will? Given the broad range of potential conflict around the world, can the United States and other nations that might provide troops for the standing force be assured that the UN's political interests will always coincide with their national interests?

UN political interests result from a bureaucratic process and are flexible, uncertain, and, at any given time, exceptionally unpredictable. It is simply a political collection of states with (allegedly) altruistic goals. It may use force for enforcement if international peace and security are threatened. But it will survive if it chooses not to wage or even if it loses a war. It has no motivation for economic gain and no territory to expand; it need not win any elections to maintain its power. Its political goals depend on the consensus of the qualified majority of the membership of the Security Council at any given time. *Not all threats to international peace and security justify UN use of force.* Not all changes in status quo are undesirable.

The United States has, as do the other permanent members of the Security Council, the ability to veto proposed use of an Article 43 force that is inconsistent with its national interests or otherwise objectionable or ill-advised. Nations capable of providing important military forces but lacking similar veto power would be justifiably reluctant to commit forces,[36] and could in any case forbid the use of their forces against their own interests. And, the United Nations can anticipate receiving criticism that the force will more readily serve the national interests of the five permanent members of the Security Council than the UN as a whole.[37] The difficulty of anticipating the circumstances that might lead to the employment of the force should cause all potential force contributing nations to challenge the wisdom of contributing forces without first knowing, more precisely, the political will to be enforced.

Problems of Entanglement

Previous concerns of Congress. There has been historical opposition to the notion of a standing UN force. For example, the 1966 U.S. Senate Committee on Foreign Affairs Report on the matter of a standing or permanent UN military force expressed concern that once established, a permanent force could be committed when the use of those forces may not be in the nation's interests. Given that possibility, it suggested that UN forces be "born of crisis and temporary in duration."[38]

In 1973, Congress codified its fear of military entanglement abroad in the War Powers Resolution, which asserts limits on the President's employment of military force in "hostilities or into situations wherein involvement in hostilities or into situations wherein involvement in hostilities (are) clearly indicated."[39] Unless the Congress is willing to give the Security Council more authority to deploy U.S. troops into combat than it gives the President,[40] it is unlikely that it (or many other nations' legislatures) would approve the unconditional commitment of forces to the UN. During his address to the UN in September 1992, President Bush clearly noted that UN members "must retain the final decision on the use of their troops."[41] Agreeing to provide the troops while withholding the authority to commit such troops into hostilities could frustrate the purpose of Article 43.

Force capabilities. The UN force must be powerful enough to deter or stop aggression by a well-organized and equipped enemy. Combat power is a relative concept, depending on factors such as the size and composition of the opposing force(s), terrain, and size of the area of operations. The force should be mobile and flexible, properly equipped; have adequate logistics; and intelligence gathering, analysis, and dissemination capability. U.S. military forces are trained and equipped to be best employed in joint task forces, and should be committed to combat only when absolutely necessary and when able to take advantage of superior technological or other capabilities. For example, even a single infantry battalion should be supported with a full range of mechanized support, artillery and other combat and combat service support, both deep and close air support, air superiority, air defense, satellite intelligence gathering capability, and so forth. It therefore would be prudent for the United States, if it is to make forces available, to make available a sufficiently large joint task force to ensure that the U.S. troops are fully supported and can be and are employed according to doctrine.

If the force is not powerful enough to deter or overcome aggression, but is nevertheless engaged in combat, nations which provided those forces may be compelled to commit additional forces to protect those already in battle. In other words, unless withdrawal (due to a change of political will) is contemplated, the commitment of some forces to support the standing army is assurance that reinforcements will be available. This is potential entanglement of the highest order. That fact does not make it inappropriate in and of itself—but it does recommend all possible caution and extreme care in the crafting of the Article 43 implementation agreement.

Command and Control

The Chain. The President determines the chain of command for U.S. military forces.[42] Assuming that a U.S. joint task force is made available for employment as part of an Article 43 force, it is likely that the U.S. forces will bring to the UN the predominant, most technically sophisticated force, and therefore will be justified to expect the field leadership role. This would be a reasonable precondition of the Article 43 agreement, and usually would be consistent with world expectations in this regard.

Even with U.S. leadership of a UN force, there are operational problems that result from a multinational force. Military efficiency is a function of training, inter-operability, unity of command, and a common language for communication, attributes in scarce supply in ad hoc units. Having the authority to command and the capability to lead are different matters.

Command relationships with other U.S. forces could be complicated as well. By law, U.S. combat forces are assigned to a U.S. specified or unified command.[43] Although a certain U.S. force (or more appropriately, a joint task force) could be designated as both part of the standing UN force and as a force assigned to a combatant command, the UN assignment will effectively remove that force from the combatant commander's force package since he will be unable to rely on its availability. Additionally, all forces operating within a geographic area are normally assigned to, and under the command of, the geographic combatant commander.[44] The reason for this requirement is obvious: it provides unity of command and ensures efficient use of resources. Whether commanded by a U.S. officer or not, a U.S. joint task force employed under UN auspices that is not under the command of the geographic combatant commander in chief (who is responsible for U.S. military operations in the region) could weaken U.S. military capabilities in the area. Further, there could be significant problems coordinating the release and dissemination of some intelligence. U.S. forces in a multinational force *should not* be at greater risk because control of sensitive intelligence demands it go to U.S. eyes only. The potential for the United States to have to prioritize intelligence source protection against U.S. forces protection is not appealing, but is real.

Planning. A clear, responsive connection between the Security Council as political and military objective setter and the military planners supporting and achieving those objectives is indispensable to translate political decisions into action and to avoid action which could undermine political endgame considerations and goals. UN infrastructure to support these tasks simply does not currently exist.

The standing force could face world-wide contingencies in all environments; desert and mountain, urban and jungle, creating a daunting planning task. No less than five separate joint headquarters of the various U.S. unified commands accomplish a similar planning task for U.S. forces.[45] Critical functions requiring interoperability, such as intelligence, training, operational planning, logistics, and communications are complicated by language, equipment capabilities, and doctrine differences—multinational headquarters do not operate smoothly without considerable practice. Anticipating the transition from peace enforcement to peacekeeping, plans for peace enforcement would need to include a peacekeeping plan for cease-fires, civil administration, elections, mediation, and nation building. Further, the UN force would be responsible to fulfill all of the duties of an occupying power under the laws of war. This would require significant rotation of forces and transition of command structures to accommodate missions essentially intended for engineering, staff corps, lift/logistics, or military police units.

Under the Charter, as well as in the Secretary General's view,[46] Security Council plans for the application of armed force are to be supported by the Military Staff Committee (MSC).[47] Composed of military representatives of each of the five permanent members of the Security Council, but lacking a permanently assigned enforcement force and frozen by cold war adversity, the MSC has never attempted to do military planning.

Overlooking problems of nationally classified information in a multinational headquarters, and with appropriate staff augmentation, presumably by nations which have provided standing forces,[48] the MSC could be expanded to plan worldwide operations. Considering the planning burden, and the need for each supporting nation to be "connected" to the headquarters, the necessary complication of planning the follow-on peacekeeping efforts,[49] and the difficulty of reaching political consensus in fluid situations, [50] the MSC bureaucracy needs to be immense, and its inefficiency and inflexibility is unfortunately predictable.

FUNDING

Congress asks for discussion and analysis of the following Secretary General proposal to strengthen UN peacekeeping: "that contributions for peacekeeping and related enforcement activities be funded out of the National Defense function of the budget rather than the 'Contributions to International Peacekeeping Activities' account of the Department of State."[51]

In his "Agenda for Peace," Secretary General Boutros-Ghali highlights the substantial increase in peacekeeping operations as well as their unpredictability. To achieve greater flexibility, and therefore broader capability, he proposed that contributions for peacekeeping and related enforcement activities be funded out of the national defense budgets.

The United States is the largest single financial contributor to the United Nations. Congress funds U.S. assessments for UN peacekeeping operations either through Department of State authorization and appropriation bills for separately created peacekeeping operation accounts, through security assistance program accounts, which are voluntary payments, or through its regular budget payment to the United Nations.[52] Unprogrammed assessments are funded by reprogramming undisbursed funds, an undependable method from the UN perspective.

It is not uncommon for supporting forces to initially fund peacekeeping expenses, for example, air transportation, with unit operations and maintenance funds. Until and unless those funds are reimbursed, other more useful training (from the combat unit perspective) cannot be undertaken. Using operations and maintenance funds to meet unprogrammed peacekeeping duties can therefore detrimentally affect unit readiness.

The funding burden is substantial. "Five years ago, peacekeeping cost UN members states $223 million in assessments. (In 1992) the bill (was) $2.7 billion, with no indication that the price tag will stop growing."[53] Eighty-seven percent of the peacekeeping budget comes from only 10 countries.[54]

The United Nations is hopelessly in debt. Many countries, including the United States, are behind in paying their assessments.[55] Some are behind because of bureaucratic budgeting limitations, for example, the United States appropriates annually and is reluctant to make mid-year appropriations. Congress recently found that "the normal budget process of authorizing and appropriating funds a year in advance and reprogramming such funds is insufficient to satisfy the need for funds for peacekeeping efforts arising from an unanticipated crisis" and "greater flexibility is needed to ensure the timely availability of funding to provide for peacekeeping activities."[56]

Some payments are withheld for political reasons.[57] According to the Secretary General, "the real problem is a lack of political will among the member states. They are not ready to pay."[58] The situation is a constant source of frustration to the Secretary General, who must lobby for support for each operation. As the number of operations expands, the funding problem swells.

Congress has already undertaken to address this problem in 1993. It authorized the Secretary of Defense to provide assistance in an amount not to exceed $300 million, provided that the funds are required to meet unexpected and urgent requirements, and that State Department funds are insufficient and unavailable, and only upon Secretary of Defense advance notice to Congress of the source of the peacekeeping assistance funds.[59]

In essence, Congress has created authority for the Secretary of Defense to spend $300 million beyond programmed funds in the event of an emergency. This proposal specifically and correctly answers Boutros-Ghali's recommendation, and is the right way to proceed, but $300 million may prove inadequate.

PEACEKEEPING LOGISTICS SUPPORT

Congress asks for discussion and analysis of the following Secretary General proposals to strengthen UN peacekeeping: "that member states commit to keep equipment available for immediate sale, loan, or donation when required" and "make airlift and sealift capacity available to the UN force at cost or at lower than commercial rates."[60]

The Secretary General's Viewpoint

Although some nations are willing to provide personnel for peacekeeping, they are sometimes unable to provide equipment necessary to support their personnel for operations. He suggests that "a pre-positioned stock of basic peacekeeping equipment should be established, so that at least some vehicles, communications equipment, generators, etc., would be immediately available. . . ."[61] Alternatively, governments should commit themselves to keeping certain equipment on stand-by for immediate sale, loan, or donation to the UN when required.

The UN Peacekeeping Bureaucracy

UN peacekeeping operations are an ad hoc affair. When international peace and security are threatened, and the

Security Council[62] decides it would be appropriate, the Secretariat arranges for a peacekeeping force as part of the conflict resolution process. When the belligerents are amenable to the presence of UN peacekeepers,[63] the Security Council drafts a mandate tailored to address the pressing issues of the conflict, and the Secretariat negotiate with willing nations to identify volunteers for the force. Once created, the force deploys and provides services in support of the conflict resolution process.

The deployment of a peacekeeping force creates the perception of, and depends on, the collective political will of the international community to resolve the conflict. Peacekeepers provide stability to allow diplomatic processes to proceed. They must be able to accomplish a wide variety of duties, for example, monitor withdrawals, oversee prisoner exchanges and disarmament, conduct related investigations. Even-handed performance of these duties provides stability, which results in confidence. "The moral backing and legitimacy of the international community is the strength of UN forces, not the calibre of their weapons."[64]

The broad range of possible missions highlights the need to task, organize, and equip forces based upon the political mandate, the military threat, terrain, and terms of reference.[65]

UN peacekeeping experience has demonstrated that the UN bureaucracy is not optimum for leading military operations; it has insufficient staff manpower, and its internal organization is ineffective in supporting military operations.[66] In 1988, the Secretary General centralized peacekeeping activities (including good offices, mediation, negotiation) in his own staff. Planning and management of peacekeeping operations is accomplished by the Under-Secretary General for Special Political Affairs in the Office of Political Affairs.[67] There is also a military advisor, with a small staff, for the Secretary General. Because of the substantial growth in the number and complexity of peacekeeping operations, the challenge to manage current operations and plan future operations is relentless. In 1987, there were only five on-going peacekeeping operations, all of which had been in operation for 10 years or more.[68] By early 1993, there were 13 operations ongoing, and as many as 13 more in various stages of consideration.[69]

Until September 1993, logistics support of peacekeeping operations was provided by the Field Service under the Under-Secretary General for Administration. Field Services is not part of the Office of Political Affairs, which led to the awkward situation of having operations and logistics to support those operations planned in separate agencies. This is not especially crucial for self-sustained forces, but could have been fatal for those lacking that capability. The recent change was essential—but was a difficult bureaucratic change. The combination of ad hoc military units, lacking interoperability training and variously configured, with an inadequate bureaucracy, not properly aligned with operational requirements, results in support that is reportedly unresponsive and insufficient.[70]

The Problem
The proposal to make equipment available for sale to the UN is certainly not objectionable. Contracts for such equipment would benefit U.S. manufacturers—there is a certain charm to having U.S. contributions to the United Nations used to purchase equipment from U.S. firms.[71]

Donation of military equipment is a common means of disposing of surplus, obsolete, and excess material. For example, such material may be provided to foreign governments, local organizations, and drug law enforcement agencies. There are many needy agencies and organizations that could benefit from such U.S. government largess. The United Nations could apply to receive such equipment for its peacekeepers, and it could be delivered as "in kind" payment of assessed U.S. costs. Similarly, military property could be leased. Whether sold, loaned, or donated, *the real problem is maintenance of the equipment.*

The United Nations has no infrastructure to perform maintenance on equipment is acquires. Establishment of UN equipment pools is expensive, and there is no UN transportation arm to transport equipment to and from peacekeeping operations. It may be unrealistic to believe that peacekeepers that lack equipment could properly maintain equipment provided to them. Contracting for such maintenance support is expensive, although this could also be provided by the United States as an "in kind" payment of assessments. There is neither doctrine nor standards that address requirements of interoperability of equipment used by various peacekeeping forces, so large, advance acquisition of such equipment could be shortsighted or poorly suited. For these reasons, the practice of accepting the offered services of peacekeeping forces who do not have the needed equipment should be discontinued, or worked into a comprehensive arrangement which makes political, economic, and tactical sense.

The proposal to make airlift and sealift capability available to the UN force "at cost or at lower than commercial rates" is simply an effort to stretch the budget of the United Nations. Participating nations should be encouraged to share the burden of peacekeeping to the greatest extent possible. Making air and sealift capability available below the market cost discourages nations from doing what they can to support the peacekeeping effort, and therefore is not wise. The only caveat to this is where nations may be able to subtract the training value of such missions from the price tag—up to the amount that would have been assigned to accomplish such training.

CONCLUSION

UN military involvement in peace enforcement can undercut its critical role of resolving disputes through diplomatic means. Incongruence between U.S. and UN interests, the likelihood of military entanglement requiring expanding force commitment, and the immense logistics and planning burdens of worldwide joint and combined military operations all counsel against making a guarantee, before the crisis, to provide troops.

Each nation should be prepared to provide a self-contained force to support the UN efforts. The United Nations should establish goals and subsequent standards for interoperability so that those forces can be efficiently combined as necessary. Combining forces demands that command relationships, a common language, support responsibilities, and intelligence procedures be resolved.

With the Congressional authorization for the Secretary of Defense to fund peacekeeping efforts under urgent (unprogrammed) circumstances, changes in U.S. funding process for UN operations are unnecessary, though levels may require adjustments. It would be appropriate to provide excess equipment or services as "in kind" payment for UN assessments.

Services of peacekeeping volunteers who require substantial logistics support should generally not be accepted—they are a significant drain on limited UN assets. Finite military resources should be acknowledged in the Security Council's peacekeeping decisions. Diplomatic rather than military assistance is its most critical contribution to successful peacekeeping.

NOTES

1.   John M. Gosko, "The UN Summit Stresses Global Cooperation," *Washington Post*, 1 February 1992, A1, A19.

2.   He also argued for preventive diplomacy by UN agencies and regional organizations; peacemaking, measures to bring about agreement; and peace-building, to prevent the recurrence of conflict. Boutros Boutros-Ghali, "An Agenda for Peace, Report of the Secretary General Pursuant to the Statement Adopted by the Summit Meeting of the Security Council on 31 January 1992," (New York: United Nations, 1992).

3.   The President outlined several areas where peacekeeping capability could be improved: short notice availability of a trained force of men and equipment, combined training and interoperability, including command and control; logistical support and stockpiling; planning crisis management and intelligence; and adequate, equitable financing. Thomas L. Friedman, "Bush, in Address to UN, Urges More Vigor in Keeping the Peace," *New York Times*, 22 September 1992, A1, A14.

4.   United Nations, "United Nations Peacekeeping Forces Awarded 1988 Nobel Peace Prize" (Washington, DC: United Nations Information Center, December 1988), 1.

5.   Boutros-Ghali, "Agenda," paragraphs 14 and 15.

6.   UNPROFOR, Yugoslavia; UNTAC and UNAMIC, Cambodia; UNIKOM, Iraq-Kuwait; ONUCA, Central America; UNAVEM I and II, Angola; MINURSO, Western Sahara; ONUSAL, El Salvador; UNIIMOG, Iran-Iraq; UNTAG, Namibia; UNOSOM, Somalia; UNGOMAP, Afghanistan-Pakistan. United Nations, *United Nations Peacekeeping Operations Past and Present* (New York: United Nations, September 1992), 8.

7.   The following countries have been discussed as candidates for possible peacekeeping missions: Bosnia, Sri Lanka, Solomon Islands, Haiti, Sudan, Liberia, Eritrea, South Africa, Mozambique, Tajikistan, Moldova, Georgia, Nagorno-Karabakh. Unnamed Intelligence Analyst. Personal interview, 2 December 1992.

8.   On 3 December 1992, the Security Council authorized, under Chapter VII, the Secretary General and member states "to

use all necessary means to establish as soon as possible a secure environment for humanitarian relief operations in Somalia."

9. National Defense Authorization Act for Fiscal Year 1993, P.L. 102-484, 1341, 1342, 106 Stat. 2315 (1992).

10. National Defense Authorization Act for Fiscal Year 1993, 1341(b) (3).

11. UN Charter, Article 41.

12. "Such action may include demonstrations, blockades, or other operations by air, sea, or land forces." UN Charter, Article 42.

13. Boutros-Ghali, "Agenda," paragraph 42. But the use of force by UN troops to maintain civil order and expel mercenaries from the Congo in 1960-1961 (ONUC) may contradict this assertion. See R. Simmonds, *Legal Problems Arising from the United Nations Military Operations in the Congo* (Martinus Nijhoff, The Hague, 1968), 61-62.

14. UN Charter, Article 43.

15. UN Charter, Article 43 (3).

16. This command authority, unsupported by explicit Charter language, is claimed in Secretary General Boutros-Ghali's "Agenda," paragraph 44.

17. For example, judgments of the Intentional Court of Justice could be "given effect" by force if the Security Council so decided. UN Charter, Article 94 (2).

18. Boutros-Ghali, "Agenda," paragraph 20.

19. There is some support for establishing a standing *peacekeeping* force. At the January 1992 Security Council summit, French President Mitterand said France is willing to make available 1,000 troops within 48 hours for peacekeeping purposes, and would double that number within a week. Gosko, A19.

20. Section 403 of Title 10, *U.S. Code* (1992) and National Defense Authorization Act of Fiscal Year 1993, 1341.

21. National Defense Authorization Act of Fiscal Year 1993, 1342.

22. Boutros-Ghali, "Agenda," paragraph 43.

23. Section 287d of Title 22, *U.S. Code* (1964) begins: "The President is authorized to negotiate a special agreement or agreements with the Security Council which shall be subject to the approval of the Congress by appropriate Act of joint

resolution, providing for the numbers and types of armed forces, their degree of readiness and general locations and the nature of facilities and assistance, including rights of passage, to be made available to the Security Council on its call for the purpose of maintaining international peace and security in accordance with Article 43 of said charter."

24. Section 287d-1 of Title 22, *U.S. Code* (1964).

25. Ibid.

26. Ibid. The President has delegated this authority to Secretary of State in Executive Order 10206, 16 F.R.529 to request that the Secretary of Defense support such requests. As of July 1992, at least 135 U.S. military personnel were members of four UN operations: UNTAC (50), UNIKOM (20), UNTSO (35) and MINURSO (30). On October 20, 1992, the Defense Department deployed a MASH unit to Zagreb to support UNPROFOR (236). Majorie Browne, "United Nations Peacekeeping, Issues for Congress," Congressional Research Service, The Library of Congress, Washington, DC, 24 Dec 1992.

27. Carl Von Clausewitz, *On War*, ed. and trans. Michael Howard and Peter Paret (New Jersey: Princeton University Press, 1989), 87.

28. Robert Johanson, "UN Peacekeeping and the Changing Utility of Military Force," *Third World Quarterly* 12.2 (1990): 53.

29. George L. Sherry, "The United Nations, International Conflict, and American Security," *Political Science Quarterly* 101.5 (1986), 760.

30. Sherry, 761.

31. For example, peacekeeping missions Cambodia and the former Yugoslavia, both established March 1992, Somalia, April 1992, and El Salvador, July 1991 share problems originating as domestic matters. United Nations, *United Nations Peacekeeping Operations Past and Present*, 8.

32. William H. Lewis, "Commentary," in *The Future Security Role of the United Nations*, William H. Lewis, ed., (Washington, DC, National Defense University's Institute for National Strategic Studies, 1992) 16.

33. For example, consensus for intervention has been reached for cases of El Salvador, Iraq, and Yugoslavia. British Foreign Secretary Douglas Hurd has agreed that Article 34 justifies such

intervention. Glen Franchel, and Jim Hoagland, "Leaders Seek to Bolster UN's Security Role," *Washington Post*, 17 July 1991: A1, A19. The French have also recognized a duty to intervene in cases where a government is creating humanitarian catastrophe. Edward C. Luck and Toby Tristes Gati, "Whose Collective Security?" *The Washington Quarterly* 15.2 (Spring 1992): 53.

34. See also, the "Universal Declaration of Human Rights," UN General Assembly Resolution 217A (III) of 10 December 1948. GAOR, III.1, Resolutions (A/80), 71-77, generally considered to reflect customary international law on human rights. Consider, for example, the UN's decision to resolve the mistreatment of ethnic minorities within Iraq, as a matter of international peace and security. Stephen S. Rosenfeld, "Sovereignty and Suffering, Charting the New Humanitarianism," editorial, *Washington Post*, 2 Oct. 1992: A29. Intervention in this case is simplified by the fact that Iraq was "occupied" (under UN Security Council Resolution 687) at the time of the intervention.

35. At the 1992 UN Security Council summit, Li Peng of China said that noninterference in the internal affairs of UN members states should be the guiding principle of the new world order. Gosko, "UN Summit Stress Global Cooperation," A19. Considering Tienanmen Square, it is not likely to soon change its views.

36. Under Article 44, members who provide forces under Article 43 are invited to "participate" (i.e., to voice their concerns) in the Security Council's deliberations regarding the employment of that nation's forces.

37. Johanson, 59.

38. "United Nations Use of Peacekeeping Forces in the Middle East, the Congo, and Cyprus," (Washington DC: Congress, House Committee on Foreign Affairs, 1966), 8.

39. The War Powers Act, Section 8, P.L. 93-148, 87 Stat. 556-60 (1973) codified in section 1595, et. seq. of Title 50, *United States Code* (1976).

40. This assumes the constitutionality of the War Powers Act.

41. Friedman, A1.

42. See section 162 of Title *United States Code* (1988), which taken in total, confirms the President's authority to establish the chain of command for military forces.

43. Sees section 162 of Title 10, *United States Code* (1988), which requires military department secretaries to assign all forces under their jurisdiction to unified and specified commands, except forces required for military department functions and "multinational peacekeeping organizations."

44. "Except as otherwise directed by the Secretary of Defense, all forces operating within the geographic area assigned to a unified combatant command shall be assigned to and under the command of, the commander of that command." Section 162(4) of Title 10, *United States Code* (1988).

45. USCENTCOM, USEUCOM, USLANTCOM, USPACOM, and USSOUTHCOM.

46. Boutros-Ghali, "Agenda," paragraph 43.

47. Article 46, UN Charter: "Plans for the application of armed force shall be made by the Security Council with the assistance of the MSC."

48. It is possible that the MSC would be staffed with permanent five members, such as China, that may not provide such forces.

49. Planning for follow-on peacekeeping has never been a staff function of military headquarters, and will be a difficult interface to make.

50. UN members that contribute Article 43 forces can expect to be "associated" with the MSC (under Article 47(2) and to "participate" in Security Council decisions concerning the use of their force (under Article 44). The effect could be to politicize operational decisions.

51. National Defense Authorization Act for Fiscal Year 1993, 1341(b) (1).

52. UN Charter, Article 17 requires contributions to the UN's expenses. The United States pays 25 percent of the UN regular budget; the 1992 assessment was $298.6 million. But for the maximum assessment levels, the United States would pay, based upon gross national product, about 28 percent. Vita Bite, "UN System Funding: Congressional Issues," Congressional Research Service, The Library of Congress, Washington, DC, 26 Jan 93: 3.

53. William Branigan, "The UN Empire—The Cost of Peacekeeping—Missteps on the Path to Peace," *Washington Post*, 22 Sept. 1992, A35.

54. United States, 30.3 percent (more than the "General Assessment" rate for the United States of 25 percent), Japan, 12.4 percent, Russia, 11.44 percent, Germany, 8.93 percent, France, 7.29 percent, UK, 6.10 percent, Italy, 4.29 percent, Canada, 3.11 percent, Australia, 1.5 percent, Netherlands, 1.50 percent. In response to criticisms that large contributors are not fairly represented on the Security Council, one recommendation is to enlarge the Security Council membership, as was done in 1965 (11-15 members) by adding Japan, Germany, delete Article 107, and give a seat to Africa, Asia, and Latin America. Luck, 46-47.

55. U.S. arrearage to the UN regular budget, as of 31 Dec. 92, were $239.5 million. "UN System Funding," 4.

56. National Defense Authorization Act for Fiscal Year 1993, 1342(a) (5) a (6).

57. For example, since 1980, Congress has prohibited contribution for projects benefitting the Palestine Liberation Organization. "UN System Funding," 6.

58. John M. Gosko, "UN Chief Stresses Need For Money," *Washington Post*, 22 November 1992: A33.

59. Section 403 of Title 10, *United States Code*, (1992).

60. National Defense Authorization Act for Fiscal Year 1993, 1341(b) (4) and (5).

61. Boutros-Ghali, "Agenda," paragraph 53.

62. The UN General Assembly has authorized two peacekeeping operations: the UN Emergency Force I in 1956, and the UN Security force in West Irian in 1962, as a matter of political expediency.

63. UN peacekeepers historically have been employed only as part of the peace process, the most critical aspect of which is the existence of a cease-fire agreement and consent to the presence of the peacekeepers to monitor that peace. Humanitarian relief efforts in Somalia beginning in December 1992 mark a departure from this norm, and may signify a trend for future UN intervention.

64. Thomas G. Weiss and Meryl A. Kessler, "Resurrecting Peacekeeping: The Superpowers and Conflict Management," *Third World Quarterly* 12.3/4 (1990/1991): 137.

65. "Terms of reference," issued by the Secretary General to the peacekeeping force, describes such things as the mission,

command relationships, and support available.

66. James H. Allan, "Peacekeeping in the Persian Gulf," *Military Review*, August 1991, 58.

67. Weiss, 143; Lewis, 8.

68. UNIFIL (Mar 1978), UNDOF (June 1974), UNFICYP (March 1964), UNMOGIP (Jan 1949), UNTSO (June 1948).

69. Notes 6 and 7 and accompanying text.

70. Lewis, 8.

71. Recent legislation allows release of U.S. contributions to the UNTAC (Cambodia) only upon certification by the Secretary of State that U.S. firms are being given the opportunity to provide goods and services for that operation. Department of Commerce, Justice, and State, and Related Agencies Appropriation Act, 1993, P.L. 102-395, 106 Stat. 1866-67 (1992).

3

JOINT OPERATIONS IN THE AMERICAN CIVIL WAR

SCOTT W. STUCKY

THE AMERICAN CIVIL WAR HAS ALMOST CERTAINLY BEEN THE subject of more books than any other event in U.S. history. This avalanche of print shows no sign of stopping; indeed, it has been increasing.[1]

Recently, the U.S. military has embraced the doctrines of joint and combined operations with a fervor never before seen. Prodded by the Goldwater-Nichols Act of 1986, the regret of Vietnam, and the embarrassment of affairs like Grenada, joint operations now permeate official U.S. strategy and are taught to officers at all levels of professional military education. Interestingly, however, the flood of Civil War monographs and the official frenzy over jointness seem to have remained almost totally separate phenomena. To my knowledge, only one book purports to treat Civil War joint operations as an integrated whole. This is Rowena Reed's *Combined Operations in the Civil War*, which, while provocative, draws some very dubious conclusions and is over 15 years old.[2]

Scott W. Stucky, a lawyer in the Office of the Judge Advocate General, Headquarters of the Air Force, is a 1993 graduate of the National War College. This essay won the *National War College Alumni Association Award for Excellence in Writing*.

SCOTT W. STUCKY

Examination of two major joint operations in the Civil War—the Henry-Donelson campaign and the Fort Fisher operations—may determine whether any conclusions can be drawn from such joint operations in their infancy. Did, as Reed claims, the Union have a coherent joint strategy in 1861-1862 which was thrown away with McClellan's demotion from general-in-chief? Were joint operations simply ad hoc affairs that depended upon the personal chemistry between Army and Navy commanders? What part did politics and the Clausewitzian "fog of war" play in such operations? Did they have any lasting effect upon interservice cooperation?

Before examining the above operations, it is essential to examine the state of thought on joint warfare at the time war broke out, as well as previous American experience with it. By 1861, Clausewitz had been dead for 30 years, but his great work had yet to be translated into English and was essentially unknown to Americans.[3] The principal tactics manuals used at West Point, Mahan's *Out-Post*[4] and Hardee's *Tactics*,[5] did not even mention joint operations. Jomini's *The Art of War*, the principal strategy text there, contains a short article on "descents" (Jomini's term for amphibious operations).[6] Jomini stated that such operations were "rare" and "among the most difficult in war." He expressed regret that Napoleon's great plan for an amphibious invasion of England was never carried out to determine whether such a very large-scale assault could have been done. Jomini recognized the problems of weather, supply, and logistics in such operations but, in the end, stated that "It is difficult to lay down rules for operations of this character," and then set out a few maxims of deception and concentration of force, which did not differ greatly from those applicable to warfare.[7] He included as an appendix an anecdotal survey of amphibious operations from antiquity to 1862.[8]

Naval thought on joint operations was even sketchier in 1861. Traditional naval thought then (and long after) held that an aspiring officer could learn everything he needed by going to sea at an early age. The Naval Academy was not established until 1845, and then largely as a political response to the "mutiny" on the *U.S.S. Somers* in 1842.[9] The curriculum was basically nautical, although academic subjects were taught. Because no naval counterpart of Jomini had yet emerged, officers of the Navy paid little attention to theories of naval warfare, let alone amphibious or other joint operations.[10]

Actual American experience with joint operations prior to 1861 was limited. The American Revolution saw several amphibious expeditions, including the combined French-American fiasco at Newport in 1778 and the successful Yorktown operation in 1781.[11] However, the fact that the U.S. Navy was not established until 1794 (and then virtually abolished again under Jefferson) illustrates that no lasting lessons as to the efficacy of joint operations were learned. The most recent experience before the Civil War was Winfield Scott's unopposed landing at Veracruz in 1847, a superbly executed operation using the first specially designed landing craft in American history. Some 8,600 men were put ashore in a few hours without losing a man, a fitting prelude to one of the most brilliant campaigns in our military history.[12]

In 1861, Scott was still, at 75, general-in-chief of the Army, a post he had held since 1842 (he had been a general officer since 1814). Though physically unfit for field service, Scott recognized the likelihood of a long and difficult war. In May 1861, he wrote to his eventual successor, George B. McClellan, laying out his famed "Anaconda Plan" for the strangulation of the South by blockade, and its invasion by joint operations down the Mississippi to New Orleans:

> We rely greatly on the sure operation of a complete blockade
> of the Atlantic and Gulf ports soon to commence. In
> connection with such blockage, we propose a powerful
> movement down the Mississippi to the ocean, with a cordon
> of posts at proper points . . . the object being to clear out and
> keep open this great line of communication in connection
> with the insurgent State and bring them to terms with less
> bloodshed than by any other plan. . . . This army, in which
> it is not improbable you may be invited to take an important
> part, should be composed of our best regulars for the
> advance, and of three years' volunteers, all well officered.

Scott was also realistic enough to recognize the political
dangers inherent in a protracted campaign when public
anger was aroused:

> A word now as to the greatest obstacle in the way of the
> plan—the great danger now pressing upon us—the
> impatience of our patriotic and loyal Union friends. They
> will urge instant and vigorous action, regardless, I fear, of
> consequences—that is, unwilling to wait for the slow
> instruction of (say) twelve or fifteen camps, for the rise of the
> rivers, and the return of frosts to kill the virus of malignant
> fevers below Memphis, I fear this, but impress right views,
> on every occasion, upon the brave men who are hastening to
> the support of their Government. . . . I commend these
> views to your consideration and I shall be happy to hear the
> result.[13]

Scott's caution was well founded; political pressure
provoked the advance on the Confederate positions at
Manassas which resulted in the rout at First Bull Run,
Thereafter, the appointment of McClellan to command the
Army of the Potomac, clashes between the two, and Scott's
debility prompted his retirement and replacement by
McClellan on 1 November 1861.

McClellan's tenure as general-in-chief lasted only 4
months; yet it has been claimed that, during this time, he

formulated a "revolutionary" strategy of joint operations which would begin with coastal strikes at Charleston, New Bern, Mobile, and New Orleans, and then, driving inward along railroads and the Mississippi, cut Confederate internal communications and sever the parts of the Confederacy from each other.[14] In this interpretation, the Peninsular Campaign is seen as a joint operations triumph which was only kept from success by Lincoln's obtuseness in keeping McDowell's corps in Washington, by fumbling on the part of the Navy, and by the demotion of McClellan, which "prevented him from coordinating the movements of other Federal armies . . . or obtaining reinforcements from less active theaters of war."[15] The final conclusion is that a great opportunity was missed:

> The Navy, whose aid McClellan had actively solicited and used, when available, to maximum advantage, was allowed to pursue an independent strategy while the Army commanders, lacking McClellan's foresight and flexibility of method, agreed with the Lincoln administration that wars were only won by slugging it out on the battlefield. The failure of the Peninsular Campaign signalled both the demise of Federal grand strategy and the demise of combined operations planning.[16]

This revisionist interpretation is deeply flawed. First, it posits that McClellan could, with the nebulous powers of the general-in-chief, achieve results with other armies which he was unable to do with his own when in active field command. Second, the notion that McDowell's corps was essential to victory on the peninsula is nonsense. McClellan at all times vastly outnumbered his opponents, and McDowell would not have made the difference. Third, McClellan possessed no command authority whatsoever over naval forces. To assume that he could, as general-in-chief in Washington, force Army-Navy cooperation in distant theaters flies in the face of experience throughout the war. Finally, the interpretation simply passes over the very real flaws in McClellan himself—flaws that were to prove fatal. His unwillingness to move quickly and to fight, his consistent overestimation of his opponents, his paranoid secretiveness about his intentions, and his contempt for his political masters and their needs in this most political of wars destroyed him in the end. There is absolutely no reason to believe that his retention as general-in-chief and his being given everything he wanted on the peninsula would have made any difference. Spinning out grandiose plans was an activity to McClellan's liking; execution was another matter altogether. The fact is that neither the command arrangements nor the doctrine for joint operations existed at this time. Successful joint operations, like much else, would have to be improvised by those on the scene.

THE FORT HENRY-FORT DONELSON CAMPAIGN

The first large-scale joint operation in the Western theater of war was the Fort Henry-Fort Donelson campaign, which brought Ulysses S. Grant to public attention. Central Tennessee was an area of great strategic importance to the Confederacy. Not only was it a fertile farming area, but it also had large iron deposits and many forges and furnaces. Given the insurgents' lack of industrial capacity, this was a resource almost beyond price. However, the problems of defending this area, immense to begin with, were devilishly complicated by Kentucky's attempt to stay neutral in the war. Since neither side wanted the opprobrium of violating this neutral status, defensive works to protect central Tennessee had to be built outside Kentucky.[17]

Given the poor state of the roads and the lack of north-south railroads, the obvious invasion route into central Tennessee was by the "twin rivers," the Tennessee on the west and the Cumberland on the east. To deal with this threat, Confederate fortifications were constructed on both rivers during 1861, although work went slowly. Fort Henry, on the Tennessee, was poorly located on low land facing Kentucky on the other side of the river. On 15 September 1861, Colonel Bushrod Johnson, the engineer officer who selected the site, described it as "a good enclosed work, with bastion fronts, mounting six 32-pounders and two 12-pounders, requiring about 1,000 men to man it."[18] Fort Donelson, 12 miles to the east on the Cumberland, was a stronger position. It sat on a bluff 75 to 100 feet above the river and was surrounded by gullies which would hamper assault by land.[19] However, progress on Fort Donelson was quite slow, aggravated by lack of men and the reluctance of local slaveowners to rent their slaves to the government during harvest. By 4 November, Donelson only had four 32-pounders and two naval guns.[20]

Kentucky's shaky neutrality ended in September 1861, when Confederate General Leonidas Polk occupied Columbus and turned it into a fortified bastion. Grant promptly occupied Paducah, at the confluence of the Tennessee and Ohio. In November 1861, Union Army command in the area was shaken up, when Major General Henry W. Halleck assumed departmental command in St. Louis. Grant was subordinate to Halleck. However, Union forces in Kentucky were not all under Halleck's authority. rather, he shared responsibility for the state with Major General Don Carlos Buell, at Louisville, who commanded the Army of the Ohio. Buell's department included Kentucky east of the Cumberland and all of Tennessee.[21]

The idea of an advance down the twin rivers was not a new one; on 20 November, Colonel Charles Whittlesley, Chief Engineer of the department, had written Halleck, suggesting "A great movement by land and water" down the rivers.[22] President Lincoln was eager for a campaign in Tennessee, to succour the Unionists in the eastern part of the state. However, mounting such an expedition depended upon naval forces which as yet did not exist. The first naval commander in the west, Commander John Rodgers, was sent to the Mississippi primarily to interdict clandestine commerce, although he was also to begin work on the Anaconda Plan's great advance down the Mississippi. This advance, it was thought, required the construction of a fleet of ironclads, which eventually emerged as twin-engine, single-wheel craft with sloping sides, carrying 10 guns, including three of the new 8-inch Dahlgren rifles. The building of these was a joint Army-Navy affair, and squabbles over the contract resulted in the recall of Rodgers and his replacement by Captain Andrew Hull Foote.[23]

Foote, a strongly religious New Englander who was a strict temperance man, was instructed by Secretary of the Navy Gideon Welles to cooperate with the Army without subordinating himself to it. Foote threw himself into the construction of the ironclads. By November, seven of them had been launched. However, the Army Quartermaster Corps, which was responsible for paying the contractors, was immensely slow in doing so. Foote also had enormous trouble getting crews for the ships. Civilian rivermen naturally preferred the higher pay and lesser danger of contract work, while naval personnel were few. Assistant Secretary of the Navy Gustavus V. Fox discovered 500 sailors on garrison duty in Washington, and shipped them west. Nevertheless, as late as 9 January, Foote had to commission *Cincinnati* and *Carondelet* with only a third of their crews each. And as late as the beginning of the Fort Henry expedition, Halleck was authorizing Grant to detail soldiers for gunboat duty.[24] Nevertheless, by the end of January, Foote had a workable gunboat fleet.

In early January, Grant was directed by Halleck to make a reconnaissance up the Tennessee to keep Polk from sending reinforcements to Bowling Green, toward which

Buell was planning an advance in response to Lincoln's desires. This excursion turned into a miniature version of General Ambrose Burnside's "mud March" a year later. Grant said, "We were out more than a week splashing through the mud, snow, and rain, the men suffering very much."[25] The reconnaissance had its intended effect, in that Polk sent no reinforcements, and General George Thomas was victorious at Mill Springs, thereby erasing the threat of a Confederate move against Buell's flank. Grant, however, was restless and impatient; he saw opportunity in a joint operation up the twin rivers but had to persuade Halleck to approve such an expedition. He accordingly traveled to St. Louis for an interview with Halleck, which went badly. Halleck barely knew Grant but was familiar (as were most officers in the old Army) with the stories of Grant's drinking, and had no doubt heard more recent ones as well.[26] Grant recounted the scene in his memoirs:

> I renewed my request to go to St. Louis on what I deemed important military business. The leave was granted, but not graciously . . . . I was received with so little cordiality that I perhaps stated the object of my visit with less clearness than I might have done, and I had not uttered many sentences before I was cut short as if my plan was preposterous. I returned to Cairo very much crestfallen.[27]

Crestfallen Grant may have been, but his spirits revived upon his return to Cairo, Illinois, where he consulted with Foote, who agreed on the advisability of a joint operation down the rivers. Therefore, on 28 January both officers cabled Halleck, asking permission to occupy Fort Henry. Foote stated that four ironclads would suffice. Foote's endorsement of the plan changed Halleck's mind; he replied that he was only waiting for a report on the condition of the roads and then would give the order.[28] While Foote's intervention (and the knowledge that he would "keep a fatherly eye" on Grant) certainly had some effect, equally effective was a report Halleck received from McClellan on 29 January that Beauregard was on his way to Kentucky from northern Virginia with 15 regiments.[29] This turned out to be untrue (except for Beauregard himself, sent by Davis to get him out of the East), but certainly had an effect on Halleck's sudden *volte-face*.

Halleck's order provoked a violent spasm of preparatory activity. Grant and Foote worked closely together in arranging transportation and planning for the landing of troops. The expedition sailed on 4 February and landed troops early on 5 February some miles north of Fort Henry. Fortunately, Fort Heiman, a companion installation on the Kentucky side of the river, already had been abandoned. The land advance was slow because of severe rains and the poor condition of the roads. On 6 February, Foote took his gunboats down to the fort and began a bombardment.

Fort Henry, as mentioned earlier, was situated on low land along the river, which in the winter of 1862 crested some 30 feet above normal. This flood was a disaster for the Confederacy, because it made the mines anchored to the river bottom useless and put part of Fort Henry under water. Brigadier General Lloyd Tilghman, commanding there, had 3,000 men and 17 guns; however, only two of the riverside guns, a Columbiad and a 24-pounder rifle, were effective against armor. Tilghman, thinking Fort Henry indefensible, had sent most of his men to Donelson. The artillery battle between Foote's gunboats and the fort was a heavy one. The *U.S.S. Essex* was hit in a boiler by the Columbiad, causing "carnage" below decks and scalding the captain and others. The *U.S.S. Cincinnati*, Foote's flagship, absorbed over 30 hits. But then, the fort's 24-pounder burst, killing most of the crew, and the Columbiad was accidentally spiked by a broken priming wire. With the gunboats firing at point-blank range, Tilghman raised a white flag. The river was so high that the boat sent to accept the surrender floated in through the fort's sally port. Grant's forces arrived only 30 minutes after the surrender, having been delayed on the roads, and Foote turned the fort over to the Army.[30]

Foote had taken 47 casualties, 38 of them in *Essex* alone. Tilghman surrendered only about 60 men. The rest managed to escape, but left the artillery and stores behind.[31] Grant promptly determined to move against Fort Donelson, but could not do so immediately, both because of the condition of the roads and the necessity for Foote to return to Cairo, repair damage, and then drop down the Cumberland to Donelson. Foote left the *Carondelet* at Fort Henry to support Grant and took the rest of the fleet with him. Grant, hampered by the weather, did not move toward Fort Donelson until 12 February. Foote was still in Cairo, feverishly trying to repair damage and assemble crews to transit the Cumberland. When Halleck learned that he was planning on sending only one gunboat (in addition to the *Carondelet*), he told Foote that at least two must be sent. By shifting crews around, Foote managed to get three ironclads—the *St. Louis, Louisville,* and *Pittsburgh*—underway and reached Donelson on 14 February. The *Carondelet* arrived on the 12th and fired a few rounds into the fort.[32]

Foote, who felt unprepared for another attack against fixed fortifications so soon after the heavy Fort Henry action, nonetheless attacked Donelson on the 14th. This bombardment was as unsuccessful as the one on Henry had been successful. Fort Donelson, located on high bluffs, could subject the gunboats to an intense plunging fire. Donelson, by February, had eight 32-pounder smoothbores, one 10-inch Columbiad, two 32-pounder carronades, and one 64-pounder rifled gun in its waterside batteries. One after another, the gunboats were disabled and floated back downstream. The *St. Louis,* now Foote's flagship, was hit

59 times and Foote was himself wounded. The Confederates in the fort were jubilant; Grant was correspondingly depressed. He had invested the fort on the 14th, but many of his men lacked tents and had left their overcoats at Fort Henry, fooled by unseasonably warm weather. The weather had now turned bitterly cold, and Grant was faced with the possibility of conducting a siege under unfavorable conditions. On the 15th he met with the wounded Foote, who said he would have to return to Cairo to repair damage, but would return within 10 days and lay siege to the fort with his gunboats. In the meantime, the least damaged vessels would remain on station.[33] Grant now faced the prospect of a prolonged siege under bad conditions, with dubious support from Halleck; however, as he later wrote, "the enemy relieved me from this necessity."[34]

While Foote's attack had been a tactical failure, it had important operational results. The Confederate commanders in the fort, mesmerized by the naval threat, had allowed Grant to invest the post, missing the opportunity for strategic withdrawal and the saving of the substantial forces (about 17,000 were eventually surrendered) therein. The Confederate situation was not helped by a command divided among three generals, two of whom—Gideon Pillow and John B. Floyd—were inept poltroons, and two of whom—Pillow and Simon B. Buckner—despised each other. On the 15th, while Grant was away conferring with Foote, Pillow's Confederates managed to break Grant's lines on the east side, opening the way for escape. However, the opportunity was then thrown away when Pillow ordered a retreat back into the fort.[35] Grant, returning from his conference, managed to plug the hole by nightfall. After further squabbles within the Confederate command and another unsuccessful breakout attempt, the episode ended with the escapes of Pillow and Floyd and Buckner's unconditional surrender to

Grant on 16 February.

The Henry and Donelson campaign illustrates several points about the conduct of joint operations at this stage of the war. First, of course, in the absence of unified command or meaningful doctrine for joint warfare, the conception and execution of joint operatins were totally dependent upon ad hoc actions by the responsible commanders, and therefore upon their personal chemistry and communications. Foote and Grant were very different individuals—one a teetotaler who preached sermons at church services, the other a cigar-smoking quasi-alcoholic who had left the Army under a cloud—yet they worked well together. Whatever their differences, they shared a common inclination to attack the enemy, both hating inactivity. They maintained excellent communications and worked together without undue worry as to who would get the credit—a quality rare in Civil War commanders. The reverse of this is of course equally true; a lack of personal chemistry and communication between commanders could (and would) doom joint operations. Given the rudimentary command and departmental arrangements of 1862, however, this was the situation, and commanders had to deal with it.

The second point to be made is that the command arrangements which did exist on the Army side hampered, rather than encouraged, successful joint operations. Although Grant describes Foote as "subject to the command of General Halleck,"[36] he was not in any formal sense. His instructions from the Navy Department were to cooperate, and he did that admirably, but he was not Halleck's subordinate. Halleck therefore had true operational control of only half the joint operation. Moreover, Halleck's dislike and distrust of Grant almost destroyed the operation before it started; only Foote's intervention on Grant's side (and the Beauregard rumor) finally got it moving. In addition, departmental arrangements then were highly unsatisfactory. Halleck had no operational control over Buell, who was supposed to be moving in support of Grant, but who adamantly refused to budge. Another 2 years would pass before the North developed satisfactory high command arrangements, and even then they depended more upon the personalities in place than on well-thought-out doctrine.

Finally, although the Henry-Donelson campaign produced important strategic results, it was not followed up as it could have been. Halleck seemed more interested in curbing his ambitious subordinate than in exploiting the victory. Indeed, in early March, Grant was relieved of command and almost arrested in a ludicrous mixup over his not sending requested reports.[37] Halleck, who told McClellan on 15 February that "I have no definite plan beyond the taking of Fort Donelson and Clarksville. Subsequent movements must depend upon those of the enemy,"[38] personally took field command and wasted much of the spring in a glacial and ultimately useless move on Corinth, MI. Thereafter, he frittered away the forces which had been under Grant's command. As a result, Grant's services were essentially lost to the Union until fall 1862, and much that lay open to conquest after Henry and Donelson (including East Tennessee, so vital to Lincoln) had to be won by bloody attrition later.

Between spring 1862 and the end of 1864, several joint operations, both riverine and littoral, were carried about by the Union with varying degrees of success. New Orleans was taken in April 1862 by the Union Navy, which ran past the city's defenses in the south, Forts Jackson and St. Philip, to occupy the city. The Army took over occupation of the city from the Navy, after forcing the forts' surrender in a Donelson-type operation supported by mortar boats. A Union attempt to take Vicksburg in 1862 through joint operations failed; when the city fell in July 1863, it would be through classical siege warfare. In April 1863, a Union fleet under Admiral Samuel F. DuPont attempted to pound Charleston into submission, in an operation presaging the British attempt to force the Dardanelles by naval gunfire alone in 1915. The failure of DuPont's fleet convinced the Navy that joint operations would be necessary to reduce the city, as DuPont had predicted. Even so, Charleston held out until 1865. Finally, in August 1864, Admiral David G. Farragut won his spectacular victory in Mobile Bay, defeating a Confederate fleet and sealing off the port. Farragut's campaign again illustrated the need for joint operations; the Army had committed inadequate troops to the operation, and the city remained unoccupied until virtually the end of the war.[39]

THE FORT FISHER OPERATIONS

The operations at Fort Fisher, North Carolina, in December 1864 and January 1865 differ from the Henry-Donelson campaign in several important particulars. First, of course, late 1864, by which time almost any disinterested observer would have pronounced the Confederates defeated, was not early 1862, when the issue was in doubt. Second, there were great differences in scale, the assaults on Fort Fisher being a vastly larger Union operation. Third, the amicable relations that had marked the Federal high command in the Henry-Donelson campaign were conspicuously absent in the first phase at Fort Fisher. Finally, of course, Fort Fisher was an Atlantic, not a riverine, operation and its execution bore more similarity to the great amphibious landings of the Pacific War of 1941-45 than to Henry and Donelson.

Fort Fisher, "the largest, most formidable fortification in the Confederate States of America,"[40] was located on a peninsula between the Cape Fear River and the Atlantic Ocean 18 miles south of Wilmington, NC. After the Battle of Mobile Bay in mid-1864, Wilmington, always a popular destination for blockade runners, was the only port still open for such commerce—the Confederacy's sole lifeline to the outside world. A hundred blockade runners sailed in and out of Wilmington during the war, attracted by the stupendous profits to be made in the trade.[41] Even in 1864, with over 30 Federal ships on patrol there, Wilmington had taken in $3.2 million in imported goods. Blockading the port was difficult because two separate inlets into the river, separated by 25 miles of shoals, had to be watched—an arc 50 miles long, too large to be thoroughly patrolled. [42]

Colonel Willam Lamb, the fort's commander since mid-1862, had been working steadily on the fortifications for 2½ years. By late 1864, the L-shaped earthen work consisted of a half-mile landface across the peninsula, made up of 15 30-foot traverses containing bombproofs and connected by a tunnel, mounting 20 Columbiads, 3 mortars, and several field pieces. For a half-mile north, the area had been cleared of trees to present a clear field of fire. It was also protected by a 9-foot palisade. At the angle of the L was a 43-foot-high work called the Northeast Bastion. The fort's seaface ran south along the ocean for another mile of traverses, bombproofs, and tunnels. Twenty large artillery pieces, including a 150-pounder Armstrong rifle, were emplaced here. The seaface culminated in a 60-foot emplacement called the Mound Battery, which mounted two heavy coast guns. The landface was also defended by a minefield—a great innovation. Twenty-four buried shells and mines were connected electrically, to repulse a land assault.[43] By late 1864, Fort Fisher, mounting 44 large guns, was very impressive. Its principal weakness was manpower; its permanent garrison numbered only 600, too few to defend so huge a work.

The impetus for a joint Army-Navy expedition against Fort Fisher came from Navy Secretary Gideon Welles, who had been arguing for it since 1862. When Wilmington became the preeminent blockade-running port in mid-1864, Welles finally persuaded President Lincoln and Secretary of

War Edwin M. Stanton to support a joint operation. However, Grant, by now a lieutenant general and general-in-chief of the Union armies, was cool to the idea, partly because he did not want to commit a large number of troops, and partly because he disapproved of the War Department's choice to lead the Army contingent, Major General Quincy A. Gillmore, who had performed badly before Richmond earlier in the year. Eventually, Grant approved committing about 7,000 troops to the operation but he vetoed Gillmore; his choice was Godfrey A. Weitzel, a talented young West Pointer who was Chief Engineer of the Army of the James, then sitting "bottled up" at Bermuda Hundred below Richmond. Grant liked Weitzel and particularly approved of the fact that Weitzel agreed that the fort could be taken without a huge mass of infantry. Secretary Welles had his own command problems. The naval command was offered to Admiral David G. Farragut, but the hero of Mobile Bay, in poor health and believing the expedition a dubious venture, declined. The command was then offered to Rear Admiral David Dixon Porter, the brash, self-promoting son of the hero of the War of 1812. Porter, seeing a chance for glory and advancement, threw himself into the planning of this largest naval expedition of the war.[44]

The Army command arrangements were then completely upset by the commander of the Army of the James, Major General Benjamin F. Butler, in whose area of responsibility Fort Fisher lay. He decided to take personal command of the Army portion of the expedition. Butler was the stormy petrel of Federal command, who sowed controversy wherever he went. A brilliant and eccentric Massachusetts lawyer and politician, he had, as a delegate to the Democratic convention in 1860, submitted a minority report on the platform supported only by himself, and voted 57 times for the nomination of Jefferson Davis. Commissioned a major general of volunteers in 1861, he conceived the idea of treating escaped slaves as "contraband of war" forfeit to the United States. As military governor of New Orleans in 1862, he issued the notorious "Woman's Order," which stated that any woman who insulted a Federal soldier was to be "treated as a woman of the town, plying her vocation."

This affront to Southern femininity earned him a price on his head from Jefferson Davis, the nickname "Beast," and his face on chamber pots all over the South. His other nickname, "Spoons," came from the rumor that he had enriched himself at New Orleans by stealing Southern silver and by rakeoffs and bribes from contractors. Although scandal resulted in his relief at New Orleans in 1862, his position as one of the nation's leading War Democrats insured his continuation in command, despite his rascality and his almost total failure in field command.[45]

The problem with Butler's assuming field command, which annoyed Grant but which he did nothing to prevent, was that Butler and Porter despised each other. In 1862, while military governor, Butler had publicly criticized Porter's part in the New Orleans action; this led to a feud which ended only with their deaths. The immediate effect of Bulter's assumption of command, however, was delay. Some of this was the normal confusion attendant upon such a switch; most of it, however, was due to the famous affair of the powder-boat.[46]

Butler had a great interest in innovative military technology and was an unsuccessful inventor himself. Prompted by newspaper reports of destruction caused by the accidental explosion of two gunpowder barges in England, he conceived the notion of packing a hulk with explosives, running it in near Fort Fisher, and exploding it. At a meeting with Grant and Porter in November, he predicted that such a huge explosion would flatten the fort's wall and kill most inside, so that infantry could walk in and take it. Grant was unenthusiastic but let the scheme proceed Porter, despite his dislike for Butler, was taken in and agreed to provide the ship, the explosives, and the transportation. The ship selected was the *U.S.S. Louisiana*, a flat-bottomed, shallow-draft vessel then doing blockade duty. She was disarmed, cut down, camouflaged to look like a blockade runner, loaded with 200 tons of gunpowder, and fitted with an elaborate ignition system.[47]

The expedition left Hampton Roads on 13 and 14 December. Butler's transports carried 2 divisions, a total of 6,500 men. Porter had 57 ships, including ironclads, frigates, and gunboats. The expedition arrived off Wilmington 19 December, but a gale began to blow and the transports returned to Beaufort, NC, to wait it out. The storm, which lasted three days, enabled Colonel Lamb to bolster his defenses; by 23 December he had some 1,400 troops in the fort, although a third of them were "Junior Reserves"—boys 16 to 18 years old.[48]

Butler, at Beaufort, sent Porter word that he would return on the 24th, with the bombardment and the landing on Christmas Day. Porter, whose ships had ridden out the gale without serious damage, now decided to set off the powder-boat early on the 24th—in the Army's absence—and begin the bombardment the same day. When he heard this, Butler exploded. The old animosity between the two fused with the Navy's seeming desire to get all the glory to provoke Butler into a rage. He promptly steamed south ordering his transports to follow as soon as they had finished taking on coal.

The *Louisiana*, under Commander Alexander C. Rhind, was towed near Fort Fisher on the evening of the 23rd. Her engines were then started and the ship brought closer. However, the night was clear and a blockade runner, *Little Hattie*, then inconveniently appeared. Not wanting to alert the fort's sentries, Rhind anchored the boat at a point he thought was about 300 yards away, but which was actually about twice as far.[49] The fuses were lit and the crew got away. The *Louisiana* went up in a huge explosion shortly before 2:00 A.M. on the 24th. Nevins called it "one of the most ludicrous fiascoes of the war." Rhind, watching his work go up in smoke, remarked "There's a fizzle," and went below. The explosion, though impressive, had done absolutely nothing to the fort except waken its garrison and badly frighten some of the teenaged recruits. There would be no easy entry into Fort Fisher. [50]

On 24 December, Porter began an exceptionally heavy naval bombardment, firing over a hundred rounds a minute into the fort. The fort replied, but with fairly limited fire, both because the bombardment made the gun emplacements exceedingly uncomfortable and because ammunition needed to be saved. Nevertheless, several of Porter's ships were damaged by the fort's fire. More serious were five separate accidental explosions of Parrott rifles in the fleet, causing 37 casualties. Eventually, Porter had to order the 100-pounder Parrotts out of the battle.

Butler finally arrived late in the day, exceedingly disgruntled by Porter's actions. Porter was equally peeved at the transports, arriving too late to attempt a landing that day, and suspended the bombardment. Some 10,000 shells had been thrown into Fort Fisher with, it turned out, very little effect.[51] The landing took place on Christmas Day, north of the fort. About 2,000 troops went ashore, under Weitzel's command, while Porter resumed the naval bombardment. Although the landing was unopposed, it soon became apparent that the fort was still full of resistance. Canister exploded in the advancing ranks, and the minefield took its toll as well. Furthermore, the wind was coming up, which meant that reembarkation might become impossible. Finally, Confederate prisoners boasted that 6,000 men under General Robert Hoke were on their way from Wilmington. Although Butler's orders from Grant explicitly directed him to entrench and besiege the fort if necessary, he thought it impossible to carry the place by storm and simply did not want to undertake a siege. He therefore ordered the withdrawal of the troops, although officers on the scene felt that a determined attack would have worked. The withdrawal had to be broken off when the surf became too high to bring in the boats. Butler sailed for Hampton Roads, leaving 700 men on the beach.[52]

Porter was livid. Even before the attack, relations between the two men had become so bad that they only communicated through intermediaries. Now Butler had abandoned the joint effort, leaving his men and Porter in the lurch. Porter, to his credit, kept up a continuous fire and managed to get the 700 men off the beach when the wind changed the next day. He then gradually withdrew to Beaufort.

The Confederates were naturally jubilant at the repulse of the huge expedition. Colonel Lamb telegraphed, "This morning, the foiled and frightened enemy left our shore." General Braxton Bragg, the department commander, wrote President Davis with the news, commending Lamb and his superior, Brigadier General W.H.C. Whiting, for "gallantry, efficiency, and fortitude displayed under very trying circumstances."[53]

Reaction in the North was stinging. Grant wired Lincoln that "The Wilmington expedition has proven a gross and culpable failure. . . . Who is to blame will, I hope, be known." Porter, writing General William T. Sherman, whom he hoped would replace Butler, included a sharp barb at the Army: "When you have captured [Savannah] I invite you to add to your brow the laurels thrown away by General Butler after they were laid at his feet by the navy, and which neither he nor those with him had the courage to gather up." To Secretary Welles, Porter wrote: "I feel ashamed that men calling themselves soldiers should have left this place so ingloriously . . . . [In] a war like this, so many incompetent men in the Army are placed in charge of important trusts . . . . If this temporary failure succeeds in sending General Butler into private life, it is not to be regretted." Later, when Butler attempted to blame the failure on the Navy, Porter pronounced Butler's report "a tissue of misstatements from beginning to end."[54] The fiasco ended Butler's military career. Lincoln had been reelected and no longer needed to tread as lightly with the War Democrats; after a quick calculation of Butler's support, which was still strong among black troops and abolitionists, he authorized Grant to relieve him. In early January, Butler was replaced as commander of the Army of the James by Major General E.O.C. Ord.[55]

Although Porter had wanted Sherman to replace Butler, Grant's choice, Major General Alfred H. Terry, was an excellent one. Terry, a Yale Law School graduate and court clerk who played the flute for recreation, was as unlike the flamboyant Butler as could be imagined. Though not a professional soldier, Terry had risen to corps command by his own merit. He was quiet, dependable, and easygoing—qualities that would help in dealing with the mercurial, self-promoting Porter.[56] Grant's instructions to Terry left no doubt that he did not want a repetition of the former command friction:

> Grant wrote to Porter in the same vein: "I send Major-General A.H. Terry with the same troops General Butler had, with one picked brigade added, to renew the attempt on Fort Fisher . . . . [He] will consult with you fully, and will be governed by your suggestions as far as his responsibility for the safety of his command will admit of."[57]

Porter was somewhat dubious of Terry, both because he had been a subordinate of Butler's and because the additional soldiers he brought were U.S. Colored Troops, of whom Porter disapproved. However, once the two men met, at Beaufort on 8 January, things went well. After a 3-

98

day gale, the expedition set out on 12 January, the largest ever to sail under the American flag to that time. Porter had 59 warships mounting 627 guns, while Terry had nearly 9,000 men in the 21 transport vessels.[58]

The fleet arrived at Wilmington late that night. Porter had been dissatisfied with the accuracy of his naval gunnery in the first bombardment; far too many shells had sailed over the fort and landed in the river, or simply buried themselves in the sand. His instructions to his fleet directed commanders to fire "deliberately . . . never . . . fire at the flag or pole, but . . . pick out the guns." The Parrotts, whose explosions had caused such problems the first time, were to be fired, if at all, only with reduced charges.[59]

The fort's garrison was only some 700 men; Hoke's division, which had arrived just as Butler withdrew, had itself been withdrawn to Wilmington by Bragg, who did not think that the Union would attack again before spring. Colonel Lamb, upon sighting the fleet, send an urgent appeal to Bragg, who ordered Hoke back, telling him to prevent a landing, and if it had already occurred, to establish a defensive line to protect Wilmington.

Porter began the bombardment before dawn on the 13th, hoping to provoke the fort's guns into disclosing their location by muzzle flashes. This worked, and after sunrise the rest of the fleet joined in, sending into the fort a fire as heavy as, and substantially more accurate than, the December bombardment. The landing began between 0800 and 0900 hours. To guard against a repetition of the December fiasco, where the men had been marooned for a day, they carried 3-days' rations. Terry's biggest fear was an attack during the landing by Hoke's troops; therefore, the Federals were ordered to establish a defensive line facing north. The landing was unopposed, however, and by mid-afternoon 8,000 men were ashore. Porter kept up the bombardment until dark, and left his ironclads at work all night to discourage repairs to the fort. Several ships were damaged, but none severely.[60]

By this time, Hoke's division had advanced from Wilmington and set up a defensive line. Despite appeals from the fort, Bragg, who thought the Federal force too strong to resist, at first refused to order Hoke to attack the forces on the peninsula. Colonel Lamb was reinforced by some North Carolina troops and sailors, bringing his force to about 1,550. Later, on the 14th, Bragg ordered Hoke to attack and went out to the scene. Upon seeing the well-entrenched Federal troops (whose numbers he overestimated), Bragg thought the assault futile, especially given the power of the fleet. He countermanded his order and Hoke remained quiescent.[61]

Porter resumed the bombardment on the 14th. It had a substantial effect; General Whiting, who thought Bragg a fool and had come to share the fort's fate, said: "It was beyond description, no language can describe the terrific bombardment." The fort took some 300 casualties from the bombardment, and only one gun on the landface was still operational.[62]

Porter and Terry met that night aboard Porter's flagship and planned the land assault. The fleet would continue its bombardment until 1500 hrs. on the 15th. At that time, two columns would assault the fort, one Army, one Navy. The Army assault, made up of 4,000 troops, would hit the landface near its western end, while the Navy one, 2,000 sailors and marines, would attack the Northeast Bastion. The remaining 4,000 Army troops ashore would protect against an attack in their rear by Hoke. The naval assault was a dubious proposition, consisting as it did of sending men innocent of infantry tactics and armed only with cutlasses and pistols, against strong works. Perhaps Porter, despite his excellent cooperation with Terry, was loath to give the Army all the glory of storming the fort. In any event, the assault failed; the sailors were badly cut up by musketry and cannister, taking about 300 casualties. Pinned down by fire, they desperately attempted to dig holes in the sand and finally broke and ran.

However, the naval assault had done the Army attackers a great service; convinced that this was the main assault, the defenders' manpower and attention were diverted from the landface. Even as the exultant Confederates saw, in Lamb's words, "a disorderly rout of American sailors and marines," Federal battle flags appeared on the western end of the landface. A counterattack was mounted, but then the fleet opened up on the Confederates massed in the fort, creating havoc. Fierce hand-to-hand fighting ensued at the landface, where the ships could not fire without hitting their own men. The fight moved from one traverse to another, not ending until about 2200 hrs.[63]

The fort surrendered some 2,000 men and 169 guns. Terry had 955 casualties and Porter 386. Approximately 250 more Federal casualties resulted from the accidental explosion of the fort's main magazine on the day after its surrender. The surrender of Fort Fisher prompted a national celebration. Grant ordered the firing of 100-gun salutes at his City Point headquarters, and Congress tendered its thanks to both Terry and Porter. The strategic value of closing the South's last blockade-running port was apparent to both President Lincoln and the Northern public, while southern response was gloomy in the extreme.[64]

The essential part that joint operations had played in the Fort Fisher campaign was readily apparent to participants from both Services. Porter wrote to Secretary Welles: "[General Terry] is my *beau ideal* of a soldier and a general. Our co-operation has been most cordial; the result is victory, which will always be ours when the Army and Navy go hand in hand."[65] Secretary of War Stanton wrote to Terry and Porter: "The combined operations of the squadron and land forces of your commands deserve and will receive the thanks of the nation, and will be held in admiration throughout the world as a proof of the naval and military prowess of the United States."[66]

CONCLUSIONS

Two campaigns—one early, one late; one riverine, one from the ocean—have been reviewed in detail. What conclusions can be drawn from them about joint operations in the Civil War?

The first, quite straightforwardly, is that *joint warfare existed and could work effectively.* Joint operations were not, as some seem to think, something which sprang full blown, like Athena from Zeus's brow, in World War II or 1986. They existed in the Civil War; commanders like Grant, Porter, and Foote were "thinking jointly" in that they were considering campaigns in terms of what resources the Army and the Navy could bring to the objective, and how the two could work together to accomplish it. Both the Henry-Donelson campaign and the Fort Fisher operation presented difficult problems of terrain, weather, logistics, tactics, and strategy. Joint operations solved these problems, or at least dealt with them to the extent necessary for success. Joint operations may not have been "essential to victory," as *Joint Pub l* asserts today, but they certainly contributed in very important respects to the attainment of victory.

Second, *by the end of the Civil War, joint operations had achieved a high degree of sophistication.* The contrast between the rather small-scale Henry-Donelson operation, pushed by Grant in the face of opposition from the Army command, uncoordinated with other movements, and not followed up, and the Fort Fisher operation, with its huge scale, full support from both War and Navy Departments, and detailed planning, is instructive. Fort Fisher illustrates as well the industrial and organizational maturity which the war vastly accelerated in the north and which, to Allan Nevins, was its most important contribution to the nation.[67] Much of this sophistication would be lost with the end of the war (as the logistical nightmares and command squabbling of the Spanish-American War were to show), but for the United States to have attained this level of sophistication in operations in the 1860s, with a volunteer army, was a remarkable feat. No other nation in the world—including the vaunted Prussians and French—could have carried out the Fort Fisher operation. Indeed, operations of this scale and maturity were not to be seen again until World War II.

Finally, notwithstanding the very real advances set out above, *the command structure for joint operations remained deficient throughout the war.* Ultimately, the success or failure of these operations depended upon the personalities of the Army and Navy commanders. In the absence of a commander in chief, it was only by cooperation and good relations between them that victory could be attained. The hatred existing between Butler and Porter was enough to doom the first expedition to Fort Fisher, notwithstanding the military, economic, and political power that lay behind it. It is only in our own age that we have succeeded, we think, in exorcizing interservice rivalries by giving real powers to joint combatant commanders. Will this in fact work? The experience in the Persian Gulf was positive, but he who thinks that formal command arrangements can reduce men to smoothly-functioning machines understands neither history nor the fog and friction of war. All command arrangements can do is provide the best possible framework for what must be done, and those in the Civil War were deficient in that respect; ad hoc relationships, not formal organization, were the essence of success in joint operations.

The American Civil War was a war of tradition—dazzling Napoleonic maneuvers, bayonet charges, cavalry skirmishes—and of innovation—minefields, submarines, and rifled artillery. Lincoln, in his Second Annual Message to Congress in 1862, told Americans: "The dogmas of the quiet past are inadequate to the stormy present. The occasion is piled high with difficulty, and we must rise with the occasion. As our case is new, so we must think anew, and act anew. We must disenthrall ourselves, and then we shall save our country."[68] Those who carried out joint operations in the war had indeed disenthralled themselves from military dogma; the occasion, "piled high with difficulty" as it was, brought forth innovation, organization, and ultimately victory on a grand scale.

NOTES

1. Harry Pfanz, *Gettysburg: The Second Day* (Chapel Hill: University of North Carolina Press, 1987).

2. Rowena Reed, *Combined Operations in the Civil War* (Annapolis: Naval Institute Press, 1978).

3. Karl von Clausewitz, *On War* (Princeton, N.J.: Princeton University Press, 1976).

4. Dennis Hart Mahan, *An Elementary Treatise on Advanced-Guard. Out-Post, and Detachment Service of Troops* . . . (New Orleans, LA: Bloomfield & Steel, 1861).

5. William J. Hardee, *Hardee's Rifle and Light Infantry Tactics* (New York, N.Y.: J.O. Kane, 1862).

6. Antoine Henri Jomini, *The Art of War* (Philadelphia, PA: J.B. Lippincott & Co., 1862), 248-52.

7. Ibid., 248, 250-51. He did warn the defender "not to divide his forces too much by attempting to cover every point," advice which would have been useful for the Confederacy. Ibid., 251.

8. Ibid, 361-390.

9. Jack Sweetman, *The United States Naval Academy: An Illustrated History* (Annapolis, MD: Naval Institute Press, 1979), 3-17.

10. Geoffrey S. Smith, "An Uncertain Passage: The Bureaus Run the Navy, 1842-1861," in Kenneth J. Hagan , ed., *In Peace and War: Interpretations of American Naval History, 1775-1984* (Westport, CN: Greenwood Press, 1984), 86-87.

11. Bruce Lancaster, *From Lexington to Liberty* (New York, N.Y.: Doubleday & Co., 1955), 358-59, 430-55.

12. K. Jack Bauer, *The Mexican War 1846-1848* (New York, N.Y.: MacMillan, 1974), 236-44.

13. Charles W. Elliott, *Winfield Scott: The Soldier and the Man* (New York, N.Y.: MacMillan, 1937), 722-23.

14. Ibid., Reed, Chapter 2.

15. Ibid., 188.

16. Ibid., 189.

17. The obvious place for fortifications on the Tennessee and Cumberland Rivers was at the Birmingham "Narrows" between Paducah and Eddyville, where the rivers are only three miles apart. However, this site is well within Kentucky and therefore was politically off-limits in 1861. Benjamin Franklin Cooling, *Forts Henry and Donelson: Key to the Confederate Heartland* (Knoxville,TN: University of Tennessee Press, 1987), 46.

18. U.S. Army Service Schools, *Fort Henry and Fort Donelson Campaigns Source Book* (Fort Leavenworth, KS: The General Service Schools Press, 1923), 158.

19. Cooling, 46.

20. Ibid., 56; *Source Book*, 182.

21. Bern Anderson, *By Sea and by River: The Naval History of the Civil War* (Westport, CT: Greenwood Press, 1977), 91.

22. *Source Book*, 14.

23. Cooling, 23-24.

24. Ibid., 25-27; *Source Book*, 79, 307.

25. Ulysses S. Grant, *Personal Memoirs of U.S. Grant* (New York, NY: Library of America, 1990), 189.

26. William S. McFeely, *Grant: A Biography* (New York, NY: W.W. Norton & Co., 1981), 96-97.

27. Grant, 190.

28. *Source Book*, 139-44; U.S. Department of the Navy, Naval History Division, *Civil War Naval Chronology 1861-1865* (Washington, DC: Department of the Navy, 1971), 11-14.

29. McFeely, 97; *Source Book,* 142: Herman Hattaway and Archer Jones, *How the North Won* (Urbana, IL: University of Illinois Press, 1983), 65-66.

30. Cooling, 101-6; Hattaway and Jones, 66-67.

31. *Source Book,* 327; Cooling, 106.

32. Anderson, 94-96; McFeely, 98-99.

33. Anderson, 96-97; *Chronology,* 11-22; Grant, 204; and Cooling, 136.

34. Grant, 204.

35. Accounts as to why Pillow made this seemingly inexplicable decision vary. Some say it was a withdrawal to regroup and remove stores from the fort, others that his tactical victory convinced him that the fort could be defended. Cooling, 180-82.

36. Grant, 190.

37. McFeely, 105-10; Grant, 219-21.

38. *Source Book,* 691.

39. Richard E. Beringer, et al, *Why the South Lost the Civil War* (Athens,GA: University of George Press, 1986), 185-202.

40. Rod Gragg, *Confederate Goliath: The Battle of Fort Fisher* (New York, N.Y.: Harper Collins, 1991), 2.

41. A ton of coffee could be purchased in Nassau for $249 and resold in Wilmington for $5500; the blockade runner could then buy cotton for 3 cents a pound and resell it in Great Britain for $1 a pound. A bottle of gin purchased for $4 in Bermuda could be resold in Wilmington for $150. Ibid., 8.

42. Ibid., 11-12.

43. Ibid., 18-21.

44. Ibid., 34-37; Reed, 331-33.

45. Gragg, 38-39. See generally Dick Nolan, *Benjamin Franklin Bulter: The Damnedest Yankee* (Novato, CA: Presidio, 1991).

46. Allan Nevins, *Ordeal of the Union, Vol. 8: The Organized War to Victory: 1864-1855* (New York, NY: Charles Scribners' Sons, 1971), 190; Hattaway and Jones, 658-59.

47. Grant, 663; Gragg, 40-42; Reed, 337-38. For the scientific calculations supporting the idea see U.S. Navy Department, *Official Records of the Union and Confederate Navies in the War of the Rebellion,* Series I, Vol. 2 (Washington, DC: Department of the Navy, 1900), 207-14.

48. Shelby Foote, *The Civil War: A Narrative. Vol. 3: Red River to Appomattox* (New York, NY: Random House, 1974), 715-17.

49. Gragg, 50-51; U.S. Navy Dept., I, 2, 226-27.

50. Nevins, 190; Gragg, 51-53. After the war, Bulter blamed the failure of the powder-boat on Navy incompetence. A typical Butlerian squabble followed. See U.S. Navy Dept., I, 2, 237-40.

51. Foote, 719.

52. U.S. Navy Dept., I, 2, 149-50, 250-51; Gragg, 88-97; Foote, 720.

53. Foote, 720; U.S. War Department, *The War of the Rebellion: A Compilation of the Official Records of the Union and Confederate Armies*, Series I, Vol. 44 (Washington, DC: GPO, 1893), 825.

54. U.S. War Dept., I, 44, 832; U.S. Navy Dept., I, 11, 264, 268; Grant, 668.

55. Foote, 739-40; Gragg, 103-4.

56. Gragg, 105-6.

57. U.S. Navy Dept., I, 11, 404-5.

58. Gragg, 107-09.

59. U.S. Navy Dept., I, 11, 425-27; Anderson, 281-82.

60. Foote, 741-42; Gragg, 114.

61. Gragg, 126-27.

62. Chronology, V-11.

63. Gragg, 157-90.

64. Grant, 670; Foote, 746.; Gragg, 322-42.

65. U.S. Navy Dept., I, 46, part 2 (Washington, DC: GPO, 1895), 140.

66. U.S. Navy Dept., I, 11, 458.

67. U.S. Joint Chiefs of Staff, *Joint Warfare of the U.S. Armed Forces*, Joint Pub 1, 11 November 1991), iii; Nevins, Chapters 13 and 14.

68. Roy Basler, ed., *Abraham Lincoln: His Speeches and Writings* (Cleveland, Ohio: World Publishing Co., 1946), 688.

4

COALITION WARFARE:

PREPARING THE U.S. COMMANDER
FOR THE FUTURE

TERRY J. PUDAS

Current enthusiasm about coalition military operations as a result of *Desert Storm* might suggest this is a new idea in political-military thinking. It is not. One of the earliest examples of coalition warfare was the Peloponnesian War between the Delian League led by Athens and the coalition of city-states led by Sparta.[1] The Gulf War is only the most recent example of countries forming a coalition of combined military operations to achieve mutual objectives. U.S. participation in any future regional conflict will probably be with a coalition.

The experience of *Desert Storm* and the global security uncertainties since the dissolution of the Soviet Union have highlighted the need for major revisions in military strategic thinking. Collective security has been articulated as a central theme of United States strategy. Both the

---

Captain Terry J. Pudas, U.S. Navy, was a student at the Naval War College when his essay was honored as a Distinguished Essay in the 1993, Chairman, Joint Chiefs of Staff, Strategy Essay Competition.

August 1991 and the January 1993 National Security Strategies stress collective security. The National Military Strategy also recognizes the benefits of collective security arrangements and the utility of multinational operations. It stresses, however, that the United States must not only be ready to fight as part of an ad hoc coalition, but that it must also retain the capability to act unilaterally if required.[2]

The ever-increasing interdependence of the world's economic system has produced an environment within which the United States and other nations share uncounted vital interests. Threats to these interests will most probably be dealt with in a combined fashion with some traditional allies and coalition forces from other affected nations. Renewed emphasis on collective security and the U.S. policy to promote multinational operations sanctioned by the United Nations suggests that coalition operations are likely to be the dominant mode for employment of U.S. military forces in the future.

The U.S. experience includes participation as an alliance or coalition partner in five major 20th-century conflicts.[3] The United States fought in World War I as a partner to England and France. In World War II the United States fought in an alliance in which it coordinated operations with Russia and took the lead in commanding and executing combined operations with England, France, and other countries. The United States also led the United Nation's in Korea; in Vietnam coalition operations were conducted in with the South Vietnamese and contingents from other Pacific nations. In *Desert Storm*, however, the United States fought as a member of a "hybrid coalition," which included traditional and nontraditional allies. The hybrid coalition has been suggested as the new model for future U.S. military operations.

Wars at the higher end of the conflict spectrum, such as major regional conflicts and global wars, will still be fought by alliances and coalitions. The applicability and desirability of coalition warfare at the lower end of the conflict spectrum have received only limited discussion. The advantages and disadvantages of coalition warfare vary across the spectrum and have both political and military implications. Documents such as the Allied Tactical Publications of the North Atlantic Treaty Organization (NATO) and volumes of other material govern the conduct of operations in the U.S. standing alliance relationships. Comparatively few detailed resources are available to prepare an operational commander for the more likely future scenarios involving ad hoc coalitions. An examination of coalition complexities will provide an understanding of the benefits and disadvantages of coalition operations across the warfare spectrum from both the political and military perspectives.

COALITION AND ALLIANCE DYNAMICS

Nations join coalitions and alliances for many different reasons. These motives can determine both the relationship between those nations and the effectiveness of their formal arrangements. Mutual advantage and shared interests are the primary reasons but other considerations can include what a coalition partner can offer in terms of economic, political, or military power.

Unity of purpose for achieving mutual objectives binds partners together. Consensus on what constitutes unity of purpose though may merely be an overlap in all the partners' broader objectives, rather than the total agreement on each nation's objectives.[4]

Each alliance is first and foremost a political coalition. A nation's contribution and participation depends on its own political agenda. The more the coalition's objectives in a specific case differ from those of an individual member nation the more likely it will be to withdraw from the coalition.[5]

Collective security as a method of defense against threats to a nation's survival has been the historical basis for founding military alliances. Each nation contributes to an agreed strategy for pursuing security interests. These coalitions can provide a unity of military effort to achieve common security interests and a burden-sharing arrangement by which a nation can relieve some of the economic waste caused by duplication of military capabilities.

The ability of alliances and coalitions to function is also influenced by each nation's historical perceptions. Before World War I a complicated web of collective security arrangements existed in Europe. After the war collective security arrangements were widely believed to have contributed more to causing the war than to preserving the peace. This may explain the reluctance of many nations during the 1930s to commit themselves to collective security organizations and their selective contributions of military support in ad hoc relationships.

Certain similarities characterize coalitions, but each is unique in its power relationships, ideologies, and the beliefs of the people who create the coalitions and make them work. The linking objectives and consensus process also vary in each coalition. Three types of collective security organizations have been used by modern nations to conduct coalition operations.

The United Nations is an example of a *global organization*, the most formal and enduring example of nations united for a common purpose. The overriding objective of each member is perpetuating its national survival. Although members rarely reach unanimity, military action in support of a UN resolution normally enjoys a high degree of legitimacy. The disadvantage of these large, more diverse organizations is the difficulty in reaching consensus for action; therefore, the effectiveness and the timeliness of its decisions can be degraded.

Regional organizations such as NATO and the Organization of American States (OAS) are generally more homogeneous and focused in terms of mutual interests and strategic objectives. Reaching a consensus on common objectives and strategies is sometimes easier and quicker in regional than in worldwide organizations. The enduring nature of a standing regional security alliance also provides its members' military forces with significant advantages. Military commanders have the opportunity to organize and train their forces in combined operations. Problems hampering ad hoc coalitions (command and control, interoperability, logistics, and differing doctrines) can be overcome or minimized. Although these alliances have been credited with promoting regional peace and providing a forum for conflict resolution, none has been put to the test as a warfighting organization.

The third and most prevalent organization for conducting military operations is the ad hoc coalition. Every conflict in which the United States has participated since World War II has been fought either unilaterally or as a member of an ad hoc coalition. None of the military actions has been conducted, practically speaking, as the combined effort of a standing regional security alliance in which the United States was a member. Even though the United Nations played a major role in Korea (1950-53) and the Persian Gulf (1990-91), the military forces that fought the wars operated as members of an ad hoc coalition. The United States has carried out numerous other operations as a member of an ad hoc organization in support of UN resolutions or sanctions. Even the U.S. "war on drugs" is being prosecuted as an ad hoc coalition. Historically, when the United States has conducted multinational operations, it has done so as a member of an ad hoc coalition.

Multinational organizations are guided by considerations of political advantage in decisionmaking.[7] The contributions of coalition partners in armed conflict are directly related to a nation's political objectives. The two remaining dominant factors in coalitions are that decisions are reached by consensus and military considerations are generally subordinated to political matters.

COALITION WARFARE: PROS AND CONS

Coalitions provide the framework within which nations pool military resources to attain common political objectives. Though most often thought of in positive terms, coalitions are often a source of weakness as well as strength. Coalitions are not the same as friendships and are entered into for reasons of political self-interest.[8] A March 1991 Congressional Research Service Report on the Anti-Iraq Coalition observed that "Any multi-state coalition is unwieldy and fragile. Areas of commonality binding members together are usually less than the policy differences which remain."[9]

A commander must not only understand the dynamics that influence a coalition but must also be aware of their political and military advantages and disadvantages. The benefits of coalition warfare are determined by comparing these advantages and disadvantages from both a military and a political perspective.

Coalitions offer weaker nations a vehicle for expressing their political views in combination with stronger coalition members, and thus for increasing their influence on world events. Conducting military operations as a member of a coalition contributes to the legitimacy of the military action—a big political advantage. Unilateral operations, as in Grenada and Panama, often require the United States to provide overwhelming evidence and extensive justification to the world community. In comparison, military operations in support of a UN resolution are accepted as legitimate. Rarely are coalition military operations viewed negatively either.

Political unity of purpose and military unity of effort among coalition partners have historically been strong as long as a threat existed to their shared vital interests. In World Wars I and II, as the defeat of the common enemy became inevitable, individual coalition members' interests began to diverge in pursuit of national rather than coalition objectives. Individual national war aims and political objectives detracted from the combined military strategy, as each partner attempted to promote its own political agenda. The coalition of allies made the agreement of war aims more complicated. The World War I Treaty of Versailles became a treaty negotiated among the principal allies rather than a peace negotiated with the former Central Powers. As a result, the settlement was influenced by each country's individual and expanded war aims. France demanded territory for security and economic reasons in addition to large war reparations. England's main concern was maintaining the economic security of the empire and preventing the French from gaining too much influence. The United States negotiated on the basis of Wilson's 14 points, which emphasized borders based on self-determination, open treaties, and creation of a League of Nations. This settlement negotiated among the coalition partners following World War I has been identified as contributing to the start of World War II. Likewise, the diverse political objectives and ideologies of partners in the World War II Grand Alliance have been blamed for creating the postwar political instability that produced the Cold War.

A disadvantage of coalition operations is the existence of unique political objectives which become "hidden agendas" and influence a nation's position on strategy and the effort and resources it will contribute to the coalition.[10] This situation is very similar to the one in the recent Anti-Iraq Coalition, whose unity of purpose did not necessarily mean unity of effort. Nations based their contributions to the effort on their own political interests. Contributions ranged from ground forces, naval assets, and certain specialized equipment to economic aid for the countries in the region.

The political leadership by the coalition partners is a significant factor that often restricts a commander's ability to achieve military unity of effort. Coalition political leaders are often reluctant and sensitive about placing their military under the command of another coalition partner. Political considerations often dictate command relationship and can lead to an ambiguous and uncertain chain of command.

During *Desert Storm* the contributions of coalition partners were sometimes subject to the dynamics of changing political events. For example, the possibility that Israel would enter the conflict produced uncertainty about whether Arab forces would remain in the coalition. Additionally, last minute signals from Baghdad and Russian diplomatic proposals produced a less than unanimous reaction among coalition partners. Uncertainty about which nations would deploy combat forces and to what extent they would actually contribute to the liberation of Kuwait was detrimental to the overall operation.

The timeliness of decisionmaking also influences the desirability of coalition operations. The process of achieving consensus on the alliance's political objectives and military strategies takes time. Though necessary, this process can be a disadvantage to the military commander. The larger and more diverse the coalition, the more ineffective this decision process becomes.

Membership in, or leadership of, a coalition may be disadvantageous to the United States and may limit its ability to achieve its own political objectives. The United States may be capable of operating unilaterally and constitute the majority of the coalition forces, but political considerations may limit its freedom of action.[11] To achieve political consensus, the United States may have to make concessions in its war aims to appease other coalition partners and thus, be denied the military actions that would achieve its own political objectives.

Ad hoc coalitions can also dictate the tempo of operations. In *Desert Storm* the coalition was never formalized by a treaty. Additionally, many members did not share long histories of mutual cooperation. The result was an organization with a fragile and less enduring relationship. Therefore, the ad hoc nature of the coalition influenced the urgency of planning and execution of decisions as well as the pace of events.

Historically, a coalition's primary advantage has stemmed from its ability to combine and coordinate military effort to achieve common political objectives. Coalitions can generate significant amounts of combat power in a relatively short time. The ability to combine the unique and complementary forces of different military organizations can provide a synergistic advantage to coalitions. An example during *Desert Storm* was the anti-mine capability provided by the British.

A coalition's success normally depends on its ability to achieve unity of effort among the contributing nations' military forces. Nearly all military advantages and disadvantages of coalition warfare stem from this single concept. In military terms it is expressed as one of the principles of war, "unity of command." In many instances it may not be politically feasible, as was the case in both Vietnam and *Desert Storm*. In both conflicts, nations agreed to aims and strategies for using forces without agreeing to a unified command structure.[12] In Vietnam there were parallel Vietnamese, Korean, American, and Australian chains of command, but no overall combined commander. In *Desert Storm*, unity of effort was achieved between Allied and Arab forces, not through a supreme commander, but through the cooperation and mutual support of the U.S and

Arab coalition commanders, General Schwarzkopf and General Khalid.

Other disadvantages of combined military operations in ad hoc coalitions are a result of national differences in language, culture, standards of living, military doctrine, and military equipment. These differences normally result in major interoperability problems. Interoperability difficulties, as a result of combining dissimilar forces, may degrade overall force capability. Early in the Tunisian Campaign of World War II, elements were integrated into allied units as far down as company and battery level. This mixing of inexperienced allied units may have actually degraded the overall combat potential of theater forces.[13] Logistics coordination is another potential disadvantage of coalition operations. Logistical sustainment is the cornerstone upon which the success of a military operation depends. Varying support requirements, ranging from unique ammunition to specific, dietary or cultural, requirements may restrict the employment options for coalition forces.

In coalitions, each nation's forces want to occupy an important and responsible position in relation to the other allied forces.[14] Additionally, the burden sharing and risk associated with each coalition partner should be equitable. In coalitions, true unity of command is normally not attainable since each nation's force contributes only through the consensus of its political leadership. The uncertainties of relying on another nation's forces can be disadvantageous in terms of risk. These uncertainties are of major concern for the United States, which most often contributes the preponderance of forces to a coalition and thus risks more by relying on coalition partners.

The success of a coalition military commander depends less on his operational expertise or the combat power of his forces than on his ability to promote cooperation and create an atmosphere of mutual respect. Personalities of senior commanders play a major role in the success or failure of coalition warfare.

While coalitions have the advantage of providing nations the means to pursue their common interests through coordinated military efforts, their political fragility can become a military vulnerability with political costs of its own. Clausewitz refers to a center of gravity as the hub of all power and movement on which everything depends. For coalitions, the center of gravity is the common objective that binds them together.[15] If a military advantage can be achieved by disrupting harmony and unity in an alliance, then the coalition's cohesion becomes its center of gravity. This understanding of the importance of allied unity influenced Roosevelt's decisions in World War II. He appeased Stalin and made strategic decisions to ensure that Russia did not dessert the alliance and make a separate peace with Germany, as it had during World War I. Saddam Hussein tried to disrupt coalition unity with SCUD attacks against Israel. He attempted to goad Israel into an active military role and thereby prompt the Arab states to abandon the coalition.

RELATIVE BENEFITS OF COALITION OPERATIONS

The political and military benefits of coalition warfare also vary across the warfare spectrum. The military advantages of coalition warfare normally exceed the disadvantages in a major global conflict such as World War II. When the survival of nations are at risk, the urgency to combine forces through coalitions and create combat power normally takes precedence over individual national interests. The political and military objectives translate into military power to defeat the common enemy. Thus, the necessity to create a superior combat force by combining military resources makes coalition warfare, from the military perspective, extremely desirable and more compelling at the high end of the spectrum. In World War II, the national political interests of individual coalition partners became secondary to the overall military objective.

At the low end of the spectrum, the political benefits of coalition warfare become a more important factor. When the United States acts as a member of a coalition, it is more politically acceptable than unilateral action and contributes to the legitimacy of the operation. Militarily, ad hoc coalitions with nontraditional allies, more often than not, can detract from and complicate operations in a limited military operation. The disadvantages resulting from complex command relationships and interoperability tend to make coalition warfare less desirable at the low end of the spectrum.

PLANNING FACTORS FOR COALITION WARFARE

Ad hoc coalitions are based on temporary agreements and are less formally structured than standing alliances. The psychological and sociological problems created by differences in culture, customs, religions, and standards of living require a unique approach to planning for coalition operations.[16] Historical experience with combined operations reveals that integrating multinational forces is a complex task, requiring a great deal of skill and understanding on the part of the commander. By understanding the unique considerations required by coalition warfare, the operational commander can more intelligently plan and anticipate issues and prevent their exacerbation through insensitivity and ignorance.[17] Creating this awareness among command and staff personnel is an essential element in preparing for future coalition operations.

A coalition commander's mission is to plan operations and direct the combat power of member nations to accomplish their common objective. Key planning considerations for combined operations must include command relationships, interoperability, logistical support, and risk to U.S. forces.

The most important element in preparing for combined operations is developing sound and effective coalition command relationships. A recent congressional report on the Gulf War noted that command relationships "met with difficulties, were complex, but workable."[18]

When unity of command cannot be achieved, unity of effort and an agreed strategy must be secured through the coordination and the cooperative efforts of allied commanders. Unity of command cannot be guaranteed in future ad hoc coalitions. Operational commanders can prepare themselves to achieve unity of effort by understanding the various factors that influence a coalition's ability to coordinate forces. Unity of effort can not be achieved unless commanders understand the political and military objectives of their allies and agree on how to fulfill these common objectives.

Dealings with allies must be accomplished with patience and respect. Commanders must establish and maintain trust among the coalition forces. Coordination and cooperation are the key ingredients to successful coalition command. Harnessing the personalities of allied military leaders and the problems associated with personal relationships can be one of the greatest challenges of coalition command.[19]

Effective use of the coalition's combat strength is most easily achieved when a combined staff, including capable and credible representation from each coalition nation, plans the operations. This coordinated planning is essential for unity of effort. In *Desert Storm* this was accomplished by creating a Coalition Coordination Communications and Integration Center (C³IC). Even though the planning must always be a coordinated effort, the responsibility for planning and execution should not be separated.[20] The overall planning responsibility for a specific operation should be vested in the commander responsible for its execution.

Several general considerations should guide the coalition planning efforts. A combined plan should reflect an appreciation of the unique capabilities of each national contingent in assignment of missions. Multinational forces should be employed so as to optimize their specific strengths and avoid duplicating or degrading their unique capabilities. Likewise, the plan must accommodate the comparative vulnerabilities of participating forces. Forces are normally most effective when employed under a military commander from their respective nations.

Other considerations affecting the planning process and mission assignment of coalition forces are common doctrine, logistical sustainment capabilities, and systems interoperability. One principle of war that has significant applicability to planning for coalition operations is "simplicity." It is essential that the plan be easily understood and executed by all combat forces in a coalition.

The second most important consideration in coalition planning is interoperability. The military success of the coalition depends on the commander's ability to harmonize the capabilities, doctrines, and logistics among forces of varied cultures and languages. In ad hoc coalitions such as *Desert Storm*, where nearly 40 different nations conributed to the effort, this can be a monumental task. Some general principles and planning considerations can contribute, however, to overcoming these interoperability problems. Unity of effort requires that forces coordinate on air defense, intelligence, electronic warfare, and the timing of operations. Establishing a communications network and interoperable connectivity are key to effectively coordinating these aspects of operations.

Liaison Officers have been one of the most effective and invaluable resources in assisting the coordination efforts of coalition forces. Colonel Hixon's study, *Combined Operations in Peace and War*, concludes that the Liaison Officer is essential to the success of combined operations, but also notes that "little thought is usually given to this problem prior to the commencement of operations."[21] Hixon devotes an entire section to this subject, describing the necessary attributes Liaison Officers and the considerations that should govern their conduct. The utility of Liaison Officers was confirmed again during the Persian Gulf War. During *Desert Storm*, nearly all non-U.S. coalition forces were accompanied by one or more Liaison Officers from the U.S. Special Operations Forces. The use of these language-trained Liaison Officers helped overcome interoperability problems and provided the communications links to coordinate the efforts of the coalition forces.

In ad hoc coalitions, interoperability problems are normally managed but are rarely solved completely. One proven method of minimizing interoperability problems is assigning each national force separate geographical or specific functional areas of responsibility. This preserves their unique capabilities and prevent dilution of combat powers. Such dilution occurs when incompatible units are combined. This also helps minimize "Blue on Blue" fratricidal engagements.

Dissemination of intelligence can impact the success of coalition military action. Planning and preparations must provide for timely dissemination of military intelligence to all partners in an operation.[22] Undoubtedly the degree of dissemination will vary with the coalition's membership. In ad hoc coalitions the United States may be operating with partners—with which it may be reluctant to share intelligence, especially anything that might reveal a sensitive source or collection capability. In *Desert Storm*, no preplanned system or mechanism governed the release and dissemination of essential military intelligence other than to traditional U.S. allies.

Logistical considerations are major factors affecting the success of every military operation. The support and the sustainment needs of multinational forces vary significantly and are influenced by factors such as different tactical doctrines or specific cultural dietary requirements. Experience in coalitions confirms the desirability of logistical support remaining a national responsibility. The combined staff must, however, ensure the coordination of any host national support including transportation networks and major facilities such as ports and airfields.

In coalition planning, the U.S. commander must always consider the risk to U.S. forces involved in combined operations and assume that other commanders have the same concerns. The assessment should concentrate on the dependability of other coalition forces, as well as their combat strengths and capabilities. Rules of Engagement (ROE) are a significant consideration in planning coalition operations. U.S. forces are governed by ROE and by the Law of Armed Conflict in war. Differing ROE among coalition partners, especially in operations short of war, could provoke an unexpected enemy response and put another nation's forces at risk. Coordination must ensure that ROE is consistent among coalition members. In *Desert Storm*, coordination among coalition military commanders and liaison teams ensured an effective degree of ROE consistency.[23]

The vulnerability of the coalition's center of gravity must also be evaluated. As mentioned earlier, the common political objective that binds the members becomes the coalition's center of gravity. In this case the plan must minimize risk to the center of gravity, even when this means extending protection beyond the coalition's members. For example, during the Persian Gulf War extensive actions were undertaken to defend Israel against SCUD attacks. Had Israel been provoked into a counterattack against Iraq the cohesiveness of the coalition might have been jeopardized. Such a breakup would have considerably increased risk to U.S. forces.

The next coalition war and the membership of the alliance cannot be predicted. The U.S. military can, however, take steps to prepare and enhance its capabilities for future coalition operations. Education on the subject of coalition warfare for senior officers is a prerequisite to future success. Increased studies emphasizing the planning considerations and execution decisions in ad hoc combined operations must also become a central element of service college curricula.

Preparations must focus on the most probable planning scenarios for future conflicts such as the Pentagon planning scenarios publicized in the *New York Times*.[24] Planning for these regional contingencies must take into account all the ramifications of potential future coalition operations. The United States should attempt to increase multinational training exercises in each theater with potential coalition partners. Combined exercises, regardless of size, are productive as they create a spirit of cooperation and enhance awareness of interoperability problems.[25] Increased language training for potential Liaison Officers can provide a significant advantage in future combined operations. The planning scenarios could tailor the language training program to specific regions and even the countries most likely to be coalition allies. Sales of U.S. military equipment to potential coalition partners and the training of foreign military forces is another means of enhancing interoperability in future ad hoc coalitions. Security assistance for critical infrastructure and International Military Education and Training (IMET) can enhance the potential success of future coalition operations.

EXECUTING COALITION WARFARE

Successfully executing coalition warfare requires a unique combination of both military and political prowess. As Clausewitz said, "Everything in war is very simple, but the simplest thing is difficult."[26] His observation is even more relevant in the case of ad hoc coalitions.

The key element for successful coalition warfare is the commander's ability to achieve a unity of effort among his forces. In an ad hoc coalition such as *Desert Storm*, this will normally be accomplished through cooperation, rather than through appointment of a supreme coalition commander. The prerequisite for unity of effort is unity of purpose which involves reaching consensus on military objectives and coalition strategy. The warfighting commander must ensure consensus before committing military forces to combined operations.

Both the planning and the execution phases should be accomplished as a coordinated effort. Combined staffs are the ideal means of ensuring that multinational forces are being utilized in compliance with their national, political, and military restrictions.

In actual execution the multidimensional battlefield requires special considerations when fighting a coalition war involving naval, land and air forces from a wide variety of coalition partners. Many of the concepts discussed as planning considerations were actually applied in the execution of the Gulf War. Coalition forces were assigned missions consistent with political restrictions on their use, mission requirements and force capabilities.[27]

Militarily and politically it is important that the United States and its allies fight side-by-side against the common enemy. This is particularly desirable from a national prestige perspective. In the Gulf it was important to ensure that each coalition member was provided the opportunity to contribute to the effort. At the same time, the assignment of forces and missions in ad hoc coalitions must reflect their unique capabilities and not create organizations for political purposes whose combat potential is degraded by a lack of interoperability. The options that best satisfy these requirements may be to functionally or geographically orient the various national units. Specifically, the options which should be considered are as follows:[28]

• Assign national single service or joint forces to a specific area of responsibility.

• Assign a national single service or joint force a specific function.

• Assign a combined single service force to a specific area of responsibility.

• Assign a combined joint force to a specific area of responsibility.

Each of these options provides a useful link between the means and the ends in a coalition war. Each of these assignment options was utilized in *Desert Storm*. Specific geographical areas of responsibility were assigned both to ground units and the naval units operating in the Gulf. Other units were assigned specific functions consistent with their capabilities, such as anti-mine warfare or air defense missions. The air war combined single service forces that were responsible for a specific functional area of the overall *Desert Storm* campaign. The Arab coalition functioned as a combined joint force with a specific geographical area of responsibility.

The responsibility for logistics support in ad hoc coalitions is best retained by each respective nation. Key transportation facilities and host nation support, such as POL and water, should be coordinated through the multinational combined staff. The medical treatment of casualties and medevac policies are also best left as individual national responsibilities.

The enemy prisoner of war (EPW) issue will always be a sensitive one, and because the United States normally contributes the most to a coalition in terms of military strength and political power, it will likely bear the responsibility for the welfare of enemy prisoners of war. No matter what arrangement is agreed upon, the United States must retain sufficient oversight and control to ensure appropriate treatment of EPWs and compliance with international guidelines. The United States must also ensure compliance with the provisions and intent of the International Law of Armed Conflict by all partners.

Another major consideration for a U.S. commander is the risk to U.S. forces. This means balancing the sometimes sensitive subject of equitable national burden sharing with consideration of risks that could result from desertion of coalition partners or a failure to achieve unity of effort. In *Desert Storm* some partners saw their role strictly as the defense of Saudi Arabia or the liberation of Kuwait while others committed forces into Iraq to neutralize Iraqi military power. As explained earlier, the closer the coalition is to victory, the more the individual partners diverge from the common objectives to pursue their own political agendas. In the war termination phase of coalition warfare, this phenomenon introduces an increased element of risk to U.S. forces. U.S. commanders must recognize this risk and design risk-reducing alternatives or unilateral options to protect both the interests and the military forces of the United States.

CONCLUSION

Desert Storm provides an opportunity to examine the complexities of coalition warfare on a large scale. It was, however, unique in character, and caution must be exercised when extrapolating that experience. The brevity of the war did not fully test the ad hoc coalition arrangements.[29]

A more appropriate approach would be to compare the historical evidence to the *Desert Storm* experience and view the lessons in the same context as Clausewitz viewed war, as an art not a science. The principles and concepts Clausewitz described are applicable in coalition warfare. Coalitions are political organizations whose primary purpose is to achieve the mutual political objectives of the member nations. The fog and friction of war, as well as the influences of the individual nation's paradoxical trinities, exacerbate the military complexities of coalition warfare. Each country must balance the political purpose, the military means, and the will of its people. As long as a nation's survival is not at risk, its contributions to a coalition will be motivated first by political self-interest.

From this examination of coalition warfare, the historical evidence and the recent *Desert Storm* lessons reveal four enduring principles that the operational commander must always consider when planning for and conducting coalition operations.

First, *unity of purpose* is the political adhesive that binds a coalition. The operational commander must understand the ultimate political objective and create the "military condition in the theater which will achieve the strategic goal."[30]

Second, he must ensure *unity of effort* to achieve military success in any combined coalition operation. When unity of command is not achievable, cooperation and coordination are the key ingredients to unity of effort. Using coordinated planning staffs and assigning Liaison Officers greatly enhances this effort.

Third, *interoperability* problems in ad hoc coalitions are best managed by using the appropriate force assignment options and by allowing individual nations to retain responsibility for logistical support. Issues related to intelligence sharing, treatment of EPWs, and ROE must be managed through cooperative planning and coordination.

Interoperability is often the major obstacle to achieving unity of effort, but measures can be undertaken to minimize these problems. Language training for Liaison Officers, targeted foreign military sales and security assistance, and combined exercises can all promote interoperability with potential coalition partners.

The commander must always be prepared to minimize and prevent potential risk to U.S. forces in combined operations. Ad hoc coalitions with nontraditional allies and no formalized treaties create a situation where the dynamics of changing political events may influence the military contribution of each partner. This may equate to increased risk to U.S. forces. Additionally, diverging national aims in the war termination phase or a vulnerability to the coalition's center of gravity may be sources of risk for U.S. forces.

Finally the military and political benefits derived from coalition operations varies across the spectrum of conflict. Although coalition warfare has been touted as the new "silver bullet" for future conflicts, its utility may be questionable in operations where unique U.S. interests are at stake. In scenarios where the United States is capable of unilateral operations the benefits of a coalition must be carefully weighed against potential disadvantages. In more fragile and less enduring ad hoc relationships the urgency to act may influence the timing of an operation. Even more important, to achieve consensus on unity of purpose, the United States may be restricted from pursuing all of its own national objectives.

Future commanders must prepare themselves and their staffs now for the eventualities of participating in ad hoc coalitions. Success in achieving U.S. objectives with minimum risk to U.S. forces may depend less on warfighting skills and more on the commander's understanding of the complexities of coalitions.

NOTES

1.   Robert W. Komer, *Martine Strategy or Coalition Defense?* (Cambridge, MA: Abbot Books, 1984), 21.

2.   Chairman of the Joint Chiefs of Staff, *The National Military Strategy of the United States* (Washington, DC: GPO, 1992), 9.

3.   R. W. Komer, *Needed; Preparation for Coalition War*, P-5707 (Santa Monica, CA: Rand, 1976), 2.

4.   *Warfighting: Its Planning and Conduct*, vol. I (Carlisle Barracks, PA: U.S. Army War College, 1988), I-84.

5.   *Basic National Defense Doctrine*, JCS Joint Pub 0-1, Proposed Final Pub (Washington, DC: GPO, 1991), II-47.

6.   James Cable, *Diplomacy at Sea* (Annapolis, MD: Naval Institute Press, 1985), 14.

7.   Keith Neilson and Roy A. Prede, ed., *Coalition Warfare: An Uneasy Accord* (Ontario: Wilfrid Lalurier University Press, 1983), viii.

8.   Mark M. Lowenthan, *The Persian Gulf War: Preliminary Policy "Lessons" and Perceptions* (Washington, DC: Congressional Research Service, Library of Congress, 1991), CRS-8.

9.   *Warfighting*, I-84.

10.   Lowenthal, CRS-8.

11.   *Warfighting*, I-84.

12.   John Hixon and Benjamin Franklin Cooling, *Combined Operations in Peace and War*, U.S. Army Military History Institute Publication (Carlisle Barracks, PA: U.S. Army Military Institute, 1982), 349.

13.   Elisha O. Peckham, "Organization for Combined Military Effort," *Military Review*, November 1950, 48.

14.   Harry G. Summers, Jr., *On Strategy II: A Critical Analysis of the Gulf War* (New York: Dell Publishing, 1991), 232.

15.   *The Joint Staff Officers Guide 1991*, Armed Forces Staff College Publication (Washington, DC: GPO, 1991), 2-43.

16.   Hixon and Cooling, ii.

17.   Department of Defense, *Conduct of the Persian Gulf War, An Interim Report* (Washington, DC: GPO, 1991), 20-4.

18.   Jacob L. Deavers, "Major Problems Confronting a Theater Commander in Combined Operations," *Military Review*, October 1947, 14.

19. *Warfighting,* I-86.

20. Hixson and Cooling, 360.

21. *FM 100-5 Operations* (Washington, DC: Department of the Army, 1986), 166.

22. *Conduct of the Persian Gulf War,* 16-1.

23. Patrick E. Tyler, "7 Hypothetical Conflicts Foreseen by the Pentagon," *New York Times,* 17 February 1992, A7.

24. Hixson and Cooling, 363.

25. Carl Von Clausewitz, *On War,* ed. and trans. Michael Howard and Peter Paret (Princeton, NJ: Princeton University Press, 1989), 119.

26. *Conduct of the Persian Gulf War,* 20-2.

27. *Warfighting,* I-85.

28. *Conduct of the Persian Gulf War,* 20-2.

5

MOVING THE FORCE:
DESERT STORM AND BEYOND

SCOTT W. CONRAD

In a tale of war, the fierce glory that plays on red trium-
phant bayonets dazzles the observer. Nor does he care
to look behind to where along the thousand miles of rail,
road and river, the convoys are crawling to the front in
uninterrupted succession. Victory is the beautiful, bright
colored flower. Transportation is the stem without
which it would never have blossomed.

> *Winston Churchill*
> The River War, 1899

THE DEATH KNELL OF SUPERPOWER COMMUNISM HAD SOUNDED.
To those who had not heard it, Saddam Hussein served to
refocus America's global containment strategy to one of
regionalism. While years of planning had centered on a
U.S.-Soviet standoff, a regional flashpoint actually drove us
to war. We may debate whether *Desert Storm* represented
the last page of the Cold War or the first of

Lieutenant Colonel Scott W. Conrad, U.S. Army, was a student
at the Industrial College of the Armed Forces when he wrote this
paper. It was selected as a Distinguished Essay in the 1993
Chairman, Joint Chiefs of Staff, Strategy Essay Competition.

the new world order. Of one thing we can be certain: The function of movement that had so often taken a back seat in America's military buildup of the eighties was suddenly thrust into the forefront. For the massive Persian Gulf War deployment was perhaps the greatest in the history of the world. General Jimmy D. Ross, then the U.S. Army's Deputy Chief of Staff for Logistics, likened the feat to "moving the entire population, and all movable objects, from Atlanta, to Saudi Arabia"—a distance of well over 8,000 miles.[1] On the battlefield, transporters then spearheaded the now famous "Hail Mary" flanking action, sealing the Gulf War victory.

In July 1990, with the Soviet Union in disarray, the U.S. military appeared on the verge of a budgetary freefall. The desert war provided a reality check, of sorts: Perhaps America *should* maintain the capability to project a decisive land force to distant shores, after all. Throughout the buildup, many recognized that all the planning, training, and equipping imaginable wouldn't get forces to the fight. They had to have the capacity to deploy anywhere, with the right mix of firepower and support, in sufficient time. The Gulf War's successes aside, various aspects of our movement capacity did not measure up to this test.

Although Gulf War deployment triumphs were highly publicized, shortcomings were not. History shows that logistical lessons are usually the most easily forgotten aspects of any conflict. During crisis, there is no opportunity for reflecting on the lessons of that event. Ultimately, the victor will recall the successes and forget failures and the contribution of good luck along the way to success. If we believe that *our* side was the source of all meaningful understanding of the war then we have missed a vital point. Aspiring adversaries will surely exploit Iraq's mistakes in future conflict. In victory, our greatest danger is to learn and apply the wrong lessons.

Desert Storm euphoria could overshadow an accurate assessment and clear articulation of transportation successes and failures. What worked and what did not work? What capabilities are worth preserving or improving upon and which are not? What uniquely occurred or, unexpectedly, did not occur? If we changed some conditions of *Desert Shield/Desert Storm*, could they prevent complete success in future confrontation?

As we embark on a course to meet tomorrow's defense challenges, extreme national introspection could blur necessary global vision. This is contradictory for a nation whose security and economic well-being are interwoven in the fabric of other nations. Will tight budgets, a renewal of the *fortress America* view, or the apparent movement success of the Gulf War convince decisionmakers to reject improving this nation's military movement capability?

At a time when America's military priorities are being reordered, we must answer a critical question: Is the ability to move quickly, sustain forces anywhere in the world, and pre-position equipment and materiel near likely areas of crisis, still important? The capacity to foster global stability and defend America's national interests rests upon the outcome of this debate.

The military spending decisions ahead will be fraught with difficult tradeoffs. Logistics—especially mobility—has been a traditional bill payer for combat equipment. Despite the robust defense budgets of the 1980s, improving the nation's military mobility never kept pace with the requirements identified in many Congressionally mandated mobility studies. As we downsize, the Services' temptation will be to take the traditional "salami slice" approach, making defense cuts equally across the board. This will leave us with less of everything, including lift.

Perhaps, a reappraisal is in order. America's military now confronts a declining budget, shrinking manpower, increasing weapon costs, erosion of the available industrial base, slow access to high-tech advances, and, increasing dependence on foreign sources. In the midst of these challenges, our stewardship has got to target resources where they count the most: To empower the National Security Strategy. If moving the force—providing robust transportation support—is considered an essential enabling requirement, our commitment should provide the most cost effective, rapidly deployable and sustainable combat capability—logistical bang for the buck.

The lessons of the Gulf War can help reshape America's defense transportation system in the post-Cold War era. But, beyond this, we must reforge links with industry, secure quick access to state-of-the-art technology, achieve lower costs with higher quality, and assure rapid response to crisis demands. Set sights not only on tomorrow, but the long-range—20 or 30 years away—as well.

We have undergone a remarkable strategic metamorphosis in an amazingly short period. The free world has moved from a high threat, highly stable conflict environment, to one of low threat, but low stability. The risk of conflict with the USSR provided a benchmark for defense planning. The road to meet the next threat is not signed so well. America's resolve, though, should be just as clear.

The Middle East continues to simmer, as does the Western Hemisphere, the Pacific Rim, Eastern Europe and the Horn of Africa. While the United States has no major league adversaries, we live in a world that is more unstable than ever. By the year 2000, the Department of Defense estimates, 15 developing nations will have ballistic missiles; eight of these may be nuclear-capable. Some 30 nations will have chemical weapons and ten more will have biological weapons. More than a dozen developing nations already possess large and capable armored forces.[2] Thus, we should not assume that future conflicts, even in lesser developed areas, will be low intensity or low risk. They may be with very well-armed adversaries.

Leaf through any atlas and you will discover that ours is a globe of quickly changing maps, with no respite in sight. There is good reason for caution about tomorrow. An enemy's strategic surprise has launched three of this nation's last four major conflicts (World War II, Korean Conflict, and the Gulf War). Thus, the road ahead may be paved with known threats, as well as unknown ones. As Secretary of Defense Les Aspin recently described, "this new world order is long on the new world and a little short on order."

The shape of conflict is changing, too. It may be waged with little or no allied backing, and with unknown host-nation support or infrastructure. Any fighting that we do will probably occur where we are not—far from our borders, and in a land that cannot adequately receive our ships and planes. Can our forces go the distance and get there quickly? Will the power we project be effective upon arrival, be sustainable, and be able to quickly defeat any enemy? On the leading edge, the *Army Strategic Mobility Plan* ambitiously establishes critical deployment time lines: The lead brigade must be on the ground in 4 days; the first light division by day 12; and two more heavy divisions, with support, in place by day 30.[3] This calls for well-equipped mobility power. If we cannot project contingency forces rapidly, they will not deter or shorten conflicts. But, what is the requirement? What is necessary to maintain relevancy for modern conflict and emerging missions?

Defining the essential elements of a successful campaign is equally important. While this is often a matter of perspective, the view we should explore is that of a unified commander—the warfighting Commander in Chief (CINC). Because movement is logistics bridge between strategy and tactics, the commander's perspective is focal. The words of the quintessential operator and logistician, Admiral Henry Eccles, resonate:

The logistic viewpoint is essentially that of the commander. The command point of view is that logistics itself has no purpose other than to create and to support combat forces, which are responsive to the needs of the commander. The end product of logistics lies in the operations of combat force.[4]

Transportation has been a critical factor in strategy since fighting men carried equipment on their backs and lived off countries where they were engaged. It has grown more important as the scope of hostilities has widened, and the burden of military equipment and supplies have increased.[5] Transportation enables any operation to begin and end. Movement includes transport of soldiers, their equipment, and their logistics requirements to the battlefield. More than just the use of sea, air and land, it also includes planning, setting priorities, controlling, and allocating transportation resources. Movement is the glue that binds sustainment and all other battlefield functions.

Frequently overlapping, there are three levels of movement:

• *Strategic Movement* involves transporting forces and their accompanying equipment, and supplies from the United States and other theaters to the theater of operations. Sealift, airlift, and the pre-positioning of supplies and equipment form the strategic triad. Each has advantages and disadvantages, and each technique's strengths compensate for the other's limitations. Sealift has the largest capacity and is inexpensive, but it is slow, and relies on available ports and open sea lanes. Airlift is fast and flexible, but is expensive, has limited capacity, and depends upon available airfields and open air routes. For example, the first two fast sealift ships deployed to Saudi Arabia took 3 weeks from initial alert to arrive. But they carried more equipment and cargo than all aircraft had delivered to that point. Pre-positioning, either afloat or on land, places cargo and equipment closest to where they may be most needed, in advance. So, pre-positioning minimizes onward movement. It was the Marine Corps' afloat pre-positioned ships that saved the day during the early stages of *Desert Shield*. They enabled sufficient military supplies to be delivered when not much else was available in the theater of operations.

• *Operational Movement* marshals available military and host-nation transportation assets—watercraft, airplanes, trains and trucks—to provide reception and onward movement of forces and their logistics support within the theater. Operational movement varies from theater to theater. In a European scenario, the conflict is with civilian traffic over an extremely crowded transportation network. In a regional conflict, the challenge may be just the opposite—dealing with a limited movement capacity unable to support heavy and oversized equipment demands. Normally accessible ship off-loading cranes, and other materials-handling equipment, may be scarce or nonexistent. And, host-nation support may be insufficient to augment military transportation.[6] Ports in the theater of operations represent the transition point between strategic and operational movement.

• *Tactical Movement* affords combat units the ability to position forces and critical supplies on the battlefield with assigned trucks or helicopters, before, during and after engagements with the enemy. As you might expect, the available transportation assets at this level are significantly less than at the operational level.

CAMPAIGN PLANNING

As we review the Gulf War, let's step into the shoes of a warfighting CINC. The planning process—from drawing arrows on the map to putting troops on the ground—is a long and difficult road. Envision what you might need most to support the next operation. How can you effectively shape the strategic landscape through combat power and logistics? What capability is necessary to accomplish operational aims? What are the movement requirements? Look outward. How quickly must the force be in place to be effective? Do you count on any warning time? How big and what type force do you need to get the job done decisively? Now, look inward. Upon their arrival, over what routes and how far do you intend to move forces to reach operational and strategic objectives? What support can the host nation render? How long and at what pace do you need to sustain the force—the time line for conflict termination? Movement directly affects the critical answers to these questions from the vantage point of the theater commander. "A higher commander must think *big*," Field Marshall Slim once advised. But, while the tendency may be to apply the broad brush approach ("get there fast with lots of stuff!"), detailed planning is essential. More on this perspective later.

We have too frequently come to believe that armies can magically move anywhere, in any direction, at almost any speed, once their commanders have made up their minds to do so—as if it were all a giant board game. Perhaps this is due to the great military history saga—or maybe CNN. In reality, they cannot, and failure to recognize this fact has probably ruined many more campaigns than ever were by enemy action.[7]

How will America face tomorrow's challenges to its vital interests, or respond to the requests of our allies or the United Nations? The resources that we now assign to improving our global reach and operational agility (read movement capacity), will define us as a nation into the 21st century. Improving those capabilities will increase our options in any given scenario, instead of being limited by them. Only through this effort will the United States maintain its freedom to achieve national aims—the ultimate purpose of any strategy. As we conjure the new world order, let us put the recent past into perspective, so that it provides relevance for our future.

SETTING THE MOVEMENT STAGE

On 2 August 1990, forces from Iraq invaded neighboring Kuwait and successfully seized control of the Emirate within 24 hours. Iraq's battle-tested army of 1 million men was touted as the world's fourth largest. It was equipped with some 5,500 tanks, 5,000 armored vehicles, 5,700 tank transporters, 5,000 support vehicles, 700 modern combat planes and vast supplies of guided missiles and artillery pieces.[8] They appeared formidable.

To defend against such a foe, any challenger would have to counter with critical mass of a highly mobile, armored force—the most taxing on any strategic movement system. The less a unit weighs, the easier it is to move strategically. Upon arrival, though, its ground mobility depends on how mechanized the unit is. Our interventions into Grenada and Panama were conducted with light forces of limited battlefield mobility and lethality. These forces and their equipment were flown or amphibiously landed into the areas of operation. In contrast, most regional armies today possess hundreds or thousands of tanks. To confront this threat requires early deployment of strong antitank power.

The Gulf War was to be one of highly lethal, set piece battles—requiring many tanks and attack helicopters, and the requisite ships to get them there. The most mobile force on the battlefield includes armored and mechanized infantry divisions. Their primary weapons are the M1 Abrams Main Battle Tank (weighing over 125,000 pounds), and M2 Bradley Fighting Vehicle (weighing about 45,000 pounds). These systems usually deploy by sea because they are so large (e.g., only one M1 can be transported aboard the gigantic C-5 Galaxy). This force is the most draining on strategic mobility resources because of heavy weight, associated high volumes of ammunition, and support requirements.

Strategic mobility has eroded as the force has steadily put on weight. According to *Armed Forces Journal*, the weight of a mechanized division has grown 40 percent since 1980, and it can use 3,500 tons of ammunition, 50 tons of spare parts, and 75 tons of food and medical supplies, when on the offensive.[9] The highly mobile M1 can cruise at 35 mph while engaging far away targets. But, its parent organization—the armored division—consumes up to 600,000 gallons of fuel a day. That is twice the amount sold by the average service station in a month.

We move toward making our weapon systems more effective so that they can put more rounds on target, in less time. Target acquisition and fire control processes are now the limiting factors to maximum effectiveness. Soon, lack of strategic transport to deploy equipment and battlefield transport to move the additional ammunition will assume this role.[10] Unless we improve strategic lift and operational transport, the United States will have an even harder time getting forces to war in the future. Taking the longer view, though, technological efforts should aim at lightening the heavy load of high mobility, while improving lethality.

The 9 months preceding had been historically momentous. The fall of the Berlin Wall, NATO's victory in the Cold War, the successful ouster of Panama's Manuel Noriega in Operation *Just Cause*, German reunification, dismemberment of the Warsaw Pact, and the Soviet Union fragmenting in disarray, were seemingly unforgettable milestones. Then, this previously unanticipated enemy attacked and seized its neighbor in such a sinister manner that it overshadowed those events. Along with the defeated nation, the tyrant held much of the world's oil supply hostage. Regional hegemony—if not global control of the precious commodity—loomed real. The free world was galvanized and the prospect of intervention seemed inevitable.

During that first week in August, 11 Iraqi divisions were in, or deploying to, Kuwait.[11] They appeared to be massing for further advance against the region's linchpin, Saudi Arabia. Iraq's armor force was already positioned and poised for further advance. Gulfs and oceans separated adversaries who could bring a comparable heavy force to the fray.

Strategic geography and surprise were on Iraq's side. King Fahd, Saudi Arabia's head of state, at first hesitated against American attempts to use his country as a stronghold. Key U.S. envoys (including U.S. Central Command's General Schwarzkopf and Secretary of Defense Cheney) ultimately convinced him of the approaching danger. He requested U.S. military assistance to deter such an attack and defend his nation. Had the United States not gained ready passage to the ports of Saudi Arabia, the determination to deploy forces may have been far more tenuous. There were few practical military options. American forces could have moved slowly over the unsecured beaches of Kuwait, or let Iraqi aggression go unchecked. The Saudi decision to allow access was pivotal.

Saddam Hussein viewed his "bold annexation of Iraq's 19th province"—Kuwait—as a means to assume the mantle of leadership of the Arab world. In doing so, he also gained 40 percent of the world's oil reserves and believed he could then resolve his country's pressing economic problems.[12] Others saw it differently. The brutal aggression was so wanton that it greatly simplified the task to muster world response and unify a coalition. The United States believed that the unprovoked attack threatened the world's oil supply and wanted to "redress a great wrong."[13] To Arab neighbors that joined the coalition, conflict appeared inevitable, if distasteful. Saddam's fanaticism and deception had worn thin, and he had crossed over the line—figuratively and literally—once too often. Others throughout the world appeared less threatened immediately by Iraq than by the potential long-term repercussions of doing nothing. Forces from America and 38 other nations took on the task of deterring Iraq from further attack. At the United Nations, even the Soviet Union and China, backed the responses and did not interfere with the U.S.-led military operations.

Once President Bush decided to intervene, public sentiment for action appeared unwavering. The United States was joined in the coalition by many other nations, while Iraq remained in near complete isolation. This coalition, and the alliances forged over the years, brought America essential strategic access. Besides Saudi Arabia's cooperation, more than 80 percent of deploying flights flowed through en route staging bases in Spain and Germany. Global deployment required overflight agreements from many governments. At this critical time, European countries also made key transportation contributions beyond the limit of America's resources—then fully employed moving U.S.-based forces. Iraq was denied freedom of action because it had no meaningful strategic alliances.

Years of lip service and precious little real accomplishment toward interoperability meant that the United States remained self-reliant for all equipment and resupply. There was almost no sharing of supplies and equipment among allies in the operational theater. This further drained U.S. transportation resources. Witnessing the success of *Desert Shield/Desert Storm*, Americans may not be willing to support violent intervention without the added strength of a UN or other coalition. Today, resource considerations, alone, militate toward this conclusion.

While some nations contributed money, many provided critical operational transportation assets as their contribution to the coalition. These barges, tank transporters, trucks, and land rovers proved indispensable to the total success of the war effort and they made the war less expensive for the United States.

When Americans ask, "What price victory?" the currency we deal in is the lives of our sons and daughters. Coalitions share the burden of casualty and economic cost. While United Nations support provided legitimacy to the coalition's military operations, can we expect similar worldwide popularity or cooperation in future operations? Cold War issues appeared clear cut: If the East struck, the West would retaliate. The new world order may not be so predictable.

America's commitment to the region had been long-standing. In 1943, President Roosevelt declared that "the defense of Saudi Arabia is vital to the defense of the United States."[14] President Carter conceived the Rapid Deployment Force concept in 1979. It aimed to protect America's national interests in the Middle East. President Reagan gave the idea teeth when he activated the very real, if not fully manned, U.S. Central Command (CENTCOM) in 1983. Previous Middle Eastern operation plans had focused on responding to a potential Soviet onslaught into Iran. Iraq's invasion of Kuwait, though envisioned by a few, surprised many policy makers and military planners.

On 6 August President Bush ordered U.S. forces to deploy as part of Operation *Desert Shield* (to emphasize that it shielded Saudi Arabia from further attack). It was the right force for the wrong scenario—Fulda Gap and Kola Peninsula replaced within the blink of an eye by Wadi Al-Batin and the Persian Gulf. Following Vietnam and the Soviet buildup in Germany, U.S. Army doctrine had taken on a distinctly Central European flavor. There, a significant transportation infrastructure was in place and, although substantial, America's presence was as a part of a larger alliance. The anticipated warning time and support structure of a war in Europe caused many to discount the notion of preparing for a *come as you are* war. The Gulf War should have changed this mind set.

Our ability to project forces rapidly and massively, halfway around the world—contemplated but never accomplished—was put to the ultimate test. Within days, the nation energized its defense mobility resources.

The United States had four stated national policy objectives in response to Iraq's aggression:
- Immediate, complete, and unconditional withdrawal of Iraqi forces from Kuwait
- Restoration of Kuwait's legitimate government
- Security and stability of Saudi Arabia and the Persian Gulf
- Safety and protection of the lives of American citizens abroad.[15]

Noticeably absent from the list was perhaps our true vital interest—preservation of access to oil. Many coalition members had similar motivation. America's objectives also did not directly address a desire to balance military power in the region. This balance had shifted significantly in Iraq's favor because of its war with Iran. Finally, although rallying public opinion included branding Saddam Hussein as "another Hitler," stated policy did not include his removal from power.

The JCS translated these political aims into military objectives:
- Develop a defensive capability in the Persian Gulf region to deter Saddam Hussein from further attacks
- Defend Saudi Arabia effectively if deterrence failed
- Build a militarily effective coalition and integrate coalition forces into operational plans
- Enforce the economic sanctions prescribed by UN Security Council Resolutions.[16]

These initial objectives did not include forceful restoration of Kuwait's rightful government, if sanctions failed. This would require deploying a significantly larger force—which the United States could not, initially, move to the battlefield. The overall intent of deterrence and defense options was to confront Iraq with the prospects of unacceptable costs and a widened conflict with the United States.[17] This required deploying a force at least equal to Iraq's.

MOVING THE FORCE IN *DESERT STORM*

Early estimates suggested that a potential adversary's armor columns could reach defensive positions near the Saudi Arabian port at Al-Jubayl in just 4 weeks (19 days of pre-hostility buildup and 9 more days of movement to reach the objective).[18] To counter this threat, planners calculated that adequate forces would take at least 17 weeks to deploy—too late to defend Saudi Arabia, much less deter aggression.[19]

The Army's lead elements launched their deployment to Saudi Arabia on August 7 (designated as C-day, for the first day of deployment). This began Phase I of the fastest buildup and movement of combat power across the greatest distances in history.[20] Distances were immense—7,000 airlift miles and 8,700 sealift miles from the east coast of the United States. During that first deployment phase, which lasted from August 7 until November 8, the United States moved about 1,000 aircraft, 60 Navy ships, 250,000 tons of supplies and equipment, and 240,000 military personnel to the Gulf.[21] In historical contrast, 168,400 U.S. forces were airlifted to Vietnam in 1965, during the most intense 1-year buildup of that conflict.[22] In the first month of the Korean Conflict, America sealifted 79,965 tons of equipment and cargo.[23] We moved over two and one-half times that amount—300,000 tons—during those first thirty days of the Gulf War.[24]

While impressive in gross terms, these numbers conceal that it took over a month to get the first full heavy division, the 24th Infantry Division (Mechanized), in place. Nearly 7 months passed before a sustainable force, capable of offensive operations, was fully positioned, in large part, because of transport limitations.[25] Hardly rapid! On the other side of the coin was the success story of the Maritime

Pre-positioning Squadrons (MPS) that completely outfitted two Marine Expeditionary Brigades. This was our most responsive means of delivering necessary supplies and equipment during the first days of *Desert Shield*. The MPS ships took less than half the time to deliver their cargoes than if transported directly from the United States.

When Iraq attacked Kuwait, the CENTCOM Commander quickly reviewed the bidding. With a focus on rapidly injecting a deterrent combat power, it became clear to him that something had to give: There was not enough quickly available strategic lift to move the range of forces necessary to attain stated objectives. The threat was real that Iraq would exploit Saudi Arabia's vulnerability and continue the drive south. So, the theater commander had to figure out what he could live without for the short run to defend Saudi Arabia. He decided that the answer was logistics. Thus, Schwarzkopf made the early decision to front load mobile combat units into Saudi Arabia.

In the initial stages of the conflict, there was just a thin line of Saudi forces along the border with Kuwait. This became known as the window of vulnerability to the threat of Iraqi attack. Saudi Arabia would remain vulnerable until decisive, mobile power could arrive. As the curtain raised on *Desert Shield*, the theater commander's military options were limited by the time required to move heavy forces over significant distances. Available strategic transport could not meet his required delivery dates. Because of this, holding the key desert ports and airfields was weighed to be more important than closing logistical power into the theater of operations.[26] This decision, though apparently prudent, nearly became our Achilles' heel.

Allocating the most and the fastest strategic lift to combat units results in a force that is critically unsustainable for some period. It also throws an already complex operation—the synchronized buildup of a theater support structure—out of kilter. In *Desert Shield*, the early preferential movement of combat forces delayed organizing theater support that future operations would dictate. This limited operational choices. Deployed units became tied to host-nation sources and the strategic lifeline. The entire support structure was built ad hoc. The resulting impromptu design was then tied to a defensive posture. It was severely stretched when called on to support the offensive in Operation *Desert Storm*. When tested, it showed early signs of fatigue after only 100 hours of intense combat.[27]

The first show of force units in theater, from the 82nd Airborne Division, lacked significant mobility, survivability, or sufficient firepower to match an Iraqi armored assault. In many ways they were no more than a speed bump in the path of the fourth largest army in the world. It was, however, one of the only forces that could deploy quickly enough to the region. Because the 82nd is relatively light, CENTCOM planners believed that most of its requirements could be met by the host nation. With the deployment of the airborne division, the line in the sand was drawn. Several realities emerged: Light forces, poised for rapid deployment, grow markedly when faced with a modern armored threat (or, based on our Somalian experience, any threat at all). Upon alert, steps were taken throughout the 82nd Airborne Division to increase on-hand equipment and supplies not normally authorized—especially additional TOW weapon systems. These 11th-hour upgrades nearly doubled the planned sortie requirement for the 82nd—adding a new meaning to the term light forces.[28]

Host-nation support requirements were heightened beyond original estimates because of the decision not to deploy the normal complement of XVIII Airborne Corps logistics elements. Shortage of easy to load, roll-on/roll-off (RORO) fast sealift ships meant that the sought after heavy combat units would have to deploy incrementally. Sealift shortages resulted in slow buildup of heavy forces during September and October.[29]

Within America, the decline of the shipping industry—ship building, manpower and shipyards—has led to reliance upon available allied and foreign flag shipping. For example, of the 359 ships that formed America's steel bridge to Saudi Arabia during *Desert Shield/Desert Storm*, 180 of the 212 chartered vessels flew foreign flags. Twelve ships were on loan from allies.[30] In planning for the future, there is danger that foreign ships will not meet military needs (RORO ships versus commercially preferred tankers) and may not be there when the chips are down. Since 1987, only two noncombatant ships have been built in America. And, the widely recognized shortage of American merchant mariners would likely stifle unilateral crisis response. As we look over the horizon, these facts beg the question, "Can America 'go it alone' in sealift?"—as the 1987 National Security Council Directive 28 mandated. The answer is quite clearly "No!" But, if global responsiveness, unconstrained by the international marketplace, is what we seek, then renewal of American sealift is critical.

If Iraq had continued its attack in early August, Saudi Arabia would surely have been lost. Sufficient American forces could not have been brought to bear quickly enough to defend her. Iraq's strategy of inaction and the monumental efforts of deploying units and military and civilian transporters allowed the window of vulnerability to be narrowed by early October. The local commander was then satisfied that a successful defense could be mounted. Time became an unforeseen ally. Deployment of forces necessary to execute this primary objective had taken nearly 2 months to complete. Fortunately, the threatened Iraqi assault never appeared. Ability to quickly overcome distance with a sizeable force has always been an underpinning of U.S. strategic success. In *Desert Shield*, inability to surge mobile forces *en masse* was our most insurmountable obstacle.

What are the implications? First, there are few places in the world that possess wealth of resources comparable to the Gulf States. Yet, even with this host-nation support, the absence of firm support agreements complicated planning. It placed U.S. and other coalition combat forces at risk when deployed with the full complement of their organic and supporting logistical organizations. As in the past, the fog of war affected the strategic situation. The intent of the military operation shifted from defense to offense to eject an invader. The early decision to deploy shooters constrained the effective establishment and ongoing support of the theater logistics structure.[31] An unsustainable force may be deployed for legitimate reasons. But, the associated risks of failure in combat and inability to support continuous, lengthy operations, should be recognized.[32] Finally, light forces are not as light as advertised when facing a heavy threat. This leads to under-estimating already critical strategic lift requirements within a system that is unable to meet the planned theater requirements (much less the unplanned).

The debate now wages over how we should restructure our forces. Rallying cries such as "Not a smaller Cold War Army!" abound. Some advocate lighter, more easily deployable forces, and others argue for mobile, more survivable formations. We often frame force structure decisions by comparing the faster delivery times of air, versus those of the slower sea deployment. But, other than the light divisions, closing a ground combat force into most regions of the world will likely involve sealift, unless we have pre-positioned massive amounts of materiel. When logistical support is included in the movement requirement, the deployment time difference between light and heavy combat forces is much less pronounced. Even the light fighters will require sealift. In fact, when the size of the force exceeds airlift capacity, the rapid deployability advantage of light forces almost disappears.[33] This should weigh into the force structure calculus.

Let me reframe the argument. Just as a threat-driven mix of light and heavy forces is essential, each leg of the strategic mobility triad must be balanced. Sealift, airlift, and pre-positioning are mutually exclusive, and bring distinctive and necessary traits to our movement arsenal. Airlift will always play the paramount role in delivering people, and high priority cargo early. Sealift is the key to deployment of any force larger than one light Army division. Once the deployment requires sealift, the weight to be moved is less important than the early availability of capable ships.[34] Pre-positioning of the right supplies and equipment in or near crisis locations enables sharp reductions in response time and total required lift.

A balanced approach to strategic mobility will provide America the power to respond aggressively to regional crisis. All elements are essential. Currently, this balance is weak. In the zeal to save defense dollars, some have suggested tradeoffs among components of the triad (for example, Air Force C-17 long-range transport planes for fast sealift ships, or vice versa). But, as the congressionally mandated *Mobility Requirements Study* of 1992 concluded, "to support national interests, deployment capability must increase through expanded investment in sealift, pre-positioning, and transportation infrastructure in the United States, and in sustained investment in aircraft."[35]

Other factors not unique in our history contributed to the slow pace of the deployment. One was the glut of "stuff" that piled up at piers and marshaling areas, virtual iron mountains, caused by lack of asset visibility through the transportation pipeline. Two views, from different conflicts, prove that our learning curve building up to conflict is as steep as our forgetting curve after conflict:

LtGen William "Gus" Pagonis, who commanded the ad hoc 22nd Support Command and headed the Army's logistical effort, recounts that one of his biggest challenges was handling the thousands of containers throughout the Gulf War buildup. Shippers were intent on filling every 40-foot container to the brim to assure that ship capacity was maxed out. This practice made good sense in terms of the known shipping shortage but drained terminal resources. Most of the containers were intended for multiple consignees or were loaded with unidentifiable loads. Some 28,000 of the 41,000 arriving containers had to be opened pierside to find out their contents. Then, many were hauled 2,000 miles out into the desert just to find that most of their contents really belonged to units near the ports. Pagonis was caught on the horns of a dilemma. Shippers were trying to get as much cargo to Saudi Arabia as quickly as possible. The mission was being disrupted because port operators and truckers in the theater of operations were swamped.[36] This had a cascading effect that highlighted shortages of storage space, materials-handling equipment (MHE) at all levels, and of trained equipment operators. It also dramatically demonstrated what can happen when you've lost visibility of incoming cargo. Ultimately, because units lost confidence in the distribution system, they submitted multiple supply requisitions on the same items. This further choked the system and slowed the delivery of critical items.

This was symptomatic of a problem that has historically plagued logisticians. The House Government Operations Committee concluded in 1970, that: "Supply support to Vietnam was at once a demonstration of superb performance and appalling waste."[37] LtGen (Ret.) Joseph Heiser, who was Pagonis's counterpart for much of the Vietnam conflict, echoed this conclusion. "First with the Most" became a banned motto in Heiser's 1st Logistical Command. It represented, to Heiser, the philosophy that had created the logistical *mountains* found in Vietnam in 1968—almost 2 million tons—of which only about a third could be identified.[38] No one makes the point more clearly than LtGen Heiser:

> In three different wars, I've faced many different, serious logistics problems. In each war, because supplies were low or nonexistent or could not be located, we lost critical time getting the support required by the combat

troops. The worst situation is to arrive at combat with an excess of noncritical items and a shortage of critical items.[39]

Like so many other aspects of the Gulf War movement epic, what was a heralded success story from one vantage point, frequently obscured a known shortfall at another. This is a defining point to the theater commander's perspective. If you are in his shoes, it is inconsequential that gross amounts of tonnage are being off-loaded at the ports. The commander wants to know, "Is it the right stuff?" Like the difference between information and intelligence—the cargo delivered must be meaningful to carrying out the commander's plan. If it is not, we are reduced to moving mountains of stuff! The Gulf War was to be waged from an allied country with a magnificent logistical base. With ongoing U.S. assistance, the Saudi government had built a huge and modern complex of military installations. The terminal ports in Saudi Arabia were a transporter's dream. They were second to none in throughput capacity because the country imports nearly everything it uses. The Saudis had built facilities for just such a contingency. Persian Gulf seaports at Ad-Dammam and Al-Jubayl were among the most modern in the world (for example, Ad-Dammam could berth and off-load 39 ships simultaneously, including the gigantic fast sealift ships). Airports at Dhahran, Riyadh, King Fahd, and King Khalid Military City were equally impressive.

All coalition partners relied heavily upon the infrastructure along the Saudi coastline. Most worldwide ports could not have handled the types and volume of ships and planes offered up. For example, few seaports can berth a fast sealift ship because of its tremendous size. Thus, future intervention may require an alternate, much slower method of cargo discharge—such as over-the-shore.

As spectacular as the Saudi ports were, the country had limited improved roadways away from the coast and almost no logistical infrastructure to sustain the gigantic inbound force. Saudi Arabia was half a globe away—with a climate and landscape that were notoriously inhospitable to humans and equipment. But, the desert provided the most advantageous terrain to showcase U.S. strengths in armor and air power. The desert floor and wadis eased the tactical freedom of movement so essential to win the ground war.

Air supremacy meant that truck convoys and air resupply could flow unimpeded. If Iraq was planning a follow-on attack, intelligence reports suggested the most likely avenue of approach was along the Saudi coast road. This high speed road ran from Al-Khafji to Al-Jubayl and Ad-Dammam.[40] It seemed tailor-made for an armor attack. Such an advance would offer the most lucrative targets in the port complex, desalinization plants, oil refineries and other coastal facilities. Loss of, or serious damage to, the port facilities would have made any force buildup in theater extremely difficult. In many ways, this coastal port complex was Saudi Arabia's center of gravity.

Iraq did not follow up its initial success in Kuwait. Had Iraq taken Saudi Arabia's ports, strategic access would have been denied, and that nation would surely have fallen. Unbelievably, the enemy did not attempt to capture, disrupt or destroy the port complex. As the coalition began massing ships, planes and tanks in Saudi Arabia, Saddam Hussein did little to respond. He took few steps to impede the coalition's preparations for war—no serious interdiction of the sea lanes or air routes. (Ironically, threats of releasing his terrorist "hit squads" sent a chill through the airline traveling public and freed up precious air transport assets for the deployment). He allowed the coalition to assemble, acclimate, and train in Saudi Arabia for 5 months. Then, he allowed them to attack. His inaction was often perplexing—but gave the coalition with an unexpected advantage. Initiating a conflict, then passively waiting for the other side to lose interest is nearly unprecedented.

The key variables in movement are requirements (forces), capabilities (ships, planes, etc.), and time. By giving us time, Iraq minimized the effects of shortfall in capabilities. The United States benefitted greatly from the luxury of time to deploy its forces. As the weeks passed, Saddam Hussein showed no signs of abiding by the UN resolutions calling for his withdrawal from Kuwait. Operation *Desert Shield* appeared to have met its objective of deterring an Iraqi drive into Saudi Arabia, but Kuwait was still under Iraqi occupation. By mid-October, some 435,000 Iraqi soldiers, supported by more than 3,600 tanks, almost 2,400 armored personnel carriers, and more than 2,400 artillery pieces occupied Kuwait.[41] Besides other coalition partners, American forces then opposing those 27 Iraqi divisions in October, consisted of the XVIII Airborne Corps (with 4.5 Army divisions), one Marine Expeditionary Force, three carrier battle groups and one battleship battle group, an amphibious task force, and over five fighter and bomber wing equivalents.[42] Our ability to defend Saudi Arabia then appeared secure. Not even with superior weaponry, however, did coalition forces yet have the overmatching forces to drive Iraq from Kuwait.

The Gulf War was unique. This is how the *movement stage* shaped up:

• Because there was no enemy sea or air threat—enabling freedom of strategic movement—our forces were deployed to the region without disruption.

• This was to be a war fought in open terrain, well suited for coalition air and armor power—requiring significant and rapid resupply, but allowing nearly uncontested convoy movement.

• Unlike nearly any other scenario, the battlefield was to be free of noncombatants—easing unimpeded movement along otherwise congested main supply routes.

• The coalition knew generally where the enemy was, its numbers and disposition of equipment. The reverse was not true. This is best exploited by concentrating movement assets in concert with the advance of the battle.

•   No enemy safe havens or sanctuaries were to be honored—minimizing potential diffusion of the sustainment effort.

•   Although the battlefield was to be nonlinear, the battles would be set piece—requiring the synchronization of combat power, movement, and sustainment.

Compare this movement scenario with past conflicts, such as Korea or Vietnam, or to possible future ones in a regional setting.   The deck was very clearly stacked in our favor.   Iraq negated the key advantages it had possessed: Surprise and strategic geography!   America cannot be assured of such accommodating terrain, ports, freedom of movement, or enemy strategy in future conflicts.

The UN embargo reinforced Saddam's intent to keep the Iraqi army in fixed positions.   This minimized fuel consumption and wear and tear on its equipment—but it did not free Kuwait. By quickly projecting a symbolic presence we had engineered a delay.   The static situation afforded America precious time for more movement—a strategic pause. Iraq's inaction opened the door to enable the joint force commander to inject an offensive potency. So, at the end of October, the National Command Authority decided to increase force levels for deployment to Saudi Arabia. The strategic calculus then changed.   No longer was an equal force sufficient.   To eject Iraqi forces from Kuwait an overmatching force would have to be employed. Ultimately, U.S. expansibility—the power to generate forces—provided the joint commander the capacity to eject Iraq from Kuwait.   The key to victory was the employment of a decisive force.

Many people agreed that applying U.S. power gradually has been our major error of the Vietnam Conflict.   The hope was that the enemy would realize what it was up against, and sue for peace.   Instead, North Vietnam used this *gradualism* to improve its strategic advantage.   Post-Vietnam doctrine has focused on the fast concentration of

American firepower to destroy the enemy's military power and will to fight. Senior decisionmakers remembered all too well this "underkill" approach that ultimately led to U.S. failure. They were intent that it not be repeated in the Persian Gulf. This required the employment of a decisive force. The impact upon movement was dramatic. Fortunately, the enemy allowed the time and freedom of access to make this strategy attainable.

At Cold War force levels, and with significant forward presence, the United States was readily able to exercise strategic leverage around the world. Force levels on the horizon make this unrealistic. What risks will America accept in one region to assure strategic reach to other theaters? The lengthy Gulf War deployment may have appeared simple, but suppose future deployments occurred simultaneously and without warning. At current surge lift capacity, a quick and decisive offensive formation could not be mounted in one theater, much less multiple theaters.

On 8 November Phase II deployments began with the President's announcement that the theater would be reinforced by approximately 200,000 additional military personnel. So, what had been done once now had to be repeated. Most of the forces deployed during the second wave were forward based in Germany and, thus, were closest to the pending fray—with truly realistic forward presence. These included VII Corps headquarters, two armored divisions and an armored cavalry regiment. (Ironically, many of these were deactivated immediately upon war termination and redeployment). Other American forces moved during this phase included over 400 U.S. Air Force aircraft, three carrier battle groups and one battleship battle group, and the 1st Infantry Division (Mechanized) from Fort Riley, Kansas.[43] With the deployment of these forces, there could be no doubt that the coalition was readying to go on the offensive.

Forward-based units and prepositioned supplies and equipment shortened previous deployment distance and movement time considerably. These factors were critical to our employment of an offensive strategy because they partially offset the requirements for greater strategic lift. The forward presence of over 300,000 U.S. forces in Europe, as well as the four divisions' worth of prepositioned equipment, had camouflaged the previous strategic lift shortfall. The value of forward basing combat power in strategically located areas was proved in this instance. There has been a subtle, but important, paradigm shift. We can no longer count on the transport slack that pre-positioning large amounts of equipment and supplies afforded us in NATO. The global demands of regionalism and reduced forward basing will yank this slack instantly taut, instantly aggrevating a tough movement situation.

By mid-January, all units that were to participate in the liberation of Kuwait had arrived in Saudi Arabia or were en route. The *movement stage* was set. The total U.S. movement effort to the Persian Gulf was impressive. By all modes, transporters moved:

- 4 million tons of dry cargo—about the weight of 40 modern aircraft carriers[44]
- 31,800 tons of mail—that would cover 28 football fields in mail six-feet deep;[45]
- 12,435 tracked combat vehicles and 117,157 wheeled vehicles;[46]
- Over 33,000 containers—that, if laid end to end, would have stretched 188 miles;[47]
- More than 6 million tons of petroleum products; and,
- More than 9 divisions of troops (about 560,000) and equipment.[48]

The coalition's intense air campaign was launched on January 17, 1991, and the "thunder and lightening" of Operation *Desert Storm* began. The campaign wore down the Iraqi military, taking away their ability to detect mounting movement of massed coalition forces in what General Schwarzkopf called the "Hail Mary" play. LtGen

Pagonis, who engineered much of the movement, best captured the unparalleled scope of this operation:

> Simply put, the two Army corps and all their equipment had to be trucked westward and northward to their jumping-off points for the assault. VII Corps was trucked 330 miles across the desert, and XVIII Airborne Corps leapfrogged more than 500 miles west and north. This required us to assemble a fleet of nearly 4,000 heavy vehicles of all types, many of which had to be contracted for. Just before the ground assault began, peak traffic at a checkpoint on the northernmost of these supply routes approached 18 vehicles per minute, seven days a week, 24-hours a day. This volume of traffic was sustained for almost 6 weeks.[49]

As equipment and supplies entered the theater's front and pushed inward, key operational shortfalls became apparent. The Army deployed nearly 75 percent of its truck companies in support of only 25 percent of its combat divisions, there was still insufficient ground transport to move the force.[50] Many believe that had the ground war gone longer than 100 hours, operations would have ceased until the logistical tail caught up.[51] Secretary of Defense Aspin, then Chairman of the House Armed Services Committee, suggested that by the end of the 100-hour ground war, "we were pretty much at the end of our string in being able to fight this thing."[52]

Whether irony or a forgotten lesson of history, we nearly met the fate of so many in the past. A similar circumstance had defeated another desert warrior in North Africa, in 1941. The "Desert Fox," Field Marshal Erwin Rommel, was outfoxed by logistics. He pumped plenty of combat power into the port at Tripoli, but continued to over extend resupply lines. There simply were not enough trucks to sustain the fast paced offensive. Supplies piled up at the wharves while shortages grew at the front.[53] And, who can forget Patton's pursuit of retreating German forces through France in the late summer of 1944? Patton's

Third Army (the forerunner of the Army's Gulf War contingent to CENTCOM) was seizing everything in sight. It was spread over a 700-square-mile area extending from the port of Brest in the west to the banks of the Seine River in the east. Initially, Third Army had accomplished in 19 days what planners had thought would take at least 75 days. A logistical halt was to occur, but the opportunity for greater gains convinced Supreme Allied Headquarters to continue. The pace grew faster and snowballed—some would say out of control. On 12 September, General Patton's advance came to a halt because of a lack of fuel, ammunition, and the transportation to distribute those supplies. The breakneck pace, length of required sustainment, and inaccurate consumption estimates had clearly caught planners by surprise. Ironically, it had been Patton who defeated an initiative to add a supply battalion, equipped with 96 two-and-one-half-ton trucks, to each armored division. Patton's shortsightedness returned to haunt him.[54]

Considering these lessons from history and our recent Gulf War experience, will we too be acccused of shortsightedness through out inaction? During the Army's armor modernization of the 1980's, its transportation fleet had not kept pace. In the zero-sum game of defense spending, we had bought more tanks and fewer trucks. Nowhere was this more apparent than with heavy equipment transporters (HETs). It was argued that Europe had plenty of railroads to carry tanks eastward to combat areas. So, HETs were relegated to evacuating only disabled tanks. There were very few in the Army inventory. Our Gulf War Army divisions had an average of only six tank transporters apiece. In total, the Army had only 112 HETs available in the theater, and the Marines but 34 (compared to Iraq's 5,000+).[55]

In Saudi Arabia, HETs saved us from two major problems: First, wear and tear on our tanks; and, second, wear and tear on the fragile roads. If our tanks were driven on the 120 °F hot roads, for example, the resulting damage to the roads would have made it impossible to move the precious logistical bases up to the front. The mountains of supplies would then have continued to pile up at Dhahran. The theater Army's head logistician explained:

> Logisticians are paid to look at reality. We might not have made it in the Gulf without the HETs that Saudi Arabia, Germany, Egypt, and the Eastern bloc so generously provided. In how many contexts can we count on our allies, let alone our former Warsaw Pact adversaries, to equip our armed forces?[56]

Most American military trucks were designed for the European scenario—where road networks are prevalent in nearly every square kilometer. They were incapable of moving off-road in a theater with not much more than a dirt track road system and could not move supplies far in the desert. This constrained the fast paced forward offensive of the ground campaign. Trucks designed for the German autobahns did not fare well on the sandy desert wadis. And, there weren't enough drivers for the round-the-clock operation. Peacetime manning had reduced many transport battalions to 60 percent of authorized personnel.[57]

The much-anticipated coalition ground campaign began on February 24, massively moving to reclaim Kuwait and deliver a devastating defeat to the Iraqi Army. Prompted by the widespread destruction, President Bush declared a cease-fire on February 28, only 100 hours into the ground war. Stated political and military objectives had been attained—an apparent victory!

But, what of the future? How might our potential adversaries exploit the lessons of the Gulf War to disrupt America's deployment and sustainment flow?

• Capture, disrupt, or destroy rival ports to slow or eliminate U.S. ability to close and sustain equipment and forces.

- Mine harbors to prevent amphibious assaults or over-the-shore cargo discharge, and take advantage of American weakness in mine clearing. (At sea, the lack of U.S. minesweeping ships may have been a factor in our decision not to stage an amphibious landing into Kuwait.)[58]
- Interdict sea and air lanes to bottle up the movement flow of U.S. forces and equipment. (Impossible? Iran recently bought three Russian submarines, with an option to buy two more).
- Employ nuclear, biological or chemical weapons on ports and main supply routes.
- Take first strike action and follow through, before America can deploy forces.
- Employ terrorism or other means to destroy or disrupt key American ports, intermediate staging bases and coalition ports.

While the accomplishments of Gulf War transporters were truly herculean, lack of transportation was the key limiting factor to our Gulf War victory. The mark of a successful movement system is one that is invisible to combat forces—gauged by how little it influences the commander's actions and available options. In *Desert Shield/Desert Storm*, transportation shortages were a constance concern.

As we seek to maintain relevance in a world of strategic *white water*, several realities emerge that we may expect to guide our actions:

- Geography separates America from most of our vital interests by long distances over water, requiring a realistic means of long-range strategic lift.
- Crisis response strategy requires more strategic lift that can quickly surge, and the ability to place necessary war materials nearer to a potential battlefield. We had to rely on others during the Gulf War. Their assistance may not be available the next time around.
- The United States will never have enough lift for all scenarios. But, America's role on the world stage demands

sufficient capability to project a decisive force to any regional flashpoint in time to ensure success.

• To save cost and lives, we will need to go with enough force to get the job done quickly.

• The defense budget will continue to shrink.

• Pressure will increase to find economies of scale to save acquisition and transportation costs.

• Few regional scenarios have sufficient infrastructure to support U.S. force requirements.

• The value of information, communication and space systems will a play a critical role in optimizing the global transportation network.

• Americans will work more closely with our allies in intervention operations.

• The farther forces must travel, the greater the transportation requirement. As forward presence decreases, the likelihood of strategic deployment from the continental United States increases. Thus, surge lift—quickly available transportation—will take on ever increasing importance.

• The civilian transport industry cannot economically maintain a capacity to move massive amounts of heavy military equipment—a requirement without commercial application. America's next conflict may not call for the full mobilization of the armed forces. So, unlike the Gulf War, we cannot expect to rely so heavily upon commercial transportation to support future deployments. Only increased organic military transport can meet this challenge.[59]

• Early response to crisis reduces risk—requiring quick deployment capability. This will reduce the forces required later, when more lift options may be available to deploy them.[60]

• The duplicate supply systems among the Army, Navy, Air Force and Marines complicated and slowed the movement flow. Such inefficiencies and redundancies, if not corrected, will plague us again in future operations, at the expense of timely deployment and effective sustainment.

• Our *Desert Shield/Desert Storm* success, as in past conflicts, was accompanied by inefficient logistical—particularly movement—practices. Too much was accomplished by placing a terrific strain on a tenuous movement system. Not enough can be attributed to sound organization and efficient procedures.

Compared to the Cold War model, there is a paradigm shift in the type of conflict we can expect to encounter. This commands a sea change in our framework for moving and sustaining forces, and the mobility tools we will use to project that power. Transportation has been, perhaps, the most fre-quently limiting factor of modern war, including our recent endeavor in the Gulf. The hope has always been that everything would somehow come together on the day of reckoning. As national strategy evolves, the United States will have less warning time to react to regional flashpoints than during the Cold War. America will rely more acutely than ever upon viable strategic and operational mobility.

MOVING THE FORCE BEYOND *DESERT STORM*

The bedrock that once formed the basis of this nation's defense planning—a U.S.-Soviet confrontation—has crumbled into ashes. We are left with a host of potential regional flashpoints. The former Soviet Union no longer stabilizes the actions of its client states—and lack of this glue has stirred the global pot. (Can anyone believe that Saddam Hussein would have conducted his Persian Gulf adventure under the auspices of Iraq's former Soviet sponsor?) Now that the Communist threat has dissipated, domestic agendas throughout Europe and the United States have altered previous priorities.

In the afterglow of the Cold War and *Desert Storm*, the United States should not be lulled into a false sense of security. Just as the threat of Soviet domination galvanized the free world, the hibernation of that threat now strains the ties that bind America with its traditional allies. While a global coalition successfully conducted multilateral contingency operations against a common enemy in the Gulf War, the reasons that brought us together will rarely exist in the future. Our regional military alliances, no longer challenged by the Soviet threat, may fail to provide a reliable basis for strength. The United States should prepare to act alone when vital national interests are at stake.

Perhaps the most obvious challenge within the developing world is the broad proliferation of modern arms and, particularly, of weapons of mass destruction. Throughout the globe, nations have obtained nuclear, biological, and chemical weapons, along with means to deliver those weapons. Once-unsophisticated militaries now have high technology conventional weapons capable of threatening regional stability.

This is not business as usual! It calls for a dramatic transformation:

• First, we must move past *containment* to *regionalism*. While the threat may be harder to define, the essential elements are not. American forces should be mobile, flexible, lethal and sustainable from long distances. The challenge of achieving these capabilities, within the bounds of decreasing budgets, reduced force levels, and shrinking forward basing must be overcome with smart planning and efficient spending.

• Next, to break the traditional military spending mold, fix the focus of the national power *lens* on potential economic gains, not just military threats. Uniquely, among the elements of mobilization, strengthening military movement capacity directly contributes to the well-being of the nation. Renewing infrastructure—highways, ports, and railheads; increasing manufacturing—ships, aircraft, and trucks; and, exploiting transportation technology, all create jobs and help our nation's economy grow.

Preparations should continuously improve ways to save transportation, acquire additional lift platforms where absolutely necessary and adopt techniques to lighten the cargo load. This will require a new approach to integrate disparate elements into a balanced and unified mobility strategy. We cannot afford to reinvent the wheel. Nor should we have to relearn the logistical lessons of the past—including *Desert Storm*—by repeating the same mistakes through omission or commission.

Regionalism relies on rapid global reach. The growing military threat posed by many developing nations, especially when facing two regional flashpoints simultaneously, would probably exceed current U.S. mobility resources. America must bridge this requirement/capability gap to enable intervention when and where necessary—while saving cost, time, and potential casualties.

Strategic surge lift and pre-positioning capability must be improved. Limited strategic lift and prepositioning constrain the number of forces U.S. leaders can send to a crisis. Of the power resources theater commanders need most, strategic lift ranks at or near the top. Because the United States will probably not have enough forces immediately on the scene of future conflicts, or nontraditional missions, strategic lift will determine the scope and duration of our commitment. This dictates balanced inter-theater mobility—with increased forward deployed equipment and supplies, additional fast sealift capacity, aircraft that can operate from unprepared sites, and continued civil air access. Cost benefit and risk analysis and the warfighting CINC's needs assessment are guiding considerations for improvement.

Actions in the first 2 weeks of a conflict are crucial to preventing the enemy from gaining key theater objectives. Swift political action and the demonstrated ability to move forces eases the task of regaining lost territory and, ultimately, defeating the enemy. Because they significantly shorten deployment times, prepositioning and airlift can best minimize that early risk. Rapid deployers must hold the line while we build a decisive force capable of offensive operations. Sealift best addresses this latter need.

Pre-positioning. Short of forward-based forces in the theater of operations, afloat pre-positioning provides essential quickness, strategic agility and flexibility to swing to different regional scenarios. Afloat pre-positioning is less costly and better able to close heavy forces than airlift. It provides a low-keyed, but ever ready response to crisis. Often overlooked, this may be the simplest way to gain necessary strategic leverage. Land-based pre-positioning could make a big difference if close enough to the fray. It more likely would provide the edge in building up a decisive force.

Sealift. America's maritime industry was once a formidable national resource. Without coordinated government and private sector reinvigoration, the United States will possess limited ability to decisively respond to crisis via sealift. Lessons learned from the Gulf War, coupled with the follow-on *Mobility Requirements Study* (MRS), has generated enough momentum to begin to scratch the surface in shipbuilding. The first large, medium-speed RORO ship keel was expected to be laid in late 1993. The MRS indicates, though, that doing nothing more will result in a further 15 percent reduction of available sealift by 1999.[61] If this continues, the option to deploy a heavy force to a future distant battlefield is in question. This essential element of national power has been hibernating, with no new strategic sealift construction in over 30 years.

For several reasons, American-flag shipping has fallen— to 4 percent of all U.S. commerce.[62] Dwindling economic markets and skyrocketing operating costs have forced U.S. shippers to register their vessels under foreign flags. Thus, they take advantage of lower labor and other costs. Additionally, the commercial trend has been toward more, and larger, container ships and tankers, that the military has not embraced. The result is fewer U.S. flag carriers, fewer shipyards, fewer merchant mariners, and fewer ships suited to handling military cargo.[63]

A balanced approach to revitalize the maritime industry is necessary:

• Acquire existing RORO ships with Maritime Administration acquisition funds.

• Construct modern diesel-propelled RORO ships in U.S. shipyards with funding already appropriated by Congress for strategic sealift.

• Refurbish and renew the Ready Reserve Fleet. This sustainment fleet, with too few militarily useful ships, provided lackluster performance during the Gulf War.

• Set up a merchant marine reserve to ensure sufficient seamen are available during crisis, although nothing will help the merchant marine like an increase in U.S.-flagged ships.

Airlift. Changing world geopolitics and an aging military air fleet point to the need for improved airlift. The workhorse of the Air Force fleet, the C-141, flew a year's worth of service life in only seven months during the Gulf War.[64] An answer to our rapidly aging C-141 fleet is the C-17. By design, it can bypass congested destination airfields and move large quantities of supplies and equipment directly to forward areas. It is estimated that the C-17 will increase access to over 6,000 airfields worldwide that are currently inaccessible to C-141s and C-5s—that's an approximate 300 percent increase. This means more versatility in responding to crisis and greater speed in closing a force into a bare base theater. For example, recent estimates show that if the C-17 had replaced the C-141 during *Desert Shield/Desert Storm* we could have met our airlift deployment requirements 20 to 35 percent faster.[65] The aircraft's lower manpower requirements, reduced operating costs, and exceptional ground maneuverability make the C-17 an efficient and effective choice for the future.

The Civil Reserve Air Fleet (CRAF) program is based on military accessibility to U.S. commercial air carriers, who maintain modified aircraft in the fleet for considerably longer than five years. Now, over 30 percent of the U.S. commercial air fleet is leased, and this could reach 60-70 percent within the next ten years.[66] Leasing provides airlines greater flexibility to change aircraft types and saves large capital costs associated with purchasing aircraft. Like the shipping industry, increasing segments of the aircraft industry—through expanding ownership of flying or leasing firms—are controlled by foreign corporations. These facts raise the specter of further decline in the CRAF, since foreign owned aircraft are excluded from participating. In addition, the flexibility inherent in the leasing option will work against fleet stability that is so essential to CRAF. The needs of the airlines no longer parallel those of the national defense. In crisis, can the United States rely on the provision of commercial aircraft controlled by the corporations of other nations? What occurs in board rooms around the world could inextricably control our ability to conduct independent military action.

An underlying current emerges. America's contingency transportation capacity has become a hostage to domestic and international economic forces that have little to do with the realities of national defense. There is no mechanism in place to maintain the essential link between industry and government. Our ability to adequately respond to future crisis relies on reforging this link.

Service advocacy has frequently hindered acquisition of strategic lift assets. Let's face it: Airlift and sealift are not the stuff of Air Medals or Navy Crosses. Weapon systems—carriers and fighters—have usually taken primacy at the expense of strategic mobility. As we draw down and the competition for acquisition dollars grows, the Services will naturally gravitate toward supporting high-tech weapon systems. The handwriting is already on the wall.

Why not take the burden of Service parochialism out of the strategic mobility equation? Accomplish this by passing budgetary responsibility for strategic lift to U.S.

Transportation Command. Vest that command with the responsibility to prepare, justify and execute a separate mobility budget line.

No capability requires bolstering more than the wide spectrum of operational transportation. This is where the rubber, quite literally, meets the road for the warfighting CINC. Many necessary improvements extend beyond the foxhole, all the way to the producers and depots. An overarching battlefield distribution system, integrating total asset visibility of cargo in the transportation pipeline, increased and improved ground lift capability, and smarter allocation of transport resources is necessary. What good is knowing where the goods are unless we have enough trucks to get them to the customer units? So, let's address some of these key issues.

Total Asset Visibility. Our distribution system, that includes supply and transportation, is based on Cold War thinking and antiquated technology. We must fix it! In the Central Front scenario, units knew exactly where they were to locate, where they would draw their support, over what routes and by what schedule they would move. Things were neat and predictable.

Well, things have changed. We must progress from a Cold War supply point logistical system, which relies on getting the goods to fixed locations, to one that is distribution based. This would focus on getting the goods to customer units, wherever they are at in the theater of operations. To accomplish this, though, logisticians must know where critical supplies are and direct them where most needed. Otherwise, we will continue to do no more than react and improvise, instead of anticipate support requirements.

The battlefield is mobile and transitory—and it must remain so for us to win. That is America's warfighting strength. But, our logistics just haven't quite caught up. When units move, we don't use available technology to track and update their actual battlefield locations. With this meaningful information, updated through secure satellite links, battlefield distribution can become seamless—not accidental. Without it, we are reduced to aimless movement—like the mailman trying to guess where you've moved without a forwarding address. The mail winds up in the dead letter bin. In *Desert Storm*, our dead letter bins—those thousands of containers filled with undeliverable goods—proved to be a vast waste of resources that we cannot afford in the future.

Many believe that Gulf units lacked supply discipline. Critics allege that repetitious supply ordering glutted the distribution pipeline. While duplicate requisitioning did occur, mere mention of this hides the important truth: Units lost confidence in the distribution system's ability to deliver the goods. Unlike combat operators who were deluged with information, logisticians thirsted for it. Without timely and accurate requisition status; up-to-date unit location information; or, sufficient ship, aircraft, and container manifest visibility, logisticians could not optimally support battlefield operations. As the former commander of the Army Materiel Command, General (Ret.) William G.T. Tuttle, Jr., described:

> We could get parts to the arrival ports, but there we lost asset visibility. We have done little to improve our distribution process since Vietnam, and we have seen similar—though not as poor—results on other occasions. **We should tolerate this no longer**. United Parcel Service and Federal Express can tell you precisely where your package is located in their system at any given time. Similar processes could be applied to track combat-essential components or even to monitor the location of entire units.[67]

Today, shippers around the world expect not only dock-to-dock service, but transportation tracking from producer-to-consumer. In world shaping matters, America's military should not accept less. The needs of DOD must merge with the available distribution technology of the civil sector to produce total asset visibility of critical cargo items through the transportation pipeline. Otherwise, we will be left, once again, to lost confidence in the distribution system and moving mountains of stuff. Tuttle's movement vision would:

> Employ satellite systems, and querying transponders on each shipment unit that would relay time-tagged locations to digitized map displays in movements management centers. Each shipment unit would have its unique identity. The movements management teams could then forecast arrivals, reroute convoys around enemy action . . . or take actions necessary for the reliable delivery of cargo or units. This process applies equally well to the strategic deployment and sustainment systems.[68]

The cost to get this system up and running will be high, but the rewards in logistical support to the warfighting CINCs, inventory and storage cost efficiency, elimination of support redundancies, and improved sustainability.

Joint Theater Logistics Command. Future conflict will be short-notice, and require quick and lethal response. There will be no time to get things organized. The necessary theater logistical structure necessary must integrate command and control for quick redirection of reinforcement and materiel flows—especially common item support for people and equipment. It must exhaust all available host-nation support capability with formal contracting teams. Currently, there is no such joint theater organization to manage logistics for the CINCs. The 22nd Support Command became the locus of Gulf War victory, but it was strictly ad hoc. We must move to formalize, stand-up, and minimally staff similar Joint Theater Logistics Commands for each theater.

Intra-theater Transport. Streamlining the transportation "push" of supplies and equipment forward should be the goal of an efficient movement system. Ground mobility and materials-handling procedures should be fully integrated, using equipment to eliminate in-transit unloading and reloading. The Palletized Load System (PLS), recently approved for limited procurement, consists of a five-axle, high-mobility truck; a two-axle trailer; and, a 16.5-ton load capacity flatrack. The driver can load and unload the flatrack from the cab of the vehicle, without a crane or forklift, in less than two minutes. Flatracks conform to international shipping standards and could be tailored as far back as the ammunition plants and depots in the CONUS. From there, pre-positioned afloat aboard RORO vessels on the host PLSs. Finally, they could be driven off of these ships in crisis-torn ports, directly to forward units. Delivery without delays builds victory—true inventory in motion.

Take this concept a step further using high technology and battlefield pre-positioning—a technique known as caching. Squads of PLS vehicles, loaded with essential supplies, could "orbit" the battlefield, awaiting delivery instructions. Equipped with global positioning systems, the trucks could be directed to precise locations to drop their loads, forming caches, just before needed by advancing units. Transponders or radio transceivers mounted on the flatracks would allow units to locate and identify these caches by satellite monitoring devices or simple radio receivers. This PLS-cache concept would provide an impetus away from delivering to fixed supply points, and anticipate battlefield distribution needs. Unlike the past, logistics would enable, instead of halt, the initiative.

If we are to wage mobile warfare, the key lesson of the Gulf War is that we need more Heavy Equipment Transporters (HETs). Heavy divisions should have enough to move one brigade with a single lift. Besides the operational advantage of agility—the capability to move heavy forces rapidly—HETs preserve tank combat readiness, extend service life and decrease expensive operating costs. Cost advantages are enormous: Moving tracked vehicles in a heavy brigade-sized task force just 1 mile, under their own power, costs over $180,000 (based on life cycle, per mile operating costs). It costs just $15,000 to move them one mile on HETs—a $165,000 saving per mile.[69] While cost is not normally a driving factor in determining warfighting requirements, this staggering saving increases the quantity and quality of training affordable during the peace.

• *Other Equipment.* Provide *warfighting* CINCs with enough of the right transport assets to get the job done. Equip contingency forces with trucks able to operate off-road—like the Heavy Expanded Mobility Tactical Truck (HEMTT)—instead of commercially designed vehicles, unsuited to traverse sparse road networks.

Containerization and palletization of unit equipment would streamline the movement process. Most commanders, though, fight against these. They know that there is not enough materials-handling equipment to off-load the boxes and pallets at final field locations. To overcome this often overlooked shortfall, outfit early deploying units with rough terrain container handlers, and front and side loading forklifts.

Don't use Ad-Dammam, Saudi Arabia, as an example of typical ship discharge operations in a regional setting. Instead, let's use Mogadishu, Somalia, which could unload only one small ship at a time. Other vessels were discharged in the harbor onto smaller boats, while being beaten by heavy surf. With that basic premise, there is strong justification to possess a robust logistics-over-the-shore (LOTS) capability. Without it, the United States cannot gain greater than meager entry into most worldwide ports.

STREAMLINE THE FORCE

After the military draws down, U.S. planners will have too little force structure to afford the redundancy of designating forces to specific regions. With fewer available forces there will be greater need for efficient employment.

Adapt force structure to be rapidly deployable and, with a minimum of preplanned adjustments, capable of fighting across the spectrum of future conflict. Keep a fraction of units in a high state of readiness. Tailor this force so that the functions (such as logistical support) that are the most difficult to achieve after the opening of hostilities receive higher priority than those that can be quickly developed. Shift some support units, particularly those that speed theater buildup, from the reserves to the active force to increase readiness. In these ways we can focus our transport effort and limited resources.

Unless checked, the widespread use of unguided ordnance—rather than more expensive guided munitions or smart bombs—will continue to grow. The costs to stock and move ammunition within and to the theater are high, and amounts are significant. Unguided ordnance can be justified only when the combat effect sought is prolonged neutralization, harassment, or reconnaissance by fire.[70] We should place greater reliance on smart munitions to decrease the demand on strategic lift to move large stocks of less accurate munitions and delivery systems.

Additionally, the threat allocation process—determining how much ammunition is really needed to achieve objectives—has run amuck. There were 78 ammo-laden ships still awaiting off-load the day the Gulf War ended. And, 3.2 million rounds of 155mm howitzer rounds were moved to Saudi Arabia, while 2.9 million of these rounds had to be returned. Correcting this problem will allow more strategic lift for the rapid buildup of U.S. forces.

Finally, based on their proven lethal advantage over the nearest adversary, restructure armored units with fewer tanks. This will lighten the load of projecting armored formations and lessen requisite support structure. Taking this a step further, we need an improved and easily transportable capability to defeat armor and other hard targets, such as a medium-weight armored gun system.

For too long, transportability—equipment design to reduce mobility requirements—has been an afterthought in the acquisition process. Just as roles and missions redundancy has come into question, DOD has to really scrutinize and enforce the transportability of each piece of developing equipment. While lethality must be the order of the day, we cannot afford mobility guzzlers any longer.

We must also continue to promote collective security arrangements—especially those that gain us strategic access. The importance of staging bases and overflight rights cannot be overestimated in planning for future operations. Additionally, the relevance of developing equipment interoperability with allies will increase as these ground forces draw down and multinational corps are formed. This can lead to greater resource efficiencies. While coalitions may be ad hoc, firmly established alliances could make the strategic difference in the next confrontation.

EXPLOIT AMERICA'S HIGH-TECHNOLOGY ADVANTAGE

We must examine new technologies aimed at easing the logistics burden of long-distance commitments. Exploit our technological edge to enable U.S. contingency forces to overcome the constraints of time and distance in reacting to contingencies. For ground forces, these technologies might include electromagnetic guns and other new weapons that do not require significant ammunition supply; engines using alternatives to fossil fuel; and, weapons, like automatic or robotic tanks, that use fewer people and need less transport.

A different approach will be necessary for theater resupply. Large surface effect ships of 1,000- to 2,000-ton capacity with self-defense armament could load farther off shore, perhaps from larger ships of 20,000 to 40,000 tons displacement. The speed and flexibility of such ships would totally redefine theater logistics as to routes, timing, echelons of stockage, require supply quantities, and vulnerability to enemy attack.[71]

CONCLUSION

Regional focus and reduced forward presence will significantly increase America's reliance on movement in the future. The slightest delay or inefficiency in harnessing our movement resources may cost us victory. To carefully restructure military capabilities will lessen the risks of distance and time in an unstable world.

To execute a credible crisis response strategy, a world power must be able to readily surge strategic mobility, and reliably move equipment and supplies on the battlefield. There is sober logic in demonstrating that development of these capacities is among the strongest possible deterrents to conflict. And, there is good economic sense in suggesting that America's fiscal renewal will be enhanced by reinvestment in the military transportation base. After all, military *and* economic strength will define our future.

In moving the force beyond *Desert Storm*, it is vital that we assure America's strategic role in the world by shaping movement preeminence. To do so prudently provides, perhaps, the greatest conventional deterrent to war—global reach. To do less invites confrontation with adversaries willing to test the substance and purpose of that reach.

NOTES

1. LtGen Jimmy D. Ross, USA, *Today's Challenge: Tomorrow's Army* (Washington, DC: Department of Defense, January 1992), 6-1.

2. Col. Joseph J. Collins, USA, "Desert Storm and the Lessons of Learning," *Parameters* (Carlisle: U.S. Army War College, Autumn 1992), 87.

3. MGen Fred E. Elam, USA, and LTC Mark Henderson, USA, "The Army's Strategic Mobility Plan," *Army Logistician* (May-June 1992), 3.

4. RADM (Ret.) Henry E. Eccles, *Logistics in the National Defense* (Washington, DC: 1959; NAVMC 2799, reprinted 1987), 9, 18.

5. Chester Wardlow, *The Transportation Corps: Responsibilities, Organization, and Operations in World War II* (Washington, DC: Office

of the Chief of Military History, 1951), 2.

6. Col. Gilbert S. Harper, USA, "Army Logistics in 2010," *Army Logistician* (September-October 1991), 20.

7. Martin Van Creveld, *Supplying War* (New York: Cambridge University Press, 1977), 3.

8. Michael Klare, "Pax Americana Redux," in *The Gulf War Reader*, Micah L. Sifry and Christopher Cerf, eds. (New York: Times Books, 1991), 470.

9. Joseph Galloway, "The Point of the Spear," *U.S. News and World Report* (March 11, 1991), 41; and, Charles Lane, et al, "The Killing Ground," *Newsweek* (January 28, 1991), 30.

10. Murray Hammick, "Logistics Comes of Age," *International Defense Review* (July 1992), 665.

11. Department of Defense, *Conduct of the Persian Gulf Conflict: Final Report to the Congress* (Washington, DC: GPO, April 1992), Vol. I, 38.

12. James Blackwell, et al, *Interim Report of the Center for Strategic and International Studies Group on Lessons Learned from the Gulf War* (Washington, DC: CSIS, July 1991), 1.

13. Dick Cheney, Secretary of Defense, Department of Defense, *Conduct of the Persian Gulf Conflict: Final Report to the Congress*, Vol. I, iii.

14. Joe Stork and Martha Wenger, "From Rapid Deployment to Massive Deployment," in *The Gulf War Reader*, 34.

15. *Conduct of the Persian Gulf Conflict: Final Report to the Congress*, Vol. I, 38.

16. Ibid., 40.

17. Ibid., 43.

18. Ibid., 43.

19. Ibid., 40.

20. Ibid., Vol. II, E2.

21. Ibid., Vol. II, E16.

22. Association of the United States Army, *Special Report: Operations Desert Shield/Desert Storm—The Logistics Perspective* (Arlington: AUSA, September 1991), 4.

23. The first month of the Korean buildup was July 1950. *U.S. Army Chief of Transportation Briefing: Operation Desert Shield/Desert Storm* (Fort Eustis, Virginia: August 1991).

24. The first month of the buildup was August 7-October 7, 1990.

General Accounting Office Report: Operation Desert Shield/Desert Storm (Washington, DC: GPO, February 1991).

25. Blackwell, 34.

26. *Conduct of the Persian Gulf Conflict: Final Report to Congress,* Vol. I, 41.

27. Col. Douglas W. Craft, USA, *An Operational Analysis of the Persian Gulf War* (Carlisle: Strategic Studies Institute, U.S. Army War College, 1992), 20.

28. Transportation planners traditionally worked with estimates of 766 C-141 plus 24 C-5 sorties for an Airborne Division. It actually required approximately 1,200 C-141 equivalent and 24 C-5 sorties. Ibid., p. 19, 47.

29. *Conduct of the Persian Gulf Conflict: Final Report to the Congress,* Vol. I, 59.

30. U.S. General Accounting Office, *Part of the National Defense Reserve Fleet is No Longer Needed,* Report to Congressional Requesters (Washington, DC: GPO, 1991), 16.

31. Craft, 21.

32. Michael D. McManus and Frederick M. McNamee, *Logistics Management Institute Report: Relationships Between Mobility, Sustainability, and Firepower* (Bethesda: LMI, February, 1991), iii-iv.

33. Ibid., 12.

34. Ibid., 13.

35. Department of Defense, *The Mobility Requirements Study* (Washington, DC: GPO, January 23, 1992), Vol. I, ES-2.

36. LtGen William G. Pagonis, USA, *Moving Mountains* (Boston: Harvard Press, 1992), 206.

37. Congress, *Military Supply Systems: Lessons from the Vietnam Experience,* House, 91st Cong., 2nd sess. (Washington, DC: GPO, October 1970), 3.

38. LtGen Joseph M. Heiser, Jr., USA (Ret.), *A Soldier Supporting Soldiers* (Washington, DC: Center of Military History, United States Army, 1991), 151.

39. Ibid.

40. *Conduct of the Persian Gulf Conflict: Final Report to the Congress,* Vol. I, 40.

41. Ibid., 51.

42. Ibid., 103.

43. Ibid.

44. General Hansford T. Johnson, USAF, Commander in Chief, U.S. Transportation Command, *Presentation to the U.S. Senate Committee on Armed Services* (Washington, DC: March 13, 1992), 1.

45. Pagonis, 2.

46. Ibid., 6.

47. Ibid.

48. Johnson, 1.

49. Pagonis, 9.

50. *Conduct of the Persian Gulf Conflict: Final Report to the Congress,* Vol. II, F-2.

51. Joel Nadel, "Logistics Lessons," in *The Gulf War Reader,* 168.

52. Rick Maze, "Storm Report: Logistics Hit Their Limit," *Army Times* (May 4, 1992), 10.

53. Headquarters, Combined Arms Support Command, "Sustainment Imperatives in History—Integration: Rommel's Nemesis," *Army Logistician* (March-April 1992), 10.

54. Maj. Anthony H. Kral, USA, "Sustaining Patton's Pursuit," *Army Logistician* (January-February 1991), 26-30.

55. General Accounting Office, *GAO Report: Operation Desert Storm—Transportation and Distribution of Equipment and Supplies in Southwest Asia* (Washington, DC: GPO, December 26, 1991), 10.

56. Pagonis, 203-204.

57. Congress, *House Armed Services Committee Report on the Persian Gulf War* (Washington, DC: GPO, April 23, 1992).

58. Ibid.

59. Johnson, p 4-5.

60. LCDR Robin E. Rathbun, USN, "Strategic Mobility for the 1990s: The Mobility Requirements Study," *Strategic Review* (Summer 1992), 4-5.

61. *The Mobility Requirements Study,* Vol. I, ES6.

62. Doug Bandow, "Merchant Marine Sinks Oceans of Money," *The Wall Street Journal* (September 12, 1988), 20.

63. Kent N. Gourdin and LTC Robert E. Trempe, USA, "Contingency Transportation in a Changing World: Meeting the Challenge," *Logistics Spectrum* (Spring 1992), 11.

64. Gen. Hansford T. Johnson, "The Defense Transportation System," *Defense Transportation Journal* (October, 1991), 56

65. Ibid.

66. Gourdin and Trempe, 11.

67. GeneralWilliam G.T. Tuttle, Jr., USA (Ret.), Sustaining Army Combat Forces—Part II," *Army Logistician* (November-December 1991), 12-13.

68. Ibid., 14.

69. Joe A. Fortner, Capt. Jules T. Doux, USA, and Capt. Mark A. Peterson, USA, "Bring on the HETs!," *Military Review* (January 1992), 42.

70. Re Dave McCurdy and Re John G. Rowland, *Center for Strategic and International Studies Report—Conventional Combat Priorities: An Approach for the New Strategic Era* (Washington, DC: CSIS, May 1990), 37.

71. Ibid., 55.

6

ATTACKING ELECTRIC POWER

THOMAS E. GRIFFITH, JR.

Electric systems have been a favorite target of air power since the Air Corps Tactical School (ACTS) first considered it in the 1930s. Electric systems have been critical target systems in every war since, and will likely be targeted in future air campaigns.[1] Nevertheless, there has been little thought given to understanding the conditions which determine when these attacks will be successful in obaining the political objectives of any given application. Often, attacks on this system are advocated more out of institutional inertia than clear strategic thinking. If the Air Force believes in the utility of attacking electric power, then some effort must be make to define the conditions for these attacks and for predicting the effects of such attacks.

It is not surprising that there has been little thinking about targeting electric power because there has been little thought given to the topic of conventional strategic attack in general and, as a result, there has been little debate about what targets should be attacked and why.[2] It is important to provide an intellectual foundation for strategic

Major Thomas E. Griffith, Jr., U.S. Air Force, wrote this paper while he was a student at the Air Command and Staff College. It was named a Distinguished Essay in the 1993 Chairman, Joint Chiefs of Staff, Strategy Essay Competition.

planning because interest in the idea of conventional strategic bombing as a tool for U.S. policy makers has been revived by a number of recent events, including the increasing number of crisis situations in a multipolar world; the growing sophistication of weapons which sharpen the blunt instrument of military force; and the belief that a strategic air attack can enforce political demands without committing large numbers of ground forces and enduring the concomitant domestic political problems.[3]

The conventional wisdom about targeting electric power holds that such attacks have wide-ranging effects on a variety of institutions. Two political effects believed to result from the loss of electricity are, first, that it will diminish civilian morale, thereby forcing a change in the government's behavior, and second, that these attacks will raise the costs for the political leaders of a country, increasing pressure on them to change. Likewise, there are two important military effects usually mentioned: that the loss of power will have a direct impact on the fighting military forces and that it will cause a reduction in war production. These four arguments, either separately or in combination, have been used in the past to advocate attacking electric systems.

Not all of these arguments are sound. Attacks on electric power to reduce civilian morale have not been effective in changing political behavior. Attempts to influence governments through increasing costs by targeting their electric systems have also been ineffective because leaders of most regimes generally embark on actions with high resolve, and thus are unwilling to change their policies simply because of losing electric power. Moreover, political leaders and military forces are prepared for such contingencies, and are therefore well-insulated from the loss of the national power grid and able to continue functioning. In contrast, attacking electric power can be effective in slowing the production of war material, and in a prolonged war against a self-sufficient nation attacking electric power is necessary. Given the current limited nature of war against small powers, however, it does not appear that war production will be a factor in the near future. In addition there are several drawbacks to attacking electricity, including the largely negative impact of deaths and disease on the civilian population, and the potentially negative international censure which could result from such actions. In today's world the military benefit gained from attacks on electric systems are small, while their potential to be politically counterproductive is large.

NATIONAL ELECTRIC POWER SYSTEMS

Though electric power systems may be organized differently from country to country, the basic technical requirements for generating electricity are the same, making it possible to discuss, in general terms, the basic components of an electric power system[4] and the effects of losing power. A generic electric power system is composed of four separate subsystems: generation, transmission, distribution, and control. An understanding of how each of these works offers some insight into determining the vulnerability of the system.

The generation subsystem is the heart, or source, of the electric system and is characterized by the method in which the turbine is turned. A steam, or thermal, plant burns a fossil fuel, primarily coal or oil, to generate heat and produce steam which then moves the turbine blades. A nuclear power plan is a variation of a steam plant which uses nuclear energy to produce the steam. A hydroelectric plant uses the water stored behind a dam as its source of power for moving the turbine blades.[5]

After electricity is generated, it is then sent to a step-up transformer, located in the substation or transformer yard, close to the power plant. Here the voltage of the generated power is raised (or stepped up) to a higher voltage for transmission, and sent along high-voltage power lines to the various users.[6] The transmission system terminates at a transformer yard (substation) or other load center, such as a large factory of military installation, where the voltage is reduced (or stepped down) and the electricity sent through the distribution network to the various consumers.[7] The transmission system is also the means by which generating facilities are interconnected. These interconnections allow for the economical exchange of power and, most importantly, improve the reliability of the entire power system by providing redundant power sources in an emergency.[8]

While the interconnection of electric systems is physically accomplished through the transmission subsystem, it is the control network that coordinates the interchange of power.[9] Control systems may be automated by computers or rely on manual operations for transferring power, and are typically capable of controlling power throughout the system and accessing other systems.[10] As a result of this integration, extensive intelligence is required about how the specific national power grid is organized, and how much of the total power capacity of the country is interconnected.

The effects of attacks on power systems can be divided into two broad categories: military and civilian. Military effects are defined as the impact of the loss of electricity on purely military operations, such as the loss of communications capability or the inability to employ air defense radar equipment. The civilian effects would include the impact of the loss of power on the social, political, and economic sectors of a nation. Clearly there is overlap in these two areas. Generally, though, the loss of electricity impacts the civilian sector more immediately and more pervasively than the military.

Most militaries are relatively unaffected by a loss of power for three reasons. The first is that the military consumes very little of a nation's electricity. In the United States, for example, the entire Department of Defense consumes only about 1 percent of the electricity in the country, and much of that is for peripheral functions such as heating and air conditioning.[11] The amount consumed for essential functions like communications or computing is minute in relation to national consumption. Further, although the military consumes only a small amount of power, generally they are a high priority user, meaning that if any power is available in the national power grid, military needs will likely be met.[12]

Even if it were possible to completely eliminate a country's power system, only a portion of the military would be affected, because most ground tactical units (division level or below) rely on organic sources of power.[13] As a result, the areas most affected would be fixed installations, such as air bases, naval ports, or theater headquarters. However, because these sites are vulnerable to power interruptions they are normally supplied with emergency power equipment. In both the Korean and Vietnam conflicts, American forces relied almost entirely on generators because the host nation's electric system could not supply the necessary power.[14] During *Desert Storm*, staged mostly from a country with a sophisticated national power system, there was nevertheless a need to supply auxiliary power systems to U.S. forces.[15]

If a nation chooses to rely on a national power system for daily military operations, there may be some initial confusion as the change to emergency power is made, but the long-term effects on the military are more likely to be a result of a loss of war production rather than the direct impact on operations.

While the military is largely insulated from a loss of power, the civilian population is heavily affected.

Although there is little statistical quantification of the civilian effects from the loss of power, some anecdotal evidence has been gathered from various power outages.[16] Based on these observations we can predict that the loss of electricity will likely cause the following civilian effects:

• Transportation: Trains, subways, street lights, and air traffic will all be slowed or stopped.

• Emergency service: Hospitals will be forced to use backup power. Police and fire department response times will be longer.

• Public utilities: Water, gas, and sewer services will be interrupted, eventually causing health problems.

• Industrial: Manufacturing will largely stop until power is restored (unless the plant has its own generating facility). In addition, losses may occur in sensitive processes such as steel manufacturing because of the sudden loss of power.

• Computers and telecommunications: The loss of power will interrupt computer operations and may result in the loss of data or other damage. Depending on the availability of emergency power, telecommunications will also be affected.[17]

While these general effects offer some indication of the impact of a loss of power, the precise result will depend, to a large degree, on the specific situations, making it difficult to quantify or predict the exact civilian effect of an attack on electric power in advance.

Overall, national power systems are exceedingly vulnerable to air attack and interruption. Generators and turbines rotate at high speeds, making them very susceptible to damage from bombing.[18] Transformer yards are in open areas and are readily identifiable because of the many power lines that converge there. In addition, spare parts for generators and transformers are not readily available because of the expense and custom-manufacturing required. The control system, however, can mitigate against the damage caused by air attack by providing a means to transfer power between areas, and ensuring that the priority consumers are supplied.[19] The interconnections disperse the generation of electricity by making the power from more plants available to any given area.

Although these interconnections can limit the vulnerability of the national power system, they cannot eliminate it, and when discussing power systems the tendency is for the military planner to become enamored with this vulnerability without asking the more fundamental question, "Why are these attacks being proposed?"

PAST ELECTRIC POWER TARGETING

Air Corps Tactical School

The first conceptual work in identifying specific strategic bombing targets in general, and electric power in particular, was done during the 1930s at the service school for airmen.[20] The bomber advocates at ACTS used meticulous logic to explain how strategic bombing could win wars through the attack of specific targets. They began with the premise that the will or morale of a country, and not the destruction of the field forces, was the true objective in war, not because the army had been defeated.[21] Thus, disintegration of the nation's civilian morale became the true objective in war.[22]

The quickest and most efficient way to directly attack a nation's will, they felt, was by "paralyzing its economic structure and threatening its very existence" through precision bombing.[23] Strategic bombing advocates hypothesized that because a modern nation was very specialized and interdependent—an industrial web in their terms—it would be vulnerable to interruption at certain critical points which could be identified through a scientific analysis of its economic system.[24] Instructors expounded on the validity of this concept in a lecture called the "national Economic Structure," which analyzed the United States. A second study offered a more in-depth analysis of New York City. This detailed study was taught to acquaint the students with selecting targets, discovering their vulnerabilities, and estimating the effects of the attack.[25] One of the targets most frequently cited for destruction in these lectures was the electric power system.

Electric power was seen as a key target set in the industrial web theory because of the success which attacks on this system promised. An attack on electric power was attractive for several reasons: it would affect, simultaneously, the social and economic spheres of a nation; the targets were relatively easy to locate and were considered vulnerable to air attack; the generators and transformers would be difficult to replace; and, perhaps most importantly, this type of attack would be economical, because a small amount of destruction would yield impressive results.[26] According to their calculations, 100 bombs could destroy three-quarters of the electric generating capacity in the Northeastern United States.[27]

By 1938, the New York City electric system was well known to these instructors, and they used a hypothetical attack on it to demonstrate the effectiveness of their theory.[28] They knew, for instance, that there were 26 steam generating plants in the city for general use, and 8 steam generating plants solely for the transportation system. The instructors believed that lack of power would stop almost any form of modern transportation—there would be no rapid transit and no elevators. Also the lack of traffic signals would cause difficulties on the road. Shipping would be disrupted because ships could not be unloaded at the port. Eliminating power would also cause water supply distribution problems and increase fire hazards.[29] The overall impact would be twofold: first, and most importantly, it would hurt the morale of the population "by making life under war conditions more intolerable to them than the acceptance of our terms of peace," and secondly, these attacks would destroy the enemy's capacity to wage war.[30] The presumed end result, though left unstated, was the immediate capitulation of the foe.

Because the ACTS instructors believed that victory in war depended on the civilian population's will to continue fighting, their target analysis emphasized civilian rather than military effects. This is evident in their justification for selecting electric power. Their analysis of the attack of New York City, which highlighted the value of an attack on electric power, however, included no specific mention of how this attack would affect war production—only manufacturing in general.[31] These ideas about strategic attack developed at ACTS eventually became more than academic theories—they strongly influenced target selection in the first air campaign plans for World War II.

World War II—Germany

The first opportunity for air planners to present their ideas on strategic bombing outside the Air Corps Tactical School came in 1941, when President Roosevelt requested that the Army and Navy submit plans for their war production requirements.[32] The aircraft portion of the Army's request was formulated by the newly constituted Air War Plans Division (AWPD) in August 1941.[33] While this plan, christened AWPD/1, was technically only a production forecast and not an employment plan, the air planners used the opportunity to present their ideas on how the United States could defeat Nazi Germany through strategic bombing.

The four primary planners for AWPD/1 were Col. Harold L. George, Lt Col Kenneth N. Walker, and Majors Laurence S. Kuter and Haywood S. Hansell, Jr. All had been students and then instructors at ACTS. This common intellectual foundation gave them a strong belief in the efficacy of strategic bombing and the importance of electric power as a target system.[34] They believed that victory could be had by using strategic bombing to cause "the breakdown of the industrial and economic structure of Germany."[35] In order to fulfill this mission, the planners selected targets that were essential to war production and to the will of the civilian population, such as electric power, transportation, and oil. Once these were struck and civilian morale began to break, they projected that area bombing of cities might be required to achieve the final capitulation.[36]

The team systematically analyzed the information available about the German electrical system to establish its value as a potential target. They believed that destroying 50 electric power plants would eliminated approximately 40 percent of Germany's electric generating capacity.[37] They were confident that despite the small size of the targets (calculated as 500 feet by 300 feet for the entire plant), they would be easy to find in daylight and that "about 17 hits in that area will guarantee destruction of the plant."[38] Because of their feeling that electric power was so important to both industry and society, they made "Disruption of a major portion of the Electric Power System in Germany" the number one priority of AWPD/1.[39] Attacking this system would immediately follow what the planners called the "intermediate objective of overriding importance"—gaining air superiority.[40]

In identifying targets, the planners relied heavily on the targeting theory they had refined at ACTS.[41] The effects they hoped for as a result of bombing electric power were split between military production problems and civilian discomfort. Among the war industries listed in AWPD/1 as dependent on electricity were aircraft, ship, aluminum, synthetic rubber, and armaments production. The plan also targeted textile production, which was important because "of the shortage of wool and warm clothing in Germany."[42] Other civilian targets impacted by a reduction in power were automobile production, the cold storage of food, and urban transportation—areas chosen for their impact on civilian morale rather than military production or forces. As a faithful reproduction of ACTS theory, the strategy in AWPD/1 relied heavily on affecting the will of the people.

The target priorities and air strategy of this first air plan were reviewed 1 year later, in August 1942, when President Roosevelt directed the Services to prepare a new plan for the production requirements of aircraft in order to achieve "Air Ascendancy" in 1943.[43] In light of this new guidance, the new plan, called AWPD/42, revised the target priority list, displacing electric power to fourth, preceded by the German Air Force, submarine construction yards, and transportation.[44] This put less emphasis on hitting economic targets like electricity and more on traditional military targets such as the transportation system.[45] AWPD/42 was issued on 9 September 1942 and became, according to official historians, the "basis for all AAF [Army Air Forces] strategic planning prior to the Casablanca conference of January 1943."[46]

Even before the Casablanca conference, however, the targeting assumptions in AWPD/42 came under intense scrutiny. The chief criticism of AWPD/42 was leveled by the members of the Joint Intelligence Committee, who objected to the assumptions involved in the target selection process.[47] This questioning led to the creation of an Army Air Force headquarters organization whose sole purpose was to perform an independent analysis of Germany and make target recommendations.[48] This committee, first known as the Bombing Advisory Committee and later as the Committee of Operations Analysts (COA), was composed of civilian and military personnel instructed by General Henry H. (Hap) Arnold, the commander of the Army Air Forces, to analyze the deterioration of the German economy through bombing and to determine the "date when deterioration will have progressed to a point to permit a successful invasion of Western Europe."[49] This marked an almost complete reversal of targeting objectives of the initial air plan.

There were several factors that influenced COA in its assessment of the German electrical system. The first was the belief that the German national power grid was highly flexible and could shift power sources quickly between regions. Because of this flexibility, the COA concluded that the German electrical system contained excess power of between 15 and 20 percent, which, they believed, constituted an "enormous reserve."[50] The COA also postulated that the poor results of the Luftwaffe bombing of British power plants demonstrated that, "The vulnerability of electric power plants is debatable."[51] Finally, they felt that targeting other systems such as ball bearings, petroleum, and steel production would have a more immediate impact on the military capability of Germany.[52] The net result was that, relative to other target systems, electric power did not appear to be a high priority, and in the formal COA report to General Arnold it was ranked 13th—eliminating it from any real consideration as a target.[53] Arnold forwarded this list to the 8th Air Force headquarters in England where it reflected, in effect, the target priorities for the Combined Bomber Offensive (CBO) Plan.[54]

At least one other American targeting organization in Europe addressed the possibility of attacking electric power—the Enemy Objectives Unit (EOU). As part of the Economic Warfare Division in the U.S. Embassy in London, this unit was assigned the task of formulating criteria for target selection and applying them to different target systems. Such a process would, theoretically, produce the best targets to attack.[55] The methodology developed by the EOU was based on the premise that targets would be "chosen in light of an explicitly defined military goal, linked to the full context of war strategy." The members of the unit opposed attacks designed to weaken the economy[56] or to affect morale and instead concentrated on the impact bombing would have on the German military capability.[57] The EOU Handbook specifically states, "The target systems in this Handbook have been selected on the basis of their direct military effects only."[58] While this organization operated autonomously from 8th Air Force, much of their target analysis was used by the 9th in its efforts to prioritize targets. Electric power was rejected by the EOU analysts primarily because attacking it would not lead to "an early reduction in military strength disposable in the field."[59]

There were two main factors that caused both the COA and the EOU to disagree with the ACTS instructors and early air planners that German electrical power should be a key target. The belief that the interconnections within the German electrical system would allow power to be transferred and thus reduce the vulnerability of the system was the first element, but more important was the change in air strategy from one of affecting the will of the civilian population to one of support for a land invasion. As a result, the German power system was never systematically attacked during the war.

World War II—Japan
In contrast with the extensive planning for a strategic bombing campaign against Germany, the study of Japan did not seriously begin until early 1943 when General Arnold directed the COA to analyze the Japanese economy to determine appropriate strategic targets.[60] Prior to this time, the "Germany first" strategy that the United States and Britain had adopted dictated that the COA's targeting attention would initially be focused on Europe and only after that was completed would they need to consider targets in Japan. In addition, the Army Air Forces possessed little capability, even by 1943, of attacking mainland Japan on a sustained basis.[61] Finally, and most

importantly for target selection, there was a severe lack of intelligence about Japan.[62]

In October 1943, the COA began consolidating subcommittee reports prior to making targeting recommendations to General Arnold. The electric power subcommittee noted that isolated attacks on the power system would be of "little more than nuisance value."[63] They felt that large-scale attacks on the power system would be effective in weakening the fielded Japanese forces, but only in the long term (estimated to be between 6 months and 1 year).[64] In addition, the committee discovered that the Japanese obtained the bulk of their power from a large number of small hydroelectric dams. Because of their location, number, and construction, these dams presented poor targets for strategic bombing.[65] The subcommittee's pessimism about the effectiveness of bombing electric power resulted from this dispersion of the power plants, which lowered the vulnerability of the system and the delay in affecting the military capability of Japan. Based on this report, and perhaps the COA's ambivalence toward electric power based on the their German targeting experience, they concluded that, while the electrical power system was vulnerable, it would not be a profitable target overall.[66] The net outcome was that the Japanese electrical system was not mentioned in the six target systems the COA recommended to General Arnold, and the Japanese power system was never targeted during World War II.[67] Following the war a high-level commission, called the U. S. Strategic Bombing Survey (USSBS), was formed to evaluate the effectiveness of strategic bombing on the outcome of the war.[68] Their study of electric power offered some vindication of the ACTS thinking because they found that an attack on the German power system would have seriously impacted Germany's ability to wage war.[69] It is important to note, however, that the USSBS comments are in relation to the importance of electricity to war production, rather than the original objective of winning the war by collapsing civilian morale. In addition, while the USSBS did discuss the potential value of electricity in Nazi Germany, they made no recommendations regarding its value as a future target. Despite these important differences, for air planners the lesson was clear—hit electric power, regardless of the situation. This attitude prevailed despite the changes in the nature of war and in the enemies the United States faced in the post-World War II era, and is still the basis for current attitudes about the value of attacking electric power.

Korean War

When North Korean forces launched their invasion on 25 June 1950, the U.S. Air Force, much like the rest of the world, was caught by surprise. Prior to the invasion, the Far Eastern Air Forces (the Air Force component responsible for air matters in Korea) had accomplished little contingency planning and once the war began, there was little more they could do but react. It wasn't until 3 July that Strategic Air Command, which retained operational control of the bomber force, began looking for potential strategic targets.[70] This investigation identified five hydroelectric plants in eastern North Korea: Fusen, Choshin, Kyosen, Funei, Kongosan, and one large power plant, Suiho, in western North Korea, as potential targets. Together these plants produced 90 percent of the power used in North Korea. Suiho was considered the most important because of its size (the largest power plant in the Orient) and because it supplied electricity to Manchuria.[71] The rationale at the beginning of the Korean War for attacking electric power bore a striking resemblance to the strategy of AWPD/1. The objectives were spelled out in a memorandum to the Far Eastern Air Forces by Air Force headquarters in Washington, which stated, "Destruction of the plants was expected to lower North Korean morale by putting out lights, bring some electrically-powered industry to a halt, and eliminate most of the surplus power being exported."[72] Based on this report and other analysis the Fusen plant was attacked on 25 September 1950, 3 months to the day after the war began. This mission, however, would be the first and last attack on electric power in the opening phase of the war. General Douglas MacArthur had obtained permission to cross the 38th parallel and the Joint Chiefs of Staff (JCS) ordered that the bombing of targets in the north cease.[73]

MacArthur's drive to reunite Korea was halted near the Yalu River when the Chinese Communist Army intervened in November 1950, forcing the United Nations (UN) command to retreat south. Following this attack the war stalemated near the 38th parallel and in July 1951, peace talks began. The UN ground forces' objective changed from the traditional aim of defeating the opposing army to a new objective of simply holding ground against any further territorial gains by the Communist forces while minimizing UN casualties during the negotiation process. Air power became the primary military means available to directly influence the North Korean government.[74]

The initial attempt, through bombing, to compel the Communists to accept a cease-fire agreement was an interdiction campaign which began in September 1951, known as *Operation Strangle*. This effort, aimed at both the North Korean rail and road systems, attempted to stop the flow of supplies from the rear areas to the front lines and to force a North Korean withdrawal and subsequent peace agreement.[75] Although this interdiction campaign stopped 95 percent of the supplies going to the front lines and may have delayed or even prevented a ground offensive, it nonetheless fell short of its stated goal of "strangling the enemy and forcing an armistice. In attrition, the effort was costly to the UN forces: from August 1951 to March 1952, FEAF alone lost 236 aircraft on interdiction missions.[76] The lack of success in stopping the Communist resupply effort coupled with the cost of the operation (both in terms of aircraft lost and in the loss of prestige to the newly independent Air Force) resulted in a search for alternative methods of employing air power to bring pressure on the enemy.

A new plan, based on a study commissioned early in 1952 by Major General Jacob E. Smart, the FEAF Deputy Commander for Operations, was written by Colonel Richard L. Randolph and Lieutenant Colonel Ben I. Mayo, both Korean combat veterans and members of the FEAF staff.[77] They concluded that the most promising avenue to bring pressure on the North Korean government was to use air power to "destroy or damage enemy supplies, equipment, facilities and personnel."[78] This plan, which they termed an "Air Pressure Strategy," would include some of the interdiction targets that were already being attacked, such as locomotives, vehicles, and supplies, but would add electric power, which they considered "one of the most lucrative air targets remaining in North Korea."[79]

While the primary rationale for attacking electric power may have been a desire to inflict costs on the North Korean leadership and convince them to stop the war, the official explanation was based on curtailing war production. According to this rationale, previous bombing had largely eliminated North Korean industry, forcing them to take defensive measures by dispersing war production to small workshops and underground facilities that made the destruction of manufacturing by conventional bombing difficult at best. Hence, eliminating electric power at its source was deemed the most efficient and effective method of curbing North Korean war production.[80]

The continued institutional perception about the value of electric power as a morale target was also a factor. In addition to stopping war production, eliminating electricity would cause an "adverse psychological effect on [the] civilian and military population."[81]   An unwritten but nevertheless real reason for striking electric power was to inflict costs on the Chinese, who were providing much of the support for the North Korean forces. Because North Korea exported surplus power from the Suiho plant to Manchuria, attacking this target would not only cost the Communists monetarily, both in terms of repair and lost production, but also inflict indirect damage on Manchuria, a sanctuary for Communist forces.[82]

The effects of bombing the electric power system were easy to judge from a tactical or military viewpoint. In 4 days, beginning on 23 June 1952, U.S. Air Force and Navy aircraft destroyed 11 of the 13 generating facilities in five plants, eliminating 90 percent of the power in North Korea.[83]   The impact of these attacks was widespread. Throughout North Korea there was a 2-week blackout that hindered and even stopped much of the war production in the small factories and shops. The outage hampered vehicle and rail car repairs that required electric welders[84] and impeded agriculture by disabling the electric pumps used for irrigation and stopping the machines used for milling rice.[85] The damage to the Suiho facility resulted in a 23 percent loss of the electric power requirements of northeast China for 1952. As a result, 30 out of 51 important industries in Manchuria did not make their production quotas for the year, and 4 were as much as 75 percent below their goal.[86]

Although the reports on the effectiveness of these attacks indicate that they were successful in crippling the supply of power, the real impact must be judged light of their aim, which was to increase the costs to the North Korean, Chinese, and presumably Soviet leaders for continuing the war. The Soviet and Chinese leaders reacted by immediately sending technicians to repair the damaged facilities.[87] The North Koreans worked around the power interruptions by staggering shifts at the workplaces to take advantage of the power available, and buying small generators for mines and manufacturing plants.[88]

The attacks had a negative impact on Allied leaders. Both the British press and the Labor Party vehemently protested the attacks, out of fear that they would cause the Communists to break off the peace talks. They were also indignant about lack of consultation prior to the bombing.[89] American congressional leaders were also agitated, but for a different reason. Congress was upset that such important targets had not been bombed earlier.[90] These two widely disparate reactions probably presented mixed signals to the Communist leaders about the intentions of the U.S. bombing.

In the end, the attacks failed in their fundamental purpose of pressuring the North Koreans to sign a peace accord. Despite the increased costs caused by almost eliminating the national power system, the concomitant impact on production, and the division among the Communist allies, the war, and the "Air Pressure Strategy," continued for over a year after these attacks.

Vietnam War
While attacks on electric power, and the strategy behind them, did not force an end to the Korean War, this failure did not diminish the high regard planners placed on electric power as a target system. As a result, the North Vietnamese power grid was struck during both the *Rolling Thunder* and *Linebacker* bombing efforts.

The *Rolling Thunder* air campaign was an attempt to fulfill a variety of political objectives by bombing North Vietnam. At various times these objective included boosting the morale of South Vietnam, demonstrating American resolve, interdicting the supplies used to support the insurgency of South Vietnam, and breaking the will of the Hanoi government to support the Viet Cong insurgency.[91] While attacking the primitive electric power system of North Vietnam may have had some small effect on morale and interdiction, the primary purpose in attacking it was to inflict sufficient costs on the North Vietnamese leadership to convince them not to support unrest in the south.[92]

Although *Rolling Thunder* began in March 1965, and included occasional attacks on power plants, the electrical system was not attacked systematically until the spring of 1967. The Joint Chiefs of Staff (JCS) urged a concentrated attack on electric power in the fall of 1966, when the failure of the interdiction and oil campaigns became evident. In *Rolling Thunder 52*, the eight major power plants in North Vietnam were nominated to the President for attack. These attacks were designed to eliminate power in the Red River valley area, which would serve two purposes: one was to reduce production in the railway shops and the shipyard; the second was the hope that destroying these targets would disrupt normal life and affect the will of the people to support the war effort.[93] On 21 February 1967, President Johnson approved the attacks of all the North Vietnamese thermal power plants with the exception of those in Hanoi and Haiphong.[94] Authorization to attack the Haiphong thermal power plants was given on 22 March 1967, and they were struck on 20 April. An attack on the Hanoi central power station was authorized on 8 April, and it was finally hit on 19 May. Attacks continued sporadically throughout the rest of *Rolling Thunder* in an attempt to prevent repairs to the power plants and to keep power production at low levels.[95]

By the end of May 1967, 14 of the 20 electric power targets, including generating plants and transformer substations, had been attacked, virtually eliminating electric power production in North Vietnam. The bombing destroyed 85 percent of the generating capacity of North Vietnam and heavily damaged the transmission network.[96]

The overall impact of these attacks, however, was minimal, though the government did ask residents to voluntarily cut consumption and requested that the foreign embassies turn off their air conditioners.[97] The lack of electricity forced many factories to use manual tools rather than automatic machinery, and compelled the government to disperse much of the production. Although one of the stated goals of the attacks was to stop or hinder work at the Haiphong shipyard, there is no evidence to suggest that the lack of power had any impact on their ability to offload cargo.[98] Overall, according to a Central Intelligence Agency report, the loss of the central power system did degrade the industrial production of North Vietnam, but did not reduce their ability to continue the war.[99]

The North Vietnamese leadership reacted to the loss of power in several ways. The first was to ensure that the priority users still had electricity. They did this through the use of some 2,000 portable generators and five underground diesel generating stations.[100] The North Vietnamese compensated for their loss of industrial capacity by relying on increased support from the Soviet Union and China, which by 1968 amounted to $600 million in economic aid and $1 billion in military equipment, and no doubt also increased the dependency of North Vietnam.[101] Although the social and economic costs inflicted on North Vietnam were quite severe, they were not enough to coerce Hanoi into accepting U.S. demands.

Support among American policy makers for the bombing waned after the attacks on electricity in early 1967. While some, like Walter Rostow, urged President Johnson to continue the bombing in order to continue imposing costs on the Hanoi government,[102] others, like McGeorge Bundy, urged a stop to the bombing. He wrote to the President in May 1967, "The lights have not stayed off in Haiphong, and even if they had, electric lights are in no sense essential to the Communist war effort." He felt that continued attacks would prove politically counterproductive at home and abroad and would distract from the war in South Vietnam.[103] In short, as in Korea, the attacks on the North Vietnamese electric power system did not prove decisive in achieving American policy goals.

Rolling Thunder ended in October 1968, and strikes on the North Vietnamese power system did not take place again until April 1972 with the *Linebacker I* bombing campaign. This bombing effort was focused primarily on interdiction, and the primary air tasks were reducing the flow of supplies into North Vietnam, destroying existing stockpiles in the north, and slowing the flow of supplies south.[104] The electrical system was attacked as part of the effort to attack any target that supported the war effort.[105] The attacks during *Linebacker I* eliminated 70 percent of the total power generating capacity in North Vietnam. North Vietnamese political leaders and military facilities were virtually unaffected by the loss because they were assured of electricity supplied through potable generators.[106]

The bombing of the North Vietnamese power system resumed on 18 December 1972, with the initiation of the *Linebacker II* bombing effort. The objectives of this campaign were purely psychological. President Nixon hoped to destroy the North's will to fight, forcing them to sign a peace agreement, while demonstrating U.S. resolve to the South Vietnamese government through the use of air power.[107] In 11 days the USAF attacked six electric power targets in North Vietnam using 166 sorties.[108] Laser-guided bombs were judged the most effective munitions for attacking electric power plants, and their use on the Hanoi facility reportedly put it out of operation for 6 months.[109]

Overall, the attacks on electric power reduced the amount of operational generating capacity from 115,000 to 29,000 kilowatts. These attacks, coupled with the damage done during *Linebacker I*, eliminated almost 90 percent of the generating capacity in North Vietnam. Despite the extent of the damage, there is little evidence that the lack of electricity had much negative influence on daily life in the North. Certainly the people lost electricity in their homes and manufacturing stopped, but many of the government programs instituted during *Rolling Thunder* were still in place, and, if needed, previous methods could have been implemented, such as increasing imports, using manual machinery, and other substitutions for the loss of electricity. The lack of power had little impact on the function of the government or the military. As the official USAF bombing survey noted, "The limited amount of power available [through the national system and portable generators] was probably supplied only to priority users, such as the more important industrial installations, foreign embassies, and selected government buildings in Hanoi."[110] The best that can be said of the bombing of electric power during *Linebacker II* is that while it had some effect, the influence on the Hanoi government eventually signing a peace agreement is still unclear.

Desert Storm

Because most of the information from Operation *Desert Storm* is still classified, it is difficult to make definitive judgments about the impact of attacks on electric power. What is known, however, is that once again electric power was a high priority target. The primary purpose in bombing was not to stop war production, but rather to induce strategic paralysis on the leadership in Baghdad.[111] The focus of these attacks was on the military, with the loss of power intended to affect facilities such as radar sites and communication facilities.[112] In addition to the military effects, there was also the hope that because electricity touched all aspects of Iraqi society it might have a psychological impact as well.[113]

During the Gulf War, attacks on electric power required 215 sorties, or about 1 percent of the total U.S. sorties flown.[114] These attacks virtually eliminated any ability of the Iraqi national power system to generate or transfer power.[115] Further, a DOD study notes, "the synergistic effects of losing primary electrical power sources in the first few days of the war helped reduce Iraq's ability to respond to coalition attacks."[116]

Despite the destruction of Iraq's electric power system, at least some high-priority users had access to electricity. It appeared that the priority users in Baghdad were never seriously affected by the virtual elimination of Iraq's national power grid.[117]

There is little doubt, on the other hand, of the impact of the loss of power in Iraq on the civilian population. The civilian effects from the loss of power were quire severe, including the loss of power to hospitals, the breakdown of water purification systems and damage to sewage systems, which then contaminated the water supply. One report attributed 70,000 casualties to this "indirect" collateral damage cause by a lack of electricity.[118] The negative political backlash of such reports is unquantifiable but nevertheless real, and must be considered in future air campaign planning.

WHEN TO TARGET ELECTRIC POWER

Historical evidence suggests that, while electric power systems are inherently vulnerable to attack, the application of air power against these systems, especially in limited war, is usually ineffective in achieving strategic objectives, despite accomplishing the intermediate goals of diminishing electric generating capacity, hindering war production, and causing civilian discomfort. In light of the often contradictory evidence, air planners must asks, "When is it feasible to attack electric power?"

In assessing a nation's vulnerability to losing power, the dispersion of the generating facilities and the interconnections within the country must be analyzed.

Simply put, the more dispersed the generating facilities the harder it is to attack the electric power system. The greater the number of plants, the less power each one contributes to the system, and eliminating a few plants does little to affect the total output.

The dispersion of the Japanese power system was a key reason why it was not attacked. Likewise, the Enemy Objectives Unit (EOU) analysis, although mistaken, rejected the German power system in part because they thought it was highly dispersed. While determining the number of power facilities may be relatively easy, it is difficult to discover how the system is interconnected.

As mentioned earlier, power facilities are primarily interconnected for reliability—to allow power to be transferred from areas with a surplus to areas that are experiencing difficulties.[119] If only a portion of a country's generating capacity is eliminated, it would still be possible to get power to the affected area from undamaged facilities further afield, as long as the transmission system is intact. Thus, interconnections of the national power grid allow each generating plant to serve as an alternate power source for every other area. The assumption by the Committee of Operations Analysts and the Enemy Objectives Unit during World War II that Germany had a very interconnected system was a key reason for their not recommending the German power system as a priority target. The dispersion and interconnections of a system are two characteristics that must be analyzed in assessing the vulnerability of the national power system.

More fundamental than deciding the vulnerability of the system, however, is the strategy behind the attacks, because this determines when striking these facilities is likely to be effective in achieving the goals of the air campaign. There have been four basic strategies, used either separately or in combination, to justify attacks on electric power: to influence the will of the people; to raise the costs to the leaders; to produce direct military effects; and to impact war production. Highlighting each strategy provides insight into when it should be attacked in the future.

Attacks on Morale

One of the most persistent assumptions among air planners has been the belief that depriving civilians of electricity will lead to a change in a nation's policy. The notion drove the ACTS strategic targeting policy, and has been an enduring thought in the justification for bombing electricity in every war since. The belief in electric power as the panacea target for affecting civilian morale stems in part form the ubiquitous nature of electricity in American society. The United States accounts for 35 percent of the generating capacity in the world. In addition, our per capita usage is among the highest in the world—double the consumption of other industrialized countries, such as Germany, Japan, and the United Kingdom.[120] Oliver Todd, a journalist who visited Hanoi during the Vietnam war, summed it up best when he observed, "To a Western, so-called developed society, cutting our electricity means something. It doesn't mean very much in Vietnam. The Vietnamese for years and years have been used to living by candlelight or oil lamps."[121]

There is a more fundamental problem with attacking morale—it rarely succeeds in achieving the overall objective. While bombing attacks can lower morale in terms in attitude, causing populations to become apathetic, these changes do not influence behavior. For example, bombing in World War II did lower morale. Moreover, this decline was in direct proportion to the civilian deprivation, caused in large part by the loss of electricity.[122] But despite the decreased civilian morale, studies after World War II showed that active opposition to the current government policy was infrequent, and that bombing electric power to produce a change in civilian morale did not bring about a change in government policy.[123]   Ultimately then, air planners must decide if eliminating electricity will have any impact on lowering civilian morale, and if so, can it actually influence the political leadership toward the desired objectives?

Attacks to Influence Leaders

Attempts to influence the political leaders of a country by depriving the civilians of electricity or by destroying the costly equipment in a power plant is usually associated with a strategy of increasing costs on the leadership to force a change in policy.   This was the justification for attacking electric power in Vietnam and Korea and in neither case was it successful, nor is it likely to be in the future.

There are several reasons why this strategy fails.   The first is that nationalism and the high resolve most nations have in any conflict tend to undermine the usual calculus of cost versus benefits that may seem applicable to nations outside the conflict.   If the issue in question is of high national interest then the damage inflicted on electric power is not likely to exceed the costs that the leaders of a country are willing to pay.[124]   In addition, once national leaders become committed to a course of action they are reluctant to change. Such a change could mean the loss of prestige and political power that they may fear more than "losing" the war.   Rather than admit certain defeat in domestic politics, they would rather continue the present course of action despite the bombing.[125]

A more practical consideration is that political leaders are generally well insulated from the loss of the national power system.   As the official USAF bombing survey from *Linebacker II* noted, "An air campaign against the electric power system of a country should not have as an objective the total cutoff of power.   All critical elements of military and government agencies have alternate means of generating electric power."[126]

Attacks for Military Effects

An attack on electricity to directly affect the military forces of a country is a new phenomena, having been used for the first time in the war against Iraq. This is primarily a refection of how much more dependent the military is on electricity to perform activities such as powering air defense radars and communications than in the past. In contrast, during World War II attacks on electric power for military effects were specifically rejected because of the length of time between an attack and the impact on military operations.

While striking electric power plants might be useful as a tactical measure to create temporary confusion, such attacks will have only a minimal long-term impact, because the military, as a priority user, will have access to whatever power is available in the national grid, and will also likely have emergency power systems. Even in Baghdad, where the lights went out minutes after H-hour,[127] it is not clear if that was a direct result of attacks on the electric system or an Iraqi defensive reaction, and what, if any, long-term impact it had on military operations. No doubt the attacks against the Iraqi power system did cause some confusion in the Iraqi military, but exactly how well that advanced the goal of strategic paralysis on the Iraqi leadership is still not clearly known.[128]

William C. Arkin, of Greenpeace International, investigated the bomb damage in Iraq after the war and believes that the strategic bombing on Iraq made little difference to the outcome.[129] According to Arkin, "The air war was clean on a strategic level [meaning little direct collateral damage], but irrelevant to the defeat of the Iraqi Army."[130] The attack on electric power and the indirect collateral damage inflicted have caused others to question the target selection plan of the Gulf War as well. A recently published book states, "the aspects of [the USAF] campaign most directed against Iraq's economic and political structure [i.e., electric power] seems to have been the least relevant to the ultimate victory."[131]

Attacks on Production

The strongest argument for attacking electric power is to stop, or slow down, war production. The industries that make war goods are very dependent on electric power, and many processes are simply not possible without this resource. In most countries the majority of the electricity generated is used in the manufacturing process.

The USSBS analysis after World War II recommended attacks on electric power only to affect war production, which can be an important factor in winning a war in the long term against a country that cannot import.[132] Therefore, bombing electric power to affect war production is most effective in a total war of attrition against a major power. Likewise, in a war of short duration, where the enemy has stockpiled war material, stopping war production will have minimal impact on winning the war.

In a limited war, against a small nation with outside support, attacking electric power to halt war production will not have much impact because of the ability of the nation to substitute for the loss of power by increasing imports and dispersing manufacturing, as North Korea and North Vietnam demonstrated when their power systems were eliminated.

CONCLUSIONS AND IMPLICATIONS

Attacks on electric power can be useful in fulfilling national security aims, but only under two specific conditions. First, the target country's power system should be vulnerable to destruction by being very concentrated with very few interconnections. Second, the strategy behind the attacks should be focused on stopping war production over the long term. To strike electric power to affect civilian morale, increase costs to the leadership, or impact the military will waste missions and could prove counterproductive to the political aims of the war.

The problem with attacks on electric power is the potentially negative political impact of causing indirect collateral damage to the civilian population. There are some actions in attacking electrical power such as breaching a hydroelectric dam or bombing a nuclear generator that would be successful at interrupting power, but would not be considered because of the negative political impact generated. Although dams have been attacked in the past, in the current political climate and with the limited nature of modern war, it seems doubtful that these attacks would be seriously considered as a means of eliminating electric power.[133]

Similarly, the indirect effects to civilians in Iraq as a result of the bombing of electric power has raised questions at home and abroad. The official response is that although the attacks were more thorough than planned, they were nonetheless necessary, and the post-war suffering of the Iraqi people is the fault of Saddam Hussein.[134] Certainly this is true from the legal point of view, for the defender and the attacker bear an equal amount of responsibility for the protection of civilians, but the fact is that the negative impact of these attacks on world public opinion far outweighed the military benefits accrued by bombing electric power in Iraq.

The implication is clear—national electric systems are not a useful target. If the wars of the future will be limited wars and not total wars of attrition, then attacks on electric power should not be considered. Although national power systems are vulnerable to air attack, the military is largely insulated from a loss of power, and civilian discomfort has not been shown to influence government policy. Further, attacks on electricity may prove to be politically counterproductive. If the true aim of eliminating electricity is to affect other systems, such as communications or computers, then the time and effort would be better spent in concentrating on the intelligence and methods for attacking these systems. In future strategic air operations, the targeting of national electric power systems has little utility.

NOTES

1. The most recent example may be George Kenney and Michael J. Dugan, "Operation Balkan Storm: Here's a Plan," *New York Times*, November 30, 1992.

2. In many circles, including the U.S. Air Force, since 1945 the terms "nuclear" and "strategic" have become, regrettably, synonymous, see Phillip S. Meilinger, "The Problem with Our Air Power Doctrine," *Airpower Journal* VI, no. 1 (Spring 1992), 27-29.

3. See for examples of these points: Joseph F. Pilat and Paul C. White,"Technology and Strategy in a Changing World," and Thomas J. Welch, "Technology Change and Security," *The Washington Quarterly* 13, no. 2 (Spring 1990), 79-91 and 111-120; T. Ross Milton, "Strategic Airpower: Retrospect and Prospect," and Dennis M. Drew, "The Airpower Imperative: Hard Truths for an Uncertain World," *Strategic Review* XIX, no. 2 (Spring 1991), 7-15 and 24-31; Jacquelyn K. Davis, "Technology and Strategy: Lessons and Issues for the 1990s," *The Annals of the American Academy of Political and Social Science* 517, (September 1991), 203-216; Leon Sloss, "U.S. Strategic Forces After the Cold War: Policies and Strategies," and Barry D. Watts, "The Conventional Utility of Strategic-Nuclear Forces," *The Washington Quarterly* 14, no. 4 (Autumn 1991), 145-156 and 173-210; Frank Kendall, "Exploiting the Military Technical Revolution: A Concept for Joint Warfare," *Strategic Review* XX, no. 2 (Spring 1992), 23-30; Patrick J. Garrity and Sharon K. Weiner, "U.S. Defense Strategy After the Cold War," *The Washington Quarterly* 15, no. 2 (Spring 1992), 57-76; Richard H. Shultz, Jr., "Compellence and the Role of Airpower as a Political Instrument," *Comparative Strategy* 11,

no. 1 (January-March 1992), 15-27.

4. Laura Gosline, Defense Intelligence Agency Analyst, interview with author, DIA Headquarters, 9 February 1993.

5. Thomas G. Fink and H. Wayne Beaty, eds., *Standard Handbook for Electric Engineers*, 12th ed. (New York: McGraw-Hill, Inc., 1987), 12-4; Bruce W. Leyson, *The Miracle of Light and Power* (New York: E. P. Dutton & Co., Inc., 1955), 28-42; Robert H. Miller, *Power System Operation*, 2nd ed. (New York: McGraw-Hill Book Co., Inc., 1983), 14.

6. Richard L. Bean, Nicholas Chackan, Harold R. Moore, and Edward C. Wentz, *Transformers for the Electric Power Industry* (New York: McGraw-Hill Book Co., Inc., 1959), 8; Miller, 13, 143; Fink and Beaty, 14-3.

7. Office of Technology Assessment, *Physical Vulnerability of Electric Systems to Natural Disasters and Sabotage*, OTA-E-453 (Washington, D.C.: GPO, June 1990), 4.

8. *Electricity Transfers and Reliability* (Princeton, NJ: North American Electric Reliability Council, October 1989), 8.

9. Leyson, 47; Electricity Transfers, 25-27.

10. Leyson, 45; Fink, 16-8.

11. Energy Information Administration, Annual Energy Review 1991 (Washington, D.C.: U.S. Dept. Energy, June 1992), 14-15, 30-31, 206-207. According to this source the total amount of electricity consumed in the United States by end users was 9.41 quadrillion btus. Using a standard conversion factor of 3412 btus per kilowatt-hour, this equates to 2.8 trillion kilowatt-hours. DOD use was given as 120.6 trillion btus or 3.5 billion kilowatt-hours, approximately 1.3 percent of the total amount of electricity consumed the country. Major Jim Mandziara, Material and Resource Management Policy Directorate, Office of the Assistant Secretary of Defense (Production and Logistics), telephone interview with author, 4-5 May 1993.

12. Interview with Laura Gosline; Herman L. Gilster and Robert E. M. Frady, *Linebacker II USAF Bombing Survey*, HRA file K717.64-8 (Headquarters Pacific Air Forces: April 1973), 12-14.

13. Robert R. Ploger, U.S. Army Engineers, 1965-1970 (Washington, D.C.: Dept. of the Army, 1974), 194-95.

14. Headquarters Far Eastern Air Forces, *FEAF Report on the Korean War (draft)*, HRA file K720.04D,15 February 1954, book 3, section 20, 13-14; Ploger, 60, 194-95; John Schlight, *The War in South Vietnam: The Years of the Offensive*, 1965-1968 (Washington, D.C.: Office of Air Force History, 1988), 171; Richard Tregaskis, *Southeast Asia: Building the Bases* (Washington, D.C.: GPO, 1975), 209-210, 224,250, 257, 284-85, 370. During the Korean conflict, the South Korean system was extremely limited and the supply of power undependable. As a result, all the air bases had emergency power systems and one generated its own electricity. In South Vietnam U.S. forces found two problems with the national system. The first was that South Vietnam's commercial power used 50 cycles whereas most American equipment was designed to use 60 cycles. In addition, when American forces started arriving in large numbers in late 1965 and early 1966, the demand for power quickly outstripped the supply and most American fixed facilities used their own generating facilities for power production.

15. Department of Defense, *Conduct of the Persian Gulf War: Final Report to Congress*, April 1992, 442-44. This report also notes that the U.S. Air Force maintains a bare base construction package, nicknamed *Harvest Eagle*, which contains its own power generation and distribution equipment. This equipment is theoretically capable of supporting 55,000 people and 750 aircraft at 14 different airfields.

16. OTA report, 19. The impact of power interruptions in this report are largely from the 1965 Northeast and 1977 New York City blackouts.

17. OTA report, 23-29.

18. Leyson, 39-40.

19. *Electricity Transfers*, 39.

20. Robert T. Finney, *History of the Air Corps Tactical School, 1920-1940*, USAF Historical Study No. 100, (Maxwell AFB, AL: Air University, 1955), 5-7.

21. For a vivid example of this reasoning, see Giulio Douhet, The Command of the Air, Richard H. Kohn and Joseph P. Harahan, eds. (New York: Coward-McCann, 1942; reprint, Washington, D.C.: Office of Air Force History, 1983), 126, 139-140.

22. "Air Force Objectives," lecture, ACTS, HRA-file 248.2015A-12 (Maxwell AFB, AL, 1934-35), 1.

23. "General Air Force Principles," lecture, ACTS, , HRA file 248.2016A-3 (Maxwell AFB, AL, 1934-35), 1.

24. Air Force Objectives, 2.

25. Major Muir S. Fairchild, USA, "New York Industrial Area," lecture, ACTS, HRA file 248.2019A-12 (Maxwell AFB, AL, 6 April 1939),1.

26. Air Force Objectives, 2.

27. "The National Economic Structure," lecture, ACTS, HRA file 248.2021A-7 (Maxwell AFB, AL: 1939-40), 15. Their precision was a direct reflection on the amount of information they had on electric power in the United States. They could pinpoint the number of electric targets because they had obtained a listing of the major power plants in the United States through the McGraw Central Station Director.

28. For example, the file containing the 1939-40 lecture on the National Economic Structure also has a 59-page pamphlet, complete with overhead photography and floor diagrams, of the Hudson Avenue Generating Station in New York City.

29. Fairchild lecture, passim.

30. Ibid., 2.

31. Ibid.

32. H. H. Arnold, *Global Mission* (New York: Harper & Bros., 1949), 245.

33. James C. Gaston, *Planning the American Air War: Four Men and Nine Days in 1941* (Washington, D.C.: National Defense University Press, 1982), 14, 90; Haywood S. Hansell, Jr., *The Air Plan That Defeated Hitler* (Atlanta, GA: Hogans-McArthur/Longino & Porter, Inc., 1972), 60.

34. Hansell, 70.

35. AWPD/1, *Munitions Requirements of the Army Air Forces,* HRA file 145.82-1 (26 August 1941), 2.

36. Ibid.

37. Ibid., 3,4.

38. Ibid., 3.

39. Hansell, 81; AWPD/1, 2.

40. Quoted in Haywood S. Hansell, Jr., *The Strategic Air War Against Germany and Japan: A Memoir* (Washington, D.C.: Office of Air Force History, 1986), 34.

41. Hansell, 112-113.

42. AWPD/1, 3.

43. Robert Frank Futrell, *Ideas, Concepts, Doctrine: Basic Thinking in the United States Air Force 1907-1060* (Maxwell AFB, AL: Air University Press, 1989; originally published 1971), 130.

44. Hansell, 163.

45. Futrell, 157.

46. Wesley Frank Craven and James L. Cate, *The Army Air Forces in World War II* (Chicago: The University of Chicago Press, 1948-1958), 2:277.

47. *History of the Committee of Operations Analysts*, HRA file 118.01, 1; Futrell, 142; David MacIssac, *Strategic Bombing in World War Two* (New York: Garland Publishing, Inc., 1976), 24-25.

48. Hansell, 148; Craven and Cate, 2:349-350.

49. LtGen H. H. Arnold, USA, Commanding General Army Air Forces, to Assistant Chief of Air Staff, Management Control, HRA file 118.01, 9 December 1942; Craven and Cate, 2:353-354.

50. Ibid.

51. "Economic Targets Within the Western Axis," memorandum, Committee of Operations Analysis to LtGen Arnold, HRA file 118.04A-1; Craven and Cate, 2:362.

52. COA history, 1-19; Hansell, 161.

53. Craven and Cate, 2-363; COA history, 44; Hansell, 159. The target systems listed ahead of electric power included: the German aircraft industry, especially fighter assembly plans and engine factories; ball bearings; petroleum; grinding wheels; nonferrous metals; synthetic rubber and tires; submarine construction yards and bases; military motor transportation; general transportation systems; coking plants; steel; and machine tools.

54. COA History, 44; Craven and Cate, 2:364-365.

55. W. W. Rostow, *Pre-Invasion Bombing Strategy* (Austin, TX: University of Texas Press, 1981), 15.

56. Ibid., 23.

57. Enemy Objectives Unit (EOU), Economic Warfare Division, *Handbook of Target Information*, HRA file 512.323 (London: U.S. Embassy, 24 May 1943), 1.

58. EOU Handbook, 18. For a postwar analysis that supports the primacy of this approach for target selection, see Carl Kaysen, *Note on Some Historical Principles of Target Selection*, Rand Research Memorandum RM-189 (Santa Monica, CA: The Rand Corp., 15 July 1949).

59. EOU Handbook, 107-108.

60. Craven and Cate, 5:17; Futrell, 159.

61. U.S. Strategic Bombing Survey, Summary Report (Pacific War) (Washington, D.C.: GPO, 1 July 1946), 6, 809. Bombing of mainland Japan did begin in fall 1943 with B-29 attacks from China; however, because of logistical problems these raids were sporadic and ineffective. Sustained attacks started in November 1944 when B-20s began flying to Japan from bases on the Marianas Islands.

62. Craven and Cate, 5:17; COA History, 82. The COA history notes that a March 1943 intelligence study of Japanese targets did not include electric power (59).

63. Report to the Committee of Operations Analysts by subcommittee on Far Eastern Electric Power, HRA file 118.04F-1 (30 October 1943).

64. Ibid.; COA History, 82.

65. Ibid.

66. "Report of Committee of Operations Analysts on Economic Objectives in the Far East," memorandum, Committee of Operations Analysts to General Arnold, Chief Army Air Forces, HRA file 118.04D (11 November 1943), 4, 53.

67. Craven and Cate, 5:93; Futrell, 159. The six target systems they did endorse were anti-friction bearings, the electronics industry, the aircraft industry, merchant shipping in harbors, urban areas, and coke and steel production.

68. MacIssac, 21-23, 154-156.

69. U.S. Strategic Bombing Survey, Summary Report (European War)(Washington, D.C.: GPO, 30 September 1945),14; U.S. Strategic Bombing Survey, German Utilities Industry Report (Washington, D.C.: GPO, January 1947), 2,18, 46-51.

70. Robert F. Futrell, *The United States Air Force in Korea, 1950-1953* (New York: Duell, Sloan and Pearce, 1961; rev. ed., Washington, DC: Office of Air Force History, 1983), 183,186.

71. Air University Quarterly Review Staff, "The Attack on Electric Power in North Korea," *Air University Quarterly Review* VI, no. 2 (Summer 1953), 14; Futrell, Korea, 184.

72. Memorandum, Mr. C. H. Pruefer, to General Banfill, 21 September 1950, cited in USAF Historical Division, *United States Air Force Operations in the Korean Conflict, 25 June-1 November 1950,* USAF Historical Study 71, HRA file K101-72 (Washington, DC: Department of the Air Force, 1952) ; FEAF Report on the Korean War, Book 3, Section 2, 35.

73. Futrell, *194*. These attacks were stopped for two reasons both based on the success of the UN drive north. The first was based on the length of time between attacking electric power and the impact on the battlefield, in addition these attacks would result in more reconstitution by UN forces after the peninsula was reunited. The second reason was the fear that attacking the power facilities might provoke China into entering the war, see USAF Historical Division, *United States Air Force Operations in the Korean Conflict, 1 July 1952-27 July 1953,* USAF Historical Study No. 127, HRA file, 101-127 (Washington, DC: Department of the Air Force, 1956), 29-30.

74. Otto P. Weyland, "The Air Campaign in Korea," *Air University Quarterly Review* VI, no. 3 (Fall 1953): 18.

75. Futrell, 441-442.

76. Col R. L. Randolph and Lt Col B. I. Mayo, *The Application of FEAF Effort in Korea*, Staff Study for Deputy for Operations, FEAF, HRA file K720.01 (12 April 1952),1,

77. Futrell, 478.

78. Randolph and Mayo, 8.

79. Ibid., 15.

80. Attack on Electric Power, 13.

81. *History of the Far East Air Forces, 1 January 1952-30 June 1952,* vol. 1, HRA file K720.01, 41.

82. Secretary of State Dean Acheson claimed that the reason behind thse attacks was to reduce the amount of electricity being exported to Manchuria and affect the air defense radar system in northwestern Korea. Dean Acheson, *The Korean War* (New York:

W. W. Norton & Co., Inc., 1971), 135-136. He is the only reference to this rationale.

83. Futrell, 483-488.

84. FEAF Report on Korea, section 13, 7-8.

85. USAF Operations, 33.

86. Ibid.; Futrell, 488.

87. FEAF Intelligence Roundup and Operations Summary, No. 126 (24-30 January 1953), 22.

88. USAF Operations, 33.

89. Acheson, 135-136; Mark W. Clark, *From the Danube to the Yalu* (New York: Harper & Bros. Publishers, 1954), 73.

90. USAF Operations, 33-34.

91. Mark Clodfelter, *The Limits of Air Power: The Bombing of North Vietnam* (New York: The Free Press, 1989), 59-61.

92. Wallace J. Thies, *When Governments Collide: Coercion and Diplomacy in the Vietnam Conflict, 1964-1968* (Berkeley, CA: University of California Press, 1980), 74.

93. Clodfelter, 102.

94. Ibid., 105.

95. *The Pentagon Papers: The Defense Department History of United States Decision-making in Vietnam*, Senator Gravel edition (Boston: Beacon Press, 1971), IV:151-253, 206-208; Clodfelter, 105-107.

96. *Pentagon Papers*, IV:153, 201. See also Admiral U.S. Grant Sharp's testimony in Congress, Senate, Committee on Armed Services, *Air War Against North Vietnam*: Hearing before the Preparedness Investigating Subcommittee, 90th Cong., 2nd sess., 1967, I:105.

97. Jon M. Van Dyke, *North Vietnam's Strategy for Survival* (Palo Alto, CA: Pacific Books, Publishers, 1972), 144.

98. Congress, Senate, Air War Hearings, IV:364-365.

99. *Pentagon Papers*, IV:169.

100. Ibid., IV:153, 201; Van Dyke, 207; Clodfelter, 134-136.

101. *Pentagon Papers*, IV:225-227.

102. Ibid., 164.

103. Ibid., 158.

104. A. J. C. Lavall, ed., *Airpower and the Spring 1972 Invasion* (Maxwell AFB, AL: Air University, 1976; reprint ed, Washington, D.C.: Office of Air Force History, 1985), 105-106.

105.   M. F. Porter, Linebacker: *Overview of the First 120 Days*, HR file K 717.0414-42 (Headquarters Pacific Air Forces, September 1973), 35.

106.   Clodfelter, 167-169.

107.   Ibid., 177, 182.

108.   Gilster, *Linebacker II*, 12.

109.   Ibid.

110.   Ibid., 13-14.

111.   Headquarters United States Air Force, *Reaching Globally, Reaching Powerfully: The United States Air Force in the Gulf War* (Washington, D.C: Department of the Air Force, 1991), 12.

112.   *Conduct of the Persian Gulf War*, 96.

113.   Col. John A. Warden, USAF, interview with author, 7 December 1992.

114.   Title V report, 159.

115.   Michael A. Palmer, "The Storm in the Air: One Plan, Two Air Wars?" *Air Power History* 39, no. 4 (Winter 1992), 29.

116.   Title V report, 150.

117.   From 22 January to 4 March 1991, I was held as a prisoner-of-war in Baghdad. I stayed in four different prisons and was taken to a number of other locations for interrogations. While most places had no electricity, two locations did have electric power. The first was a building in Baghdad the prisoners referred to as "the bunker," an underground facility known officially as the Directorate for Military Intelligence. In this building there was power for ventilation, lighting, heating, and a kitchen. I was taken there several times over the course of 2 weeks for interrogations and there was never a lapse in electric power. The Iraqi Intelligence Service Regional Headquarters, known to the prisoners as the "Baghdad Biltmore," also had a constant source of power. I was moved to this prison late at night on 31 January 1991, and I can distinctly remember that the lights were on inside the prison and that I was taken down several floors to my cell in an elevator. This prison had a generator located outside the building that was turned on by the guards as needed. The formal names of these locations can be found in the Title V report, 619.

118.   The figure of 70,000 is used by William K. Arkin of Greenpeace who, by all accounts, has presented the most unbiased, though critical, review of the strategic bombing in Iraq, see "Tactical Bombing of Iraqi Forces Outstripped Value of Strategic Hits, Analyst Contends," *Aviation Week & Space Technology* 136, no. 4, 27 January 1992, 62, 63.   Beth Osborne Daponte of the U.S. Census Bureau estimated that 100,000 Iraqis died from disease after the war; Daponte, "Iraqi Casualties from the Gulf War and Its Aftermath," *Defense & Arms Control Studies Program* (Cambridge, MA: Center for International Studies, MIT, 1992).   Some estimates are given as high as 170,000 casualties. For some examples of the uproar over this damage see, Nina Burleigh, "Watching Children Starve to Death," *Time* 137, no. 23, 19 June 1991, 56-57; Bernard E. Trainor, "War by Miscalculation," in Joseph S. Nye, Jr., and Roger K. Smith, *After the Storm: Lessons from the Gulf War* (Lanham, MD: Madison Books, 1991); Nicholas G. Fotion, "The Gulf War Cleanly Fought,: and George A. Lopez, "The Gulf War: Not So Clear," *The Bulletin of the Atomic Scientists* 47, no. 7 (September 1991):24-29, 30-35; Eric Hoskins, "Killing is Killing—Not Kindness," *New Statesman and Society* 5, no. 185, January 1992, 12-13; Fred Pearce and Stephanie Pain, "Devastation of Iraq Takes Its Toll in Hunger and Disease," *New Scientist* 132, no. 179, November 1991, 14.

119.   Eugene Gorzelnik, North American Electric Reliability Council, telephone interview with author, 14 April 1993; *Electricity Transfers and Reliability* (Princeton, NJ: North American Electric Reliability Council, October 1989), 2.

120.   Fink, 16-2, 16-3.   The only two nations with a high number of kilowatt hours are Canada and Sweden.   In the case of Canada, at least, much of the power that is produced there is exported—to the United States.

121.   Quoted in Clodfelter, 136.

122.   Irving L. Janis, *Air War and Emotional Stress*, RAND series (New York: McGraw-Hill Book Co., Inc., 1951); reprint Westport, CN: Greenwood Press, Publishers, 1976), 145-146.

123.   Ibid., 147-149, 151-152.

124.   Robert A. Pape, Jr., "Coercion and Military Strategy: Why Denial Works and Punishment Doesn't," *The Journal of Strategic Studies* 15, no. 4 (December 1992): 432-433.

125.   Ernest May, *Lessons of the Past* (Oxford, England: Oxford University Press, 1976), 125-142.

126.   Gilster, 12.

127.   Richard P. Hallion, *Storm Over Iraq: The Making of an Air Power Victory* (Washington, DC: Smithsonian Institution Press, 1992), 176.

128.   Interviews with Gosline and Warden.

129.   "Tactical Bombing," 62-63.

130.   Quoted in "Tactical Bombing."

131.   Lawrence Freedman and Efraim Karsh, *The Gulf Conflict and the New World Order* (Princeton, NJ: Princeton University Press, 1993), 437.

132.   USSBS, Summary, 14; USSBS, German Electric Industry, 3, 46-51.

133.   Because dams and nuclear power plants contain what are termed "dangerous forces" the issue of attacking these targets is complicated by international law constraints (Article 56 of the 1977 Protocol I).   Addition to the Geneva Convention of 12 August 1949 lists the criteria involved with attacking these targets.   Although the United States is not a signatory to this document, such guidance could affect future air attacks (W. Hays Parks, "Air War and Law of War," *The Air Force Law Review* 32, no. 1 (1990), 202-218).   Official Air Force guidance states, "Target selection of such objects [dams and nuclear power plants] is accordingly a matter of national decision at appropriate high-policy levels" (Air Force Pamphlet 110-31, *International Law—The Conduct of Armed Conflict and Air Operations,* 19 November 1976, 5-11).

134.   "Strategic Campaign Focused on Targets and Cut Casualties, Pentagon Maintains," *Aviation Week & Space Technology* 136, no. 4, January 27, 1992, 64-65.

7

BOSNIA:
A QUESTION OF INTERVENTION

BRETT D. BARKEY

No one starts a war—or rather, no one in his senses
ought to do so—without first being clear in his mind
what he intends to achieve by that war and how he
intends to conduct it.[1]

Carl von Clausewitz

A TURBULENT HISTORY

UPON THE BALKAN SHORES HAVE CRASHED SOME OF
Europe's most tumultuous historical forces.[2] The land bears
the marks of Greek, Roman, Gothic, Slavic, and Turkish
conquest, to name a few. Foreign domination is at the root
of many of this region's uneasy divisions. The first dates
from 284 A.D., when Emperor Diocletian divided the
Roman Empire into two parts, with the separation running
north and south through Bosnia-Hercegovina.[3] In 1054, the
Christian world was divided between Rome and
Constantinople, based somewhat on Diocletian's lines, with
the line of religious demarkation running through

Captain Brett D. Barkey, U.S. Marine Corps Reserve, was a
student at the Naval War College Off-Campus Seminar when he
wrote this paper, which was a Co-winner in the 1993 Chairman,
Joint Chiefs Staff, Strategy Essay Competition. A short version
of this paper was published in *Strategic Review*, vol. 21, no. 4.

Slovenia and Serbia. In the 14th century, an Islamic tidal wave crashed into Europe as the Ottoman Turks overwhelmed the Balkan states; the Serbian kingdom was one of the last to fall in 1389.[4] For the next several centuries, the Hapsburg Empire fought the Turks and established a buffer zone through Hungary and Croatia. Many fleeing Serbs were recruited to man this zone.[5]

From this history grew many of today's cultural divisions. The northern and western areas of the former Yugoslavia, Croatia, and Slovenia were more readily influenced by Rome and later Austria. Croats and Slovenes are predominantly Roman Catholic and use the Roman alphabet. The southern and eastern portions—Serbia, Macedonia, and Montenegro—felt more strongly the influence of the Greeks, Turks, and Slavs. As a result, although their language is predominately Serbo-Croation, the Serbs use the Cyrillic alphabet and are Christian Orthodox.[6]

Muslims (until 1991 not recognized as a separate nationality) and Muslim communities are more widely dispersed throughout Bosnia than are the more concentrated Croat and Serb populations. After the Turkish conquest, many locals converted to Islam to preserve their lands and to gain influence with the sultan. Thus, Muslims are today often disparaged as traitors by many Serbs and Croats, although many generations have passed since their conversion.

As the Ottoman empire slowly weakened through the 17th, 18th, and 19th centuries, nationalist influences correspondingly increased, nowhere more so than in the Balkans. Serbia won its independence from Turkey in 1878 but fell under the competing influences of two great powers, Austria and Russia. This bitter mixture of elements produced four wars between 1878 and 1918: The Russo-Turkish War, two Balkan Wars, and the World War I. At one point in 1908, Austria sent 100,000 troops to

Bosnia to quell nationalist unrest, unsuccessfully. In 1914, the Austrians sent to Sarajevo the Hapsburg heir, Archduke Franz Ferdinand, as a symbol of goodwill—he was shot dead by Gavrilo Princip, a Bosnian-Serb nationalist.

World War I dispatched the empires of the 19th century. Its peace treaties carved out the Kingdom of Serb, Croats, and Slovenes (renamed Yugoslavia, or "Southern Slavs," in 1929), from former Austrian and Turkish holdings. To govern, King Alexander, a Serb, was installed along with a parliament.[7]

This unsteady experiment ended with the Nazi invasion and occupation in 1941 and the creation of a large Croation puppet state.[8] Unleashed by the Germans, Croatian and Bosnian fascists savagely murdered hundreds of thousands of Orthodox Christians, Muslims, and Jews.[9] In addition, some 230,000 Serbs and Slovenes were ejected from Croatian territory, foreshadowing today's "ethnic cleansing."[10]

Throughout the war, fractious guerilla forces offered resistance, with those led by Josip Broz Tito, a Croatian Communist, ultimately establishing control over all of Yugoslavia with British and Soviet assistance. After Tito's split with Stalin in 1948, Yugoslavia enjoyed relative prosperity.[11] To check the various nationalist energies, however, Tito employed a strong Communist party organization and a centralized system of government. This system included a federal army and security apparatus (the Administration of State Security, "UDB-a"). These features, along with the fear of Soviet domination and the West's strategic interest in a unified and non-Soviet Yugoslavia, dampened nationalistic fervor. Nevertheless, in 1974, ethnic unrest in the republics forced Tito to grant them more autonomy.[12]

Tito died in 1980. Without him, the federal institutions proved unable to withstand the storms following the fall of communism throughout Eastern Europe in 1990. Having long used nationalism to help maintain their power,[13] Serbia's President Slobodan Milosevic and other former Communist leaders waived the nationalist flag all the more furiously.

Croatians and Slovenians saw 1991 as the opportune moment to throw off not only communism, but what they saw as the strangling Serbian domination which had crept into Yugoslavia's federal system. Together, they declared independence from the Yugoslavian federation on 25 June 1991. The United Nations recognized these nations along with Bosnia-Hercegovina on 22 May 1992.[14]

In Slovenia, the most homogeneous region in the mixing pot of the Balkans,[15] hastily gathered independence forces routed the better equipped but ineptly led Yugoslav army (YPA).[16] Surprised, the YPA quickly withdrew from this inhospitable, mountainous area (where the Italian and Austrian Alps mix) and turned their attentions to the growing unrest in Croatia which threatened their rear.[17]

Croatia is home to large pockets of ethnic Serbians from the days of the Hapsburg buffer zone. Once they declared independence, Croatian fighters faced their neighbor Serbs (formed as paramilitary or territorial defense forces) along with the YPA (now almost entirely Serbian). In the ensuing violence, all sides reportedly committed appalling atrocities (an estimated 15,000 killed, including many civilians).[18] In addition, those units exercising control over an area forcefully ejected anyone of dissimilar ethnic background, an old practice now euphemistically called "ethnic cleansing."

The inadequately supplied Croatians fought to a draw with the larger, better equipped, but poorly led Serbian units, forces that currently hold a third of prewar Croatian territory and have proclaimed their own "Serbian Autonomous Province Krajina."[19] Some 14,000 UN Protection Forces (UNPROFOR) monitor an uneasy cease-fire (the 15th) signed in January 1992.[20] Beause so many issues remain unsettled, fighting could erupt at any time.[21] With the conflict in Croatia over for the moment, both Croatian and Serbian forces shifted their attention to Bosnia-Hercegovina.

To meet a European community imposed deadline for recognition, leaders in Bosnia held a referendum on independence from Yugoslavia on 29 February 1992. The ethnic Serbians, some 31 percent of the 4.3 million Bosnians, boycotted the election, denounced the result (99.4 in favor of independence) and proclaimed their own "Serbian Republic of Bosnia."[22] Outright war soon began. The well-armed Serbians who made up Bosnia's "territorial defense forces," Bosnian-Serb reservists from the former federal army, and paramilitary forces all assisted by the YPA sought and largely gained control of some 70 percent of Bosnian territory.[23] They were battled by the Croatian Army, Croatian volunteers, Bosnian-Croats, and Bosnian-Muslims.[24]

During the fighting, many communities were besieged, including Sarajevo. Starvation was combined with indiscriminate sniper and artillery attacks, causing great suffering among the noncombatant populations of these communities.[25] Additionally, most non-Serbian occupants of captured territory either fled or were violently ejected from these areas.[26] An estimated 600,000 have fled to Croatia.[27] All told, an estimated 2 million have been displaced by the fighting, creating the largest refugee crisis since World War II.[28] By January 1993, an estimated 17,000 had been killed in the fighting.[29]

At this writing, international attention is focused on Bosnia. An international military force of some 9,100 troops is on the ground to assist in the supply of humanitarian needs. Both the European Community and the United Nations are seeking the belligerents' agreement on a plan to divide Bosnia into 10 ethnically based regions joined by a loose federation similar to the Swiss Canton system.[30] The Bosnian and Croatian governments have agreed. The Serbs have not signed on and are thought unlikely to do so as long as their successes continue on the battlefield.

The Geopolitical Dimension

None of the present Balkan states has forces capable of projecting further than their neighboring states, much less to the United States.[31] What possible strategic danger to the United States may be present lies in the possibility that the conflict might spread beyond Bosnia. To date, Serbian incursions have been reported in Italy, Austria, and Hungary.[32] Pointing to several, as yet, hypothetical scenarios, some have argued that a spreading conflict might eventually lead to involvement of two NATO allies.[33] The first scenario involves Kosovo.

Kosovo is a province of Serbia. Once largely autonomous, Serbia proper has increasingly, sometimes violently, impressed itself on Kosovo's overwhelmingly Albanian population by taking over government processes and deploying large numbers of police and troops.[34] Serbia's heavy handedness and the express desire of many Kosovars for union with Albania has compelled Albanian nationalist leaders to commit themselves to intervene if Serbia uses military force to repress the Kosovars.[35] If Albania becomes involved, some argue that Turkey will intervene to protect their fellow Muslims, as might Macedonia with its large Albanian minority.[36] Given Serbia's pattern of focusing on the next rebellious region after settlement of the last, those in Kosovo face the real possibility of Serbia's increased attentions should the war in Bosnia end.

A similar possibility exists in Macedonia.[37] The inhabitants of this former Yugoslav republic are approximately one-third Albanian.[38] However, both Bulgaria and Greece claim an ethnic and territorial interest in Macedonia, and some analysts assert that neither will stand aside were Serbia to invade it.[39] The Turks would probably also move to protect the Muslim minority against Greeks and Serbs (both Christian Orthodox).[40] A fight between two members of the North Atlantic Treaty Organization (NATO) would greatly weaken the alliance.[41]

The prospect of Russian intervention is a somewhat more harrowing. A strong romantic connection binds Serbians, the "Southern Slavs," with the Slavic "motherland," Russia.[42] Expectations are reportedly high among Serbs that nationalists in Russia will restrain or unravel UN diplomatic efforts, particularly if President Yeltsin were ousted.[43] President Yeltsin has faced blistering criticism for his failure to forcefully support the Serbs and for joining UN Security Council resolutions detrimental to them. Although Russia has not yet done so, it could easily use its Security Council veto to terminate U.N.-sponsored military action against Serbia (this concern has delayed the imposition of tighter sanctions). President Yeltsin's electoral victory on 25 April reduced this concern, and, since his victory, Yeltsin advised the Serbs to expect no quarter from Russia.

The Military Situation
Global issues aside, the military situation in Bosnia is relevant to any evaluation of potential U.S. strategies. There are an estimated 170,000 to 200,00 combatants in Bosnia.[44] Of these, the some 80,000-95,000 Serbs are most likely to resist allied military intervention.[45] These forces consist of the Serbian regular army (allegedly transferred to the "Territorial Defense Forces of the Serbian Republic of Bosnia and Herzegovina"), local militia, mercenaries and "Chetniks."[46] As the former Yugoslavia's primary national security threat was being overrun by either NATO or Soviet forces in an East-West confrontation, Yugoslavia's defense forces were trained to conduct guerilla warfare

against an occupying force.[47] Their tactics have included hit-and-run raids, ambushes, sabotage, hostage taking, and terrorism.[48]

In addition to having its 900 tanks and 800 heavy artillery pieces, the Serbian Army in Bosnia has a huge quantity of small arms, machine guns, mortars and rockets.[49] Their air forces include 48 combat aircraft (including MiG-21s, MiG-23s, and MiG-29s) and 20 helicopters.[50] Air defense weapons reported in the area include 20-, 30-, and 40-mm antiaircraft artillery, large numbers of hand-carried surface-to-air missiles, SA-7s and SA-14s, as well as SA-2s, SA-6s, and SA-9s. For naval forces, Yugoslavia (Serbia and Montenegro) possesses several missile carrying frigates and patrol boats, patrol and midget submarines (five each), and many minelaying vessels.[51] Despite denials, Belgrade reportedly plans and controls all military operations in Bosnia.[52]

Typical Serbian operations have two stages.[53] First, using conventional armor and infantry assaults, Serb forces take "cardinal points" in the areas they wish to control. "Cardinal points" usually consist of tactically important positions along the road network. From there irregular forces begin the second stage by setting up forest camps and fanning out to attack (usually at night) Croat and Muslim communities isolated among Serbian communities. Then they attack outlying villages in non-Serbian areas. Against determined resistance, irregular forces wait until they have a two-to-one advantage (or better) and the support of Serbian artillery and tanks before attacking. They then move to the next area and repeat the cycle.

Despite their preponderance of fire power, the Serbian forces have suffered from poor coordination and leadership. They have not fared well against determined and well-organized resistance. Efforts to militarily defeat opponents have been sacrificed to satisfy the strategy of "ethnically cleansing" non-Serbian areas.[54]

Violence against civilians has been an important feature of Serbian tactics. Civilians have been specifically targeted in an attempt to drive them from their homes.[55] Terror campaigns using irregular forces to drive civilians out are said to be reminiscent of tactics the Turks used in their conquest of the Balkans.

The impact of terrain on military operations in Bosnia cannot be overstated. Bosnia's 19,735 square miles (about half the size of Virginia) are almost entirely mountainous and forested.[56] There are few roads and rail lines. Most roads are winding and single lane and have numerous bridges, tunnels, and switchbacks, all handy targets for guerrillas.[57] Largely rural, the greatest population and industrial concentration is in Sarajevo, home to Bosnia's only operational international airport.

Prewar Bosnia was landlocked but for one corridor to the small Adriatic port of Ploce (currently under Croatian control). Nine other major ports on the Dalmatian coast are in either Slovenian, Croatian or Montenegran territory.[58] Since Montenegro is joined with Serbia in the "rump" Yugoslavian federation, and Croatian interests might shift against allied military intervention, use of these ports may be difficult. The 10 federal submarines and mines could inhibit their use. Furthermore, the approximately 1,100 offshore islands provide ready havens for the many missile carrying federal boats of various sizes.

Even with secure port facilities of sufficient size, getting troops and supplies inland may be difficult given the large chain of mountains, the Dinaric Alps, running from northwest to southeast along the coastline. These rugged mountains separate the coast from the interior except for a few vulnerable roads. Sabotage would require long detours on secondary roads described as little more than dirt tracks. Building new roads would require a substantial engineering effort including numerous cuts, fills, bridges, and tunnels. Security against interdiction would demand constant effort. To avoid these difficulties, an airlift may be necessary (although it is the most expensive way to supply forces).[59]

Bosnia, however, has limited air facilities.[60] The only international airport in the Bosnian government's control is Sarajevo (which is ringed with hilly country, reminiscent of Beirut's international airport). When not closed by hostile fire, the United Nations is using this airport for humanitarian relief flights. There are several other airports in former Yugoslavia, but roadways connecting them to Bosnia are limited. The weather in Bosnia is moderate. However, the mountains often bring low clouds, fog, and precipitation, which can limit air operations.

Intelligence about Bosnia and hostile forces is limited.[61] According to reports, human intelligence sources are few. Furthermore, U.S. forces include few speakers of Serbo-Croatian, much less anyone can who speak the local dialects. Because of the broken terrain, high technology sensors could not adequately identify targets, much less distinguish friend from foe.

To summarize the military situation, Bosnia's terrain is extremely favorable for guerrilla operations because of the ease with which they can conceal their forces, as well as interdict overland supply lines.[62] Resistors would rarely present concentrated targets, would have no clear centers of gravity on which to focus, and would have a significant "home court advantage." The Soviet's experience in Afghanistan demonstrates the difficulty that a technologically superior force, even with air support, can have in defeating a determined foe in mountainous terrain. Why then, should any country decide to intervene militarity in Bosnia?

WHY INTERVENE?

The basis for military intervention can be divided into four general categories: (1) security, (2) *Realpolitik*, (3) ideological, and (4) moral. Each category encompasses certain political and miliary objectives which can be analyzed in terms of the military situation in Bosnia. Whether the strategies will successfully meet the objectives can then be estimated.

Intervention for Security
The first and most obvious basis for military intervention would be to neutralize a threat to the national security of the United States.[63] Advocates of military intervention in Bosnia must concede that the conflict presents no *direct* danger to the United States. None of the military forces in the Balkans can threaten more than their contiguous neighbors. Any *indirect* threat, such as the involvement of NATO members weakening the alliance or adding to the destabilization of Russia is disturbing but, as yet, hypothetical.[64]

Intervention To Influence Events: *Realpolitik*
Chancellor Otto von Bismarck was the most easily identifiable practioner of the use of military force shape political events.[65] To extend his example to American military intervention in civil war would see the United States use its forces to preserve American influence in the Balkans and elsewhere.

Ideological Intervention
The not-too-distant past saw the frequent use of U.S. military assets (overt and covert) to intervene in the civil wars of Nicaragua, El Salvador, and Afghanistan. The rationale for this intervention was primarily to support those fighting communism.[66] Since communism was the enemy and defending democracy the goal, these conflicts present examples of military intervention for *ideological* reasons.

The United States unabashedly supports the spread of democracy as a pillar of its foreign policy and promotes free markets. It hardly needs saying that internecine warfare is unfriendly to either concept.[67]

For democracy to take hold in the former Yugoslavia, some fundamental political issues must be resolved.[68] First, minority rights must be assured. Second, a mechanism must be established that allows for representation of the various ethnic groups but still permits efficient political decisionmaking. Third, some means must be found to resolve newly exacerbated deep, historical animosities between the ethnic group. Fourth, a peaceful mechanism must be developed to define the new borders between these republics.

Certainly, peace must come before a nation can begin to build political and economic institutions from scratch, and military intervention may be able to force a peace. But, forcing a peace may just postpone the ultimate resolution of this historical conflict. Factions can simply wait out the occupation, as the Balkan people have done many times in their history, only to resume the fighting as soon as forces leave.

Moral Intervention
Moral intervention can be defined as that involvement in another state's affairs because of actions that "shock the conscience of mankind" or violate "community standards."[69] Two broad objectives to moral intervention can be identified: the pursuit of (a) peace, or (b) justice. Peace can be defined as the absence of violence. To avoid the death and destruction that violence and aggression wreak, particularly on the weak or unprotected, some argue that it becomes morally imperative for all who can to take steps to maintain the peace. As the world's only superpower, the United States is urged to become the main enforcer of peace.[70]

In addition to enforcing peace as a basis for morally warranted military intervention, the pursuit of "justice" is often presented as a rationale. Justice can mean many things but in relation to Bosnia it has often been expressed as "punishing aggression" or "punishing war criminals."[71]

Punishment can have several purposes, including retribution, specific deterrence, and general deterrence.[72] Retribution can be most simply described by the Biblical phrase, "eye for an eye." To "specifically deter" is to punish a particular offender so as to discourage him from offending again. "General deterrence" seeks to make an example of an offender so as to dissuade others who might also like to offend.

Translating these three concepts into military objectives, retribution would probably require not just the defeat of an offending nation's armed forces and recovery of any territory or wealth lost in the conflict, but some additional punitive measures as well. Specific deterrence likely requires reversing any gain and inflicting such a loss in personnel and equipment that the offending nation will not repeat its crime. General deterrence would require much the same as specific deterrence, except that the offending nation's punishment must be so obvious that other potentially errant nations would be assured that they would likewise lose all gains from their aggression.[73]

If "punishment" becomes a policy goal, Serbian gains must first be delineated and then be reversed. In areas where Serbians gained their dominance by force, the task is easily done. However, in those areas of Bosnia where Serbians were the dominant group prior to the war (some 43 percent of pre-war Bosnia's territory), identifying the task is more challenging.[74] However delineated, to reverse Serbian gains would seem certain to require the use of force.[75]

Another dimension of the international concern over the situation in Bosnia centers on the war crimes that allegedly have been committed. To obtain justice, the use of military intervention to capture and try war criminals would probably be required. But this topic is also fraught with issues. By international law, all nations have both the right and obligation to try war criminals.[76] However, the only international war crimes tribunals that meted out significant sentences were convened after the unconditional surrender of Germany and Japan.[77] Because it is unlikely that Serbia would willingly surrender its head of state or the head of one of its major political parties for a trial, complete military victory over that nation may be the only way to secure the trial of war criminals.[78] Apart from Israel, few nations have been willing to unilaterally use force to capture war criminals in other countries, largely because it invites similar actions within their own borders.[79] Consequently, using military intervention to capture and try war criminals would seem to imply a military objective of either complete surrender of the offender nation or the use of kidnapping. Unfortunately, neither alternative seems attractive.

THE NINE QUESTIONS

The discussion just concluded can be distilled into the following questions which should be put to any proposed strategy for the use of American forces:

National security:

(1) Does the option resolve or reduce a direct threat to the security of the United States?

Influence:

(2) Does the option allow the United States to influence the actions of other states or the course of events in general?

Ideological:

(3) Does the option promote the development of democracy or economic prosperity?

Moral:

(4) Does the option reduce violence or suffering?

(5) Does it deter the offending nation from further aggressive acts?

(6) Does the option deter other nations from aggressive acts in the future?

(7) Does the option reverse the unjust gains of an aggressor nation?

(8) Does the option inflict some punishment on the aggressor nation?

(9)Does the option aid in resolving crimes against international law?

These questions will be examined as they relate to three proposed strategies for the use of U.S. forces in Bosnia: (1) deployment of ground forces, (2) use of airpower to strike targets in Bosnia or Serbia, and (3) use of air power to impose a "no-fly zone."[80]

GROUND COMBAT OPERATIONS

The most drastic step the United States could take would be to intervene militarily in the conflict by putting forces on the ground with the intention of occupying all or part of Bosnia.[81] In the simplest terms, such an operation would probably have three stages: (1) establishing security (through occupation and pacification of the assigned regions); (2) establishing civil affairs operations to maintain order; and (3) disengaging.[82]

National Security
Military conquest and occupation of all or part of Bosnia does not directly improve the security of the United States. If anything, national security may be adversely affected, in that military assets dedicated to this mission are not immediately available to address other contingencies that may have a more direct impact on national security. Moreover, unsuccessful commitments can erode national confidence in the military (which can be measured in terms of congressional allocations), thereby reducing readiness. The aftermath of the American failure in Vietnam illuminates this point. Furthermore, once troops are deployed, ensuring success may involve an ever-escalating commitment—which American history has shown to be the most slippery of slopes.

Influence
Incremental increases or decreases in American influence in this or any area would be hard to measure. U.S. influence probably depends on a myriad of factors, one of which is the credibility of a threat to use military force.[83] This credibility, in turn, must be based upon success on the battlefield. Mere threats may deter for a while, but at some point a capability must be demonstrated. As a logical corollary, though, a *lack* of success on the battlefield would probably diminish the credibility of a military threat and

reduce U.S. ability to influence events.

The success or failure of ground force intervention cannot be predicted. If success is defined as a resolution of those factors that gave rise to the conflict (which may be hard to identify), success may never be possible. The deep and long hatreds bred by history and nurtured by the atrocities of the last year are not going to be assuaged even by complete conquest and long-term occupation of Bosnia, much less a limited deployment to "protected areas."[84]

Ideological

The use of ground forces to promote democracy and prosperity in Bosnia presents other important questions. At present, Bosnia is divided into three spheres of control: Bosnian-Serbs control two thirds of the land, have proclaimed themselves a republic, and have established a parliament; Bosnian-Croats control approximately 20 percent and have proclaimed their autonomy; the original Bosnian government controls the small remainder of territory. To use ground forces to reestablish the original government's influence over the extensive portions of the nation that it no longer controls may require the extensive use of force.

Determined resistance by even a small band would risk casualties. Moreover, given the terrain and its impact on military operations, it may be virtually impossible to subdue those who might defy authority (probably both Croats and Serbs). Recall that the Balkan peoples have a proud tradition of guerilla resistance. And, even if military control were established over all of Bosnia by force, political control will not necessarily follow because military success will not resolve the deeper issues of intolerance of ethnic minorities.

Economically speaking, were military control quickly established over Bosnia, the efforts to rebuild could begin.[85] To date, few have been willing to reconstruct buildings or businesses for fear they will simply be destroyed in the next round of fighting.[86] Seemingly, establishing sufficient confidence in any peace, especially one that was militarily imposed, to rekindle the economy would probably require a long-term commitment of force.[87]

Moral
Were ground forces successfully deployed in all or part of Bosnia, the present level of violence and suffering could probably be reduced for the short term. The benefits are less obvious if a guerilla resistance continues. Also, belligerents could wait out the occupation and resume hostilities on departure of the intervening force, even if this occupation were long-term. If only part of Bosnia is occupied, such as for a "protected enclave," the intervenors must be willing to morally accept that the suffering and atrocities are likely to continue in areas outside their control.[88]

Partial occupation, therefore, presents the same moral dilemma that taking no action does—watching others suffer, with inaction arguably condoning the violence. Seeking to avoid this dilemma and having forces on the ground may propel political leaders toward ordering the expansion of protected enclaves to help those nearby (which would probably require combat). Thus, intervention for the moral purpose of reducing violence and suffering does not seem to allow for the placement of geographical limits on the deployment of ground forces.

The next of the nine questions is whether the introduction of ground troops through all or part of Bosnia will deter Serbia or Serbian-Bosnians from further military aggression. How others will react to a use of force is difficult to predict. Serbs may hesitate to resist foreign ground forces aggressively for fear of inviting full-scale invasion and occupation.[89] Even so, having a tradition of waiting out the occupation, what prevents a return to violence on departure of the troops? Once again the answer seems to be that occupation would have to be long term to deter further violence.

To the question—"Will the use of ground forces deter other nations from aggressive or immoral acts?"—a complicated response must follow. First, successful deterrence cannot be proved since, by definition, the unwanted act never occurred. Second, all deterrence theories assume, to some degree, that national leaders act rationally, another difficult proposition to establish in an age of Khomeinis, Khadafys, Husseins, an Assads. Third, an argument can be made that while the world's attention is distracted by the deployment of international ground forces to a region, opportunities are created for others to act.[90] Fourth, to be a deterrent, intervention must be effective—it has already been shown that the use of ground forces contains risks of failure that should not be ignored. Fifth, on some occasions in a nation's affairs its leaders may rationally conclude that aggressive action is in its best interest, despite the international reaction.[91] In sum, whether or not the involvement of ground forces will deter other nations from acting aggressively cannot be proved or disproved.[92]

Before ground forces are committed to Bosnia, the question of whether their deployment is intended to reverse Serbian or Croatian gains must be answered. If deployment is limited to protective corridors and enclaves, this operation supports the status quo. Implicitly then, Serbian and Croatian territorial gains would receive the imprimatur of the international community and some will claim that aggression was "rewarded" by failure to reverse it.

The only way to satisfy the axiom, "Aggression should *not* be rewarded," is to restore Bosnia to the status quo ante. To the extent that this can be done militarily, it would require the "roll back" of Serbian forces in the two thirds of Bosnia they control and the same for the Croat-dominated areas. If even token resistance is offered, a substantial commitment of forces would be necessary to fulfill this objective.

Whether a partial or large-scale deployment is contemplated, consideration has to be given to the duration of the commitment of forces. As stated before, probably only a long-term commitment will prevent opponents from overrunning these area once intervening forces leave.[93]

Turning to the issue of whether the deployment of ground troops would "punish" either Serbia or Serbian forces in Bosnia (or Croats, for that matter), partial deployment preserves the status quo and, therefore, does not punish anyone. A more aggressive deployment aimed at rolling back Serb or Croat control might incidentally exact some retribution (that is, do more than simply reverse the gain), particularly if incursions into Serbia or Croatia were necessary to defeat their forces in Bosnia.

Will the use of ground forces aid the resolution of "war crimes?" Partial deployment is unlikely to meet this aim, since again it preserves present positions. Neither Serbia nor Croatia is likely to assist in resolving war crimes by surrendering their nationals to any foreign or international tribunal. Likewise, it is unlikely that any Serbian or Croatian courts are going to act against their own merely by virtue of the fact that international forces have been deployed.[94]

A broader deployment may assist in settling war crimes if those captured in the process are turned over to the appropriate international tribunal. Complete military victory over these nations may be the only way to gain control over those most directly responsible for war crimes.[95]

In summary, the introduction of ground troops seems to address no direct security threat to the United States. Additionally, it cannot be proved one way or another

244

whether the use of ground forces will deter aggressive acts by other nations outside the Balkans. The deployment of ground forces may promote U.S. influence in the area, if successful, and may reduce violence and suffering in the short term. However, unless sizeable forces are introduced for a long time with broad military objectives, their introduction is unlikely to promote democracy or prosperity, deter or punish (much less reverse) Serbian aggression, or resolve war crimes.

THE USE OF AIR POWER IN THE BALKANS[96]

Many analysts both outside and inside the Clinton administration have proposed using air power in the Bosnian conflict. Advocates have proposed using air strikes to "take out" Serbian artillery, interdict supply routes from Serbia to Bosnia, and strike military infrastructure in Serbia.[97] These proposals will be tested against the nine questions.

National Security
The use of air power in Bosnia or Serbia will not significantly improve the national security of the United States. It must also be recognized that the loss of crews and aircraft in combat operations would diminish national security given the time and expense it takes to train and equip air forces, particularly in an era of greater fiscal austerity.

Influence
Few can deny the psychological impact of jet aircraft screaming overhead or of coming face to face with an Apache or Cobra gunship. The presence of such forces has a substantial influence on all who come into contact with them. They also demonstrate our military commitment to the area. Unfortunately, this influence can be diminished

by unintended civilian casualties[98] and by the loss or capture of the crews and aircraft.

Ideological

The use of air power will not directly support the development of democracy or prosperity in Bosnia. In fact, the economic damage done from the air may prolong the economic crisis in that area. Other than preserve the status quo, if successful, its use presents no solutions to political problems, such as treatment of minorities, which retard the evolution toward a more liberal democracy.

Moral

Will the use of air power reduce violence and suffering? Air power, it is argued, will compel the Serbs (and Croats) to stop the process of ethnic cleansing. Air strikes are also proposed as a means to halt the indiscriminate shelling of civilians. Further, air power is thought to be able to protect such besieged Muslim enclaves as Srebrenica from further Serbian assault by "counter-balancing" the Serbs' greater firepower or by directly halting Serbian attacks. If these propositions were correct, which will be discussed, then in the short-run the use of air power might reduce suffering and violence.

Air power does have limits: it does nothing to resolve the underlying sources of the violence. Until those issues are resolved, the cessation of air protection would likely see the resumption of hostilities.

Nor is the use of air power likely to stop ethnic cleansing since this terror is often inflicted by small groups (that blend into the local population after the crime) going from house to house in the middle of the night.[99] These tactics are enormously difficult to counter from the air because of the challenges of detecting, identifying, and targeting these groups.

Air power *might* make it harder for enemy artillery

units to indiscriminately shell civilian areas thus reducing casualties.[100] However, it cannot guarantee a stop to such actions given the ease with which these weapons can be moved and hidden. Moreover, air power will provide no protection from the frequent and indiscriminate sniper attacks on civilians.

Air power may be successful in interdicting Belgrade's supply of war material to Bosnian-Serbs, especially since most overland supply routes must cross bridges over the Drina River.[101] However, an estimated 250,000 tons of ammunition is already on the ground in Bosnia, enough to support combat at current levels for as long as 2 years.[102] Even when that runs out, there is no guarantee that the combatants will not continue the struggle using knives, clubs, or rifle butts.

Air power might also be able to protect the besieged areas if the Serbs (or Croats) attack with concentrations of troops and use supporting arms. If the Serbs and Croats can be deterred from attacking, then an opportunity to negotiate a settlement has been created. Notwithstanding that, however, air power alone is unlikely to break the sieges (or feed the hungry) in these areas.

The successful use of air forces may provide some "counter-balance" to the Muslims' lack of firepower by limiting the Serbs' use of artillery. Unfortunately, however, air power will not redress Muslims' other strategic weaknesses, such as shortages of weapons and ammunition. Thus, even without their artillery support, the better-armed Serbs may be able to slowly squeeze out besieged Muslims through attrition and starvation. To conclude on this question, although air power may reduce suffering and violence, it seems more likely that it will have no effect.

The next question is, "Will air power deter Serbia or Bosnian-Serbs (or Croats) from committing aggressive acts?" The answer to this question cannot be known in advance. In the face of such an international display of force, the Serbs may back down, but again, the use of air power may have the opposite effect. Look how the German bombing of British cities hardened English determination to resist the Nazis in 1940. Published accounts have indicated that despite overwhelming odds, Serbs are willing to fight on as their ancestors did against the Ottoman Turks.[103]

Similar uncertainty prevails in trying to answer the next question: "Will the use of air power in Bosnia, Serbia, or Croatia deter other nations from aggressive acts?" Note that allied intervention on behalf of the Kurds and Shiites did not prevent the outbreak of ethnic violence in the Balkans (or tribal violence in Somalia, or nationalist violence in Russia). Perhaps the nature of internecine violence is so absent of reason that concepts of deterrence are meaningless.[104] Unfortunately, this point is incapable of being proved.

The next question is, "Will the use of air power reverse Serbian or Croat gains in Bosnia?" Here, the likely answer is no. Air power, as proposed so far, is largely a means to preserve the status quo. Air power alone is unlikely to compel Serbians to give up control of the more than two thirds of Bosnia that they now occupy (or the Coats their portion).

Air strikes may, particularly if directed at Serbia, exact some retribution for perceived wrongdoing. Those who have suffered at Serbian hands may take small satisfaction in that result. However, this feeling may be quick to pass unless steps are also taken to return property and prosecute those who have committed war crimes. Air power alone will not be able to right those wrongs, which answers in advance the last question, "Will air power assist in resolving war crimes?"

In summary, air strikes against Serbia or Bosnian-Serbs may exert some influence in the region, reduce somewhat the violence and suffering, and exact some measure of retribution. It seems unlikely, however, that air power will promote the national security, of the United States, foster democracy or prosperity, reverse unjust gains, or resolve war crimes. It cannot be proved that the use of air forces will deter Serbs or others from aggressive acts.

NO-FLY ZONE

The United Nations Security Council imposed a no-fly zone which prohibits the belligerents' use of military aircraft in Bosnia. UN Security Council Resolutions have authorized the use of force to implement the no-fly zone. At present, U.S. forces are patrolling the area, along with NATO allies.[105]

National Security
The no-fly zone does not directly enhance the security of the United States. Arguably the diversion of resources from training and other missions could adversely impact U.S. security. Loss of aircraft and crews from these missions might negatively impact national security as well.

Realpolitik
The commitment of American air forces demonstrates U.S. commitment in the area which preserves some measure of influence (particularly over other U.S. allies that might want to become directly involved in the conflict.) It represents at least an initial attempt to forge an international military response to events upon which other allied military action can be built. However, enforcement of a no-fly zone shows little promise in shaping the course of events in Bosnia.

Ideology
The use of American air assets to enforce a no-fly zone does not directly enhance the prospect of democracy or

prosperity in Bosnia since it only preserves the status quo. It offers no resolution of the political difficulties which, if unsettled, will continue to fuel the conflict. Therefore, the carnage can continue at its brutal pace, with or without the belligerents' using their limited air assets.

Moral

Will the no-fly zone reduce violence and suffering? To the limited extent that violence and suffering was attributable to air attack, yes, this option will reduce it (assuming it is effectively executed). However, the level of overall violence in Bosnia has been largely unaffected by the no-fly zone to date. (Admittedly, at this writing, enforcement provisions had been only recently added.) Ethnic cleansing, done in small groups at night, will be unaffected, as will the indiscriminate targeting of civilians by artillery or snipers. Except for the use of air support, the no-fly zone has not brought a marked reduction in Serbian or Croatian combat efforts.

Will the no-fly zone deter other nations from taking aggressive action? The imposition of no-fly zones in Iraq did not deter Serbia's aggression. However, a nation that relies on its air assets to act aggressively might be deterred if it thought that it might lose expensive aircraft in the process. In contrast, nations that primarily use ground forces to inflict aggression may be undeterred when they observe the lack of impact the no-fly zone has had on Serb or Croat abilities to accomplish their military and political objectives. To them, the threat of a no-fly zone will likely ring hollow (as it apparently has in Bosnia).

The answer to the last three questions is negative. Being only a means to preserve the status quo, the no-fly zone will not reverse the unjust gains, punish aggressors, or resolve "war crimes" issues.

To summarize, the no-fly zone does not directly enhance U.S. security, promote democracy and prosperity, reduce violence and suffering, reverse unjust gains, punish aggressors, or settle war crimes. However, with relatively minimal risk, this option does maintain U.S. involvement in the area which could supply the groundwork upon which some influence over actions of other nations in the area might be based.

CONCLUSION

The discussion above attempted to explore the propriety of the use of military force in Bosnia via nine analytical questions. The answers to those questions demonstrated that none of the proposed strategies satisfies the four general categories of goals: security, *Realpolitik*, ideological, or moral. Moreover, the discussion revealed that the strategies meet only some of the goals, often at the expense of others. It is necessary, therefore, to prioritize among the goals.[106] Outside of resolving direct threats to national security, which would seem to take precedence, ranking the other goals is itself an important policy determination.

The discussion also exposed the fact that some goals may not be attainable short of a prolonged and sizeable commitment of force. Consequently, since Clausewitz warns that military objectives must be feasible given the level of military means available,[107] the broad goals discussed above will need to be pared down to something more realistically obtainable.

These issues await resolution. Their settlement is all the more imperative since the Bosnian crisis is likely to be repeated, complete with calls for U.S. military intervention, elsewhere in the Balkans (Kosovo and Macedonia, for example), in the former Soviet republics, in the horn of Africa, and in many other regions.

NOTES

1. Carl von Clausewitz, *On War* (Princeton: Princeton University Press, 1976), M. Howard & Paret, eds. & trans., 579.

2. These few pages cannot possibly give fair treatment to such a complex history. Perhaps the best one page summary of this region's troubled history is "Black History," *The Economist*, 22 August 1992. More thorough treatments include Glen E. Curtis, ed., *Yogoslavia: A Country Study* (Washington, DC: Federal Research Service, Library of Congress, 1992); Department of the Army Pamphlet 550-99; Barbara Jelavich, *History of the Balkans, Volume 2: The Twentieth Century* (Cambridge: Cambridge University Press, 1984); Wayne S. Vucinich, ed., *Contemporary Yugoslavia* (Berkeley: University of California Press, 1983); and Vladimir Dedijer, and others, *History of Yugoslavia* (New York: McGraw Hill Book Co., 19174) Kordija Dveder, trans.

3. For brevity's sake, I will occasionally refer to the area simply as Bosnia.

4. This is an important element in the Serbian national ethos, and the climactic Battle of Kosovo is often cited by today's Serbs as an example of courage in the face of overwhelming odds. *New York Times*, 24 April 1993.

5. By this time, a long tradition of partisan fighting had developed as the weak peoples of these areas sought to challenge the cycle of domination by the many empires that have conquered the Balkans.

6. The Turks allowed the Orthodox Church to operate with little interference. It became the repository of Serbian nationalism through the period of Turkish rule.

7. King Alexander was assassinated in 1934 in Paris. This period is covered in more detail in Joseph Rothschild, *Eastern Central Europe Between the Two World Wars* (Seattle: University of Washington Press, 1974).

8. At times, in addition to the Germans, Italy, Bulgaria, and Hungary all had troops occupying former Yugoslavia. By 1943, some 600,000 German troops were garrisoned throughout the Balkans. *German Antiguerilla Operation in the Balkans (1941-1944)*, Department of the Army Pamphlet 20-243 (Washington, DC: GPO, 1954)(1974 reprint), 49. It should be noted that their duties

included more than anti-guerilla actions. They extended to manning and fortifying the Dalmatian coast against allied invasion, as well as securing the production and transportation of natural resources (such as bauxite) for the Nazi war effort. Ibid. at 47-72. Although it appears that as many as seventeen divisions operated in Serbia, these often under strength units were frequently made up of overage reservists who found the going especially difficult in the mountainous terrain.

9. Although the Serbs claim 500,000 to 750,000 died at Croatian hands, others put the figure at 350,000. Jozo Tomasevich, "Yugoslavia During the Second World War," in Wayne S. Vucinich, ed., *Contemporary Yugoslavia* (Berkeley: University of California Press, 1983), 272. Obviously, there is little moral difference between the figures.

10. Vladimir Dedijer, and others, *History of Yugoslav*ia, Kordija Kveder, trans. (New York: McGraw Hill Book Co., 1974) 580. The Germans finally halted the Croats efforts to rid their country of all Serbs because it led to more unrest in the neighboring, German-occupied Serbia. Christopher Cviic, *Remaking the Balkans* (London: Royal Institute for International Affairs, 1991), 19.

11. Relative to the rest of Eastern Europe, as well as Spain and Greece.

12. More detailed treatment of this period is found in Duncan Wilson, *Tito's Yugoslavia* (Cambridge: Cambridge University Press, 1979) and Paul Shoup, *Communism and the Yugoslav National Question* (New York: Columbia Viking Press, 1968).

13. Cviic, Chapter 2.

14. Anton Bebler, "Yugoslavia's Agony: Civil War Becomes Savage Chaos," *International Defense Review*, 9/1992, 815.

15. Slovenia's population of two million is 91-percent Slovene, 3-percent Croat, and 2-percent Serb, with Hungarians, Italians, and Germans making up the rest. Leslie Vinjamuri, "Slovenia: Background and Basic Facts," Congressional Research Service Report for Congress, No. 92-674F (27 August 1992)(using 1990 data).

16. Bebler, 813-15.

17. The Yugoslav Peoples Army (YPA) began large-scale

operations in Slovenia on 26-27 April 1991. However, by 18 July 1991, the last YPA soldiers were withdrawn. Bebler, 813-15. Slovenia commemorated the withdrawal of the last federal soldier on 26 October 1991. Julie Kim and Erich Saphir, "Yugoslavia: Chronology of Events June 15, 1991-August 15, 1992," Congressional Research Service Report for Congress, No. 92-689F (25 August 1992), 15.

18. Bebler, 816. Also, David N. Nelson, "A Balkan Perspective," *Strategic Review* XXI, no. 1 (Winter 1993): 34.

19. Nelson, 34. An unfavorable critique of Serb strategy and tactics can be found in Tammy Arbuckle, "Yugoslavia: Strategy and Tactics of Ethnic Warfare," *International Defense Review*, 1/1992, 20.

20. Ibid. In 22 January 1993, Croatian forces attacked one of these areas, with UNPROFOR in no position to stop them. The cease-fire soon resumed as both Croatia and Serbia returned their attentions to Bosnia. "How Many Little Wars Make a Big One," *The Economist*, 30 January 1993.

21. Notably, the UNPROFOR mandate requires periodic extensions, usually at 6-month intervals.

22. Bosnian-Croats responded by proclaiming a "Croatian Community of Central Bosnia." Milan Vega, "The Army of Bosnia and Herzegovina," *Janes Intelligence Review*, February 1993, 64.

23. Whether Serbs truly "control" all 70 percent has been questioned, given the fluid and unconventional nature of the conflict.

24. Although international pressure ended the overt presence of the Croatian Army, the estimated 45,000 Croat troops count some 15,000 from the Croatian Army who were discharged to fight in Bosnia. Milan Vega, "The Croatian Forces in Bosnia - Herzegovina," *Janes Intelligence Review*, March 1993, 99.

25. Sarajevo was fed through an international airlift reminiscent of the efforts in Berlin. Patrice K. Curtis, "The Sarajevo Airlift: U.S. Military Humanitarian Assistance," Congressional Research Service Report for Congress, No. 92-777F (29 October 1992). Unfortunately, there are no other international airports in Bosnia and it has been necessary to airdrop supplies to some besieged areas.

26. Bosnians apparently did likewise to Serbian occupants of

Bosnian controlled areas.

27. "How Many Little Wars Make a Big One." Also, Lois B. McHugh, "Yugoslavia: Refugee Assistance," Congressional Research Service Report for Congress, No. 93-267F (23 February 1993).

28. Bebler, 816.

29. Refugee, 1. Others claim as many as 100,000 casualties. *New York Times*, 29 April 1993.

30. See *New York Times*, 26 March 1993. In continuing efforts to resolve the conflict, the EC/UN negotiators have proposed connecting the Serbian "cantons" with a six mile wide, fifty mile long, corridor. *New York Times*, 26 April 1993.

31. That is not to diminish the ever-present possibility of isolated terrorist actions. However, research (limited to unclassified material) has revealed no reports indicating that the Balkan states are presently active in this regard. That could change, of course, were the United States to get more directly involved.

32. Bebler, 816.

33. "The Future of the Balkans: An Interview with David Owen," *Foreign Affairs* 72, no. 2 (Spring 1993): 4.

34. Albanians, who are mostly Muslim, make up 90 percent of the population, or almost two million people. Steven Woehrel, "Kosovo: The Next Post-Yugoslav Crisis?" Congressional Research Service Report for Congress, No. 92-818F (16 November 1992). See also *New York Times*, 25 April 1993.

35. Albania and Serbia are bitter historical enemies. "Kosovo," summary page.

36. If Macedonia sends troops, then Greece and Bulgaria might be drawn in, for the reasons discussed below. "Kosovo," 7. Lord Owen notes that Turkey is an important American ally because it provides the United States a foothold in Asia and played a crucial role in the Gulf War. Moreover, Turkey's allegiance may be critical to containing an expansionist and hostile Iran.

37. Julie Kim and Carol Migdalovitz, "Macedonia (Skopje): Recognition and Conflict Prevention," Congressional Research Service Report for Congress, No. 93-69F (11 January 1993).

38. The former federal army withdrew from Macedonia on

26 March 1992 and did not resist Macedonian independence. Bebler, 816.

39. Nelson, 29. Serbs and Greeks, both Orthodox Christian, have strong historical and cultural ties. In return for Serbian pressure on Macedonia regarding the use of that historic name, Greeks are reportedly shipping huge amounts of oil and fuel to Serbia (through Macedonia—which has no armed force capable of halting the shipments) in violation of the trade embargo. A company of Scandinavian peacekeeping troops has been dispatched to the Macedonian border to enforce the sanctions. *Eastern European Newsletter*, Vol. 7, No. 8, 13 April 1993.

40. *New York Times*, 25 April 1993 (citing a C.I.A. report).

41. One could question the degree to which such a conflict might weaken the alliance given the Soviet Union's demise and the on-again, off-again battles between Greece and Turkey over Cyprus.

42. Russia's longheld desire for access to the Adriatic and Mediterranean Seas also plays a part.

43. *New York Times*, 26 March 1993,

44. John M. Collins, "Balkan Battlegrounds: U.S. Military Alternatives," Congressional Research Service Report to Congress, No. 92-679S (2 September 1992), 9. Bebler, 86. Croatian forces are said to amount to 41,000-45,000 men equipped with small arms, light and heavy machine guns, rockets, mortars, armored vehicles, tanks and artillery (much of it captured form the former Yugoslav army). They have several missile-carrying ships, helicopters, and three MiG-21's (supplied by defecting federal pilots). Vego, JIR 3/93, 101, 103.

Bosnian government forces (mostly Muslim) are estimated at 80,000, although only 44,000 are fully armed. Vego, JIR 2/93, p 67. Ibid. p 67. These numbers reportedly include several hundred Mujahadin volunteers from other countries. Ibid. at 63-64. They are armed with a variety of small arms, rockets, mortars (60, 82, 120mm), mines, and a few missiles. Ibid. at 65-66. Bosnian government forces are hampered by supply problems, although they reportedly control several arms factories. Ibid. at 66, Bebler, 814.

45. Millan Vego, Federal Army Deployments in Bosnia and Herzegovina," *Janes Intelligence Review*, October 1992, 445. The

New York Times, citing American intelligence sources, puts the figure at 50,000. 29 April 1993.

46. Ibid. "Chetniks" are Serbs from the southern rural area of Serbia. Arbuckle, 19. Their name harkens back to the monarchist guerrilla forces that fought against Tito's communists and, less enthusiastically, the Germans in World War II. Ibid.

47. *Defense and Foreign Affairs Handbook, 1990-1991 Edition* (Alexandria, VA: International Media Corporation, 1990), 1127-28.

48. Collins, 14.

49. Serbia claims to have withdrawn from Bosnia, but allowed members of its army born in Bosnia to remain there if they wished. Steven J. Woehrel, "Bosnia-Hercegovina: Background to the Conflict," Congressional Research Service Report for Congress, No. 93-106F (21 January 1993), 6, Vego, JIR 10/92, 445.

50. Vego, JIR 10/92, 447. Dr. Vego notes that the Serbs are having trouble maintaining their equipment and that these figures do not reflect their true combat effectiveness. Ibid.

51. Milan Vego, "The Croatian Navy," *Janes Intelligence Review*, January 1993, p. 11-16. JIR 1/93.

52. Vego, JIR 10/92, 468.

53. This discussion is drawn from the analysis of Serb tactics in Croatia found in Arbuckle, 19. I have assumed that they are using the same methods in Bosnia.

54. Arbuckle, 19.

55. Vego, JIR 10/92, 446.

56. The rugged forested terrain includes many caves and caverns making it extremely easy to conceal forces and weapons.

57. Collins, 9.

58. Colin Pielow, ed., *Guide to Port Entry*, (Surrey: Shipping Guides Limited, 1992); *Lloyd's Ports of the World 1985* (London: Lloyds of London, 1985), 541-46.

59. Collins, 20.

60. Former Yugoslavia had 184 airfields, but only 23 had runways longer than 2,438 meters, *Defense and Foreign Affairs Handbook*, 1127. Only 16 to 20 are recognized internationally. Compare *The Europa World Year Book 1991* (London: Europa Publications Limited, 1991), Vol. II, 3090, and *Yugoslavia: Country*

Profile 1991-92 (London: The Economist Intelligence Unit, 1991), 28.

61. Collins, 11.

62. Recall that guerilla operations against an occupying force was the main mission of Yugoslav defense forces. See 229-230, *supra*.

63. This statement could be broadened to include threats to "vital national interests," which might be defined as those threats which while they may not affect America's physical security, might adversely and significantly affect our way of life. The stability of Europe may be a vital national interest to the United States. Although to fairly treat the subject of whether this conflict would truly destablize Europe would require separate study, I would submit that the significant economic and military powers in Europe—England, France, and Germany—will remain unaffected, even if the war spread to Greece and Turkey.

64. Many have drawn analogies between the threat to security represented by Hitler's actions in Czechoslovakia in 1938 and the present situation in Bosnia. This analogy is misleading. First, although hoodlums, the Serbian leadership is not reported to have designs to dominate the world similar to those Hitler expressed in *Mein Kampf*. Second, Serbia does not have the cultural, economic, or demographic base from which to build a military force anything like Nazi Germany's with which it could launch attacks on the United States or Europe. Third, Hitler's invasion of Czechoslovakia fundamentally altered the security of the rest of Europe by taking over a nation strategically placed, complete with its large, well-trained army (some 750,000 men, including reserves, amply supplied with modern weapons), its natural resources, and its substantial industrial based (including the Skoda arms works). There is nothing like this in Bosnia. Fourth, the Munich Accord is so remarkable because, at England's lead, Czechoslovakia (who was not allowed to participate in the conference which decided its future) was forced to surrender its sovereign territory and to subject many of its citizens to systematic extermination by the hundreds of thousands. This allowed Hitler, without firing a shot, to circumvent the last natural barriers to German expansion and shred the collective security treaties between France,

Czechoslovakia, and the Soviet Union. Nothing of that dimension is happening in Bosnia.

For a more thorough discussion of appeasement see Andreas Hillgruber, *Germany and the Two World Wars* (Cambridge, MA: Harvard University Press, 1981, M.H. Bell, *The Origins of the Second World War in Europe* (New York: Longman, 1986); and Williamson Murray, *The Change in the European Balance of Power, 1938-39* (Princeton: Princeton University Press, 1984).

65. For a treatment of this proposition see Gordon E. Craig, *The Politics of the Prussian Army* (New York: Oxford University Press) Parts V-VII, Edward Crankshawa, *Bismarck* (New York: Penguin Books, 1981). Of course, it was Clausewitz who said, "War is nothing but the continuation of policy with other means." *On War*, 69.

66. To support intervention, international lawyers pointed to evidence of the outside involvement of other hostile powers, such as Soviet Union or its satellites. The United States, it was said, would be simply leveling the playing field. Incidentally, it could also be said that the United States was acting simply to halt the expansion of a hostile Soviet Union, as opposed to fighting the spread of communism as an ideology.

67. Ironically, all the former Yugoslav republics boast some democratic processes. Unfortunately, that fact has not prevented the horrible human rights abuses reported in the area.

68. Obviously, just identifying the sources of the Bosnian conflict would warrant a separate study. See, for example, Ivo Banac, *The National Question in Yugoslavia* (Ithaca: Cornell University Press, 1984), Robert K. King, *Minorities Under Communism: Nationalities as a Source of Tension among Balkan Communist States* (Cambridge, MA: Harvard University Press, 1973). Without attempting to be complete, I offer the four political issues noted in the text as some of the most apparent sources of this conflict.

69. These standards are represented by international law, as in the Hague and Geneva Conventions, and are articulated in such documents as the United Nations Charter. For a more thorough discussion of these issues see Michael Walzer, *Just and Unjust Wars* (New York: Basic Books, 1977), Chapter 6; John Norton Moore, ed., *Law and Civil War in the Modern World*

(Baltimore; Johns Hopkins University Press, 1977); and Richard A. Falk, ed., *The Law of Intervention in Civil War* (Baltimore: Johns Hopkins University Press, 1971).

70. In its purest form, this argument would seem to justify intervention anywhere and everywhere, "If history has taught us anything it is that aggression anywhere is a threat to peace everywhere in the world." Harry Truman, address of 11 April 1951, cited in David C. Hendrickson, "The Ethics of Collective Security," *Ethics & International Affairs*, Vol. 7 (1993), 3. "Every act of aggression unpunished . . . strengthens forces of chaos and lawlessness that ultimately threaten us all." George Bush, comments of 6 September 1990, cited Hendrickson, *supra*. Interestingly, Professor Hendrickson notes that global containment of communism has given way to a desire to contain violence on a global scale.

Unfortunately, such a doctrine presents the same weaknesses as did the global containment of communism. One, it demands the development and maintenance of huge forces to deal with the many conflicts around the globe (in a time of enormous fiscal constraint). Second, such a doctrine seemingly allows for no assessment of the strategic import of a particular breach of the peace and therefore permits no means for the rational allocation of resources should there be several crises. Third, military intervention to stop a conflagration does nothing by itself to resolve the underlying causes of the violence, it simply puts out the fire.

71. On 26 and 27 August 1992, Acting Secretary of State Lawrence Eagleburger named several Serbs and Croats as war criminals at an international conference on the situation. Those named included Vojislav Seselj and Zeljko Raznjatovic (known as "Arkan"), both leaders of major political parties in Serbia. Secretary Eagleburger called upon Bosnian Serb leader Radovan Karadzic, Bosnian Serb Army Commander, General Ratko Mladic, and Serbian President Slobodan Milosevic to demonstrate their efforts to make their forces comply with international law. *Yugoslav Republics: Country Report* (London: The Economist Intelligence Unit, 1992), No. 4, 11. The United Nations Security Council directed a study of the feasibility of convening an international tribunal to try these individuals. Their preliminary

conclusions were reported to be that it may not be possible to bring to justice those most responsible for the atrocities. *New York Times*, 25 April 1993.

72. These concepts will be very familiar to students of criminal law.

73. Interestingly, the deterrence argument has become a feature of the global containment of peace. It has been said that Serbia's gains must be reversed to deter future Serbias from breaching the peace and acting aggressively against their neighbors. For examples of the debate see "To the Rescue" and "The War that Won't Go Away," *The Economist* (24 April 1993), as well as the opinion pages of the *New York Times*, 29 April 1993.

74. The reversal of ethnic cleansing would require the return of the victims to their property. This will neither be easy or neat. Certainly, peace would have to be restored first and minority rights assured before most of those ejected will come back to their homes. Even then, some sort of tribunal would be required (which had the confidence of the litigants) for resolving the disposition of contested property. One can easily imagine the difficulties of finding titles, records, or witnesses in the aftermath of this conflict.

75. Because force would seem to be required to obtain justice for its retributive or deterrent values, the success of this policy goal is inextricably linked to success on the battlefield. As parents might say, "You have to make them sorry." Weak or ineffective use of force will neither deter the Serbs nor anyone else who might wish to test international resolve. Nor will it salve those in the area who intend to extract their pound of flesh for the crimes perpetrated against them.

76. With respect to "grave breaches" of the Geneva Conventions, all signatories are obligated to search out, bring to trial, and punish those responsible. Articles 49(2), 50(2), 129(2), 146(2) of Geneva Conventions I, II, III, and IV, respectively. See also *Law of Land Warfare*, Department of the Army Field Manual, FM27-10 (July 1954), 182. Military courts of the United States have jurisdiction to try war criminals. Uniform Code of Military Justice, Article 18, 10 U.S. Code § 818. Finally, see also Willard B. Cowles, "Universality of Jurisdiction of War Crimes," *California Law Review* XXXIII, no. 2 (June 1945).

77. I am referring obviously to the war crimes trials that took place in Europe and the Pacific after World War II, the most famous being the Nuremburg trials. See also Norman E. Greenwood, ed., *War Crimes, War Criminals, and War Crimes Trials: An Annotated Bibliography and Source Book* (New York: Greenwood Press, 1986).

78. It has been reported that the UN commission charged with investigating war crimes in Bosnia has come to the conclusion that only total victory over Serbia will resolve the war crimes issues. *New York Times,* 26 April 1993.

79. In addition, witness the strain in relations between the United States and Mexico over the involvement of federal agents in the kidnapping of the Mexican national alleged to have participated in the killing of a U.S. Drug Enforcement Administration agent in Mexico.

80. Space limitations prevent the application of these questions other strategies including (a) the use of U.S. forces to support the arms and trade embargo, (b) the supplying and training of Muslim forces, or (c) simply doing nothing (by choice or by inaction). Like those strategies considered, *supra,* none of these options offer complete satisfaction of goals. Supplying arms, however, at least allows Muslims to participate more forcefully in resolving issues very immediate to them, to the limits of their own courage and will to fight.

81. This would include efforts to establish "protected enclaves" and "Corridors." Sizeable questions arise in that case regarding that ability to find defensible terrain (to avoid repeating the situation that the U.S. Marines faced at the international airport in Berut — a low area largely ringed by hills with no mandate to secure the higher ground).

82. *The Economist* (24 April 1993), 51, anticipates that as many as 100,000 troops may be needed, including 40,000 American, 15,000 British, and 15,000 French soldiers.

83. One may also argue that there is an absolute limit to any nation's power to influence the events or conduct of others. America may have to face the fact that her influence, politically and militarily, may be limited in the Balkans.

84. Notably, Tito's 35 years of ironfisted rule proved incapable of preventing the outbreak of ethnic violence. In fact,

if resolution of Croatian war crimes had been promoted instead of suppressed, it has been suggested that the present day conflict might not have been as violent. Cviic, 19.

85. Of course, the possibility of a determined insurgency makes foreseeable the continued destruction of the remaining infrastructure in Bosnia which can only delay any future economic recovery. One is reminded of the ironic words apocryphally uttered in Vietnam, "We had to destroy the village to save it."

86. *New York Times*, 23 April 1993.

87. One ironic note needs to be made: As a democracy intending to ensure its own continued long-term prosperity, the United States may be unable to commit a large number of forces to any conflict for a long period of time, particularly when the U.S. national security is not directly threatened. Unfortunately, it is probably *only a large force committed for a long time* that will be able to promote democracy and rebuild the economy in Bosnia.

88. One could hope that the presence of international forces might morally persuade the fighters to reduce their operational levels. Unfortunately, the presence of 23,000 UNPROFOR troops in the former Yugoslavian republics so far have had no such effect on the belligerents.

89. One cannot totally discount the possibility that Serbs in Serbia and Bosnia will resist. Serbs have taken on an embattled rhetoric in many reports, denouncing the international attempts to contain the violence. As already described, given the terrain and military tradition, such resistance could produce casualties and perhaps never be truly subdued.

90. Here one is reminded of Syria's consolidation of power in Lebanon while the world's attention was focused on the war against Iraq.

91. The concept of deterrence is irrelevant in such instances. Recall that United States would have been deterred from those operations by the threat of an international military response.

92. It is possible that the presence of international ground forces may restrain Turkey, Greece, and Bulgaria from taking aggressive action in the Balkans.

93. Certainly, other measures might be taken which could shorten the commitment, such as the training and arming of those within the protected areas (although this would not be an overnight task). Training and equipping defense forces could then be coupled with a gradual reduction of international forces although a token presence would always be maintained as a deterrent.

94. The 23,100 international troops on the ground now have not sped the resolution of these issues, nor have they deterred the crimes committed on civilians by Serbs, Croats, or Muslims. *New York Times*, 22-23 April 1993.

95. Note that despite the highly publicized "war crimes" Iraqis allegedly committed in the occupation of Kuwait (as well as against Kurds and Shiites), this Gulf War objective has largely been abandoned.

96. The points made in this section could also be made for limited raids in Serbs or Bosnia conducted by special operations forces. It should also be noted that using air power in the fashion suggested does not mean there will not be U.S. forces on the ground seeking intelligence, directing air strikes, or undertaking search and rescue missions.

97. Some general comments about the use of heliborne or airborne weapons should be made.

First, air power is most effective when directed against troop concentrations, fighting equipment, and military infrastructure. Those fighting in Bosnia have been largely irregular forces, with the occasional support of armored vehicles and artillery (mortars are used frequently). Large troop concentrations appear unlikely. Moreover, troops frequently blend with civilians and wear a mix of uniforms, making identification of friend or foe extremely difficult. There is little military infrastructure in Bosnia. Serbia is more industrialized and would offer more lucrative targets for aircraft and cruise missiles. Supply lines from Serbia to Bosnia must cross several bridges and those would be lucrative interdiction targets.

Second, as has been mentioned, Bosnia is entirely mountainous. The mountains are forested and abound with caves and caverns. Consequently, innumerable covered and concealed positions exist for military equipment such as artillery, tanks, or trucks. Mortars reportedly have been mounted on all types of civilian and military vehicles. Their high mobility coupled with the terrain will make them hard to find. Once found, they will be difficult to identify as friend or foe. Third, the forested mountainous terrain offers numerous covered and concealed positions for surface to air missiles, which are reported in notable numbers in Bosnia. Therefore, anyone could be carrying a weapon lethal to aircraft. The differing points of view on these issues, even among senior military officers, was reported in the *New York Times*, 29 April 1993.

98. Given the terrain and the fact that the belligerents wear a mix of uniforms, if any, and readily intermingle with civilians, there will be great difficulty identifying friend from foe. This heightens the difficulties in avoiding civilian casualties.

99. *New York Times*, 23 April 1993.

100. Air power might deprive gunners of stationary positions. Being on the move more and being forced to camouflage positions would probably reduce the time they would have to fire on civilian areas.

101. Vega, JIR 10/92, 448.

102. Ibid.

103. *New York Times*, 23 April 1993.

104. There have been many studies of the sources of revolutionary violence. The most recent is Jack Gladstone, et al, eds., *Revolutions of the Late Twentieth Century* (Boulder: Westview Press, 1991). See also T.R. Guru, *Why Men Rebel* (Princeton: Princeton University Press, 1970); Louis R. Gottschalk, "Causes of Revolution," *American Journal of Sociology*, Vol, 50, No. 1 (1944).

105. Although air forces have played some role in this conflict, the Serbians predominately have relied on ground forces for their successes (perhaps another manifestation of Serbian command and control problems). This fact presents a major difference with the no-fly zones in Iraq, where because of the remoteness of the regions involved, Iraqi forces extensively relied on air power to strike the Kurds and Shiites. Thus, the no-fly zones in Iraq presented a means by which much of the suffering could be stopped. As a second general comment, because the no-fly zone has been implemented, analysis of this strategy is enhanced by the success (or lack of it) it has had to date.

106. How one defines success then becomes an issue. Is it when we satisfy just one, two, or three goals, even if we cannot achieve them all?

107. *On War*, 585, 606.

8

ISLAMIC RESURGENCE IN THE MIDDLE EAST

JON R. BALL

ISLAMIC RESURGENCE IS A GROWING SOURCE OF CONFLICT throughout the Middle East. American response to this expanding phenomenon has been largely overshadowed by the ideological struggle against communism and the need to keep oil flowing to the major industrial nations around the world. With the end of the Cold War and the overwhelming victory over Iraq in the second Gulf War, America has shifted its attention toward progress on the Arab-Israeli conflict and slowing the Middle East arms race. These are valid interests, but Islam will persist long after the last barrel of oil is pumped from the ground or the last shot is fired. With Islam comes conflict not only in religious matters, but in the attempt to use it as a political force. The Islamic threat in the Middle East increasingly is shifting to forces within individual states, rather than the traditional disputes between regional actors.

Lieutenant Colonel Jon R. Ball, U.S. Air Force, was a student at the Air War College when he wrote this paper, which was named a Distinguished Essay in the 1993 Chairman, Joint Chiefs of Staff, Strategy Essay Competition.

A regional assessment of Islamic resurgence as a source of conflict in the Middle East can be pursued by exploring the following questions:

- What exactly is Islamic resurgence and what are its origins?
- What are some of the current Islamic movements in the Middle East?
- Is Islamic resurgence inherently anti-American?
- What are the implications for U.S. national security strategy in the region?

Islamic resurgence, particularly the militant variety, has received increasing attention worldwide. Without thorough analysis of this phenomenon the United States could make fatally flawed and self-defeating strategy decisions concerning the Middle East. In the future, America will need to analyze the Middle East from the Islamic perspective as it seeks ways to maintain regional stability and promote American national interests.

WHAT IS ISLAMIC RESURGENCE AND WHAT ARE ITS ORIGINS?

The notion of Islamic resurgence is an umbrella term that applies to conservative monarchies, army dictatorships, and modern republics.[1] To understand the concept, it is first necessary to sort out the subtleties in the terminology. Common descriptions for Islamic resurgence include fundamentalism, revivalism, activism, and Islamism. The most popular term in Western literature is also the most inaccurate and stereotypical—*fundamentalism.*

Fundamentalism, though popular, is not an accurate description of Islamic resurgence. In the first place, all Muslims can be described as fundamentalists in that they believe the foundation of Islam is based on the flawless word of God in the Koran.[2] The term fundamentalism originates with the American Protestant movement of the early 20th century stressing the literal interpretation of the

Bible. The term is generally used in a derogatory manner and implies a resistance to change and modernization. This is not necessarily true of the Islamic movement. Furthermore, fundamentalism frequently has been connected to terrorism and extremism, when in reality many of the resurgence movements are within mainstream Middle Eastern society.[3] Therefore, a term to describe the resurgence movement that carries less emotional baggage might be either Islamic revivalism or activism.

What is Islamic activism or revivalism all about? Contrary to Western conventional wisdom, Islamism is not simply a right-wing religious movement. Instead, it is a highly political phenomenon seeking to create an ideal Islamic society based on the Koran and the way of life in the early Islamic community of the Prophet.[4] The goal is an Islamic society that encourages an upright, Islamic life at home and also protects the political, cultural, and religious integrity of the Islamic state within the international community.[5] For Americans this is a difficult concept to grasp because of the secular evolution of the relationship between Christianity and government among Western nations. Any attempt to turn the clock back to the seventh century implies something backward, utopian, and undesirable to most Americans.

Without going into great detail, suffice it to say that Islam is a faith and way of life where political and religious authorities are inseparable. The current activist movements are attempting to revitalize the 20th century (not return to the seventh century) by using Islamic law as a blueprint for a socially just society. This is leading to a higher profile of Islam in politics, society, and personal life through religious observances, dress, and values.[6]

Modern Islamic resurgence gained international attention in the 1970s, but its origins are centuries old. Modern Islamic activism originates from a combination of Islam's revivalist tradition and a response to Western domination.[7] Conflict between Europe and the Middle East goes back to the Crusades; however, the most significant impact has been the legacy of colonialism left by Western powers. This legacy brought about an awareness, during the first half of this century, that something was wrong between the religion which God gave to Muslims and the historical development of the world in which they were living.[8] Colonialism may now be a thing of the past, but its memory lives on, especially through the state of Israel. After all, Israel was created in large part as a result of Western colonial domination. The recurring theme behind Islamic activism is a disenchantment with the West (based on colonialism) and a continued failure of existing Middle Eastern political, economic, and social systems. In response, there have been a number of attempts to regain regional identity and authority. Most of these movements, though, failed to restore the preeminence which existed in the early days of Islamic society.

Secularism, nationalism, and socialism have all proved unsuccessful in providing social justice in the Middle East. In fact, it can be argued that the two most politically successful states are based on religion. It is not uncommon for young Arabs to question their own failing secular systems while looking at the political success in Israel and Iran.[9] Arab nationalism and socialism were dealt a major blow during the 1967 Arab-Israeli war. They are now all but discredited as a result of the 1991 Persian Gulf War and the new simultaneous demise of the Soviet Union. Further, the rift between the "haves" and the "have nots" continues to grow despite the oil wealth that exists within the Middle East. Thus, it is clear why there is a continued search for a new paradigm to bring justice and prosperity to the region. Islamic activism is growing in popularity as that new paradigm.

The bottom line on Islamic resurgence, from a historical context, is that it is seen as a cure for the decline in the

Muslim world. Returning to the straight path of Islam has been a standard response to the cyclical rise and fall of Middle Eastern preeminence. The difference today is that alternative solutions such as secularism and nationalism have proved to be generally unsuccessful. Islamic activism, once a minority view, is gaining populist support. It is gaining mainstream acceptance against the backdrop of poverty, social injustice, and political repression.

Although mainstream Islamic resurgence seeks to use peaceful pressure to achieve its aims, there is still a radical part of the movement that uses violence and revolution as its means to an end. This violence is based on a centuries-old struggle between the West and Islam, manifesting itself today in Western support for Israel. The other facet of the radical movement uses the theological imperative of *jihad* or holy war to be carried out against anyone who resists the Islamic cause.[10] This radical element exists and must be dealt with, but it should not necessarily taint the entire Western view of the resurgence movement. Unfortunately, from the tone of many American news articles, the connection already has been made that equates all Islamic activism to extremism and violence.

Another important point to remember about Islamic activism is that it is not necessarily against modernization. On the contrary, Islamic resurgence is very much in favor of improving society through modern technology and science. What is objectionable to Islamists are the Western and secular byproducts that automatically come with the process of modernization. Islamic groups and governments have found it difficult to filter out modern technology and convenience without retaining some of the Western culture. This is a significant distinction often overlooked by Americans who see such efforts as backward and threatening.

A final and crucial point about Islamic activism is that it is not a monolithic force ready to sweep across the Middle

East. It is not going to unite Islam against the West, nor should it be equated with the Pan-Islamic fears of the 19th century. There is sufficient diversity among the region, its people, and its governments, not to mention the diversity in the religion itself, to prevent a unifying trans-national movement. This last point will become clearer with a brief regional analysis of resurgent activities in North Africa and the Persian Gulf.

WHAT ARE THE CURRENT ISLAMIC MOVEMENTS IN THE MIDDLE EAST?

North Africa

North Africa is a wide and diverse region. It includes areas of political, ethnic, and religious diversity. From the Maghreb countries of Morocco, Algeria, and Tunisia to the eastern Sahara countries of Libya and Egypt, each has its own unique history and culture. Despite the wide diversity, this area of the Middle East has experienced a growing resurgence of Islamic activism. Contrary to popular opinion this resurgence was encouraged, not created, by the Iranian revolution. Specifically, the countries of Tunisia, Algeria, and Egypt all have expanding legitimate Islamic political organizations. Libya also has revivalist movements, but they have been effectively suppressed by Qaddafi and his own use of Islam as put forward in his "Green Book."[11] And of course, Sudan is also embroiled in a near civil war over the fate of its Islamic government. But many Islamic countries share a pattern of Islamic resurgence that for the first time involves the use of legitimate democratic processes.

The trend of resurgence in North Africa starts with a common foundation in economic desperation. Debt, low productivity, poverty, and hunger are common denominators in the growing rift between rich and poor in each of these countries. The Algerian economy was hit particularly hard by declining oil prices in the late 1980s.

Burdened by heavy debt to pay for expanding state infrastructure, International Monetary Fund (IMF) requirements forced Algeria to accept economic austerity measures. This further alienated the population as it created a class of influential Algerians who became even richer by manipulating economic reforms.[12] Algerian unemployment reached 20 percent during the 1980s and more than 50 percent of the population now lives in poverty.[13] With greater migration to the cities in search of improved living standards, Algeria experienced food riots, strikes, and a crippling loss of social services during the late 1980s. The result is a growing feeling of hostility toward government that is viewed both inept and corrupt.[14]

Tunisia experienced similar economic problems in the 1980s. Both drought and locusts severely impacted agriculture production which employs one-quarter of the working population. Rising costs of imports and government debt forced Tunisia into economic restructuring financed by the World Bank and IMF. The Tunisian economy, once considered to be prosperous by regional standards, has deteriorated over recent years. It has few natural resources and oil production accounts for only 12 percent of export earnings.[15] Difficult economic times during the 1980s exacerbated other social and political problems within Tunisia.

Tunisian and Algerian economic problems pale in comparison to Egyptian economic woes. Historically, Egypt is an agrarian society subsisting from the narrow ribbon of arable land along the Nile river. Agriculture employs more than 40 percent of the work force while producing only 19 percent of the gross domestic product.[16] Egypt's fundamental economic problem is the pressure on resources which stems from having one of the world's highest ratios of population to habitable and cultivatable land.[17] Egypt remains dependent on American aid and is heavily burdened with debt, despite the huge write-off

273

allowed as a result of Egyptian support during *Desert Storm*. The country shows little hope of creating an economic miracle to alter the fate of 15 million Egyptians in the teeming streets of Cairo. Egypt is also burdened with a large public sector debt, rising prices, and an inability to provide jobs for young university graduates. Unfulfilled aspirations and economic malaise are attracting more people to the call of Islamic resurgence.

Another common denominator in the trend toward resurgence is the demand for more Islamic practices in government and daily life. Some groups will accept nothing less than an Islamic government and under *Sharia* law. Others want simply to see a return to traditional values in public and private life through dress, prayer, and separation of the sexes in schools and religious observances.

Tunisia evolved into one of the most secular states in North Africa where elitist governments tried to dismantle the institution of Islam.[18] Habib Bourguiba, the one-party ruler for more than 30 years, closed Islamic centers of learning, ignored religious scholars, and banned the wearing of head scarves by women. He even drank a glass of orange juice on television during Ramadan in order to support his claim that fasting detracted from productivity and development.[19] Later under popular pressure to reform, the government tried to realign itself closer to Islam; however, this did not stop the rising tide of dissatisfaction with the government's secular and elitist attitude.

The next common step in the pattern of resurgence is the development of strong organizations with populist support. Islamic organizations such as the Muslim Brotherhood attract highly motivated and disciplined individuals. Its members are not just radical extremists, but also include lawyers, doctors, and educators. The Muslim Brotherhood is making progress not only in attracting professionals, but in gaining control of professional organizations themselves. Most recently in Egypt, Islamic activists won control of the Egyptian Lawyers Syndicate, Egypt's oldest and most powerful professional organization.[20]

These movements also gain popular support as they respond to the growing needs of the people. In contrast to violent extremists who wage war against governments, the strategy of moderate activists is to build a broad economic, social, and political base. In Jordan, the Muslim Brotherhood has had a long history of charitable work. As far back as 1965, the Brotherhood organized medical, educational, and social services. They currently run 20 medical clinics, 40 Islamic schools, and one of Amman's largest hospitals.[21] Support throughout Jordan extends well into the middle class, not just the poor and discontent as evidenced by the Brotherhood's success in national political elections. Islamic activists in Egypt are also creating a parallel infrastructure to supply basic social services, hospitals, and schools. In doing so they challenge government legitimacy and threaten the policy of pursuing Western secular support as a means to prosperity.[22]

Islamic societies are so well organized that they are often the first groups to respond to natural disasters. In Algeria, the Islamic Salvation Front (FIS) was first on the scene to provide tents, clothing, food, and other supplies after a 1989 earthquake. Official government relief efforts were slow to respond.[23] Egypt had a similar experience after an earthquake in late 1992. As in Algeria, Islamic organizations were the first at the scene to provide disaster relief. Seen as a threat to government legitimacy, the Egyptian authorities sought to restrict Islamic organizations from providing aid,[24] which created considerable criticism of the government and debate within the Egyptian news media. It was not until the government was able to organize its own relief efforts that it lifted the restriction on

Islamic organizations. Such situations make it clear how Islamic groups are able to gain increasing popular support.

While these groups can be highly organized, it does not mean that they are centrally controlled in a worldwide movement. Some organizations such as the Muslim Brotherhood have spread throughout the Middle East. But most groups, even the militant ones, pragmatically accept the existence of nation-states. They tend to adapt their organization to the countries unique problems and political experiences. Such was the case for the development and evolution of the Islamic Tendence Movement (MTI) in Tunisia.

Another component of the evolution of Islamic resurgence has been to gain recognition as a legal political party. This occurred in Tunisia in 1989 and a year later in Algeria. Both governments allowed the formation of Islamic political parties in attempts to reform under the threat of economic and social upheaval. At the same time these parties were allowed to participate in democratic elections. In the 1989 general election in Tunisia, the MTI won up to 30 percent of the vote in some districts.[25] In Algeria, the FIS won 55 percent of the popular vote in municipal elections the following year.[26] This unexpected popularity caused both governments to nullify election results immediately and outlaw the Islamic parties. The governments were unwilling to accept the prospect of an Islamic activity victory even in a democratic election. Since then there have been increasing repression and arrests of Islamic activists in both Tunisia and Algeria.

The situation in Egypt is proceeding more slowly, characterized by a quiet rather than a violent revolution. Islamic activism has created an increased awareness among the general population for a desire to lead "a more Islamically informed way of life."[27] Religious programming and literature are more prevalent not only in the government controlled media and newspapers but among the local street vendors as well. Perhaps the difference between Egypt and the experiences in Algeria and Tunisia is the ability of the Egyptian government to control the major Islamic institutions and religious centers, such as the 1,000-year-old al-Azhar University.[28] This ability to co-opt the Islamic establishment has tended to limit the influence of activists groups.

Nevertheless, nonviolent extremist groups such as the Muslim Brotherhood have shown the ability to gain political power. Although Islamic political parties are still illegal in Egypt, the Muslim Brotherhood has effectively taken control of the Socialist Labor Party, giving it the largest opposition voice in government. They have also made progress toward controlling the professional organizations and even scored well in some local city elections in late 1992.[29] While the Muslim Brotherhood is making inroads into mainstream Egyptian politics, the government is still well in control. Although well organized and vocal, the Brotherhood is still a minority movement in Egypt.

Along with the non-violent extremists such as the Muslim Brotherhood, the Egyptian government is also faced with numerous militant Islamic groups. These groups challenge government authority and legitimacy through violence and terrorism. Most recently, Coptic Christians and tourists have become the subjects of terrorist attacks. These violent groups have no foundation in Islam and have no popular support among the Egyptian people. Further, these fragmented groups do not seriously threaten the existing government. Egyptian public opinion flatly rejects the violent extremists' call for an Islamic state.[30] Popular opinion does not believe that such a government would be functional, nor that it could improve economic conditions. On the other hand, public opinion increasingly views the status quo government as inept and equally unable to alter the dismal economic situation. Such a dilemma provides fertile ground for continued unrest and leaves the door open for greater political gains by more moderate Islamic activists.

The final step in the evolution of Islamic resurgence in North Africa has yet to be taken. The aspirations of Islamic activists are still unfulfilled. Many leaders have been arrested and economic conditions remain unchanged. A common argument used by existing governments to justify continued repression is that Islamic groups lack a specific plan on how to govern and solve problems should they gain control of government. A similar complaint is that once Islamists use the democratic process to gain power, the same forces will simply eliminate democracy and establish a revolutionary state similar to Iran. These arguments may be more justifications to maintain inept, corrupt, or even illegitimate governments than valid criticisms. The world cannot judge the validity of such arguments until Islamic groups have the opportunity to follow through with the results of legitimate democratic elections. In the meantime, Islamic resurgence continues to grow as a major source of internal conflict in North Africa.

The Persian Gulf

Islamic resurgence in the Persian Gulf seems to be a non sequitur since Iran and Saudi Arabia are both already Islamic states. However, there is a resurgence movement among the Gulf states stemming from the 1979 Iranian revolution. Many believed, at the time, that the Arab Gulf states would be swept away in a tide of Iranian style Islamic revolution. This obviously did not happen. The question is—why not?

The excesses of the Iranian government toward its own people after the revolution are the first and foremost reason the revolution did not spread to the Arab Gulf states. Iran's treatment of its own citizens was far worse than the treatment of Shias in neighboring Sunni Arab states.[31] Furthermore, the Iran-Iraq war sacrificed a generation of young men and induced near economic ruin. It is not difficult to see why the majority of Shias and Sunnis living in the Arab Gulf kingdoms wanted none of what Iran was offering.

Another reason that the Iranian revolution did not spill into other Gulf states is that the monarchies in these states were already sensitive to the grievances of Shia minorities.[32] The government in Saudi Arabia listened to Shia concerns and attempted to increase spending in the Shia areas of the eastern peninsula. The oil wealth of Saudi Arabia and the other Gulf States went a long way toward stabilizing their form of conservative Islamic society. Even religious and minority opposition elements shared in the prosperity. Saudi Arabia's *Wahhabi* tradition, its acceptance of *Sharia* law, and its oil wealth were enough to ensure the political stability of itself and its neighbors, despite the revolutionary fervor on the other side of the Persian Gulf. That is not to deny, however, that the Iranian revolution had a significant impact on Persian Gulf states.

The Iranian revolution represents a serious challenge to Saudi Arabia's claim to be the guardian of Islam and its two holiest sites, Mecca and Medina.[33] Iran has tried repeatedly to discredit Saudi Arabia in the Islamic world. Although the attempts largely have failed, there has been a shift in the political and religious spectrum. The Saudi government, once considered to be ultra-right, now faces opposition from a more conservative Islamic revivalism. It is interesting that many of the new conservative voices are the young people of Saudi Arabia. These young people see a conflict between their parents Westernized life style and the attempt to live according to Islamic law and precepts.[34] Iranian rhetoric continually challenges Saudi Arabia's practice of "American Islam." This is a challenge that may become increasingly serious because of Saudi Arabia's deepening reliance on the United States in the aftermath of the second Gulf War.

As a result of the latest Gulf war, there will be a continuing Western military presence in the area for the foreseeable future. Many of the Gulf states, particularly Kuwait, see this involvement as the lesser of two evils. The Gulf Cooperation Council (GCC) states are willing to accept the risk of exposure to Western culture and preeminence in the face of the greater threat from Iraqi and Iranian expansion. The question is, how long will Western presence be tolerated? In the short term, the already conservative Gulf states do not face an immediate threat from the destabilizing effects of right-wing Islamic activism. But in the long term, America's continued presence in the Gulf is poisoning the very thing it is trying to preserve—stability. Criticism is already mounting over American willingness to act against Iraq in the Persian Gulf and its unwillingness to aid Muslims in Bosnia or Palestinians in Israel. Such events are likely to fan the flames of Islamic activism and instability. In the near term, however, the Gulf states appear well insulated against political instability from any type of Islamic activism.

Israel and Jordan

Wedged in the fertile crescent between North Africa and the Persian Gulf, Israel and Jordan are also very concerned with Islamic activism. The situations in each country manifest themselves quite differently. On the one hand, Israel is confronted with violent Islamic extremist groups that reject the existence of Israel. Jordan, on the other hand, is concerned with the nonviolent, but radical Muslim Brotherhood.

In the case of Jordan, Islamic resurgence has made political inroads through the democratic process. Similar to the North African countries, food riots in 1989 put pressure on the government to share power with other political parties. As a result, the Muslim Brotherhood won 22 out of 80 seats in recent elections and has taken a legitimate place in the government.[35] What is unique about Jordan's political process is King Hussein. Thus far he has been able to maintain wide political popularity including support from the Muslim Brotherhood. In light of his declining health, however, Jordan may be the country to watch in the evolution of Islamic resurgence. With the potential change in leadership it will be interesting to see if the Islamic Brotherhood maintains its political legitimacy, particularly within a democratic framework.

In the case of Israel, Islamic extremism has complicated the Arab-Israeli conflict. There are two main factors that have brought an Islamic dimension into a traditionally Arab-Israeli dispute over the occupied territories. The first factor is the inability of the Palestinian Liberation Organization (PLO) to resolve the conflict over the disputed territories. In addition, the PLO's decision to support Iraq in the latest Gulf War further eroded the credibility of PLO leaders. As a result the militant Islamic groups such as Hamas and Islamic Jihad have become more vocal and violent in trying to further the Palestinian cause and compete for leadership within the Palestinian community.

Israel's mass deportation of 415 Palestinians is the second factor that has audited to the increased dimension. Prior to the recent deportation, Hamas was one of several relatively unknown militant terrorist groups. After the deportation, this group is nearly a household word across America. It raised the group and the Palestinian cause into the public relations arena of the international news media. The Israeli government took a group who in reality posed no serious threat to the existence of Israel and instantly gave them international attention. According to Ali Jarbawi, a political science professor at Bir Zeit University, the effect was to give political stature to a group who most

Palestinians still believe has far less support than the PLO in representing the Palestinian cause.[36]

Is Islamic Resurgence inherently anti-American?

On the surface, it appears that Islamic resurgence is anti-American in nature. American newspapers are full of vivid examples: kidnapping of American citizens, bombing of tourists in Egypt, burning of the American flag by Iranian revolutionaries, and burning of the American Embassy in Pakistan. But beneath the surface and grisly headlines, the reality is that Islamic resurgence is not inherently anti-American.

As previously mentioned, Islamic activism is in part a reaction to Western colonialism and the search for a way to restore preeminence to the Middle East. There is nothing specifically anti-American in that concept. American leadership must look beyond the rhetoric that comes with Middle Eastern culture. The United States, as the most powerful representative of the Western world is naturally going to be the subject of many Islamic grievances.[37] Even though the United States does not have an extensive history of colonialism, as the world leader it will still bear the brunt of criticism brought on by years of frustrating Western colonial subjugation of Muslims. The ill feelings expressed by militant and other Islamic groups are a result of American policy, not American society per se.[38]

America's involvement with Iran during the height of the Cold War is perhaps the most significant reason for the perception that Islamic "fundamentalism" is anti-American. Starting with the 1953 Central Intelligence Agency-sponsored coup in Iran, there has been a long history of American heavy-handed involvement in the Persian Gulf. American's overwhelming concern with the Soviet Union, and subsequent support of the Shah, left deep emotional scars on the Iranians. Add to this America's continued support of Israel and it is not hard to believe from a

Muslim perspective that American policy has been consistently anti-Islamic. Hence, the rhetoric that continues today from Islamic activists is largely a result of past political practices more that an inherent or inevitable clash between America and Islam.

The result is a "mutual satanization" between America and the more radical Islamic movements.[39] It is difficult for either side to see past misconceptions and stereotypes. It only takes a glance through American newspapers to see the evil many Americans attach to the thought of Islamic "fundamentalism." Images of the Ayatollah Khomeini proclaiming the United States as the "great Satan" are forever etched on the minds of most adult Americans. Certainly the bombings and kidnappings in the supposed name of Islam have polarized the attitudes of many Americans against the notion of Islamic revivalism. Even the religion of Islam itself is considered by many Americans to be extremist in nature.[40] This condition of "mutual satanization" is becoming imbedded in some political circles as evidenced by Patrick Buchanan's implication that there is an impending conflict between Islam and the West.[41]

The recent World Trade Center bombing is a good example of how this "mutual satanization" continues to hinder constructive political relationships. Not long after the bombing, Associated Press headlines appeared questioning Iranian ties to the Trade Center bombing, both from possible financing and the use of similar bombing methods to other Iranian-backed groups. Interestingly, Tehran Radio responded by claiming the United States is "laying the groundwork to blame Iran" for the bombing.[42] It seems that even before the facts unfolded, the innuendos were beginning on both sides based on past experiences and "mutual satanization."

The supposed anti-American nature of Islam is something that can easily be exploited to manipulate

American support from both sides. Israel was certainly able to enlist the threat of Islamic activism to deflect some attention from the deportation issue. Likewise, Egyptian officials are quick to exploit fears of revolution exported to the Sudan from Iran to garner American sympathy and deflect attention away from its own internal economic and political problems. The question is where do we go from here? What conclusions can be made about Islamic resurgence and what are the implications for national security strategy?

WHAT ARE THE IMPLICATIONS FOR NATIONAL SECURITY STRATEGY?

National security strategy for the Middle East, like any other area of the world, should be based on U.S. interests and objectives. The traditional interests for the United States and its allies have been unrestricted access to the region's oil supply and trade routes, the promotion of regional stability, and the promotion of economic trade and development. These will remain the principal U.S. interests for the foreseeable future. Islamic resurgence has the potential to affect all of these interests because of its impact on government legitimacy and subsequent regional instability.

Government legitimacy is a serious underlying source of instability. Western democracies are founded on historical constitutional documents, the Middle East does not have a similar heritage. The religion of Islam does not specify a particular form of government and the legacy of colonialism certainly has added to regional identity problems. Consequently, founding and maintaining governments that are recognized by their citizens as legitimate is no simple matter. Forms of governmental authority in the Middle East cover a wide spectrum as do the methods for succession of power. Ironically, Islamic resurgence, which was once viewed as an extremist and peripheral movement with little serious impact, is not gaining political legitimacy. The political changes described earlier in Tunisia, Algeria, Jordan, and Egypt make Islamic activism a potential threat to existing governments because of unexpected victories in local and national elections. The implications for U.S. national security strategy included the need to educate senior leadership and the need to develop new thinking regarding Islamic "fundamentalism" in order to promote long term U.S. interests in the Middle East.

The First Step—Education
Americans, including civil and military leaders, journalists, and the general population require an increased awareness of the facts concerning Islamic activism. A lack of knowledge inevitably leads to stereotyping and poor or dangerous policy decisions. America does not need to look far into its own history to see the effects on policy of ethnic or religious stereotyping. American leaders have shown themselves to be less than astute with regard to Islam. President Reagan linked Qaddafi and Libyan terrorism with a worldwide Muslim fundamentalist movement following the U.S. bombing of Libya. And Vice President Quayle made a public reference linking Nazism, communism, and radical fundamentalism.[43] Such statements are ill-informed and only reinforce a perceived double standard of American policy in the Middle East.

When it comes to making national policy and strategy, it is important to remember that not all Islamic activists are violent extremists. Islamic resurgence covers a wide spectrum from those who seek more religious observances, solutions to social problems, and greater political power, to the more radical and rejectionist. However, the small extremist groups seem to get most of the media attention, as evidenced by the recent attacks on tourism in Egypt, bombing of the World Trade Center, and Hamas-related incidents in Israel. There appears to be an attempt to use the Western news media, on both sides, to combine Egyptian, Tunisian, Israeli, and Algerian experiences into a common threat of "fundamentalism." This notion has even infiltrated the Professional Military Education system of the United States. Scenarios used in Air War College seminar exercises are embellished with the use of Islamic references and threats of "fundamentalism."[44] The U.S. public and leadership need to recognize attempts to manipulate American perceptions, either intentionally or inadvertently.

Muslims in the United States also suffer from a severe image problem. Part of the education process should be to inform Americans on the facts about Islam, which is one of the fastest growing religions in the United States. One of the inevitable lessons from such education would be to make clear that violent acts in the name of Islam have no more religious legitimacy than do violent acts in the name of Christianity (the shootout in Waco, TX, between Christian cult followers and police is a good example). With a growing Muslim population in America, accurate coverage of Islamic practices would go a long way toward dispelling stereotypes and improving America's image in Islamic countries.

One of the critical goals of education process should be to avoid substituting Islamic "fundamentalism" for the disappearing communist threat. The dissolution of the Soviet Union has made formulating national security strategy and resource allocation extremely difficult. Islamic resurgence in the Middle East and Central Asia is a convenient surrogate for those who seek the comfort of an ideological struggle. Islamic activism clearly presents a challenge to existing governments in the region, especially those who are seen as increasingly elitist and illegitimate. It also presents a threat from terrorist actions of radical fringe elements. However, this does not directly translate to a threat against U.S. interests. If U.S. policy makers see Islamism as a universal threat, they will continue to alienate a large part of the Middle East and create a self-fulfilling prophecy in our national security strategy. American interests are best served by being able to discern rhetoric from reality and extremism from moderate activism. This is the first step toward developing new thinking that will guide American national security policy in the Middle East.

An Opportunity for New Thinking
Until recently, America's overriding imperative in the Middle East centered on the containment of communism. America made decisions in the region (supporting the Shah of Iran for example) that it might not have, had it not been for the overwhelming concern over the struggle against communism. With the end of the Cold War there is a need and opportunity to reevaluate Middle East policy. The opportunity to make real progress on the Arab-Israeli peace process is certainly of great concern to the United States. But there is also an opportunity to better understand and work within an Islamic perspective in order to deal with the growing tide of Islamic resurgence. The essence of a new national strategy should rest on encouraging greater internal political participation within the countries of the Middle East. Democratization is the best means in the long run to thwart the assault against existing governments in the region by Islamic political forces. Political pluralism and democracy are rapidly becoming the most important issues in the Middle East.[45]

This new vision for U.S. strategy is not a utopian effort centered on human rights. It is also not an attempt to promote liberal Western democracy at all costs. It is, however, an investment in the long-term interest of the United States—access to oil and regional stability. It represents an opportunity to establish relations with the people of the region, not just individual governments for short term gain. It is an opportunity to break away from the old east-west mentality that drove American policy for years.

Democracy remains the best hope to co-opt the energy of Islamic resurgence. Interestingly, the word "democracy" is not found in Islam. It was added to the Arabic language in the late 19th century.[46] The concept of democracy has been slow to develop in the Middle East, but it is not inconsistent with the religion of Islam. The notion of democracy has a legitimate basis in the traditional Islamic concepts of consultation (*shura*), consensus (*ijma*), and personal interpretation (*ijtihad*).[47] There are various schools of thought about the compatibility of Islam and democracy. A full discussion on this is beyond our subject. But it is reasonable to assume that "democracy has become an integral part of modern Islamic political thought and practice."[48] Islamic organizations in Egypt, Jordan, Pakistan, Algeria, Tunisia, and Malaysia have advocated the principle of democracy and participated in democratic elections. A recent survey of the Arab world indicates that Arabs "would like the chance to remove unpopular leaders through the ballot box instead of uprisings or coups."[49] Therefore, the issue no longer is whether democracy is compatible, but how it can be implemented.

The practical application of democratic principles in the Middle East is a function of the nature and degree of popular participation. On the one hand, the conservative Gulf monarchies have made some attempts to introduce popular sovereignty through consultation in politics. On the other hand, countries such as Tunisia and Algeria have introduced local and national elections. The specific application and rate of growth of democratic principles certainly will evolve differently within each country. Americans, however, should not expect the end result to be a mirror image of a liberal Western democracy. This will not happen in an Islamic state where there is a need to balance popular and divine sovereignty. The application of democratic principles will have a unique evolution in Islamic countries. It will also be a difficult process to carry out. But encouraging political participation will have a tremendous payoff in the long run. Democracy is a powerful tool to ease nagging legitimacy problems in the Middle East.

Although the potential payoff is high, there are also many risks. To begin with, Islamic groups may simply use the democratic process to solidify political power, win election victories, and then replace democracy with a radical, authoritarian government. So far, there is no evidence to support this concern since election results in Tunisia and Algeria were overturned before the Islamic parties had the opportunity to demonstrate their intentions. In general though, evidence of toleration to diversity by Islamic groups is mixed at best. In Jordan, for example, the Muslim Brotherhood gained five cabinet posts, including the Ministry of Education, following election victories in 1991. They proceeded to cause a national controversy by banning fathers from watching their daughters play sports and by introducing prayers in school that condemn the United States and Israel.[50] Events in Pakistan also have questioned the ability to consistently respect rights of minorities and women. These are not encouraging signs however; Islamic activists deserve the opportunity to follow through on the results of legitimate elections. Only time will tell how well they continue to support the democratic process that elects them.

There are also obvious and significant risks to existing governments that allow greater political participation. Election victories by Islamic parties can directly threaten the legitimacy of governments. One approach to minimize this problem has been to create "risk-free" democracy where only the government is allowed to win.[51] This outlook ignores the possibility that democratic elections could actually insulate existing governments against radical Islamic movements. Islamic groups may find it difficult to offer real solutions to the hard social and economic problems that bring them election victory. Many of these groups are still only in the "slogan" stage when it comes to constructive alternatives. In some cases, greater use of political pluralism could diffuse the undercurrent of dissatisfaction. However, governments will have to wean themselves from the current attitude of "risk-free" democracy in order to reap potential benefits. Continued attempts to block electoral progress will likely lead to greater social unrest for existing governments.

There is also a risk to the United States in accepting a strategy that encourages greater political participation. Countries such as Egypt hold tremendous strategic importance in the Middle East. Encouraging democracy may allow anti-Western Islamic regimes to emerge in place of friendly governments. On the other hand, the policy of supporting existing governments equally could fail through coup or popular uprising, resulting in a replay of the American-Iranian experience of the 1970s.

This is clearly a difficult question for the United States to answer. America also does not have the option to simply withdraw from this apparent no-win situation. It must remain engaged in the region. In doing so, the best strategy to achieve its long-term interest is through the quiet support of greater political participation. The United States needs to have realistic expectations and accept the fact that it may face criticism from newly emerging Islamic governments. It should also avoid the self-fulfilling action of condemning these regimes as threats to and enemies of the West.[52]

Encouraging democracy is only part of the strategy to deal with Islamic activism. Dismal economic and social conditions remain the basic catalyst for the resurgence of

Islamic movements. The Middle East is only one of many areas in the world that is struggling through economic, political, and social change. Middle Eastern countries will be lucky to continue receiving current levels of economic aid considering America's own economic problems. Economic development is extremely important and complex, but it is something that will have to be done largely through regional cooperation. One thing the United States can do to have an immediate impact on economic development, however, is to slow the accelerating Middle East arms race.

Security assistance and foreign military sales have been an important part of U.S. military strategy in the Middle East. But after years of arms sales involving billions of dollars, the question still remains whether the region is more stable and secure as a result of the continuing arms buildup. The mere fact that there have been major wars in every decade for the last 40 years raises a question about U.S. policy in the region. Despite the recent victory in the Gulf War, the region is more unstable and the United States is more committed to guaranteeing regional stability than any time in recent history. *Desert Storm* also served as a high-technology arms demonstration that has customers lined up to place new orders. The region continues to spend precious resources on military weapons to promote individual security concerns. Quite frankly, the current state of affairs is nearly void of logic.

The Arab Gulf states, particularly Saudi Arabia, are prime examples. Saudi Arabian leadership is concerned about the expanding Iranian influence in the region and continues to buy more and newer weapons for its armed forces. In fact, Saudi Arabia purchased $20 billion worth of U.S. foreign military sales (FMS) from 1990 through 1992. This was more than the total Saudi purchase for all of the 1980s.[53] However, no matter how many weapons Saudi Arabia buys, it will not be able to adequately defend itself (without significant outside assistance) against serious Iranian military expansion. The mismatch between the countries in population and resources is just too great. The same conclusion can be made of a resurgent Iraq. This then leads to the question of why Saudi Arabia continues to buy high technology and often "gold-plated" weapon systems? By their own projection the Saudi military does not have enough manpower to operate or maintain the new aircraft that they currently have on order.[54]

Like all good businessmen, though, Western arms suppliers do not want to lose to the competition. Americans balked to sell F-15s to Saudi Arabia in the 1980s Instead, Saudia Arabia made a deal to buy British Tornado fighter-bombers. When it comes right down to it, 20-billion dollars in contracts to American companies buys a lot of U.S. strategic national interest. But, even Saudi Arabia has finite fiscal reserves. Extravagant spending on military hardware that does not add real security value to the region seems to be sacrificing long-term interests for short-term gain.

Egypt's situation is a little different. It has more than sufficient military capability to deter or defeat a threat from Sudan or Libya. Egypt also has a peace treaty with Israel. However, it continues largely modernizing its forces, it seems, out of a latent distrust for Israel. Unlike the Saudis, the Egyptians have plenty of manpower, but little money to spend on defense. The real threat to Egypt remains internal economic and social unrest.

A discussion on the Middle East arms race would not be complete without including Israel. Israel receives the largest amount of U.S. aid in the Middle East. The United States subsidizes approximately 25 percent of the Israeli defense budget.[55] Israel also has the best trained and most respected combat force in the Middle East. This stems largely from unique security problems that dominate their national consciousness. In addition, Israel has one of the highest Ph.D. per capita rates in the world giving them tremendous human capital. However, the drain from years of high defense spending and the lack of other natural resources has also left Israel with severe economic problems.

What does this discussion on military spending have to do with American foreign policy and Islamic resurgence? The connection is straightforward. The United States needs to find ways of encouraging countries to realign excessive defense expenditures into more productive economic purposes. Economic development and related social problems are the issues used to coalesce Islamic resurgent movements. All elements of American national security strategy (political, economic, and military) should focus on investment opportunities that promote long-term development and relationships with the people of the region. Maintaining the status quo retards economic growth and reinforces the appeal of Islamic resurgence.

CONCLUSION

Islamic resurgence is indigenous and rooted throughout the Middle East rather than being created by the Iranian revolution. The movement combines a revivalist desire to return to the straight path of Islam and a political desire to reject Western domination reminiscent of the legacy of colonialism. Resurgence is also genuine in Sunni Islam and is not just a Shiite phenomenon. It is also a paradigm to return preeminence to the Middle East where secularism, nationalism, and socialism have failed.

The Islamic paradigm, however, is not well developed. The existing Islamic states of Iran, Saudi Arabia, and Pakistan are further along in their own Islamic experiments, but the indigenous movements in other countries do not necessarily have a well developed agenda. Islamic activists do well at organizing popular support; but once and if they assume power, there is little consensus on how to structure government, develop multiparty systems, or solve economic problems. This fact, in itself, dispels the monolithic fears of Islam. There is no one correct Islamic government. The Prophet never specified a particular political organization in seventh century Islamic society. Consequently, the political legitimacy problems that have besieged the Middle East throughout its history are not going to disappear with Islamic resurgence. Each organization will develop an agenda based on its own national historical experience.

Islamic resurgence is moving into mainstream Middle Eastern society. Organizations such as the Muslim Brotherhood in Egypt and Jordan, the Renaissance Movement (formerly MTI) in Tunisia, and the FIS in Algeria have shown the ability to support non-violent democratic principles.[56] These organizations attract well educated leaders, professionals, and students who work within the political system to solve social, religious, and economic problems. Americans have not done a good job of distinguishing between these moderate Islamic forces and the numerous *Jihad* extremist organizations. Americans do not give credibility to violent Western or Christian extremist organizations; consequently, it is appropriate the same distinction be applied to the forces at work in the Middle East.

It is also important to remember that Islamic activists have an impact disproportionate to their size. The organizations in Egypt, Algeria, and Tunisia are minorities; however, they are well organized, disciplined, and motivated. Working within the system they have been able to coalesce support for their cause based on a wider populist disenchantment with existing social, religious, and economic injustices. These movements pose a serious challenge to the status quo governments in the Middle East.

The challenge for America's policy makers will be to create a long-term strategy for the Middle East. The first step is to dispel the myth of the so-called "Islamic threat." It is based on reactions to extremist violence and America's bad political experiences with Iran. A new world order in the Middle East means Americans must overcome the "mutual satanization" that has influenced their judgment and policy in the past. America's most powerful leadership tool will continue to be support of self-determination and democracy. This has the best potential to help regional governments blunt the impact of Islamic activism and ease the continuing problems of establishing government legitimacy. It also means that America must come to terms with the entire Islamic movement and be prepared to offer support to an emerging Islamic government when appropriate. Likewise, the challenge for Islamic activists is to accept diversity and the legitimacy of human rights issues as Islamic groups gain support through the democratic process. Understanding and dealing with the Islam will increasingly become one of the principal levers to successful Middle East policy in the 21st century.

NOTES

1. Anthony Hyman, "Middle East II: Islamic Bogeyman," in *The World Today*, August/September 1990, 160-161.

2. Chandra Muzaffer, "Fundamentalist Fallacy," in *The Far Eastern Economic Review*, 23 April 1992, 23.

3. John L. Esposito, *Islamic Threat: Myth or Reality* (New York: Oxford Press, 1992), 7.

4. Great Britain, Foreign and Commonwealth Office, *Islamic Resurgence* (London, April 1990), 2.

5. Graham E. Fuller, *Islamic Fundamentalism in the Northern Tier Countries* (Santa Monica, CA: Rand, 1991), 2.

6. Esposito, 12.

7. Ibid., 48.

8. Ibid., 51.

9.   Christine M. Helms, *Arabism and Islam: Stateless Nations and Nationless States* (Washington, DC: NDU Institute for National Strategic Studies, July 1990), 34.

10. Esposito, 19.

11. John L. Esposito, ed., *The Iranian Revolution* (Miami, FL: Florida International University Press, 1990), 170.

12. Stephen C. Pelletiere, *Mass Action and Islamic Fundamentalism: The Revolt of the Brooms* (Carlisle Barracks, PA: Strategic Studies Institute, March 1992), 3.

13. Carol Migdalovitz, *Algeria in Crisis* (Washington, DC: Congressional Research Service, 5 August 1992), 6.

14. Pelletiere, 4.

15. *The Europa World Year Book 1992*, vols. 1 and 2 (London: Europa Publication Ltd., 1922), 2700.

16. Ibid., 977.

17. Ibid., 978.

18. Esposito, *Iranian Revolution*, 164.

19. Ibid., 153.

20. Scott Mattoon, "Islam by Profession," *Current Affairs*, December 1992, 16-18.

21. Youseff M. Ibrahim, "Jordon Feels Change Within as Muslims Pursue Agenda," *New York Times*, 26 December 1992, 5.

22. H. J. Skutel, "Fundamentalists in Egypt," *International Perspectives*, May/June 1989, 11-14.

23. Migdalovitz, 9.

24. U.S. Embassy, Cairo, Egypt, briefing and discussion with staff, 15 February 1993.

25. Tunis Correspondent, "Fear of Beardies," *The Economist*, 12-18 September 1992, 44.

26. Migdalovitz, 9.

27. Esposito, *Islamic Threat*, 139.

28. Embassy briefing, Cairo.

29. Ibid.

30. Ibid.

31. Esposito, *Iranian Revolution*, 107.

32. Ibid., 107.

33. Ibid., 108.

34. U.S. Embassy, Riyadh, Saudi Arabia, briefing and discussion with staff, 7 February 1993.

35. Pelletiere, 20.

36. G. G. LaBelle, "Many Questions Lingering About Exiles and Hamas," *Montgomery Advertiser*, AP report, 8 February 1993, 4b.

37. Fuller, 25.

38. Esposito, *Iranian Revolution*, 327.

39. Esposito, *Islamic Threat*, 172.

40. Robin Wright, "Islam, Democracy and the West," *Foreign Affairs*, Summer 1992, 134.

41. Esposito, *Islamic Threat*, 177.

42. Donna Abu-Nasr, "Iranian-Bombing Ties Under Suspicion," *Montgomery Advertiser*, AP report, 19 March 1993, 7a.

43. Esposito, *Islamic Threat*, 208.

44. Regional Capabilities Exercise Book, RECEX 2/3, Air War College, 1993, 11.

45. John L. Esposito and James P. Piscatori, "Democratization and Islam," *Middle East Journal* 45, no. 3 (Summer 1991): 427.

46. Amin Hewedy, Militarization and Security in the Middle East (New York: St. Martins Press, 1989), 96.

47. Esposito, *Islamic Threat*, 186.

48. Ibid., 187.

49. Leon T. Hadar, *Quagmire: America in the Middle East* (Washington, DC: Cato Institute, 1992), 163.

50. Daniel Brumberg, "Islamic Fundamentalism, Democracy, and the Gulf War," in *Islamic Fundamentalism and the Gulf Crisis*, ed. James Piscatori (Chicago, IL: American Academcy of Arts and Sciences, 1991), 201.

51. Esposito, *Islamic Threat*, 187.

52. Hadar, 194.

53. Embassy briefing, Riyadh.

54. Ibid.

55. U.S. Embassy, Tel Aviv, Israel, briefing and discussions with Ambassador, 10 February 1993.

56. Esposito, *Islamic Threat*, 187.

9

COPING WITH CHAOS:
DEMOCRACY AND REGIONAL STABILITY IN THE POST-COUNTERINSURGENCY ERA

JOSEPH N. McBRIDE

The ruling of distant peoples is not our dish . . . there are many things Americans should beware of, and among them is the acceptance of any sort of paternalistic responsibility to anyone.

George Kennan

REGIONAL CRISES WITH A HUMANITARIAN TWIST WILL become a major focus of national security policy in the post-Cold War era. Many less developed countries (LDCs) threaten to become ungovernable, overwhelmed by population growth, economic decline, and breakdown of social order. Intervention in one form or another may be forced on a world community unwilling to endure the anguished faces of cyclical tragedies. Neither Cable News

---

Joseph N. McBride, Foreign Service Officer, State Department, is a 1993 graduate of the National War College. His student essay was selected as a Distinguished Essay in the 1993 Chairman, Joint Chiefs of Staff, Strategy Essay Competition.

Network (CNN) nor pressure group politics will permit national leaders to claim "We didn't know" to excuse inaction.

For the longer term, the $4 billion to $5 billion required increase in international community contributions to family planning services in the less developed countries (LDCs)[1] will be "minuscule compared to the benefits."[2] In the medium run, reinforcing regional security organizations to assume greater responsibility is probably our best hope. Regional leaders like Nigeria, India, Brazil, and Mexico should be encouraged to assume leadership in subglobal security groupings and share the burden of maintaining civilized order among their neighbors that "go critical." Bosnia and Liberia show that this will take time, however, and may not always work.

United Nations peacekeeping or peacemaking and unilateral U.S. intervention all have serious drawbacks, although each may be suitable from time to time. Cold War-style counterinsurgency is now "dead on arrival" and does not warrant resuscitation: as practiced by the United States it was largely a failure in its time, is clearly out of step with the times, and could bust the budget to no purpose.

The question remains whether U.S. bilateral policy toward the LDCs can be reinvented and our instruments retooled to support a concept of "democratic security"—one focused on governments that are: willing to be held to international norms, open to rethinking their survival strategies, and able to meet their challenges relying primarily on their own resources. (Any such effort would have to be a subtheme in an overall U.S. policy to support democracy, human rights and peaceful conflict resolution as our primary thrust within the LDCs).

Should we embark on such a course, much of the old thinking and most of the old ways of security assistance should be thrown overboard. The entire purpose behind our effort should be to help the host countries do better with what they already have—and to do so at lower levels of violence. This means focusing assistance primarily on the policies and local court systems in a public safety program tightly constrained by overarching U.S. support for democracy and human rights.

Residual U.S. military aid should focus our friends on fixing their strategic shortcomings, and look beyond mere tactical improvements. Above all, we should drum home the need to build political consensus, underwriting the host government's "unity of effort," and maintaining its moral legitimacy at home and abroad.

The Shining Path (*Sendero Luminoso*) challenges the survival of Peru. The Bush administration defended assistance to Peru completely on anti-narcotics and humanitarian rationales—anything other than "the c word," counterinsurgency.[3] Put simply, following Vietnam and El Salvador the adage seems: "We don't do mountains, we don't do jungles—and we don't do counter-insurgency." With the end of the Cold War, this prevailing popular prohibition merits rigorous rethinking.

Instability, domestic disintegration and insurrection, however, threaten to become more pervasive. Many ruling elites, from the ex-Soviet Union to Africa and South America, may prove incapable of coping with the challenges of a more crowded, competitive, and interdependent world. Global population pressures will be immense as the planet struggles to feed 3.1 billion more people—a 57 percent increase—by 2025, almost all of them in the LDCs. "The worst case scenario? Human population could almost quadruple to 20 billion by the year 2100."[4] Even under the best assumptions, the world population will double by the end of the next century.

Somalia is the clearest example of a vicious downward cycle, but similar deterioration is manifest elsewhere. The majority of the population in the ex-Soviet republics of

Central Asia is under the age of 20 and in several states it is under 15. In the 1980s Latin America and the Caribbean suffered a 1.1 percent real annual decline in GNP, "savage reversal of 20 years of progress" during which annual real growth averaged almost 3 percent.[5] Trends in Haiti, Peru, Panama, Argentina and Venezuela "bear witness" to the range of problems threatening to overwhelm the "capacity to govern" in many Latin American countries.[6]

The United States has been involved in some 60 low-intensity conflicts over the past century. This includes 11 insurgencies, 2 them (El Salvador and the Philippines) in the last decade.[7] Will the United States be able to stand apart totally from the turmoil and internal disruption that is likely to wrack many LDCs in the coming decades? If history is a predictor, the answer is, "probably not." If that is the case, what interests would likely impel our involvement and what form would U.S. intervention best take?

INTERVENTION AND U.S. NATIONAL INTERESTS

The end of the Cold War has completely undercut our traditional "national security" rationale for countering Communist insurgencies in the LDCs. Similarly, jeremiads against the "widespread political and economic collapse with potentially grave consequences for the international economy"[8] are not convincing. If one LDC collapses, others will gladly step in to absorb its market share in providing most raw materials we need. (Petroleum is arguably the one exception. And Operation *Desert Storm* proved that we were ready to take decisive military action to protect our interests on that score.) Intervention to protect "stable markets" in the LDCs would have little appeal.

If standard national security and economic rationales for intervening in the LDCs fall flat with the demise of the

Soviet Union, what would compel us to intervene in these countries? Three other challenges to our interests could trigger us to act:

   • *Humanitarian revulsion* to barbarity visited on our homes daily by CNN: Some would term this an "ideological interest." However characterized, it packs the most potent political punch of the three. It is the most likely scenario and the one national security planners should primarily focus on.

   • *Mass population migrations* triggered by a breakdown in order, in Mexico for instance. The North American Free Trade Agreement (NAFTA) should be our first line of defense.[9] But if development falters and violent challenges to the established order break out, we will seek alternatives to turning the Rio Grande into another Maginot Line. The Darien jungle provides some protection against population surges from South America, but it *can* be passed—especially by sea. (In Europe, our NATO allies have no such protection if further disintegration and chaos overwhelm Russia.)

   • Risk of *regional instability* genuinely affecting our security interests: The best example would be a Muslim extremist takeover in Egypt. It would raise questions about access to the Suez canal. More important, it would rip apart the Middle East peace process of two decades, to bridge the trying gap between our oil interests and our commitment to Israel. Similarly, a repeat of Operation *Just Cause* in Panama for whatever reason would adversely affect our interests throughout the region and would be better avoided.

TYPES OF INTERVENTION

There are six general approaches for the United States in intervention in the LDCs, and they are not necessarily mutually exclusive. In time sequencing, they cover the gamut from indirect intervention before violence breaks out to after-the-fact clean up of a situation that has already gone bad. Similarly, they range from multilateral efforts at the global or regional levels to strictly unilateral undertakings.

SWAT Team Approach

Operation *Just Cause* in Panama might be termed the "SWAT team exception"—seldom invoked but quick and decisive. A good case has been made that this model incorporates the "four salient lessons of Vietnam"[10] and provides an operational doctrine for intervention against a regime that has not fully consolidated power. For it to work, however, the intervention force must hand over power rapidly to a successor government (which can gain legitimacy) and withdraw promptly.

Peacekeeper, or International Worker

Unable to get early consensus to act, it appears that by default our "preferred style" of intervention—when we can get it—would be that of Peacemaker: for example, operating as part of an ex-post facto, multilateral peacekeeping force invited in to repair the damage after the contending factions have exhausted themselves. Under this scenario, we would join with others under a multilateral banner in seeking to restore a degree of normalcy and governance where chaos had held sway. The closest example might be a Somalia intervention deferred to 1994, but with the United Nations in on the take off as well as the landing.

The "benefits" of this remedial approach may pall rather fast:

• Whole populations may die in front of CNN before the contestants stagger to a stalemate as the world gears up.

• Reconstruction costs mount exponentially when

urban infrastructure has been devastated (for example, Phnom Penh).

• Above all, leaders at home and abroad who volunteer their forces to participate will pay a growing political bill. Potential "donors" may dry up fast as Fijians-for-hire run out and the United States and Japan tire of passing the hat as the costs grow.

Peace Enforcer, or Universal Umpire

Popular sentiment seems gradually to be gradually building for multilaterally sanctioned "conflict suppression" operations or the creation of "protected zones." The Economic Community of West African States' (ECOWAS) deployment to Liberia and Operation *Provide Comfort* for the Kurds in Iraq are cases in point, not to mention the evolving situations in Somalia and Bosnia.

Peace enforcing would appear to suffer from most of the liabilities of peacekeeping—and then some, namely:

• Heightened probability of the good Samaritans' taking bullets from both sides.

• Peace enforcers' responsibility to dictate political terms, including population resettlements, that may be repugnant.

• Difficulty imposing a settlement that endures beyond the peace enforcers' withdrawal.[11]

Tutor to Regional Security Linchpins

In this alternative, United States would attempt to reinforce regional security arrangements as the first line of response to LDC crises. The United States could provide ad hoc technical support for specific interventions, but rely primarily on regional powers to muster most of the troops, provide most of the funding, and accept most of the political responsibility.

This model is very attractive and *in the long term* may be the paradigm most worthy of our attention and investment. It is, however, far from being realized—as European inaction in Bosnia demonstrates today. Moreover, even where it is put into effect (for example, ECOWAS in Liberia) the way it is done and the results it produces may not be entirely to our liking.

On balance, these four approaches show serious shortcomings. At least in the near-to-medium term, they appear to have limited applicability. The potential breakdown in internal order posited for much of Africa, some of Latin America, and part of the ex-USSR, requires a different approach. If the United States still wants to address these situations (for the reasons earlier identified), we may have to consider the final two approaches: "the world's policeman" and "facilitator/consultants."

CAMELOT AND COUNTERINSURGENCY: THE "WORLD'S POLICEMAN" DOESN'T WORK

Vietnam permanently prejudiced the policy environment against counterinsurgency—even if U.S. combat forces are not directly involved. In El Salvador the efforts of the Farabundo Marti National Liberation Front (FMLN) and President Reagan's unique obsession brought a one-time rematch that ended in a tie after 12 years. The exception, however, only confirmed the rule: "we can't do that again."

Even without U.S. combat forces, the costs were just too high:

- 60,000 Salvadoran dead (the equivalent of 2.7 million Americans);
- 25 percent of the population becoming refugees, including one million illegal immigrants into the United States;
- Moral repugnance at U.S. failure to control 40,000 death-squad killings by the Salvadoran military
- $6 billion in U.S. assistance;
- Massive repudiation of the Republican interventionist position at the polls; and

• Heavy opportunity costs to top U.S. policymakers who had to spend scarce political capital with Congress and commit time that would have been better used elsewhere.

In the end, only the preemptive collapse of the USSR (and with it the Cold War) averted "our defeat."

"Counterinsurgency" is a pariah term, hurled to stigmatize U.S. programs (or be hotly denied) in the two countries where it might most logically apply: Peru and Colombia. In both cases the term "narcoterrorist" had to be coined (with considerable analytical justification) to duck the political paralysis invoked by any taint of counterinsurgency. The end results are dual-purpose security assistance programs, which are marginal to both *their* insurgency problems and *our* narcotics objectives, certainly in Peru[12] and apparently in Colombia as well.

The objectives of both the United States and Peru could have been better served if we could have differentiated between the narcotics and insurgency problems and focused on the highest pay-off response to each. The *quid pro quo* for our helping to hurt the Shining Path, say with helicopters for the high sierra, would be cutting off narcotics trafficking from airfields in the Upper Huallaga Valley (UHV) already under government control. The U.S. *sine qua non* for continuing this kind of cooperation to maximum mutual advantage could be tangible reduction in Peruvian human rights abuses—the Achilles Heel of our bilateral cooperation.

But it was not to be. Cold War-style counterinsurgency remains too tainted for policy makers to touch—even as a vehicle to verified improvements in human rights.[13]

SO/LIC Futile Web Spinning
DOD doctrine for "low-intensity conflict" (LIC) is a bewildering *potpourri* covering: insurgency, counterinsurgency, counter-terrorism, peace contingency

operations, and peacekeeping. The Harvard Symposium on Small Wars in 1988 concluded that:

> The National Security Decision Directive on low intensity conflict signed by President Reagan has all but dropped out of sight. . . . There appears to be limited interest in creating functional experts in LIC with experience in many different small wars.[14]

An experienced observer concurred:

> People problems at the top predominate. . . . State should be a primary player, but . . . top State officials, with rare exceptions, couldn't care less. . . . The problems would quickly disappear . . . if the President, his Secretary of State, and Secretary of Defense assigned SO/LIC a high priority. [But they don't.] Meanwhile marginal improvements are the best we can expect.[15]

An NSC-chaired "Deputies Meeting" in June 1990 refused to institute an interagency LIC backstop mechanism. And DOD's 1990 *Doctrine for Joint Operations in Low-Intensity Conflict* remains in limbo, a "draft publication" lacking official *imprimatur*.

Most recent SO/LIC brainstorming, however, is a quantum step forward in sophistication. *Peacetime Engagement: A Policy for the Environment Short of War* is an impressive new framework for approaching post–Cold War regional security.[16] This draft policy proposal does not, however, pin down "the devil in the details." How the new administration treats this legacy remains to be seen.

Outdated Security Assistance Programs

Foreign Military Assistance in the Cold War essentially paid for base rights to maintain the structure of containment and the tempo of operations. Reforming host country-capabilities to deal with domestic instability was an ancillary benefit, but far from essential. What was important was to keep the aid flowing. For that we relied on big ticket hardware transfers and basic skill training in soldiering—things we could readily take off the shelf and plug in anywhere.

This "cookie cutter"[17] approach to stamping out security assistance packages applicable anytime, anywhere, by all accounts produced "not very impressive" results.[18] Former Ambassador to El Salvador, Thomas Pickering, summed it up:

> We had neither the doctrine, nor the support nor the coordination in the United States government that would really be required to deal effectively with that kind of operation. I don't think we ever developed it; we are still kind of *ad hoc* in our way of viewing the problems. That is really quite a critical comment.[19]

Finally, we will not have the funding to support security assistance programs that can pay for high-priced equipment and training as in the old days. Former SOUTHCOM commander, General Wallace Nutting lamented several years ago:

> For the cost of steaming a carrier group up and down the coast (of Central America) for a week, we could fund most of the training programs and most of the material assistance needed (for all of Latin America) for a year.[20]

And security assistance funding cuts are only getting worse. Security assistance for Latin America dropped by more than 60 percent between FY-1985 and FY-1993. (Less than half of the $630 million cut came out of the phase down of El Salvador.) Security assistance has been "zeroed out" for thirty countries in the past two years and further deep reductions are expected for FY-94.[21]

In sum, attempts to rehabilitate Vietnam-style

counterinsurgency—minus U.S. combat troops—failed in El Salvador and never had a chance to get off the ground in the Andes. As a paradigm, it is dead-on-arrival: costing more blood, dollars, and domestic political turmoil than we are willing to commit against foreseeable threats. The lack of strategic vision, coherent doctrine, effective coordination mechanisms, and appropriate personnel policies that plagued us in El Salvador should not be repeated. Were they to be tried again on a country more difficult than five million people right on our doorstep, their failings would be more obvious and more costly.

ADVOCATES FOR "DEMOCRATIC SECURITY": CONSULTANTS AND FACILITATORS

Multilateral humanitarian intervention is gaining new *cachet*,[22] but often comes "too little, too late" as in both Somalia and Bosnia. The United States may find that multilateral handholders are often unavailable. But we may have another option—aggressive advocacy of "democratic security" to prevent a breakdown of civilized governance *before* it occurs.

A proactive policy of supporting "democratic security" should entail a three-tiered approach:

• Low cost-high value support for democratic programs and human rights before trouble strikes;

• Conciliation service should violent breakdowns begin; and

• Finally, in limited circumstances, indirect intervention through the provision of security assistance cast from a brand new mold (for example, geared to the recipient's "center of gravity" rather than U.S. surplus capabilities) when a reasonably democratic, human rights-abiding, and reform-oriented regime is imperiled with ominous implications for important U.S. interests.

The elements of this three-tiered approach are not mutually exclusive (for example, the final phases of El Salvador.) As a general matter, however:

- Democratization and human rights assistance should be available largely for the asking;
- Conflict resolution assistance might be extended where both sides were ready for it; and
- "Reinvented security assistance" should be extended only in special cases.

Democracy and Human Rights as Rallying Points

Democracy and human rights must be pillars of U.S. policy in strife-torn LDCs for three reasons:

- They are intrinsically "good" in American eyes.
- They should contribute to conflict resolution through politics instead of violent upheaval.
- A reasonable track record of adherence to democracy and human rights is a *sine qua non* condition for extending U.S. security assistance to LDCs threatened by internal turmoil.

Support for democracy and human rights must replace containment as the central, unifying theme in American foreign policy. "Only by uniting our national interests with Americans' basic values can we mobilize and sustain broad, bipartisan support for U.S. global leadership in the new era."[23] Wherever we have diplomatic relations we should be prepared to offer a range of "democratization services," including:

> Programs which develop political parties; assist in administration and monitoring of fair elections; train parliamentarians, lawyers and judges; enhance the rule of law; build free trade unions; support independent media; cultivate open markets; aid private sector institutions supporting human rights; and encourage political

participation by all groups in society.[24]

In Latin America at least, our policy should include a number of specific elements to support democracy and human rights, some of which have already proven reasonably effective, such as:

- Public fair warning that we will freeze all government-to-government assistance and vote "No" on international financial institution (IFI) loans wherever democratic regimes are toppled.
- Renewed efforts to get the Organization of American States (OAS) to amend its Charter to "suspend" participation by any state that has had a *coup*.
- Conversion of all international military education and training (IMET) to the IMET-E (expanded) format which includes civilians for management of military establishments, budgets, and codes of justice, including human rights.
- Requiring that all U.S. military assistance and sales agreements be signed by host-country presidents, to reinforce civilian control over the military.
- Making human rights enhancement programs central pillars of the "annual country plans," a fact instead of lip service.[25]

Facilitating a Negotiated Settlement
Now that the tide of Communist-controlled insurgencies has receded, we should prefer peace negotiations over military victory as the way to end the "uncomfortable wars" in the LDCs. At least three mechanisms commend themselves for consideration, and others may be possible:

- Restructure significant aid programs, around presidential certifications designed to reward (or punish) *both* government and insurgents, depending on their behavior. (The insurgents get "punished" if their abuses or recalcitrance to negotiate in good faith, etc., trigger a legally mandated presidential certification providing an automatic increase in U.S. assistance to the government.) We have a real world precedent: The Dodd-Leahy amendment on El Salvador which infuriated the Administration, but had the effect of pushing all sides toward a negotiated solution.[26]

• The same approach could be adopted as a matter of declared administration policy with regard to our generally decisive vote on IFI loans.

• Finally, the United States could provide facilitative encouragement for negotiations to be mediated by third parties, as in the case of Guatemala.[27]

INDIRECT INTERVENTION

After perusing the above efforts to enhance democracy, human rights, and peaceful conflict resolution, we come to the issue of developing a new approach to security assistance—to help stave off the "breakdown of governance" in LDCs where local conditions and U.S. interests permits. Perhaps a radical redesign of counter-insurgency assistance could restore its policy utility under certain limited conditions. If so, what would those conditions be, and how would this new approach look?

The United States should consider giving reconfigured counter-insurgency assistance only when the following criteria are met:

• The U.S. national interest is sufficiently compelling to outweigh allegations of getting our hands dirty by association.

• The host government's popular support can be solidified.

• The host government is truly capable of implementing wrenching internal reforms that address relevant grievances.

• U.S. global "credibility" will not become hostage to "victory" and we will be able to walk away if things go

sour; and
- U.S. combat forces will not be required.[28]

If any of the first three criteria cannot be met, indirect intervention via security assistance won't work, and we should keep our hands off. If the last two criteria cannot be met, let's not fool ourselves: once we are involved it will soon become a matter of U.S. direct, unilateral intervention. Still, in selective cases, it ought to be possible to "do security assistance right"—if we pick our clients as well as our fights and greatly revise how we go about it.

Making Security Assistance Work:
A Concept-Intensive Approach
The United States generally approaches client states gingerly, lest we appear colonialistic—and properly so. but as a consequence field advisors in Vietnam and El Salvador soon learned the lament: "a house leaks from the roof"—and it doesn't get fixed by working at the rice roots.

A successful strategy begins at the top, but U.S. policy makers seldom embrace the responsibility that implies. It is futile to beef up marginal operational capabilities (simply because we know how to do so) and ignore the strategic vulnerabilities of the country we presume to help. This has been generally our pattern in the past. Once launched into the swamp, we tend to rely on "more bailers with deeper hip boots and bigger buckets"—instead of calling for hydraulic engineers to attack the source instead of the symptoms.

This takes a few hard-eyed policy analysts with seats at the tables of power, not a plethora of hard-charging field men from the "can do" school of counter-insurgency. Above all, this takes leadership in the country team (and backstopping in Washington—people who are focused on systemic issues and openly determined to walk away if our efforts are marginalized and our resources are squandered.

Six Keys to Their Victory

Reflecting on frustrating years in El Salvador, one American observer concluded that "the ultimate outcome of any counter-insurgency effort is not primarily determined by the skillful manipulation of violence"[29] in battle. Instead victory goes to the side that achieves more: legitimacy, unity of effort, intelligence, effective external support, discipline and military capability, and impact in reducing the opposition's external support. To the extent that the government has the upper hand in all six factors, it has a decided advantage. If, however, the government fails completely in any one of the six, or is weak in most of them, its prospects are poor.[30]

Legitimacy,[31] unity of effort, and intelligence[32] are the three most important factors for success—but U.S. programs focused most heavily on issues of external support (for example, the Ho Chi Minh Trail and "passing the supplemental appropriations bill") and military capability. And for good, but self-defeating, reasons: these were issues we could easily attack with what we had on hand—money, weaponry, and military expertise.

Legitimacy, unity of effort, and intelligence were key to our client's success—but all depended primarily on the host government's reforms. Getting these reforms required the creation and exercise of U.S. leverage with the host government. However, while we had plenty of resources to bestow on our clients during the Cold War, the more aid we gave, the more leverage we surrendered. Recipients from Saigon to San Salvador "knew" that we were inextricably bound to their survival. Only when it became clear that we were pulling out (after Tet 1968 and the November 1989 Jesuits murder) did calls for internal reform and political settlement acquire compelling force.

In the "new world," the United States does not have to defeat any global rival, nor contend with Soviet "war by proxy" in the LDCs. Our interests do not require the survival of any client regime as the key to a global mosaic. This new-found ability to "walk away" provides us with potentially decisive leverage in dealing with client states—if we dare use it and use it wisely.

REINVENTING U.S. SECURITY ASSISTANCE

Our military assistance in Peru is tied to an "anti-narcotic" rationale; at the same time, it had to address the Peruvians' top security priority: the Shining Path. Neither the A-37s we ultimately supported, nor the originally proposed battalion training center in the Upper Huallaga Valley were very relevant to either drugs or Sendero—but they were something that we were institutionally comfortable doing. Ultimately, that determined what we did, but it could have been different.

In Peru and elsewhere, the United States should adopt a new style of providing security assistance consistent with the new circumstances in which we find ourselves. That new "style" should:

• Help the host government identify and correct its key strategic shortcomings and deemphasize our traditional assistance focused around "the business end of the gun."

• Accept that the United States does not have "the answers" to mainline into other political systems. But we do have a variety of mechanisms[33] that could help the host country expand its political dialogue in search of a broad consensus on an appropriate strategy that would permit true "unity of effort."[34]

• Key on helping the government reinforce its all-important "legitimacy" at home and abroad.[35]

• Emphasize good police work and intelligence based on motivated local cadre with something to fight for.

In short, we should begin to act more like international consultants, helping our LDC clients reconcile what they do with what they have—rather than playing the aging Santa Claus rapidly running out toys for resentful pre-teens with guns. This new role as a "facilitator" rather than as a fireman would require several *changes in how we organize ourselves to do business,* namely:

• Replace U.S. operationally-oriented officers with more Foreign Area Officer (FAO)-type diagnosticians to design and manage security assistance programs.

• Shift to more country-specific tailoring of assistance and away from vertical "stove pipe" programs pumping out primarily what Washington and Regional CINC backstop offices are geared to provide on short notice. Such horizontal integration between various agency programs can only take place at the country team level and would require full ambassadorial backing.

• Renew the executive-legislative understanding on the purpose of security assistance by completely updating the Foreign Assistance Act (FAA) which has become "barnacle encrusted" since it was first passed in 1961.[36] Such an effort should clearly specify the standards the United States requires with regard to human rights and democracy for cooperative assistance.

• Repeal Section 660 of the FAA, the 20-year old legal prohibition against most U.S. aid to police. This prohibition is no longer appropriate an era when democracy and human rights have replaced an earlier obsession with anti-communist stability as the lodestars of U.S. policy. Such an effort should be located in the reconstituted Narcotics and Crime bureau directly under the new Undersecretary of State for Global Issues primarily responsible for human rights and democracy.

Along with improving LDC criminal justice systems, smarter police work should replace military aid as the cutting edge of U.S. operational assistance to threatened governments. British counter-insurgency expert Sir Robert Thompson had the right emphasis when he said that the government's (internal) defense generally should rely primarily on the police and not the military. This should be reflected in U.S. assistance programs as well.

• Military assistance should adopt a leaf out of AID's book and "subprojectize" some of its programs, each with its own "conditions precedent" attached. The purpose would be to allow us to hold host-country officials responsible for making a reasonable effort to meet agreed targets—without threats of across-the-board assistance cancellation for nonperformance.

• Last but most important, we should set priorities for our objectives and not attribute to a given level of assistance more leverage than it is intrinsically worth.

FORGING CONSENSUS

The Clinton administration is carving out a new approach to change in the LDCs. The population explosion is coming anyway; we can either cope with it or get bowled over. At the State Department, DOD, and the NSC new structures are being proposed to grapple with its implications: the Undersecretary for Global Affairs at State, the Assistant Secretary for Democracy and Human Rights at DOD, and the Global Issues unit at the NSC.

The existence of this interconnected bureaucratic architecture should help all three agencies synchronize on a new concept of "democratic security"—one that focuses more on what the United States is for than on what we are against. Proactive programs supporting democratic institution building, human rights, and constructive political dialogue must come to the fore in our assistance efforts. We should rapidly phase out most LDC conventional military assistance programs—which we can no longer adequately fund in any case. Advocates for democracy and human rights must help redesign a new

U.S. strategy for LDCs—and become central to the domestic constituency supporting it.

If the administration has a proactive program of democracy, human rights, and support for political consensus building in place, it will be more feasible politically to reinvent a security assistance program that works, in place of irrelevant hardware transfers and technical training. This new approach would be focused on programs that do the following: reinforce host government legitimacy at home and abroad, stimulate the local political class—including but not limited to the officer corps—to confront the shortcomings of its strategy and create a community-based support structure, give primacy to police and criminal justice issues over tactical military operations, and provide more "concept-driven" assistance.

The United States can be neither the world's policeman nor its universal social worker. With concentrated effort, however, we might become be a good "diagnostic consultant" and "facilitator" to countries that dare to profit from our principles and seek help in putting them into practice.

By innovative redesign of security assistance programs, the key action agencies (particularly DOD and the intelligence community) can either drive policy—or be left behind by it. To ride the wave, however, they must revise radically how they do business. On the military side, this means the Defense Security Assistance Groups (MAAGs), and Defense Attache Offices (DAOs) should be rethought from the ground up. Ditto for State where the yawning gap between security assistance and "global issues" needs to bridged.

The policy planners need to wicker all of this into a new strategy for "democratic security." Congress, too, must be drawn into a compact for constructive engagement. But above all, DOD's program operation has to come up with a new vintage, rather than rebottling aged stocks already gone bad. Perhaps policy on low-intensity conflicts never got a fair testing; but by now it has gone sour in the cask and can not be rehabilitated. That holds true in spades for Cold War–style counter-insurgency assistance.

One can not be too sanguine about early results, despite the best of intentions. The mindsets of too many players are deeply scarred by previous ideological battles, and overcoming institutional resistance will be formidable. Moreover, the "bad neighborhoods" of the LDCs will limit the success of even the best policy. Many situations cannot be resolved, and we need the wisdom and courage to let them pass us by. In the end, tough cases where U.S. policy equities contend (like Peru) may well be decided by the power of clashing advocacy groups rather than by the merits of the issues.

Coming to grips with instability and disorder in the LDCs will be an uncomfortable process. U.S. Cold War strategy had its false starts (Alliance for Progress) and failures (Vietnam) and required a number of mid-course corrections (the Nixon doctrine replacing Southeast Asian Treaty Organization and CENTO) before proving ultimately successful. Constructing a consensus to cope with chaos in the LDCs will be even more confusing and conflict-ridden. One way or the other, we will have to do so. We might as well begin now, with our eyes open.

NOTES

1. Less developed country (LDC) is used throughout to cover all non-first world states—including the ex-Soviet Union. In the context of this paper, it is more accurate, if less fashionable, than the euphemism "developing countries."

2. Carnegie Endowment National Commission, *Changing Our Ways: America and the New World* (Washington, DC, 1993), 42.

3. Peru references come from my 1988–92 tour as Embassy Lima Political Counselor.

4.   Carnegie Endowment National Commission, *Changing Our Ways*, 1993, 41.

5.   "Rethinking Security in the Americas," *North-South Issues: Democratization* (University of Miami: September 1992), 3.

6.   William J. Olson, "Low-Intensity Conflict: The Challenge to the National Interest," *Terrorism*, vol. 12, no. 2, (1989), 76.

7.   John M. Collins, *U.S. Low-Intensity Conflicts 1899–1990*, a Congressional Research Service Study for the House Armed Services Committee, (September 1990) 23, 43. Collins' definition of low-intensity conflicts is a bit different than the four-part typology used in standard DOD doctrine, viz. He includes U.S. - stimulated *coups d' etat*.

8.   Olson, "Low Intensity Conflict," 1989, 76.

9.   OMB Director and former Joint Budget Committee Chairman Leon Panetta, *Washington Post*, 1, 27 April 1993.

10. William S. Lind, "An Operational Doctrine for Intervention," *Parameters* (December 1987), 30–36 lists the four lessons of Vietnam as: First, we cannot sustain the long-term commitment counterinsurgency usually requires. . . . Second, we have not been very good at training and equipping foreign armies. . . . Third, it is not possible to go into another country and change its culture to conform with our ideas of human rights, good government, military efficiency, or anything else. . . . Fourth, war is not won on the tactical level . . . but on the operational level." (30).

11. Marshall   Hoyler   and   John   Tilson,   *Conflict Suppression/Peace Zone Operations* (Alexandria, VA: Institute for Defense Analysis, 10 November 1992).

12. To illustrate with some Peruvian examples:

• The aborted proposal for a U.S. - provided training base for three Peruvian infantry battalions in the Upper Huallaga Valley and the substituted support for A-37 attack aircraft in Peru in FY-1991 are cases in point. The training of conventional infantry battalions (made up of draftees who rotate out after two years) would have had little impact on either the Shining Path or the narcos. In the end, it proved too hard to sell in Congress.

• With regard to the A-37s, Peruvian fighter aircraft have downed narcotics traffickers. The traffickers, however, soon shifted to night flights, against which Peru had no intercept

321

capability. Nor are these A-37s likely to be much good against Shining Path terrorists, who are either hidden in jungle bases or intermixed with urban populations.

13. The potential for achieving real synergy through tacit *quid pro quo* bargaining was demonstrated in the summer of 1991 when Congress forced the suspension of all non-humanitarian aid disbursements to Peru—primarily over human rights, although the narcotics lobby tried for its pound of flesh as well. Through tacit bargaining, we got major human rights breakthrough: (1) total access for unannounced and private International Committee of the Red Cross (ICRC) inspection visits with prisoners in all military and police facilities throughout the country; (2) ICRC access to a new national registry of all prisoners which was updated daily; and, (3) a 4 percent drop in the rate of human rights fatalities attributable to the government over the following 10 months.

In return for this (and some marginal narcotics improvements) we released AID Economic Support Fund (ESF) disbursements to keep Peru's rehabilitation program with the International Monetary Fund (IMF) and World Bank on track toward reintegration in the international financial system.

14. JFK School National Security Program, Harvard University, *Small Wars Symposium: The Case of El Salvador*, a conference report, 29 March 1988, 18.14.

15. John M. Collins, Senior Specialist in National Defense, Congressional Research Service, unpublished text of remarks at unspecified SO/LIC symposium, 11 December 1990.

16. DOD/OASD (SO/LIC), *Peacetime Engagement: A Policy for the Environment for the Environment Short of War*, (Working Draft Paper 5, 14 April 1993).

17. Colonel John D. Waghlestein, USA, "Post-Vietnam Counterinsurgency Doctrine" *Military Review* (May 1985), 44.

18. Douglas S. Blaufarb, "Security/Economic Assistance and Special Operations," in Barnett, et al (eds.) *Special Operations in U.S. Strategy* (Washington, DC: NDU Press, 1984), 217.

19. Max G. Manwaring and Court Prisk, *A Strategic View of Insurgencies: Insight from El Salvador* McNair Paper no. 8 (Washington, DC: NDU Institute for National Strategic Studies, May 1990), 13.

20. Manwaring and Prisk, 22.

21. Susan B. Clark, *The U.S. Army in a Civil-Military Support Role in Latin America,* Institute for Defense Analysis Paper P-2703, June 1992, A-3 and State Department data/contacts.

22. Carnegie Endowment National Commission, 51.

23. Will Marshall and Martin Schram, eds., *Mandate for Change* (The Progressive Policy Institute, New York, NY: Berkeley Books, 1993), 297.

24. Carnegie Report, 83.

25. This should include: (a) establishing unofficial human rights performance baselines (drawn from the local human rights groups' data) to monitor trends for "extrajudicial killings"/Assassinations or "disappearances;" (b) making it clear to all concerned that specific elements of our bilateral/multilateral assistance would be adversely affected by deterioration in human rights performance; (c) coordinating with the ICRC and other transactional human rights players the use of U.S. funding leverage to reinforce their access to prisons and lists of detainees, etc.; and (d) presenting specific military human rights improvement programs for funding as part of the annual budget cycle, including such things as: [1] Judge Advocate General (JAG-to-JAG) and Inspector General (IG-to-IG) exchanges on human rights; [2] support to military human rights training, and monitoring systems; [3] human rights sensitization exposure on the Hill for key commanders prior to deployment; and [4] doctrinal assistance at armed forces Staff and War Colleges in developing internal defense strategies consistent with human rights.

On JAG human rights aid, see: Major Jeffery F. Addicott, USA and Major Andrew M. Warner, USA, "JAG Corps Poised for New Defense Missions: Human Rights Training in Peru," *The Army Lawyer* (February 1993), 78–82.

26. The Dodd-Leahy amendment to the El Salvador appropriation in October, 1990 "halved" the already appropriated funds for FY-90 *unless* the FMLN: (a) refused good faith negotiations, (b) committed excessive human rights violations, (c) militarily threatened the survival of the government, or (d) accepted external assistance—in which case full funding would be restored. Conversely, Dodd-Leahy would have totally

eliminated aid to the government if the president could not certify that it was in compliance with the established conditions—particularly prosecuting the murderers of the six Jesuits. The administration bitterly opposed the amendment at the time, but in the words of one legislative liaison, "somewhat unconsciously in this building [State] we adopted the structure of his amendment—as long as we could keep the certification trigger under presidential control." Mark Kirk, Director of Legislative Affairs, ARA, State Department. Personal interview, 13 December 1992.

27. After decades of killing and 300,000 deaths in Guatemala, both the government and the insurgents have publicly welcomed U.S. behind-the-scenes pressure to reach closure in the current negotiations "Progress Reported in Guatemala Talks," *Washington Post*, 17 March 1993.

28. Even U.S. advisors or trainers are to be avoided as generally more of a domestic liability than they're worth in the field.

29. Max Manwaring, "Toward an Understanding of Insurgency Wars: the Paradigm" Manwaring, ed., *Uncomfortable Wars: Toward a New Paradigm of Low Intensity Conflict* (Boulder, CO: Westview, 1991), 20.

30. Manwaring refers to an unpublished study which found an 88 percent correlation between these factors and the outcome of "a sample of insurgencies that have taken place over the past 40 to 45 years." (19, 20). There is an alternative typology, however, for getting at these issues from vantage point of the insurgent instead of the counterinsurgent: see Bard ONeill, *Insurgency and Terrorism: Inside Modern Revolutionary Warfare* (Washington, DC: Brassey's, 1990).

31. Legitimacy is the accepted "moral right" to govern. It largely conditions a government's ability to attract voluntary support. International legitimacy may be harder to earn than domestic support, due to different minimum acceptable standards regarding democracy and human rights as in the cases of Argentina and Peru.

32. The two most important elements of which are: ferreting out the insurgent leadership and incentive structures to develop local cadre committed to contest for control of their homes.

33. For instance, military Subject Matter Expert Exchanges (SEEMs), USIS, the National Endowment for Democracy (NED). IMET-Extended, Anti-Terrorism Training (ATT) funded by State.

34. The introduction of a specially tailored U.S. counter-terrorism seminar conducted by ex-Rand analysts, Brian Jenkins and Cesar Sereseres, for top Colombian leaders in the late 1980s is supposed to have greatly helped Bogota rationalize its strategy. The first of two similar efforts in Lima flopped, but the second, in 1991, provoked the beginning of some real interest. These are the kinds of high level, "concept-related" consulting services we should focus on—instead of Detachments for Training (DFTs) and Mobile Training Teams (MTTs) to teach the troops how to bail water among the alligators.

35. By relatively inexpensive steps such as: instituting proactive human rights programs with the military; beefing up our anemic Administration of Justice (AOJ) and International Criminal Investigation Technical Assistance Program (ICITAP) under AID and the Department of Justice, rescuing them from the backwaters of U.S. security assistance and making an effective criminal justice system a central focus of our bilateral country strategy; increasing host country tax collection capability; introducing IGs to help control corruption; and assistance through third party intermediaries (for example, the OAS) to the mechanics of local elections where needed and appropriate.

36. The International Cooperation Act of 1991, H.R. 25605, was a House Foreign Affairs Committee-inspired effort to do just that. It passed conference but fell short of administration desires on three counts and was vetoed. With a Democratic administration and a Democratic Congress the time may be ripe to try again, this time leaving the executive with some more room for policy flexibility. Conversation with State Department Assistant Legal Advisor for Politico-military Affairs Edward Cummings, 19 March 1993.

10

MEASURES OF EFFECTIVENESS FOR COUNTERDRUG OPERATIONS

WILLIAM H. DUNN

"I WISH I WERE BACK AS THE BRIGADE COMMANDER IN MY OLD mech division," thought Colonel Charles Dunangon, U.S. Army Infantry, as he nervously fidgeted with his viewgraph transparencies. He and Lieutenant Colonel Claudia Douhet, U.S. Air Force, sat waiting in anticipation that the morning briefing to the new Director of the Office of National Drug Control Policy would go smoothly. The chairperson of the Department of Defense (DOD) Counterdrug (CD) Study Team had selected them to report on the team's recent analysis of DOD's contribution to national CD operations and the resultant measures of effectiveness (MOEs).

"You may go in now," interrupted a pleasant voice as the secretary rose to escort the military members into the executive conference room. The incoming President had replaced the previous administration's director with Dr. Amos Avagadro, an energetic extrovert who had tirelessly campaigned to deliver the Hispanic vote in the

---

William H. Dunn, Department of the Army, wrote this paper while he was a student at the Army War College. Mr. Dunn's paper was named a Distinguished Essay in the 1993 Chairman, Joint Chiefs of Staff, Strategic Essay Competition.

metropolitan New York City area. Avagadro was not without respectable credentials however. His undergraduate work was in mathematics while his masters and doctoral degrees were in Public Policy. His career had blossomed as a successful Brooklyn City Administrator. He had a reputation for toughness against drug dealers and he displayed a strong personal commitment to ridding the nation's neighborhoods of drugs.

"Dr. Avagadro, I am Colonel Dunangon from the U.S. Forces Command (FORSCOM) at Fort McPherson, Georgia and this is Lieutenant Colonel Douhet from the North American Aerospace Defense Command (NORAD) in Colorado Springs, Colorado. We are here on behalf of the DOD CD Study Team."

"Good morning to you both. As you know, the reason I asked you here is to give me a better understanding of how DOD is attacking the drug war and your method to evaluate effectiveness. Other agencies involved in CD efforts have already given their presentations."

"Yes sir. This will be an information briefing. Our examination of DOD CD operations and the development of needed MOEs is centered on the use of the systems approach. To illustrate this methodology, we will begin with a background summary followed by a broad overview of general systems theory. We will discuss where we see the nation's CD effort currently, where we believe we need to be going, and describe the measurable gap between these current and desired states. To bridge this gap, we will provide a short primer on what constitute good MOE, trace the CD strategy objectives from the national to operational level, and describe in detail two examples of military CD support operations. Finally we will report the types of data currently being collected and provide the MOEs which relate to DOD's attainment of their strategy objectives."

"And I will integrate your DOD information with the

rest of the CD community by giving you my views on where I think the nation's CD efforts should be focused," said the Director. "As you are aware, one of President Clinton's first actions was to cutback the White House staff. He recommended that my office be reduced from 146 positions down to 25.[1] If this is indicative that the President is deescalating the drug war, then I must act to provide the needed direction. With that as a backdrop, please proceed with the briefing."

BACKGROUND

Colonel Dunangon began the briefing. "Sir, although the state of the economy was the paramount issue in the 1992 presidential campaign, reduction of drug use continues to command a high ranking on our list of national priorities. In the past, the drug problem was often categorized in two ways as a domestic issue if the focus was on reducing demand, or as a foreign policy issue if the attention was on reducing supply. However, in reality, the distinction between reduction of demand and reduction of supply is often artificial and meaningless. In fact, demand reduction through deterrence may be law enforcement's main effect.[2] Former President Bush presented his National Drug Control Strategy to the public for the first time in September, 1989, when he outlined his program for America's 'War on Drugs.' Policy and guidance for the military contribution to the CD effort are manifested in the National Security Strategy, National Military Strategy, and various congressional acts, joint military publications, CD plans at individual unified and specified commands, and memorandums. Because of these new policies and guidance, traditional roles and missions for the armed forces have been amended to include military participation in CD operations. The high visibility of DOD resource investments requires that reporting mechanisms be established to senior-level decision makers and Congress.

These reporting mechanisms demand the establishment of MOEs as indicators of the impact of stepped-up military intervention in the drug war."

"Colonel, so far our beliefs are not contradictory. Indeed, the public is perplexed when attempting to determine if we are making positive progress to reduce drug usage based on a myriad of conflicting information. During the recent campaign, President Bush cited examples of success while we Democrats submitted contradictory evidence that usage patterns were increasing."[3]

GENERAL SYSTEMS THEORY

"Yes sir. Now let me talk about our methodology, how we employed a systems approach to examine DOD CD efforts and how they relate to MOEs. In the late 1940s, researchers noted that similar principles relating to 'the whole' and 'dynamic interaction' were observed independently in the physical sciences, social sciences, mathematics, economics, and other fields. Ludwig von Bertalanffy, a biologist, postulated these evolving general principles into the concept of General Systems Theory (GST) A few key GST terms need to be defined:

• A *system* is any set of components that can be seen to be working together for the overall objective of the whole.

• *Components* are the primary elements that comprise a system.

• *Environment* includes all factors that have an influence on the effectiveness of a system, but which are not necessarily controllable.

• *Hierarchy* is the relative relationship between systems and their components in terms of supra- and subordination.[4]

"A system's components may be systems in and of themselves. If this is the case, these components may be called *subsystems*. Similarly, the system under investigation may itself be a subsystem of a larger system. This leads to a fundamental dilemma in GST, namely which system should be chosen to study? Said another way, which is the system and which are the components? In the CD world for example, a possible system could be the 'DOD efforts and resources targeted to curb supply of drugs system.' However, this system is a subsystem' of the overall 'multi-agency curb supply system which in turn a subsystem of the overall 'multi-agency curb demand and curb supply system.' It can be imagined that this upward hierarchy search will ultimately result in the 'drug universe system' (figure 1).

FIGURE 1: DRUG UNIVERSE SYSTEM

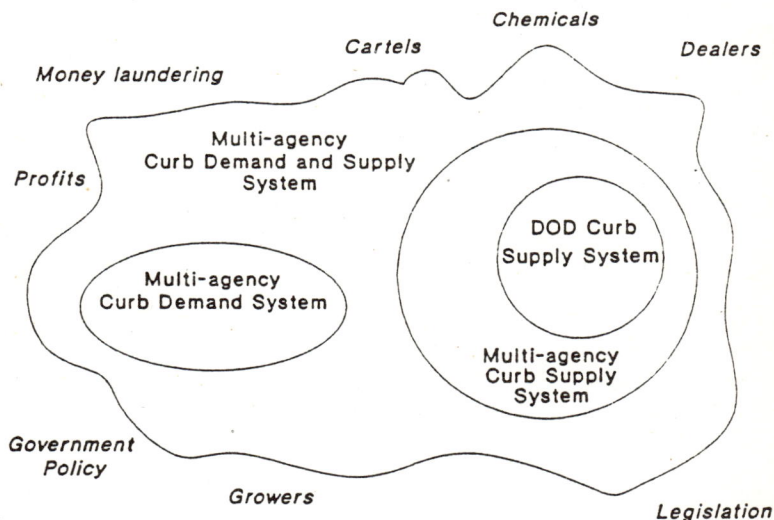

"Suboptimization may occur if the system under study is chosen too low in the hierarchy level. To remedy this, the general rule of thumb is to determine the chief decisionmaker (CMD) for whom the investigation is being performed. This person, or group of persons, also has the authority and resources necessary to affect change and implement study recommendations. In the CD case, the President (with support from Congress, as the resource supplier) could be chosen as the CDM since he is ultimately responsible for determining the focus of national effort. However, we believe that the President is too busy with other pressing domestic and foreign policy issues to be the ultimate CDM and that he must delegate his CDM responsibility for investigating effectiveness of the CD operations to a lower level. Similarly, although the Secretary of Defense (SecDef) is responsible for DOD CD efforts, the SecDef is also deemed as improper because DOD efforts address mainly the drug supply system and do not truly represent other factors such as demand which will influence the overall national objective of reducing drug use. Therefore, we believe a system that comprises the 'entire' CD hierarchy should be established. We believe the CDM should be you, Dr. Avagadro, because of your role as manager of international and domestic CD functions for the Executive Branch, and because you have the authority to coordinate and oversee the National Drug Control Strategy.[5] In addition, you have control over the budget for both demand reduction and supply reduction. The demand reduction function currently receives approximately 30 percent of the annual federal budget and supply reduction receives 70 percent.[6] Therefore, we have focused our study team efforts on a system that has you as the CDM since you have the capability to prioritize resources as well as make policy."

Avagadro nodded. "I'm in full agreement. We should identify the 'drug universe system' as the system under study so that I can provide consistency in policy and guidance."

"Fine, sir. A fundamental concept of GST is that it is necessary to describe the characteristics of the current state of the system under study and where we desire it to be. The *current state* of 'drug universe system' has three characteristics: Rampant illegal drug use prevails; a variety of agencies are conducting 'stovepipe' CD efforts based on their own agendas; and, there is minimal unity of effort. The *desired state* has one overall characteristic:

> Drug abuse and drug traffic are reduced to a level which is acceptable to United States' society and which does not seriously degrade our national security, our economic well-being, and our social order.[7]

The next step in applying GST is to determine how we can move from the current to the desired state. In other words, what is the *measurable gap?* To achieve the desired state, we must develop a seamless CD program where all agencies contribute to a unified system effort yet autonomy of the agencies as subsystems is preserved. Further, in order to chart progress toward the desired objective, MOEs must be developed for each subsystem and also for the overall system to serve as meaningful indicators.

MEASURES OF EFFECTIVENESS

"Before developing measures of effectiveness (MOEs) for selection, we will establish a definition, present a discussion of MOE selection, and provide some cautionary notes on their indiscriminate use. The term *'measures of effectiveness'* connotes different meanings dependent on usage, context, and audience. Generally, *MOE* can be defined as a quantitative expression that compares the effectiveness of alternatives or the effectiveness of continued operations. MOEs measure how well an alternative meets an operational objective or need. In our CD case, DOD objectives and other agency objectives must complement the national objective. MOEs will be developed to correlate with all these objectives. The proper choice of MOEs may be difficult, but decision makers will often mandate use of MOEs nevertheless. MOEs are used by the DOD in weapon systems development to compare potential solutions for countering recognized threat systems, thus allowing decision makers to discriminate among the competing courses of action."

Dr. Avagadro concurred. "As a decisionmaker, I believe choices usually describe costs, benefits, and counterpoints if my staff has done its analysis correctly."

"Indeed you're right," said Colonel Dunangon. DOD initially established some guidelines[8] in the preparation and selection of MOEs for various Cost and Operational Effectiveness Analyses (COEAs), these guidelines have value for establishing MOEs in other contexts as well, such as CD:

• Comparable measures for each alternative are evaluated against a baseline, generally the outcome that would exist within currently programmed capabilities.

• Measures should be selected which relate directly to the system's performance characteristics and to mission accomplishment. Decisionmakers need to know the contribution of the system to the outcome.

• MOEs should be quantitative and measurable.

• Objective measures should be used where feasible to minimize contamination by personal bias.

• Analysts should refrain from using schemes in which several MOEs are weighted and combined into an overall score."

"What about ratio data?" asked Avagadro. "If the numerator is much larger than the dominator, then small changes in the denominator may make very great ratio differences."

"You are correct. Ratios should be used with caution and only where appropriate. Ratios may mask important differences and can be misleading, particularly if uncertainty in the 'exact' measurement of the MOE exists. Especially discouraged are ratios combining MOEs and cost. It has been shown through analysis[9] that selecting a defensive strategy based on minimum cost is not optimum for outcome. At any rate, it is usually beneficial to show effectiveness and costs separately, not as ratios.

The rationale for the selection of an MOE should be documented. The rationale should include definition, dimension, limits, decisional relevance, associated measures (if any) and a methodology for the necessary data collection to compute the MOE."

"Was the concept of MOEs developed by the military," asked the Director? "They are the main advocates."

Lieutenant Colonel Douhet responded to the question. "Sir, most likely MOEs were originally conceived in the early days of operations research which traces its roots to the British in World War II. The British government recruited some leading academics to study the nature of military operations in the hope of new insights. One of their first findings was the importance of selecting proper quantifiable measures that can be investigated and which reflect the *real* problem or objective. As an illustration,[10] many British merchant ships were sunk or damaged in early World War II by enemy air attacks in the Mediterranean. The military solution was to provide merchant ships with anti-aircraft (AA) guns and crews. Decisionmakers who allocated scarce AA resources wanted to determine if the AA assets were making a difference or if they should be reallocated to other sectors in the theater. Analysis using the MOE destruction of attacking aircraft showed that only 4 percent of all attacking aircraft were being shot down. This 'poor' performance indicated that the AA could be utilized more effectively elsewhere.

335

However, further refinement of this problem gave way to the notion that the AA was not necessarily to shoot down aircraft, but rather to protect the ships they were on. When the MOE of interest was changed to 'survival of merchant shipping,' it became apparent that AA was making a substantial difference. Of the ships attacked, 25 percent of those without AA capability had been sunk whereas only 10 percent of the ships with AA were lost during the same time and under the same conditions. The choice of objective and MOE are critical and fundamental—there is no use providing the right answer to the wrong question!"

"Exactly, and at the present time the *desired state* characteristic of the 'drug universe system' is what I see as the real objective," agreed Dr. Avagadro.

Colonel Dunangon was clearly impressed with the extent to which this decisionmaker was adopting the systems approach. "Yes sir, and we must develop MOEs that relate to it. In the past, this was not always achieved and much public criticism was generated. For example, reporting the number of pounds/kilograms of drugs seized, when the composition and amounts of the total drug inventory (and replenishment capability) are unknown, does not indicate how the *overall* CD war is going. I refer to this uncertainty as the 'tip of the iceberg' syndrome. Drug seizures are measurable and quantifiable but are not the MOE for the 'real' objective.

"Similarly, the street price of drugs has not been a reliable measure of our successes. The aftermath of a big drug bust should have decreased availability, lowered purity, and increased the street price. But in general, prices in the illegal drug market have not responded as intended to increases in drug enforcement.[11] A possible reason for this is that the supply side mobilizes its reserves to pick up the slack when adversity occurs—partly because of the competition between dealers. No matter how much you interdict, there's much more out there in the pipelines.

However, recent dramatic cocaine price hikes have given a glimmer of hope that some sea state change may have occurred.

AUDIT TRAIL OF DOD OBJECTIVES

"I have been pressing the fact that MOEs must relate to the objectives under study," continued Colonel Dunangon. "Turning to military CD operations, we will trace an audit trail of CD objectives in order to develop and correlate needed MOEs. There is a myriad of CD policy directives at all levels, but we will only highlight the ones we feel are significant to DOD.

"Starting from the highest level, the National Security Strategy (NSS) of the United States lists as one of the Interests and Objectives in the 1990s:

> The United States seeks, whenever possible in concert with its allies, to reduce the flow of illegal drugs into the United States by encouraging reduction in foreign production, combatting international traffickers, and reducing demand at home.[12]

The NSS has components that include political, economic, diplomatic, and military strategy.

"The National Military Strategy (NMS) of the United States addresses the military component of the NSS and incorporates additional issues from the Defense Planning Guidance and other policy documents. The NMS has four pillars: Strategic Deterrence and Defense, Forward Presence, Crisis Response, and Reconstitution. Under Forward Presence, the NMS states[13] that 'we (the military) are charged to help lead the attack on the supply of illegal drugs from abroad.' The NSS objectives of *demand reduction and supply reduction* have been transmitted through the NMS as only *supply reduction!* Thus, the NMS has translated an overall national objective into a military objective which the DOD has the responsibility, authority, and resources to accomplish. Although the 'demand reduction' objective is not transferred, the DOD has made demand reduction, abstinence from drugs, a priority for its own military members, civilian employees, and defense contractors. Through education and testing, an 88 percent reduction of drug use has been achieved since 1980.[14] Further, DOD conducts drug education through its DOD Dependent Schools awareness and prevention programs.

"Explicit guidance was promulgated in the National Defense Authorization Act (NDAA) of 1989 which is still in effect today. For the first time, the NDAA assigned DOD three significant responsibilities:

• Take the lead for the detection and monitoring of aerial and maritime transit into the United States.

• Integrate those U.S. command, control, communications, and intelligence (C³I) assets which are dedicated in whole or in part to drug interdiction into an effective communications network.

• Approve and fund State governors plans for the National Guard to expand their support of drug interdiction and enforcement operations with the law enforcement agencies (LEAs).[15]

"Thus the DOD objective of supply reduction, as stated in the NMS, has been further refined by the NDAA to detection and monitoring of aerial and maritime transit into the United States, plus a new objective of C³I network integration has been added. To reflect this new direction, Title 10 U.S. Code, Chapter 3, Section 124, was changed to incorporate: 'Detection and Monitoring of aerial and maritime transit of illegal drugs: DOD to be lead agency.'[16]

"In September 1989, a SecDef guidance memorandum stated that DOD would assist in the attack on the supply of drugs at the source, in transit, and within the United States:

- *At the source.* DOD will execute security assistance programs in coordination with the Department of State. The U.S. Armed Forces will provide foreign forces assistance in training, reconnaissance, command and control, planning, logistics, medical support, and civic action. An improved intelligence collection effort will assist foreign governments and provide for the next phase of defense.

- *In transit.* With DOD as the lead agency in detection and monitoring aerial and maritime transit, the Commanders in Chief (CINCs) of unified and specified commands are directed to elevate the mission priority of CD within their commands.

- *Within the United States*, DOD will support requests from local LEAs and the National Guard in non-Federalized status. Also, DOD will assist the Department of Justice (DOJ) in training Federal, State, and local personnel in the conduct of rehabilitation-oriented training camps and providing overflow facilities for incarceration.[17]

In summary, the SecDef guidance offers further breakdown in exactly 'what support is available' plus it directs CINC priorities and offers DOD resources and facilities to assist DOJ. Thus, the audit trail has proceeded from the highest national levels through the SecDef and is now an elevated priority for the CINCs. The aggregation of CD objectives for DOD is reflected in figure 2.

"So where do you and MOEs fit into this, Colonel?"

"Dr. Avagadro, decisionmakers in DOD want to review CD trends to determine what works, what doesn't and what additional measures need to be taken. Other oversight agencies such as Congress, through the General Accounting Office, want to determine if the resources allocated to DOD are being used wisely and efficiently and if any progress is being made in the CD effort. At the same time, DOD needs MOEs to justify its own expenditure of public funds and rationale for any future budget requests. These desires and wishes drive the need for appropriate MOEs.

MOEs FOR DOD COUNTERDRUG OPERATIONS

"The Chairman of the Joint Chiefs of Staff has assigned major CD support missions based on area of responsibility to the CINCs of Atlantic Command (LANTCOM), Pacific Command (PACOM), Southern Command (SOUTHCOM), Forces Command (FORSCOM), and North American Aerospace Defense Command (NORAD). Two examples of how CINCs have approached this problem will now be explored. I will relate my experiences at FORSCOM and Lieutenant Colonel Douhet will follow with her brief of NORAD accomplishments.

FIGURE 2: DOD COUNTERDRUG OBJECTIVES

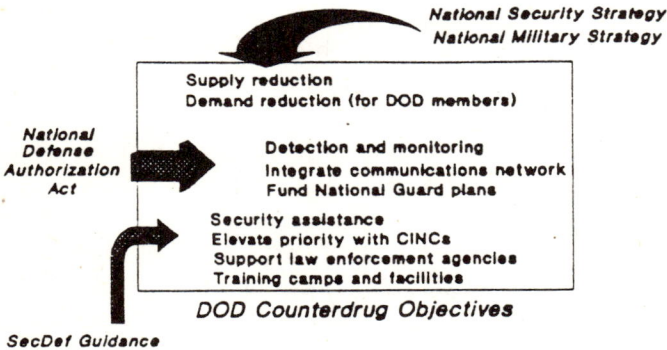

National Security Strategy
National Military Strategy

Supply reduction
Demand reduction (for DOD members)

National
Defense
Authorization
Act

Detection and monitoring
Integrate communications network
Fund National Guard plans

Security assistance
Elevate priority with CINCs
Support law enforcement agencies
Training camps and facilities

DOD Counterdrug Objectives

SecDef Guidance

"My boss, the CINC of the U.S. Forces Command (CINCFOR) at Fort McPherson, GA, has responsibility for CD within the continental United States. Additionally, since he is the Army component of LANTCOM, he provides support to LANTCOM CD operations, primarily in the Caribbean Basin. The CINCFOR's vision statement[18] acknowledges CD strategy is the latest form of the 'total or coalition force' which is a multinational, multiservice effort and that many of the new players are unfamiliar with CINCFOR (or Army) capabilities. CINCFOR envisions building a reputation for responsive and appropriate support while utilizing the 'unique training opportunities' that CD missions represent. He goes beyond reflecting on supply reduction and sees the ability for the military to assist in demand reduction through its available educational programs. These educational programs, provided to civil authorities within the applicable legal environment, will support rehabilitation endeavors. Ultimately, he foresees diminished illicit drug use resulting in reduced military involvement.

"I am Chief of the CINCFOR's staff for CD. We have translated his vision statement to five axes which support both supply reduction and demand reduction. The first four axes are to provide *operational, intelligence, planning, and training support* to LEAs, other CINCs, cooperating friendly governments, State governors, and local authorities for supply reduction. The fifth axis is *demand reduction* throughout the FORSCOM community. The caveats to the four supply reduction efforts are that they must be within the confines of the law, comply with intent of Congress, enhance combat readiness, and be coordinated with the National Guard.[19]

"A central focus for our MOE development effort is data. The paramount theme is that data should be recorded, manipulated, and retrieved in a relational data base. With a nationwide data base, trends and MOEs can be developed according to current desires or agendas, but additional MOEs can later be computed if necessary, as in the British World War II shipping example. It is outside the scope of this effort to develop the exhaustive list of data and MOEs that could be applied to every CINC and supporting agency. Rather, a sample set of data and MOEs will be developed and correlated to the established objectives for a typical CINC, in this case CINCFOR, using the five axes that support his vision statement.

Operational Support

"Ground transportation, air transportation, reconnaissance, engineer, communications, maintenance, and logistics are components of CINCFOR operational support.[20] The number of CD missions conducted in 1992 by CINCFOR increased by 1,110 percent over 1989 efforts.[21] MOEs to indicate trends in ground transportation and air transportation, in support of LEAs for example are:

- Number of LEA mission requests per calendar quarter
- Percentage of mission requests supported
- Total miles driven/flown (OPTEMPO measure) for missions supported per quarter
- Mean miles driven/flown per mission
- Probability of support success, calculated by dividing number of successfully supported missions by total number of missions requested. Support success is jointly defined by the transporters and LEA representative[s] transported for each mission. This definition should not define a success based on pounds of drugs seized, arrests, or property seizures. Rather it is a mission that was successfully supported by DOD in terms of time, place, and operation.

"The element of time for both scheduled and unscheduled mission requests can also be brought to bear on MOE determination. If an LEA request schedules a mission, the time that the DOD transporter was late or unavailable should be recorded. For a request which is an unscheduled event such as a contingency or emergency, the time elapsed from request to arrival indicates responsiveness and readiness of the support. MOEs are:

- Percentage of missions requested for which support was available within time constraints
- Median length of time support requested was late for scheduled missions
- Median waiting time from request to arrival for contingency or emergency events.

"Typical MOEs relating to ground or air reconnaissance are:

- Number of reconnaissance missions conducted
- Mean time on target (how long was the duration of the reconnaissance portion of the missions?)
- Mean number of targets acquired per mission
- Percentage of targets identified as potential traffickers, given acquisition
- Percentage of targets handed off to LEAs for intercept, given identification
- Number of targets which turn back (deterrence).

"Engineer, communications, maintenance, and logistics support. Logistics support include the equipment, supplies, repair parts, personnel, medical and other applicable military capabilities to support LEAs, State governors, and cooperating host nations. These categories complicate inclusion as successful support missions since they are performed whether or not there are any missions even performed. However, for workload considerations (OPTEMPO for support functions), MOEs are:

- Number of engineer, communications, maintenance, and logistics requests per quarter
- Mean number of personnel performing support
- Percentage of requests successfully supported
- Median delay time in required support.

"A qualitative and quantitative way of combining several of these factors has been used by CINCFOR's Joint Task Force (JTF) Six at Fort Bliss, TX. An assessment is completed based on responses by LEA (or State governor or host nation) representatives to a JTF Six questionnaire for each operational mission. The questionnaire asks LEAs to score the following mission elements on a scale from 0-4: whether or not the LEA objective was met, the impact on resources, whether LEA would repeat the mission for a similar threat, the C^3I execution, LEA's perception of the support unit, timeliness of unit support, planning by support unit, LEA training benefit, support unit morale, the LEA-unit relationship, and the overall mean. MOEs are the mean scores for these factors for a calendar quarter which are interpreted as indicators of multi-agency effectiveness and customer satisfaction. An example of these questionnaire results for LEA assessment is shown in figure 3.

Intelligence Support
"LEAs, State governors, and host nations require intelligence support to conduct their operations. Examples of intelligence support are the collection, analysis, production, dissemination, and retrievability of drug-related intelligence. Also included are intelligence. Also included are intelligence logistics such as computer data base management and logistics support. The Defense Intelligence Agency supports intelligence efforts at the national level and the CINCs support the operational or tactical level. Within the host nations, the CINCs provide Tactical Analysis Teams to be the focal point for DOD CD intelligence support and the link to DOD detection and monitoring efforts.[22] "MOEs for intelligence support are:
  • Number of intelligence support requests per quarter
  • Percentage of intelligence support requests supported

- Number of intelligence products provided
- Assessment of questionnaire responses which indicates the quality and timeless of the intelligence support provided to the LEA, host nation, or state governor missions.

FIGURE 3: LEA ASSESSMENT

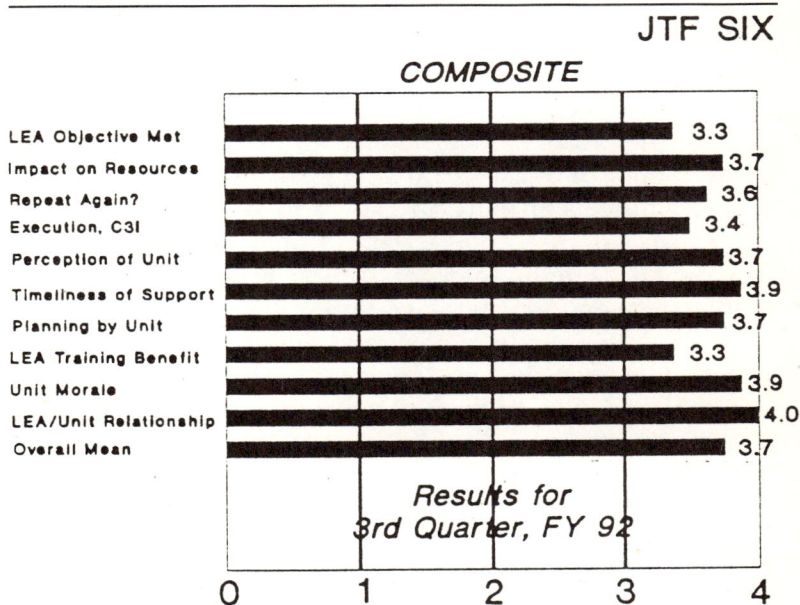

JTF SIX

COMPOSITE

	Value
LEA Objective Met	3.3
Impact on Resources	3.7
Repeat Again?	3.6
Execution, C3I	3.4
Perception of Unit	3.7
Timeliness of Support	3.9
Planning by Unit	3.7
LEA Training Benefit	3.3
Unit Morale	3.9
LEA/Unit Relationship	4.0
Overall Mean	3.7

Results for 3rd Quarter, FY 92

0   1   2   3   4

Source: Russell Morrison, Colonel USAF, "Counterdrug Measures of Effectiveness, A Dilemma," briefing slides, presentation at Military Operations Research Symposium, Monterey, CA, 25 June 1992.

Planning Support

"Planning is an area that the military has done extremely well and has high payoff potential for support to LEAs, State governors, and host nations. Military planning efforts such as forecasting, determining equipment acquisitions, development of strategy, campaign planning, communications, and intelligence preparation of the battlefield can all apply to CD as well. Planning effectiveness is difficult to single out since it is a component of operational and intelligence support; however, MOEs are the assessment of questionnaire responses relating to planning which have been solicited from LEAs, State governors, and host nations.

Training Support
"The primary definition of Training Support is training that: complements equipment, systems, and other capabilities which the U.S. government provides to foreign governments; or assists LEAs and State governors. Foreign force training is usually in the form of mobile training teams (MTTs) that conduct traditional military training skills, such as light infantry tactics, riverine operations, maintenance and logistics, aviation skills, communications, night maneuver, navigation, and intelligence gathering. Direct data on the effectiveness of training support applicable to CD is virtually nonexistent, but Military Attaches report fewer injuries and deaths of foreign forces in South American countries when trained by MTTs.[23] DOD has trained LEA officials to be pilots and in foreign language skills, helicopter maintenance, tactical survival, bomb detection, canine drug detection, and riverine operations.[24] MOEs are the assessment of the questionnaire responses solicited from host nation forces, LEAs, and State governors to evaluate the effectiveness of training support provided.

"A spinoff of training support is the value of the training received by U.S. personnel while conducting CD operations that is directly applicable to the mission essential task list (METL) for their unit. For example, a METL for an intelligence ground surveillance radar unit may include target acquisition and target identification. If

CD operations provide training value for target acquisition and identification comparable to intelligence training received while attending an accredited training course of instruction, the value is directly applicable to the METL. MOEs are questionnaire responses for individual skills, unit skills, leadership skill development, and noncommissioned officer skill development as part of after-action unit assessments of operational missions. These MOEs are used to reflect the quality of current CD operations in fulfillment of CINCFOR's caveat that combat readiness be enhanced. An example of these questionnaire results for support unit assessment is shown in figure 4.[25]

FIGURE 4: SUPPORT UNIT ASSESSMENT

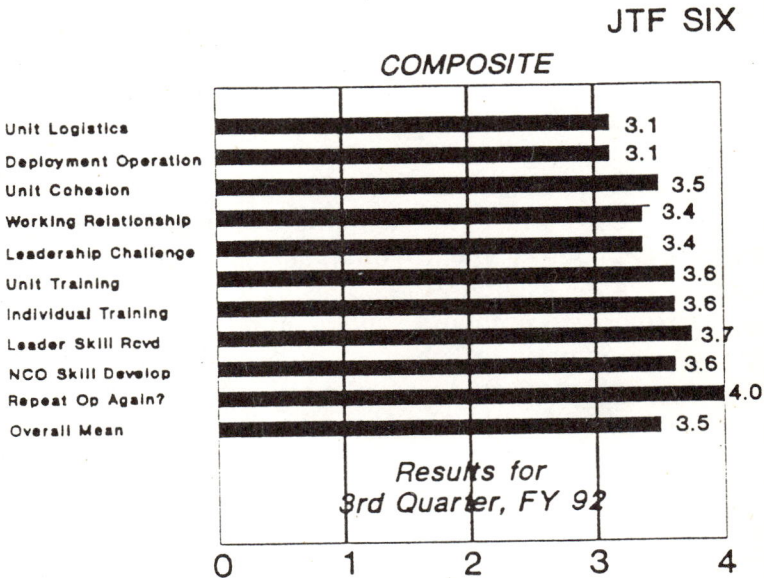

JTF SIX

COMPOSITE

	Value
Unit Logistics	3.1
Deployment Operation	3.1
Unit Cohesion	3.5
Working Relationship	3.4
Leadership Challenge	3.4
Unit Training	3.6
Individual Training	3.6
Leader Skill Rcvd	3.7
NCO Skill Develop	3.6
Repeat Op Again?	4.0
Overall Mean	3.5

Results for 3rd Quarter, FY 92

0 1 2 3 4

"New trends underway are wargaming and simulation for host nation and multi-agency training support. SOUTHCOM, for example, has initiatives utilizing simulation to represent the political, economic, social, and military aspects of the narcotics industry. After players and analysts develop courses of action for training and experimentation, simulation output provides valuable insight of the impact and interaction of individual or combined CD operations and the subsequent reaction by the narcotics industry.

Demand Reduction
"FORSCOM demand reduction is performed in conjunction with Army Regulation 600-85 'Alcohol and Drug Abuse Prevention and Control Program.'[26] This program has its own reporting requirements and the MOE indicates percentage decrease of usage through education and testing.

"That ends the FORSCOM example. Lieutenant Colonel Douhet will now detail the second example from CINCNORAD."

"Sir, CINCNORAD's CD mission is the surveillance and control of U.S. and Canadian airspace by conducting operations to detect and monitor suspected aerial drug traffic. CINCNORAD also integrates into the counternarcotics command and control network and supports the activities of other federal agencies. We collect real-time intelligence using a variety of radar sensors such as tethered aerostats, the Caribbean Basin Radar Network, the over-the-horizon backscatter radar, and the Airborne Warning and Control System (AWACS). Our long range sensor strategy is to track aircraft from their origin to destination. On-board controllers pass aircraft track data from AWACS to ground-based intelligence centers for fusion and relay to LEAs for apprehension, detention, and seizure.[27] We obtain timely identification of routine legitimate traffic and facilitate rapid response for suspicious flights. A side benefit of AWACS is its ability to use the origin-to-destination data to identify airfields both inside and outside U.S. borders which are used for drug activity. MOEs are:

- Number of LEA requests for support per calendar quarter
- Percentage of requests supported
- Mean AWACS flight hours (OPTEMPO)
- Mean number of sensor person-days of operation
- Mean number of low-flier tracks observed per mission
- Percentage of low-flier tracks identified as potential traffickers, given observation
- Percentage of low-flier tracks handed over to LEAs, given identification
- Percentage of low-fliers which 'turn back' (a measure of deterrence).

NORAD also benefits from operational mission feedback questionnaires from the LEAs on the degree to which the LEAs consider the mission a NORAD support success."

Douhet continued. "Pounds of drugs seized should not be used in conjunction with NORAD MOEs to indicate the end result of the handoff to LEAs. Pounds of drugs seized are not applicable to DOD because it is not DOD's mission to seize drugs. However, it may be a reasonable MOE for the customs people, local police, DEA, and others whose mission involves seizure and apprehension." Colonel Dunangon followed. "The MOEs just described are at the CINC level. CINCs with seaborne detection and monitoring missions have MOEs similar to NORAD except from a maritime viewpoint. Each CINC has MOEs that are common to all, for example percentage of mission requests supported, and each CINC may have unique ones. The common ones can be 'rolled up' to the SecDef level by ensuring that the supporting data are in the relational data base. A DOD initiative currently underway is called Corporate Information Management (CIM). One of CIM's objectives is the standardization of data elements. CD data elements for MOEs need to be standardized to establish common data names, formats, and most important, data definitions so that they will convey the same meaning to all people. After standardization, CD data elements should subsequently be entered into the DOD Data Dictionary. By doing so, common CD data can be combined at the SecDef level to obtain DOD corporate MOEs."

"I'll bet that DOD doesn't find these MOEs very exciting. Most people want to see some tangible results like pounds of drugs seized, arrests, convictions, and that sort of thing," said Avagadro. "But, as you described in your systems approach, DOD's role is mainly detection and monitoring with support to other agencies."

"Right again, sir. What the DOD MOEs *can do* is indicate if our nation is winning the war on drugs. That brings us to our closing remarks.

"We have utilized the systems approach because DOD is only a component of the 'drug universe system.' The MOEs that DOD has developed are important for our own use but cannot be directly translated to the national CD objective of reducing drug abuse to an acceptable level. We believe that we need to continue our work with the entire CD community to develop the ultimate MOEs which will consolidate demand reduction and supply reduction elements. We also believe that the community should adopt our relational data base and develop common data elements."

BEYOND DOD

Avagadro seemed pleased. "You have covered the military aspects of CD which are mainly concerned with supply reduction, and the other agencies' representatives have briefed me on the roles that they play. But the portion of your briefing I am most excited about is your use of GST. I have been searching for a methodology that will make my vision a reality. In the larger sense, your utilization of GST has given me the framework upon which to build a senior level multi-agency task force to serve as a steering committee to lead the national CD program. The steering committee will integrate all agencies' collective efforts and provide an overall synergistic effect. Each agency will have autonomy to conduct their operations as long as their overall efforts contribute toward the whole. Let me discuss some of the other agencies' achievements to show you what I mean."

"Regarding supply, shortly after President Bush's strategy was released in 1989, he met with presidents from three coca producing countries Peru, Colombia, and Bolivia. This February 1990 meeting in Cartagena, Colombia, produced the 'Andean Strategy.' It established a basis of cooperation for the multilateral CD effort to reduce production, consumption, and trafficking. The four near-term goals of the strategy are condensed as: strengthening each country's political commitment and capability, increasing the effectiveness of host-country law enforcement, disrupting and dismantling trafficking operations within each country, and strengthening each legitimate economy.[28] Using the terminology of your systems approach, these are elements under the category of external environment. The U.S. Government has had checkered success in achieving these goals. One reason for this is that we haven't always attacked the problem at the central reference point. Doesn't the military have a term for this?"

"Yes sir, it's called center of gravity," answered Douhet. "Clausewitz referred to it as *the hub of all power and movement on which everything depends. That is the point against which all our energies should be directed.*"[29]

Avagadro nodded. "The question is, what is the center

of gravity for supply against which we should direct our efforts? I personally believe it is the giant drug trafficking organizations and their key members. The Drug Enforcement Agency has focused on targeting large-scale drug trafficking operations, such as the cartels, through wiretaps, informants, and money laundering.[30] Destruction of *this* center of gravity should put the supply side in disarray.

"Now regarding demand, the National Drug Control Strategy has many short and long range goals for demand reduction. These sets of goals revolve around 'standards' obtained during a 1988 survey of drug usage patterns. As an example, the goals related to cocaine are reflected in table 1.

TABLE 1: DEMAND REDUCTION GOALS FOR COCAINE

Objective	Short-term (1993) reduction (percent)	Long-term (2001) reduction (percent)
Occasional use	40	60
Frequent use	30	65
Adolescent use	60	75
Incidents in emergency rooms citing use of cocaine	30	60
Reporting of ease of purchase	20	65
High school seniors not disapproving of illegal drug use	40	65

"Earlier I mentioned a Democratic Party citation which reference a 1992 study that indicated increased drug usage. Politics aside, a survey instrument and analysis based on the methodology in the 1988 study above are essential. The 1992 study conducted with a completely different methodology cannot be used to make meaningful comparisons. Thus, until the 1993 followup survey based on the 1988 study is completed, it is not known whether usage reduction objectives have been met or not. Care must be taken to ensure that survey respondents are representative of the population. Further, we must understand how the respondents were selected. Did they volunteer? Were they under pressure, from their parents for example, to provide a certain answer? I believe that these demand goals are important to keep and that the survey results are themselves MOEs for demand reduction.

"Let's take another component. There is some great work being accomplished at police departments across the country. In New York City, the police have introduced a strategy which has increased collaborative decision making. Rather than looking at the drug menace as strictly a police problem, the department has reoriented itself toward solving the drug problem from the community perspective. It has not only established an overall Executive Drug Control Strategy Committee but has also formed borough-based and neighborhood-based drug control strategy committees which are comprised of mostly nondepartmental representatives. From this broad support base, the various community goals are articulated, monitored, and improved. This grass roots approach works toward supply reduction through sharing intelligence and harvesting cooperation from the neighborhood working together."[31]

"Do you see any trouble spots in the near term?" asked Douhet.

"Unfortunately, I do," said Avagadro. "I am worried

about a possible downside of the North American Free Trade Agreement (NAFTA). Although NAFTA would increase trade in this hemisphere, this trade may provide a lucrative opportunity for the traffickers. It will be up to us to maintain the pressure on them. After NAFTA is implemented, statistical process control (SPC) techniques can be employed to look at rates of drug seizures. If they stay within the SPC boundary limits, then the counterdrug process is in control; if the rates are not within the SPC limits, then further investigation is warranted."

"Yes sir," said Colonel Dunangon. "We can't believe that we will ever be fortunate enough to stop all the drug flow. Looking at outliers from the SPC makes sense, but we need to monitor society's usage rates. If surveys find that usage is increasing, then the drug seizure rates are not outliers, but rather are indicative of increased attempts to service demand."

"In this context, SPC results might be able to assist in investigating the allocation of budget resources," continued Avagadro. "I believe that a 30-70 split in resources for demand-supply reduction, respectively, is not the right mix, and that the ratio should move incrementally toward the demand reduction side. We've seen demand reduction education work for smoking, and DOD has made great successes in reducing its members demand for drugs. We need to target demand reduction more effectively. Intuitively, I feel that approximately 50-50 would be the optimal percentage mix."

"Sir," interrupted Dunangon, "I can't fault your premise that demand reduction through education and grass roots police work are certainly important to the process and should receive more funding. But with the uncertainties of NAFTA, I don't believe we want to start cutting supply reduction resources just yet."

"In the near term I believe you are right, Colonel. I will ask the steering committee to study this budget mix."

Now Avagadro rose and walked to his white board. He began drawing a Venn diagram and labeling the various components that he had been discussing (figure 5). He concentrated now on his main point: "In Brooklyn, I saw first hand the effects of drug abuse. Drugs shatter family structure and values. Drugs undermine our school systems and are responsible for children dropping out at an early age. Drug use spreads AIDS through the neighborhood as a result of shared intravenous paraphernalia and unsafe sexual practices. Drug cases clog the court system and overwhelm rehabilitation facilities. The most prominent neighborhood role models are drug dealers. As a direct result of my Brooklyn experience, addressing these urgent social problems is more than my job, it is my passion.

FIGURE 5: STREET LEVEL MOEs

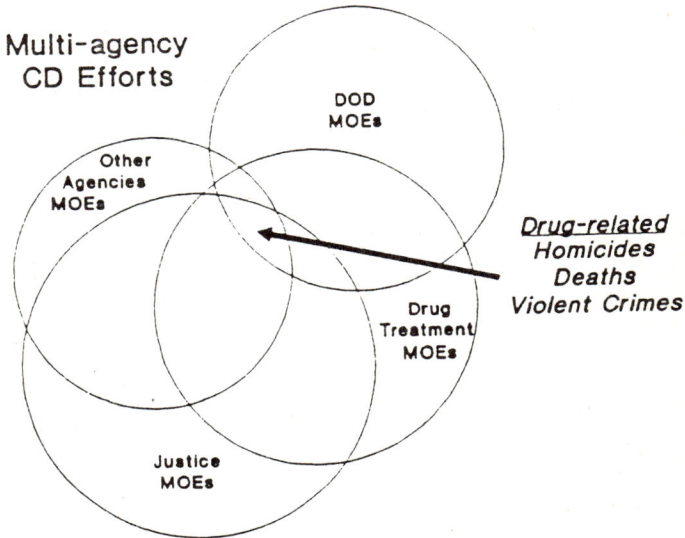

Multi-agency CD Efforts

Other Agencies MOEs

DOD MOEs

Drug Treatment MOEs

Justice MOEs

Drug-related Homicides Deaths Violent Crimes

"And society is fighting back too!" Avagadro continued. "Each agency in the CD program is making contributions to reduce supply and demand, and each agency has developed its independent MOEs. From my perspective, the significant MOEs are where the circles overlap—at the street level. All of the agencies supply reduction and demand reduction efforts are for naught if we can't see a reduction in the number of drug-related homicides, drug-related violent crimes, and drug-related deaths. The advantage of using these three measures is that they address both crime and individual usage information. We are challenged by the fact that data are often difficult to categorize as whether or not they are drug-related, and individual cases may need to be isolated. Plus, any trends developed with this data will require adjustment for population growth or decline. But the MOEs offer insight on the efficiency of the drug control policy since data on homicides, violent crimes, and deaths are available and they are all-inclusive. The data are not a result of voluntary participation as in demand reduction, and we aren't dealing with unknown 'tips of icebergs' as in supply reduction. It is a statistician's dream: we have the entire population of deaths and violent crimes to analyze, not just samples of the population. We need to standardize the definitions for these data at the national level and promulgate them down to the local levels. Coordinating this effort seems like a good mission for the steering committee too.

Avagadro paused for effect. "The success of this steering committee will depend in part on its members understanding the value of GST and how to apply it to the problems at hand. With your permission, I will ask your bosses to let me use both of you for a few months to represent DOD on the steering committee."

"I'd be honored," said Dunangon.

"Me too," answered Douhet. "Creating a steering committee is the catalyst that Colonel Dunangon and I have needed to finally bring our systems theory concept to fruition. Using this concept will allow DOD and the other task force agencies to incorporate their ongoing initiatives with the objectives of the new administration. The Clinton-Gore platform focused more on "harm-reduction" than on enforcement. Your people-oriented vision dovetails perfectly into their tenets of community-based policing, drug treatment on demand, drug education in schools, and an effective drug interdiction program that curtails the flow of drugs to schools, streets, and communities.[32] However, they may have seriously neglected issues surrounding enforcement and incarceration. An estimate of the total governmental budget (federal, state, and local) for drug control in 1990 was $28 billion, of which $21 billion went to enforcement.[33] This ratio will probably change as the administration emphasizes the health consequences of drug use and begins to target drug treatment systems for increased funding. Tasking the steering committee to study this critical budget mix will aid in determining the proper balance between demand and supply efforts. Understanding the effects of this mix on the drug universe system will ensure that enforcement is not the inadvertent billpayer.

"I'm glad to see that you share in my passion to solve these urgent social problems," concluded Dr. Avagadro. "Thanks for your briefing and your obvious enthusiasm."

"Our pleasure, sir," smiled Dunangon. The military briefers left the conference room and headed toward the elevator.

NOTES

1.   Peter Reuter, "Truce in Needle Park," *Washington Post*, 28 February 1993, C1.

2.   The White House, *National Drug Control Strategy* (Washington, DC: GPO, February 1991), 3.

3.   *Pride Questionnaire Report: 1991-1992 National Summary Grades 6-12*, 1992, Atlanta in *Mandate for Change*, Ed Kilgore, (New York, NY: Berkley Publishing, January 1993), 194.

4.   Thomas H. Athey, *Systematic Systems Approach* (Englewood Cliffs, NJ: Prentice-Hall Inc., 1982), 12-14.

5.   Department of Defense, Joint Chiefs of Staff, *Joint Tactics, Techniques, and Procedures for Counterdrug Operations*, Joint Pub 3-07.4, Initial Draft (Washington, DC: DOD, 15 August 1992), III-5.

6.   *National Drug Control Strategy*, 134.

7.   Murl D. Munger and William W. Mendel, *Campaign Planning and the Drug War* (Carlisle Barracks, PA: Strategic Studies Institute, February 1991), 77.

8.   U.S. Department of Defense, DODI 5000.2, "Defense Acquisition Management Policies and Procedures" (Washington, DC: DOD, February 1991), 4-E-3, 4-E-4; with U.S. Department of Defense, DOD 5000.2M "Defense Acquisition Management Documentation and Reports," (Washington, DC: DOD, February 1991), 8-7, 8-8, 8-12.

9.   U.S. Naval Academy, *Naval Operations Analysis* (Annapolis, MD: Naval Institute Press, 1984), 10.

10. Ethan A. Nadelmann, "The Case for Legalization," *The Public Interest*, no. 2 (Summer 1988), 6.

11. The White House, *National Security Strategy of the United States* (Washington, DC: GPO, August 1991), 3.

12. U.S. Department of Defense, The Joint Chiefs of Staff, *National Military Strategy of the United States* (Washington, DC: DOD, January 1992), 15.

13. Secretary of Defense, *Annual Report to the President and Congress*, (Washington, DC: DOD, January 1993), 111.

14. Joint Pub 3-07.4, Initial Draft, I-15.

15. Public Law 101-189, 29 November 1989.

16. Secretary of Defense, "Guidance for Implementation of the President's National Drug Control Strategy," Memorandum, (Washington, DC: DOD, 18 September 1989).

17. Department of Defense, Center for Low Intensity Conflict, "CINCFOR Counterdrug Management System (CDMS)," Final Draft, (Langley AFB: DOD, 5 April 1991), C-1, C-2.

18. Ibid., E-2.

19. Ibid., D-1.

20. *Annual Report*, 109.

21. Joint Pub 3-07.4, IV-31.

22. Robert R. Peavey, "DOD Counternarcotics Program: Viable Alternatives to Measuring Effectiveness," Executive Research Project for Industrial College of the Armed Forces (Washington, DC: DOD, 1991), 23.

23. *Annual Report*, 113.

24. Morrison, Russell, "Counterdrug Measures of Effectiveness," Briefing Slides, Presentation at Military Operations Research Symposium Monterey, CA, 25 June 1992.

25. CINCFOR CDMS, E-2.

26. Joint Test Pub 3-07.4, VI-52.

27. *National Drug Control Strategy*, 78-79.

28. Carl von Clausewitz, *On War*, trans. Michael Howard and Peter Paret, eds. (Princeton, NJ: Princeton University Press, 1989), 595-596.

29. Gordon Wilkin, "A New Assault on Cocaine," *U.S. News and World Report*, 11 January 1993, 21.

30. *National Drug Control Strategy*, 9-18.

31. Briefing and discussion as part of Army War College small group visit to New York City Police Department, 13 October 1992.

32. Governor Bill Clinton and Senator Al Gore, *Putting People First* (New York, NY: Times Books, 1992), 71-74.

33. Reuter, C-1.

11

IMPACT OF THE SOVIET UNION'S DEMISE ON THE U.S. MILITARY SPACE PROGRAM

GREGORY A. KEETHLER

One small ball in the air, something which does not raise my apprehension, not one iota.

President Eisenhower[1]

INTRODUCTION

Despite his apparent lack of appreciation for the extent of the atmosphere, Ike's reaction to Sputnik was technically correct: the thing was basically just a radio beacon in orbit, and it should have surprised no one because the Soviets had openly expressed their intent to launch a satellite for over 2 years.[2] Nevertheless, the President's attempt to downplay the event fell on the deaf ears of a nation gripped by the specter of Soviet nuclear weapons reaching the United States through space. Virtual panic set in, and the so-called "space race" was born. Over

---

Lieutenant Colonel Gregory A. Keethler, U.S. Air Force, wrote this paper while a student at the Air War College. The essay was named a Distinguished Essay in the 1993 Chairman, Joint Chiefs of Staff, Strategy Essay Competition.

the ensuing 34 years, the United States and the Soviets conducted over 3,000 successful space launches, about two-thirds having primarily military purposes.[3] By 1991, the United States was spending over $14 billion per year just on the military portion of its space program.[4]

Then, in December of that year, the Soviet Union collapsed. Given the intensity of the aforementioned "space race," there are surely profound implications for the U.S. military space program. Intuition suggests the time is ripe to scale back U.S. military space efforts—to adjust our force posture away from space in the absence of our traditional space competitor to not only save money but also to revert the use of space to peaceful purposes. Examining the impact of the Soviet Union's demise on the military space arena in light of other developments in the world and U.S. national security strategy, no opportunity to scale back exists. Indeed, the course of events in the former Soviet Union argues not only for maintaining and improving our existing space force structure, but, more importantly, for even greater emphasis on the military space mission areas known as space control.

THE OLD SOVIET SPACE PROGRAM

Soviet leaders relished their country's reputation as the world's "premier spacefaring nation," and they touted the space program "as proof of the superiority of socialism over capitalism."[5] The program's propaganda value contributed to "almost indiscriminate expenditures" being lavished on it, and by almost any measure, it became the world's largest space program.[6] The industry to support it grew to between 800,000 and 900,000 workers in over 2,000 enterprises, 90 percent of which were in Russia. The Soviets developed over 50 types of spacecraft and 10 different launch systems, which were employed in over 101 launches in 1982, the peak year in terms of launches. On the verge of collapse in 1991, the Soviet Union still mustered 59 successful launches, far exceeding the combined efforts of the rest of the world.

Cloaked in secrecy and tightly controlled by the Communist party, the program was dominated by the needs and desires of the military. According to one former Russian space science official, military activities accounted for 85 to 90 percent of the program's budget. Not only did the five military services finance most of the Soviet satellites, but they also launched them, trained the cosmonauts, performed all spacecraft recovery, and did most of the satellite tracking.[7]

The phenomenal number of launches manifests a very fundamental difference between the Soviet and U.S. approaches to their respective space programs. In his book, Nicholas Johnson summarized this difference as follows:

> Simply put, the United States has come to rely upon a very few long-lived and sophisticated satellites to fulfill specific tasks, while the Soviet Union maintains many shorter lived and simpler spacecraft to perform the same functions. . . . The frequency with which satellites must be launched dictates that launch vehicles as well as satellites must be standardized [sic] . . . and virtually mass-produced.[8]

Whereas launch preparation and checkout times for the Soviets were normally measured in days, comparable U.S. times are measured in months. This is according to General John L. Piotrowski, USAF, the former commander of U.S. Space Command, who also found a graphic example to illustrate the contrasting launch capabilities of the two countries: "During the Falkland Islands crisis in 1982, the Soviet Union conducted 29 space launches in 69 days, comparable to the U.S. launch totals in 1986, 1987, and 1988 combined.[9] In all fairness, U.S. launch figures for those years were depressed because of the *Challenger* disaster and other booster problems, but the point is well taken. Nicholas Johnson developed this as his primary thesis:

> Soviet satellite philosophy closely parallels the philosophy evident in other areas of Soviet industry and military weaponry: the paramount design qualities are ruggedness, simplicity, relatively low cost of manufacture and operation, mission effectiveness, and proliferation. These attributes are not only the trademark of the Soviet presence in space, but reflect a military space strategy designed, should the need arise, to fight and to win a war in outer space.[10]

Still later in the book, Johnson says, "To Moscow the prospect of war in space is not a notion to be shunned for romantic ideological reasons, rather it is a logical eventuality for which serious preparations must be made."[11] At the time, such high officials as Secretary of Defense Weinberger and Secretary of the Air Force Aldridge held similar views of Soviet space strategy.[12] The important point is that to the Soviet military, space forces were clearly an integral part of warfighting strategy and doctrine, and it stands to reason that this strategy and doctrine were passed on the military institutions that survive in the Soviet successor states. Thus, from a military perspective, space is likely no less important to the military institutions of the former Soviet Union than it was to their Soviet predecessors.

As space funding began to dry up, the Soviets started looking for ways to cut costs while maintaining the same capability. A 1991 DOD publication, *Military Forces in Transition*, reported "trends indicate that Soviet satellites are gradually becoming more sophisticated and longer lived. This increased efficiency is the mark of a more mature military space program that can reduce redundancy while accomplishing its missions."[13] While undoubtedly the same time-tested design features persisted, the point is that it is a fallacy to conclude that Soviet satellites were technological dinosaurs that no one else would ever want.

Nevertheless, selling space products and services to outsiders was not of particular interest to the Soviets. Commercial activity was a low priority, accounting for no more than 4 percent of the program.[14] Under *Perestroika*, more emphasis was placed on commercial activity with the creation of *Glavkosmos* in 1985 to internationally market Soviet space services and products.[15] Although the Gorbachev government had high hopes that the space industry would be an "engine of growth," the commercial endeavor met with little success.[16] When the space budget was made public in 1989, there was a public outcry against the level of resources being spent at a time when the economy was rapidly deteriorating, prompting Boris Yeltsin and others to campaign for freezing the space budget.[17] By 1991, the financial pressures on the Soviet space program had reached the point that, according to *Aviation Week and Space Technology*, the Defense Ministry "offered its secret Military Satellite Control Center for sale to any non-Soviet group for use to command commercial or scientific space missions" in order to generate hard currency.[18]

It had already been noted that 90 percent of the space industry was in Russia. Ukraine produced various equipment such as sensors and launch vehicles, and it hosted a major satellite tracking station as well.[19] Two of the three launch complexes, or cosmodromes, were in Russia, including Plesetsk, the most active one with 60 or more launches per year in the mid-1980s. The third launch complex was Baikonur Cosmodrome in Kazakhstan, which was the site of the first Sputnik launch and the launch site for all manned, lunar, planetary, geosynchronous, and high-altitude navigation missions as well as about one-third of the photographic reconnaissance satellites.[20]

To summarize, a number of features of the old Soviet space program are relevant to analyzing the current course of events:

- The program was an immense source of pride for the Soviet Union
- The space industry was, collectively, a tremendous endeavor that employed large numbers of highly skilled people
- The space program was the beneficiary of virtually unlimited funding
- The military was far and away the largest customer of that industry, was deeply involved in the program, and considered space warfare to be fundamental to warfighting doctrine and strategy
- Access to space through unparalleled launch capability was a strength of the program
- Soviet satellites were rugged and low cost, yet reasonably capable
- Until very late, commercial applications of the space program were a very low priority
- The primary "space republics" were Russia, Ukraine, and Kazakhstan, with Russian possessing most of the infrastructure.

The Soviet Union's collapse in December 1991 intensified political and financial pressure on the space program. To fully appreciate the current state of affairs in the former Soviet space program, it is useful to explore the context in which the program is trying to survive.

THE SITUATION IN THE FORMER SOVIET UNION

For obvious reasons, the world's focus on the former Soviet Union's woes gravitates to Russia. As Tom Brokaw reported one night, "Events in Russia were their usual mess today."[21]   His comment amply captures the seeming endlessness of Russian political machinations in the wake of the Soviet Union's collapse. The episode in question had the Russian parliament failing in its attempt to impeach President Boris Yeltsin in an ongoing battle for control of the government. There are many complex dimensions of the situation, suffice it to say that the political future of Russia is uncertain at best: predictions run the gamut from a return to authoritarianism to ultimate success of Yeltsin's democratic and economic reform movement to chaos and civil war.[22] Meanwhile, as confusion reigns at the highest levels of government, various other factions such as government *appratchiks*, the military, factory managers, and the like struggle to consolidate and retain their own share of power. As early as November 1992, *The Economist* assessed the country as all but ungovernable due to the competing policies of such groups.[23]

The political entropy pales in comparison to the precipitous plunge of the failing Russian economy, which has been variously described as "imploding," "collapsing," "an economic swamp," and a "basket case." The economic indicators paint a gruesome picture: 1992 production was nearly 30 percent below 1990 levels; the ruble, which exchanged at 200 per dollar as late as September 1992, slipped to almost 700 per dollar by February 1993; debt payments in 1993 will reach $40 billion, or $5 billion more than expected revenues from exports; and the U.S. Treasury Department estimates the 1993 GDP to be $75 billion, only $10 billion more than the output of the embattled IBM Corporation. Real per capita income has declined 57 percent in 2 years, and in January 1993, Russians were paying 8,688 rubles for a basket of goods that cost them 100 rubles in December 1990. To put this in perspective, as of September 1992, the average Russian wage was about 6,000 rubles per month, while pensioners averaged less that 1,000 rubles per month.[24] The upshot of all this is that the space program in Russia at this juncture is affected far more by economics than by politics.

The factors contributing to the economic calamity are both many and interrelated—again, a complete analysis is beyond the scope of this paper. However, one very significant factor germane to the issue at hand is the military-industrial complex, of which the space industry is a part, because it reportedly constituted half of Russia's industrial production prior to the Soviet collapse. Declining arms sales have combined with defense budget cuts of over 65 percent to render this capacity largely excess. Hence, weapons production is off at least 50 to 60 percent, while research and development work fell 33 percent in 1992 after a 50 percent reduction in 1991. Yet, many managers have attempted to keep employees on the payroll although they produce nothing. In the critical absence of either export revenues or Western investment and aid, the government is thus faced with the dilemma of either printing more money to prop up these industries or letting the unprofitable enterprises fail and increase unemployment dramatically. Thus far, it has attempted the former course by operating the presses that print rubles at full capacity, around the clock, every day of the week. The predictable result is runaway inflation.[25]

The Russian government announced in January that it would no longer ceaselessly print money and thereby allow unprofitable enterprises to go under, but inflation continues as other former Soviet Republics continue to print rubles.[26] The unprofitable enterprises are more often than not design bureaus and machine-building enterprises of the military-industrial complex with large numbers of engineers and highly skilled workers. Those who are not joining the ranks of the unemployed receive one-half to one-third of the wages earned by workers in more commercially profitable enterprises like textiles. Out-of-work engineers, many of them women, often take low-skill, low-paying jobs as necessity—if they can find such jobs at all.[27]

Rampant inflation, steeply declining industrial output, a dismal market for military exports, a shriveling standard of living, increasing unemployment, and an overall export level below that needed even to service the national debt all translate to an absolutely desperate need for hard currency. This is the principal motivation behind the Russians' frantic pleas for Western aid and investment. It is, therefore, an astonishing and very significant fact that in the face of such an urgent need, the government cannot control the exodus of precious hard currency from the country. A French banking analysis firm estimates that $17 billion in hard currency left the country illegally in 1991 and 1992—about $1 for every $4 in legitimate exports. This is largely done through diversion of export commodities via "unofficial channels." Estimates are that one-third of all Russian oil reaching the West is handled this way, as is one-half of the nickel.[28] General Valery Krasnovsky of the Russian Security Ministry succinctly summarized the situation: "Our country is begging for money from the West. If someone gives us a credit for $1 billion, we are very happy. But we could make much more money than that if we simply organized our trade in a proper way."[29] In this light, Western countries' reluctance to infuse large quantities of cash into Russia via aid and investment is understandable. This circumstance starkly affirms the previously cited assessment by *The Economist* concerning the government's inability to govern—in this case, to provide even a modicum of control over vitally important functions.

Political circumstances are not quite as dynamic in the other two major "space republics" of the former Soviet Union. However, without delving into the same level of detail, suffice it to say that they share Russia's economic woes. For example, the Ukrainian deficit is 44 percent of the gross national product, and the country is on the brink of hyperinflation.[30]   Like Russia, the Ukrainian economy was based on huge factories that built military products. In fact, when Khrushchev once boasted that the Soviet Union could churn out rockets like sausages, he was speaking of a rocket plant in Ukraine.   Many space components continue to be manufactured there, as does the Zenit, one of the space program's more important boosters. The political relationship with Russia is at best uneasy, at worst downright distrustful—witness the standoff over nuclear weapons and the Black Sea fleet.[31] Indeed, during a visit to Ukraine in September 1992, the author heard a Ukrainian colonel solicit promises of U.S. intervention in the event of a Russian attack, and even conversations with ordinary citizens revealed a wary opinion of Russia—they seemed to prefer being associated with Europe.

Unencumbered by experiments in democracy, Kazakhstan has actually enjoyed some measure of economic success under the iron-handed rule of President Nursultan Nazarbaev.   Western businesses have been attracted to its mineral wealth and a predictable (albeit centrally controlled) atmosphere for striking deals.   Yet, unlike Ukraine, the country remains shackled by having retained the Russian ruble as its currency, and hence, it suffers from all the monetary foibles discussed above. For this and other reasons, *U.S. News and World Report* characterized the relationship with Russia as "ambiguous at best." To complicate matters, industrial output is down 15 percent, Islamic activism looms on the horizon, and Kazakhstan's regional neighbors are not exactly icons of stability (Tajikistan, for example, was in the midst of a civil war in mid-1993.   Control of the staff at the Baikonur Cosmodrome and the question of who pays and feeds them are major sources of difficulty between Russia and Kazakhstan, and conditions there are reportedly deteriorating as a result.[32]

In short, the politico-economic environment in which the former Soviet Union space program finds itself is marked by rampant inflation, growing unemployment, a desperate need for hard currency, an industrial complex struggling to survive, tenuous relationships between the "space" governments, various internal and external sources of instability, and, at least in Russia, a government increasingly unable to govern.

SPACE PROGRAM IN TRANSITION

That the continued viability of the space program is important to the Commonwealth of Independent States (CIS) is beyond question: the very first agreement among the successor states, signed even before the Soviet Union dissolved, concerned the space program. The agreement established a CIS Space Agency, the efficacy of which is subject to question, as the three major space republics have each set up their own separate agencies. The agreement also committed the signatories to "retain and develop" the rocket technology infrastructure, the viability of which would benefit the beleaguered industrial sector significantly.[33]

Moreover, it has been said that "for a country, a viable space program is a source of pride and prestige,"[34] and clearly this is as true for the former Soviet republics as it was for the Soviet Union. With little else to be proud of, this dimension takes on even added weight. *The Washington Post* reports, "A sense [in Russia] that only its nuclear and space technologies separate it from Third World status"[35] and that there "is a growing anxiety about Russia's perceived loss of superpower status." All these factors combine to reflect what Marcia Smith, a veteran Soviet space program analyst with the Congressional Research Service, calls a "strong desire to keep everything going."[36]

As previously observed, the Soviet space program was dominated by the military, and according to *Aviation Week and Space Technology*, "the outlook is for the military to continue dominating Russian space operations."[37] However, the Russian military appears to be nearing complete shambles: navy recruits have recently starved to death, ships rarely steam, fighter pilots rarely fly, and the military leadership apparently had great difficult rounding up enough sufficiently competent troops to send a 3,000-man peacekeeping force to a rebellious region.[38] Given the strategic importance of space assets and the legacy Russians surely inherited from the Soviets on integration of space capability into warfighting strategy and doctrine, it is clear that military space projects will remain near the top of the Russian priority list for funding. That such funding will be a paltry fraction of what is was in the heyday of the space program almost goes without saying. Recently, Kuptev himself said, "Russian space activities are going through a very difficult time. These difficulties are primarily due to a significant cutback in military procurement."[39]

Thus, the previously lavish funding for the space program has "virtually been cut off." The effects of the cut-off have been severe and horror stories abound: ground controllers in Moscow protested low salaries with a strike; low salaries and inhuman working conditions prompted military conscripts at the Baikonur Cosmodrome to riot; a satellite plant was told it would be given no more metal unless it provided timber in return; ground stations have charged other elements of the same program for services; prices charged for components manufactured in other republics have gone up 30 to 50 times; and "astrophysicists earn less than bus drivers."[40]

Given the stated intention to keep the whole space program alive and the military's vested interest in seeing that happen, where is the money going to come from? The Russian scheme: "Break into the world market for space technology. . . . The focus of the fundraising will be Western countries, especially the U.S."[41]

ENTERING THE INTERNATIONAL SPACE MARKET

Unlike the half-heartedness of the Soviets' efforts, the space program is now attempting to break into the world space market with zeal. *Aviation Week and Space Technology* says Yeltsin "appears ready to cut any and every deal on space that he can."[42] *Time* Magazine reports "virtually every branch of the space infrastructure, once financed by the Soviet military, has trade representatives in the U.S."[43] Apparently, everything is for sale—even "once highly classified programs are up for grabs,"[44] which continues the tradition started by the Soviets with their Satellite Control Center leasing scheme. The Russians have gone their predecessors one better, however—they are now even peddling once ultrasecret spy photographs taken by their most powerful spy satellites to satisfy their insatiable appetite for hard currency.[45] According to one source, "One general rule seems to be emerging: Money talks, and Western currency talks loudest of all."[46] Although they "are seeking to sell their products to anyone with hard currency,"[47] the Russians believe that "America—and to a limited extent, the West—has streets that are paved with gold"[48] and that we can hardly wait to snap up the space technology of which they are so proud.[49]

Unfortunately, there seems to be very little room in the international space market, particularly in the already oversupplied area of launch vehicles and services. There are only 30-35 commercial launches per year—despite projections of a short-lived surge in commercial launches in 1994-1995, even winning every contract would hardly be enough to sustain an industry with a demonstrated annual launch capacity in excess of 100 launches. And, as was previously observed, launch services are where the Russians have a clear-cut advantage. Similar advantage is less apparent in other endeavors, where the market is often quite small.[50]

Those Western companies that have signed up to deals have sometimes encountered rather bizarre problems. For example, Motorola apparently signed a contract with Krunichev Enterprise in Moscow to launch Motorola's planned iridium communications satellite constellation on Proton rockets built by Krunichev. However, KB Salyut, another space enterprise that designed the rocket, claims it owns the engineering specifications for the Proton and anyone wanting to purchase one has to deal with them. KB Salyut says the Motorola-Krunichev deal is invalid and that no Proton can leave the plant without its blessing. Russian law does not address how to determine who owns the rights to the rocket—it was never important before. Meanwhile, hapless Motorola is caught in the middle, and as *Space News* puts it, "this kind of dispute threatens to scare away prospective bidders for Proton launch services."[51]

An additional impediment to marketing the space program in the West is pricing. For example, as the result of an agreement between Yeltsin and President Bush, the Russians were allowed to bid on the launch of a U.S.-built INMARSAT satellite. The cost to launch the satellite on a Western booster is about $62 million. The bid from KB Salyut through the Russian Space Agency was $36 million, a price that Krunichev protested as *absurdly high*. Krunichev claims to track costs accurately and that they are considerably lower, which may indeed by true because of very low labor costs. It seems more probably that most Russian enterprises would have no way to accurately calculate costs, which would hardly be surprising in a country that used to measure electronics production by weight. But actual cost is not the issue—hard currency is. Any hard currency income is essentially pure profit because it is cash that would not otherwise be generated. In fact, the Mir space station project is now funded largely by selling "rides" to guest astronauts from foreign countries for about $15 million.[52]

The difficulty that pricing causes is that by selling launch services (or any other space product or service) at cut rates—whether or not those rates reflect real costs—the Russians threaten the very survival of Western space industries.[53] Thus, in the interest of preserving these space industries, Western governments are unlikely to permit unbridled competition from former Soviet republics. Indeed, the U.S. response to all the Russian marketing efforts has been somewhat cool—U.S. companies and the U.S. Government tend to be interested in specific technology projects and pieces of hardware rather than large undertakings involving complete systems, the Motorola deal being a notable exception. This has become a source of exasperation to the Russians, who cannot understand why we are not buying their "wonderful stuff."[54] After recently visiting Moscow, Nicholas Johnson described the situation: "They were willing to sell anything that wasn't tied down. It's a lot like a flea market—there's a lot of junk, a lesser number of items that are a real bargain, and even fewer things that you really need."[55]

Not everyone agrees that the former Soviet space program is so desperate. After all, the program managed at least 47 launches in 1992 (again, more than the rest of the world combined), no programs have been cancelled, and the United States has recently shown interest in the Energia heavy lifter to boost the NASA space station into orbit. However, the number of 1992 launches (still anemic by Soviet standards) may reflect use of leftover inventory more than it does the health of the program, and it would appear that "cancellation"—or lack thereof—has a different connotation in the former Soviet space program than it does in the U.S. aerospace industry. Moreover, resuscitation of Energia is hardly enough to reverse the declining fortunes of the program, references to which are common in the literature. For example, a February 1993 *Aviation Week and Space Technology* article reported serious rifts between high-ranking military and civilian space officials, largely over economic issues. Thus, the former Soviet space program is in dire straits and its curators are willing to "cut any deal," as someone else said, that will bring in hard cash—with, as shown below, little regard for the source.[56]

WHERE TO TURN

Clearly, the former Soviet "space republics" need much more hard currency to keep their space industry afloat than they are likely to earn in America. Where else can they go? Not to Europe or Japan, who are just as likely as the United States to balk at the pricing problems, legal uncertainties, shaky political relationships, and decaying infrastructure (like Baikonur) associated with the former Soviet Union space program. The only other place to turn is to the Third World, where the appeal of thrift can overcome these kinds of disincentives. Herein lies the danger—and the most significant impact on the U.S. military space program. There are those who will scoff at this notion, but as has been shown, the survival of the former Soviet space program is at stake. Judging from the herculean efforts already displayed by the Russians to hawk their wares, why should we think they will simply fold up shop when Western countries do not sign up?

Koptev's threat seems a strong indication that the Russians, at least, have no intention of giving up. Whether this was "a slip into Soviet-style bluster"[57] makes little difference. Actions speak louder than words. The Russians have made a deal to sell advanced liquid-fuel rocket engine technology to India's Space Agency in blatant violation of the Missile Technology Control Regime (MTCR), which is an international agreement designed to prevent the proliferation of ballistic missile technology (rocket engine technology applies equally to ballistic missiles and space boosters). State Department sanctions against the offending enterprise and continuous diplomatic pressure have had no effect—the deputy director of the Russian Space Agency was recently quoted as saying, "Our position is completely clear: we are cooperating with India and will continue to cooperate," and Yeltsin lent his support to the arrangement as well.[58] Even if the Russian government, such as it is, were inclined to stop such deals, its capacity to do so is questionable.

A truly devout optimist might posit a dramatic turn of events: the Russians will see the light, embrace principle over hard currency, and develop airtight control mechanisms to somehow spare themselves the embarrassment of having to sell their space products, services, and technology to the Third World just to make ends meet. Such an unlikely turn of events would only hasten what is clearly inevitable. The former Soviet space program is doomed to shrink. One projection takes it to a level of employing a mere 100,000 to 200,000 people.[59] Ironically, even this would have little impact on the proliferation of Soviet-developed space technology to the Third World.

The reason is captured in a simple question: Where will all the rocket scientists work? As it is, they earn only a few hundred dollars per year. Displaced engineers are having to take menial jobs. It hardly seems risky to predict that many of these technically skilled people will be willing and available to work for anyone willing to hire them. Consider that before the Gulf War Saddam Hussein hired a group of Brazilian scientists for $6,500 *per month* each to develop an Iraqi copy of the Sidewinder air-to-air missile.[60]

Space experts would surely command at least as much, as it would be difficult indeed for someone like a Russian engineer making the equivalent of $10 or $20 per month not to be tempted by such a relatively astronomical offer. Russia's dysfunctional government would be hard pressed to control the emigration of such people.

So, whether it is through fire sales on extant systems and services or through hiring the "know how," Third World countries now have access to Soviet-developed space technology at prices well within their financial reach. This access is a direct result of the Soviet Union's demise. Recall that until that demise essentially had become a foregone conclusion, the Soviets had only token interest in selling their space wares. And they certainly did not have today's pressure to generate cash at virtually any price.

A logical questions at this point is, "So what happens if Third World countries have access to former Soviet space technology?" The answer requires a short digression on the military advantages that accrue from space assets.

THE IMPORTANCE OF SPACE ASSETS IN MODERN WARFARE

The explicit mention of space in the new Air Force mission statement reflects a growing awareness of the vital contribution made to the nation's defense by space: *Defend the United States through control and exploitation of air and space.*[61]

Many visionary thinkers have long grasped this notion. But, it is only recent military operations such as Operation *Desert Storm* that have made common knowledge—even within the U.S. military—of the tremendous leverage and force multiplying value of space systems.[62] Noted author Arthur C. Clarke even went so far as to describe *Desert Storm* as "the world's first satellite war,"[63] but the use of space systems to support ground combat actually dates at least to the Vietnam War.[64]

The military advantages of space accrue primarily from the fact that satellites enjoy global access—unimpeded, that is, from the standpoint of legal, political, or sovereignty considerations (there are numerous constraints that derive from the laws of physics). The most obvious of these advantages is observation. Satellites provide a "God's eye" view of the earth. One need not be a military expert to understand the tremendous advantage of being able to observe one's enemy. Reconnaissance from space in support of ground combat is "the foremost example of the impact of the space age on modern warfare," notes Nicholas Johnson.[65] A related advantage is surveillance—using appropriate sensors and orbits, satellites can provide timely notification of such things as missile launches and nuclear detonations. A second very important so-called "force enhancement" capability is communications. With communications satellites, it is possible, in short order, to establish communications between any two points on the globe. The only alternatives are to rely on the unwieldy and unpredictable bouncing of radio waves off the atmosphere or on some combination of landlines, submarine cables, and microwave relays. Again, the layman can easily appreciate the military value of quickly establishing clear and secure communications from the theater of operations to the national command authorities as well as between theater headquarters and subordinate units. In fast moving modern warfare, effectiveness of this so-called "command, control, and communications network" can be the difference between victory and defeat. According to General Colin Powell, Chairman of the Joint Chiefs of Staff, "Satellites were the single most important factor that enabled us to build (that network)" for *Desert Storm*. All communication into and out of the theater was via satellites, as was up to 85 percent of the communication within the theater. As much as 20 percent of this traffic used commercial satellites, which constitute the fastest growing category of civilian satellites.[66]

A third important force enhancement capability is navigation. No one would question the importance of knowing one's location during combat. Besides being limited to two-dimensional information, terrestrially based navigation systems such as LORAN suffer from inaccuracy and spotty global coverage. The United States had partially fielded the Global Positioning System (GPS) constellation of navigation satellites at the time of *Desert Storm*. Its extremely accurate three-dimensional information was so valuable to troops on the ground that it was not uncommon for them to overcome the shortage of receivers by taking up a collection among them to purchase additional receiving units through commercial channels.[67] The military significance of being able to determine location within a matter of meters encompasses the spectrum from cooks being able to rendezvous with troops in the field to aircraft finding their targets at night and in bad weather.

The subject of weather leads to a fourth important force enhancement capability. To say that meteorological information is vital to successful military operations is an understatement. Admiral Halsey's ill-fated encounter with a typhoon during World War II and the critical impact of weather on the timing of the Normandy invasion are but two cases in point.[68] It is virtually impossible to duplicate the timeliness and comprehensiveness of satellite-derived weather information with strictly ground based systems. Lieutenant General Thomas S. Moorman, commander of Air Force Space Command during *Desert Storm*, noted that during that conflict, "understanding the vagaries of weather became crucial to air operations" as aircraft weapons loads were optimized for weather conditions over the target.[69]

Finally, "earth sensing" is emerging as one of the most critical space-based force enhancement capabilities. Actually just another form of observation using alternative sensors, it was originally undertaken for scientific purposes. It encompasses a variety of activities ranging from measuring the earth's shape and magnetic field (which impact the accuracy of ballistic missiles) to monitoring deforestation and the health of crops (a capability that also allows camouflage to be differentiated from real vegetation). The U.S. Landsat and French SPOT are two examples of such satellite systems whose products are available to the general public as well as the military. The United States made extensive use of these "multispectral" imaging systems for purposes ranging from targeting to mapping during *Desert Storm*.[70] General Charles A. Horner, who was the Joint Force Air Component Commander in *Desert Storm* and now commands both the U.S. Space Command and the Air Force Space Command, said "the accuracy of SPOT satellite imagery was an invaluable asset to the offensive air campaign."[71]

When all of these space-based force enhancement capabilities are properly integrated into military planning and operations, their impact can be decisive. As General Moorman observed about *Desert Storm*, "For the first time, space systems were an integral part of terrestrial conflict and were crucial to its outcome."[72] This lesson was not lost on the rest of the world.[73]

THE PROLIFERATION OF MILITARY SPACE CAPABILITY

In March 1991, Israeli Defense Minister Moshe Arens stated, "Nobody should be surprised if one day, without anything to do with the Gulf Crisis, we also sent into space a satellite with an intelligence capability."[74] Mr. Arens' threat was not an idle one. Israel has put two satellites into orbit, at least one of which was a retrograde launch (against the direction of the earth's rotation), which is no easy feat. So, it is not a question of when space systems will proliferate to other countries. That process has long been underway. In 1993, 14 nations had their own communications satellites, and five more had definitive plans for them. India has significant space capabilities and planned to spend $190 million in 1993 on its space program. China's considerable accomplishments in space are well documented. It entered the commercial launch market with its Long March booster. Brazil, Pakistan, Indonesia, Taiwan, and South Africa have space programs as well. Simply put, it is widely recognized that space offers economic leverage to any nation with the means to pursue it.[75]

What the Gulf War has done is spotlight the associated security leverage of space systems and thereby kindle new interest in acquiring militarily useful space capabilities. The United Arab Emirates recently asked to buy a spy satellite from the United States. South Korea and Spain have expressed similar interests. The other Europeans' interest in satellites for military purposes has also been piqued.[76]

Those skeptical that Third World countries would enter the military space arena should bear in mind that proliferation of military space capabilities does not require dedicated military satellites. All of the force enhancement capabilities explained earlier can be purchased today on the open market. For example, Iraq used commercially available satellite photography extensively in its war with Iran and was trying to do the same after it invaded Kuwait, only the UN trade embargo stymied the effort.[77] Perhaps in anticipation of such difficulties, Iraq launched a rocket in 1989 that it claimed was a space launch, although no satellite was orbited.[78] Fortunately, nothing came of it, for as one analyst put it, "The grand deception carried out by coalition forces in the recent Persian Gulf War would have been greatly complicated, if not made impossible, had Iraq possessed timely data from observation satellites."[79]

As previously noted, earth sensing satellites have military utility, and thankfully, the French limited SPOT sales during the war strictly to allies.   Ironically, EOSAT—which markets images from the less capable U.S. Landsat system—remained legally bound to openly sell Landsat imagery and was doing so as late as mid-February 1991. Whether any of the imagery fell into Iraqi hands may never be known, but Iraq did have access to U.S. weather satellite imagery throughout the war because the responsible agency feared blacking out the signal might cause a backlash from friendly countries also affected. The military utility of weather information can also show troop dispositions. An Englishman using homemade equipment during the war to download imagery from the European Space Agency's Meteosat 4 satellite found he could discern concentrations of troops.[80]

Hence, the genie is out of the bottle and it is impossible to put it back in.[81]   But any country with designs on incorporating space capabilities into its military posture would be foolhardy to rely on commercial systems or systems owned by other countries because access to those can always be denied.   Conversely, an indigenous capability to design, build, launch, and operate military space systems has been, up to now, prohibitively expensive to all but a few countries.

The state of affairs in the former Soviet space program clearly changes this picture in a number of ways worth recounting:

• Anything and everything is for sale at bargain prices
• The space republics' governments (particularly Russia's) have dubious ability to control either these sales

or the emigration of rocket scientists who can be hired for a relative pittance

•   The former Soviet technology results in rugged, relatively simple yet capable equipment suitable for operation by underdeveloped countries

•   As the failure of the MTCR to stop the transfer of rocket technology to India shows, international controls on arms and technology transfers are ineffective in stopping this technology hemorrhage.

IMPACT ON THE U.S. MILITARY SPACE PROGRAM

As with all other aspects of our military force structure, our space force structure must be grounded in the National Security Strategy:

> We have four mutually supportive goals that guide our overall national security efforts. . . . (Among them is) ensuring that no hostile power is able to dominate or control a region critical to our interests.[82]

and the supporting National Military Strategy:

> The threat is instability and being unprepared to handle a crisis or war that no one predicted or expected. . . . It is certain that U.S. military forces will be called upon again, but predicting the time, place, and circumstances will be difficult. . . . As the only nation with military capability to influence events globally, we must remain capable of responding effectively.[83]

What is clear from the excerpts above is that these strategies no longer focus on a specific threat as their predecessors focused on the Soviets.   Unspecified, unpredictable "regional threats" are the adversaries which we must be capable of victoriously employing military forces against.

To the many who dream of "de-militarizing" space, this shift of threats means "an opportune time to signal a change of emphasis from military to civil space activity is right now," as one writer suggested when the Soviet bloc began to crumble. To others such as members of the U.S. Congress, the problem is economically driven. The 1993 Defense Authorization Bill mandates a 15-percent cut in the military space budget. The Senate proposed an even larger 25-percent cut.[84] After all, if we were in a "space race" against the Soviets and they dropped out, it only seems logical to stop wasting money on sending military systems into space, which by international treaty is supposed to be used only for peaceful purposes anyway. This leads to two conclusions which fly in the face of both of these understandable but misguided reactions:

First, there is no "peace dividend" in space. Contrary to the implication of all the "space race" rhetoric over the years, our military activities in space after the initial flap over Sputnik were not really driven by the Soviet military space program,[85] with one exception—the Soviet anti-satellite or ASAT program. In other words unlike terrestrial forces, our space forces were not "sized" to counter or match similar Soviet space forces. Rather, the assets we placed in space were there for the kinds of force enhancement purposes discussed earlier, all of which were first pursued by the United States rather that the Soviets.[86] Thus, a decline in space activity, per se, on the part of the former Soviet Union should have no bearing on our own military space program.

However, it might seem logical to suggest that since our space systems largely support our terrestrial forces, a reduced terrestrial threat should translate to a reduced number of space-based systems to enhance those forces. This is also incorrect. The space force structure is driven far more by the functions space systems perform than by the size of any potential threat. For example, physics determines the number of satellites in a constellation required to continuously observe the surface of the earth at a given altitude. Similarly, the number of satellites needed for global tactical weather support is independent of the size and number of potential adversaries. On the other hand, to the extent that the previous national strategy may have resulted in surveillance and reconnaissance satellite constellations optimized to observe the territory of the Soviet Union, the new strategy's focus on unspecified regional threats around the globe may actually argue for more such satellites on orbit.

In the case of military communications satellites, however, an argument could be made that the demise of the Soviet Union means fewer are needed. Such an argument would be thinly based on the idea that a smaller terrestrial force structure should require fewer communications channels. But experience does not support this thesis. The fact that augmenting commercial capacity had to be acquired during *Desert Storm* reinforces General Moorman's observation on the subject: "Communications capacity and channel availability have historically been shortfalls in conflict."[87] Space-based assets offer the only practical solution to rapidly establishing communications between far flung corners of the world—precisely the problem our forces are likely to face. Command, control, and communications are so vital to modern warfare that it is clearly a false economy to try to shortchange assets like communications satellites.

Only in the context of nuclear warfighting can a case be made for scaling back our space force posture as a result of the demise of the Soviet military threat. Most observers agree with the statement in the National Security Strategy that says "the threat of thermonuclear war has been radically reduced."[88] Accordingly, the need for communications satellites that can survive a nuclear attack—which can cost as much as a billion dollars each—diminishes as the threat of all-out nuclear war subsides. The Air Force has recognized this fact by scaling down the incorporation of such survivability features into the new MILSTAR satellite program and placing more tactically oriented capabilities on the space vehicle.[89]

Thus, contrary to intuition, neither reduced military space activity by the former Soviet Union space republics nor a reduced military threat from former Soviet Union states in the aftermath of the Soviet Union's demise argue for any significant reductions in U.S. space force structure. If anything, the new strategy's requirement to deal with threats that may appear anywhere on the globe at any time would mitigate for a more robust space-based force enhancement capabilities. Hence, logic that suggests a "peace dividend" in space analogous to that realizable for terrestrial forces does not withstand scrutiny.

But, yet to be addressed are the far more severe implications of the principal consequence of the Soviet space program's demise—namely accelerated proliferation of space technology, which leads to the second major conclusion.

Second, it is time to get serious about space control. As a result of the Soviet Union's demise and the economic woes left in its wake, even countries with modest means are in a position to avail themselves of space technology from the former Soviet Union, either in the form of actual systems and/or services, or in the form of expertise. It must be assumed that within that group of countries are some or all of the unspecified potential adversaries that our military strategy identifies as our principal threat.

Largely as a result of the critical role played by space systems in *Desert Storm* there is a growing realization in the world of the tremendous military leverage systems offer. Again, it must be assumed that our potential adversaries are party to this revelation. It follows, then, that we must prepare for the likelihood that, unlike Iraq in *Desert Storm*, our adversaries in future conflicts will employ against us the military advantages of space systems upon which the success of our own forces has become so dependent.

The more budget cuts shrink our combat forces while our strategy calls for prevailing over globally dispersed threats, the greater becomes our already considerable dependence on space-based systems—possibly bringing it to the point of becoming what Clausewitz defined as a center of gravity—"the hub of all power and movement, on which everything depends."[90] One need only ponder for a moment the consequences of losing some or all of our space-based communications, observation, navigation and meteorological capabilities to realize the value to an enemy of eliminating or neutralizing those systems. On the other side of the coin, however, lies the fact that eliminating or neutralizing an enemy's space-based force enhancement capabilities would be of great value to us. The obvious thing to do in the event of hostilities is to deny the enemy the benefits of space-based systems while preserving our own.

The mission area concerned with this double-edged problem of space control has long been recognized as a necessary tenet of military space doctrine. Serious efforts to control access to space date at least to the U.S. deployment, in the 1960s, of a nuclear-tipped ASAT system as a defense against a Soviet fractional orbit bombardment system. In 1968, the Soviets first tested a co-orbital ASAT system capable of destroying satellites in orbits as high as 5,000 kilometers (the system's current utility is subject to debate). In response, the United States attempted, in the mid-1980s, to field a more technologically advanced system with comparable capabilities. That system was cancelled by Congress after becoming bogged down in debates ranging from who depended more on space to the idealistic anathema of crossing the "Rubicon of active weapons in space." Often emotional, the arguments against deployment of the system varied between this latter idealistic vein and the arcane application of arms control and nuclear deterrence theories to the dual premise that U.S. interference with Soviet satellites would somehow be destabilizing while Soviet attacks on U.S. satellites with their ASAT would be harmless.[91]

Throughout the Cold War, many forward thinking writers argued and pleaded for pursuit of the space control mission area.[92] There was recognition of the need at the highest levels: the National Security Strategy of 1987 called for "unimpeded U.S. access to the oceans and space."[93] In 1989, General Piotrowski published a list of six major initiatives that should be pursued to overcome space control deficiencies that he attributed to "an attitude which persists in the U.S. . . . which seems to reject the military utility and necessity of space operations."[94] Yet, despite the valiant attempts of these and many other space-conscious strategic thinkers to prevent the emerging center of gravity represented by our space force structure from becoming a potentially fatal vulnerability, and despite the new Air Force mission statement's explicit mandate to control space, it is not clear that very much has been done to seriously pursue space control capabilities.

We must leave behind the Cold War mentality and revisit the space control issue if we are to fulfill the mandate of the new Air Force mission statement. What matters today is that we are required by our strategy to be capable of engaging in conventional warfare against a multiplicity of threats potentially equipped with space-based force enhancement capabilities. Arguments about who would depend more on space systems or whether, in the interest of preserving the sanctity of space, potential foes would refrain from attacking our space systems are completely moot. Try to imagine Saddam Hussein pondering these kind of thoughts. Through blatant violations of the Nuclear Non-Proliferation Treaty, Iraq and North Korea have both shown that determined nations consider themselves to be unconstrained even by arms control agreements to which they are a party, let alone esoteric arguments over the "militarization" of space. If one of these types of "regional threats" becomes our enemy, the control of space could be a critical if not decisive factor in determining the outcome of the conflict.

There are two key facets of achieving space control—the first is invulnerability to space countermeasures. It is not always necessary to attack the space segment of a force enhancement system to temporarily or permanently deny its use to its owner. A terrorist attack on a satellite ground station somewhere in the world could just as easily deny or inhibit the use of a satellite system. Similar countermeasures run the gamut from camouflage, concealment and deception (CCD), to "spoofing" a satellite's command signals, to electronically jamming a satellite's transmissions. With the availability of "know how" from the former Soviet Union, all of these are now potentially (if not actually)[95] within the means of our potential regional adversaries. Even a crude ASAT in the hands of a regional power is conceivable. After all, it was not that long after Sputnik that the Soviets developed their ASAT. It stands to reason that measures to neutralize space countermeasures would be kept secret to preserve their effectiveness, so it is impossible to glean from the public record everything that might be underway to reduce our vulnerabilities.

What can be said is that because execution of our military strategy has become so reliant on space systems, the ability to retain the use and benefits of those systems must be vigorously pursued. One initiative appearing to need serious attention is replacement of overseas ground stations with relay satellites. Another is to once and for all solve the problem of access to space. The well documented deficiencies in our launch vehicle force structure severely inhibit our ability to replace satellites that are disabled either by deliberate attack or by chance.[96]

The second facet of space control is to acquire the means to negate the space capabilities that our future adversaries might employ against us. Obviously, we have the capability to attack ground stations and one would presume that we have pursued means of jamming and spoofing satellites. However, it is not clear to this writer, for example, that CCD in the context of a regional enemy with access to space systems has received adequate emphasis in the doctrine and training of our combat forces. Further, *Desert Storm* suggests that there is some work to be done regarding denial of information from friendly space systems to an enemy. And, notwithstanding all of the emotional arguments on both sides of the ASAT issue, the fact remains that we have no ASAT with which to negate the space segment of an enemy's space system should all other means fail. As General Moorman put it, "An operational ASAT designed to eliminate an adversary's space capabilities must be considered an integral part of this country's force structure."[97]

The old paradigm that abhors this so-called "militarization" of space has transcended the innocence of naivete'. Such thinking truly endangers our national security in the post-Soviet environment of rapid space technology proliferation. Space was "militarized" long ago. Even civil systems have tremendous military utility and there is nothing in the Outer Space Treaty that prohibits conducting the kind of force enhancement activities that have been discussed.[98] A far more significant concern for the nation should be the danger that our space force posture will be driven by arbitrary budget cuts rather than sound analysis of national and military strategy in the contest of the evolving world environment.

GREGORY A. KEETHLER

SUMMARY

In sum, the perilous economic situation in the Soviet Union's aftermath has put its once proud space program in dire straits, prompting a desperate attempt to keep the program whole via entry into the Western commercial space market. With little potential for this market to sustain the former Soviet Union program intact, selling space products, services and technology to the developing world is the only alternative. Even if so inclined, the space republics have little ability to control either the hemorrhage of space technology to the Third World or the inevitable "brain drain" of former Soviet scientists. The result is an unavoidable acceleration of the proliferation of space technology to nations in the Third World, who—like all nations—have been awakened by *Desert Storm* to the tremendous military advantages that accrue from space.

What the Gulf War also exposed is how much we have come to depend on space systems. As the budget shrinks our combat forces, this dependence begins to take on the character of a center of gravity. Thus, contrary to intuition, the Soviets' demise yields no peace dividends in space. We must maintain and improve our existing space force structure to support our strategy of defending U.S. interests against unspecified regional threats that are globally dispersed. Moreover, as space technology proliferates to these potential threats, we become subject to employment of space-based force enhancement assets. During a conflict, either could render a crippling blow. If both occurred together, the result could be devastating. Accelerated proliferation of space force enhancement assets is the most significant impact of the Soviet Union's demise on the U.S. military space program. Therefore, it is imperative for the United States to vigorously pursue any and all technologies that will provide the capability for space control, both in the sense of preventing an enemy from denying us the use of our space assets and in the sense of denying him the use of his own space-based force enhancement assets.

NOTES

1.   Quoted in Alasdair McLean, "The Military Use of Space," *Centerpiece* 19, Aberdeen, Scotland, Centre for Defense Studies (Summer 1991):5.

2.   Nicholas L. Johnson, *Soviet Military Strategy in Space* (New York: Jane's Publishing, Inc., 1987), 20; McLean, 4.

3.   Marcia S. Smith, *Space Activities of the United States and Other Launching Countries/Organizations: 1957-1991,* CRS Report for Congress No. 92-427 SPR (Washington, DC: The Library of Congress, CRS, 11 May 1992), 82.

4.   Ibid., 91.

5.   Michael D. Lemonick, "Space Programs for Sale," *Time*, 16 March 1992, 54; statement of Ronald Sagdeev to the American Astronautical Society, paraphrased in Leonard David, "Boosters versus Bread Lines, *Ad Astra*, July/August 1992, 6.

6.   Tom Cremins and Elizabeth Newton, "Changing Structure of the Soviet Space Programme," *Space Policy*, May 1991, 129; Craig Covault, "Russians/CIS Space Outlook Chaotic But Critical to Global Planning," *Aviation Week and Space Technology*, 16 March 1992, 125.

7.   Vice President's Space Policy Advisory Board, *The Future of the U.S. Space Industrial Base—A Task Group Report* (Washington, DC: The White House, November 1992), 20; Marcia S. Smith, *Prospects for the Post Soviet Space Program*, CRS Report 92-123 SPR (Washington, DC: Library of Congress, CRS, 1992), 4; John L. Piotrowski, "A Critical Juncture," *The Officer*, September 1989, 20, 21; Smith, *Space Activities*, 12; Lemonick, 55; Cremins, 129-130; Sagdeev, 6; Nicholas L. Johnson, *Soviet Military Strategy in Space* (New York: Jane's Publishing, Inc., 1987), 48.

8.   Johnson, 49-50.

9.   Piotrowski, 21.

10. Johnson, 85.

11. Ibid., 191.

12. Secretary Aldridge: "Space is viewed by the Soviets as a 'no holds barred' environment and they view 'space power' as essential to ultimate military victory and the subsequent success of the USSR" (quoted in Johnson, 159). Secretary Weinberger: "The Kremlin appears to have focused its space effort to support and conduct combat operations" (quoted in Piotrowski, 22).

13. Military Forces in Transition (Washington, DC: DOD, 1991), 42.

14. Sagdeev, 6.

15. Cremins, 135.

16. Ibid., 129; Rich Vera, "Soviet Space Saver," *New Scientist,* 14 March 1992, 13.

17. Cremins, 130.

18. Craig Covault, "Soviet Military Space Center Offered for Commercial Lease," *Aviation Week and Space Technology,* 16 September 1991, 28.

19. Smith, *Prospects for Space Program,* 3-4.

20. Johnson, 79-82.

21. Tom Brokaw, NBC Nightly News, 29 March 1993.

22. Dimitri Simes, "What Clinton Must Do To Aid Democracy in Russia," *The Washington Post National Weekly Edition,* 8-14 February 1993, 24.

23. "Gloom, not Doom," *The Economist,* 28 November 1992, 16.

24. Sergei Kruschev, "Capitalism and Chaos: Russia's Next Implosion," *The Washington Post,* 16 August 1992, C7; Steve Coll and Michael Dobbs, "From Russia With Cash," *The Washington Post National Weekly Edition,* 15-21 February 1993, 6; Peter A. Fischer, quoted in Fred Hiatt, "Bailing Out Russia," *The Washington Post National Weekly Edition,* 15-21 March 1993, 8, 9; Fred Coleman, et al., "Deja Vu All Over Again," *U.S. News and World Report,* 8 March 1993, 39; Douglas Stanglin and Victoria Pope, et. al., "The Wreck of Russia," *U.S. News and World Report,* 7 December 1992, 40, and "Two Cheers for Demokratiya," *U.S. News and World Report,* 5 April 1993, 46; Tamara Sineshikova, Intourist guide for author's visit to Moscow September 1992.

25. Julie Corwin and Jeff Trimble, "Russia's Swords and Plowshares," *U.S. News and World Report,* 18 January 1993, 54, 55; sales in 1992 were 70 percent below those of the Soviet Union

before its collapse, according to Gennady Yampolsky, Dep. Chairman of the State Committee on the Military-Industrial Complex, paraphrased in "Russian Arms Trade," *The Washington Post*, 23 February 1993, A4; Craig Covault, "Russians Forge Space Pact, But Military Transition Chaotic," *Aviation Week and Space Technology*, 13 January 1992, 20; Sagdeev, 6; Keith Bradsher, "Russia Loans Being Delayed By Bureaucracy and Anxiety," *The New York Times International Edition*, 28 September 1992, A7; "Mass Appeal,: *The Economist*, 29 August 1992, 16; Keith Bush, "An Overview of the Russian Economy," *RE/R Research Report*, 1:25, 19 June 1992, 51; Jeffrey D. Sachs, "It's Time for the West to Put Up," *The Washington Post National Weekly Edition*, 5-11 April 1993, 24.

26. CNN, *Headline News*, 20 January 1993, 4:30 pm; Stanglin, 44.

27. Sergei Zhdakayev, "A Job No Longer Lasts Forever," Isvestia, in *World Press Review*, November 1992, 11-12.

28. Coll, 6-7.

29. Steve Coll and Michael Dobbs, "The Free Market's Ugly Face," *The Washington Post National Weekly Edition*, 1-7 March 1993, 10.

30. Chrystia Freeland, "Ukraine Facing Economic Shifts," *The Washington Post*, 1 January 1993, A23; Simon Johnson and Oleg Ustenko, "Ukraine on the Brink of Hyperinflation," *RE/R Research Report* 1:50, 18 December 1992, 52.

31. Freeland, A23; Covault, "Russian/CIS Space Outlook," 125, and "Russians Rejuvenate Military Space Assets," *Aviation Week and Space Technology*, 4 January 1993, 54; Adrian Karatnycky, "The Ukrainian Factor," *Foreign Affairs* (Summer 1992): 90-107, reprinted in *International Security Studies—WS 635: Book 1* (Maxwell AFB, AL: Air War College, 1993), 66, 68.

32. All the information in the paragraph up to the point of this note is from Victoria Pope, "Back to Future in Central Asia," *U.S. News and World Report*, 8 March 93, 42-44; Covault, "Russian/CIS Space Outlook," and "Russians Locked in Struggle for Space Program Control," *Aviation Week and Space Technology*, 1 February 1993, 57; "Baikonur Gets Bad Publicity," *Space News*, 16-22 November 1992, 1.

33. Covault, "Russians Force Space Pact," 20, and "Russian/CIS Space Outlook," 125; Smith, *Prospects for Post Soviet Space*, 6.

34. Cremins and Newton, 129.

35. Fred Hiatt, "Russians Favoring Retention of Nuclear Weapons," *The Washington Post*, 25 November 1992, A1.

36. Marcia S. Smith, interview "Newsmaker Forum," *Space News*, 23-24 November 1992, 22.

37. Covault, "Russian/CIS Space Outlook," 125.

38. Fred Hiatt, "If Yeltsin Falls, Will the Cold War Rise From the Ashes?" *The Washington Post National Weekly Edition*, 29 March-4 April 1993, 16; Bruce B. Auster, et al., "The Armed Forces: How They Line Up," *U.S. News and World Report*, 5 April 1993, 48.

39. Bruce A. Smith, "Russians May Boost Civil Space Funding," *Aviation Week and Space Technology*, 14/21 December 1992, 54.

40. Vera, 13; Lemonick, 55; Covault, "Russians Locked," 57, and "Russia Seeks Joint Space Test to Build Military Cooperation," *Aviation Week and Space Technology*, 1 February 1993, 18; Michael Dornheim, "France and Germany Will Help Fund Russian Mars 1994 Space Mission," *Aviation Week and Space Technology*, 25 May 1992, 79; Peter Aldhous, "Russian Space Science Limps On," *Science* 256 (12 June 1992): 1508.

41. Vera, 13.

42. James R. Asker, "U.S., Russian Space Pact Pledges Unprecedented Trade, Joint Flights," *Aviation Week and Space Technology*, 22 June 1992, 24.

43. Lemonick, 55.

44. Cremins and Newton, 131.

45. William J. Broad, "Russia is Now Selling Spy Photos from Space," *The New York Times*, 4 October 1992, 10; Daniel J. Marcus, "Firms Stretch Dollars in Russia," *Space News*, 23-29 November 1992, 4.

46. Aldous, 1509.

47. Carole A. Shifrin, "Geopolitical Changes Spark New Strategies," *Aviation Week and Space Technology*, 7 September 1992, 54.

48. Smith, interview, 22.

49. Marcia S. Smith, *Russian/U.S. Space Interaction: A Trip Report with Observations and Options*, CRS Report 92-774 SPR (Washington, DC: Library of Congress, CRS, 1992), 2.

50. Peter B. de Selding, "Low-Cost Proton Purchase Confirms Competitor's Fears," *Space News*, 16-22 November 1992, 29.

51. All information on Krunichev-Motorola contract taken for Peter B. de Selding, "Krunichev, Salyut Rivalry Threatens Proton Marketing," *Space News*, 15-21 March 1993, 1.

52. Asker, 24; prices taken from de Selding, "Low-Cost Proton," 3; Marcia S. Smith, interview with author, 22 December 1992, Washington, DC; James Oberg, "Psst! Wanna Buy a Spaceship?" *Omni* 14 (January 1992): 12; Esther Dyson, "Just-so Stories, or Plain Tales From Russia," *Forbes*, 14 September 1992, 366; Cremins, 131; Hamilton, 1510.

53. de Selding, "Low-Cost Proton," 3.

54. David P. Hamilton, "In Space Technology, Small May Be Beautiful," *Science* 256 (12 June 1992): 1510; Craig Covault, "U.S., Europe, Japan Vie For Russian High Technology," *Aviation Week and Space Technology*, 27 January 1992, 37; Smith, "Newsmaker Forum," 22.

55. Nicholas Johnson, quoted in Hamilton, "Small May Be Beautiful," 1510.

56. Marcia S. Smith, of CRS and a veteran analyst of the Soviet space program, visited Russia in September 1992 and came away with the impression that the former Soviet program is "doing quite well, all things considered." She does acknowledge, however, that the program is not "as strong as it was five years ago" and is not sure it is possible to keep the whole thing going. See also, Smith, "Newsmaker Forum." Covault, "Russians Rejuvenate," 54, and "Russians Locked in Struggle," 57; William J. Broad, "U.S. To Cut Costs, Seeks Russian Role in Space Station," *The New York Times*, 7 April 1993, A1.

On a visit to Russia in September 1992, the author had the opportunity to visit the Central Aerohydrodynamics Institute near Moscow, where all Soviet advanced aircraft design work and wind tunnel testing took place. Among its projects was the former Soviet space shuttle, and the author was allowed to visit a large thermal/vacuum chamber in which shuttle components were tested. The facility appeared disused, and although a redesigned shuttle nose section was installed on a testing jig in the chamber, the level of dust gathered on it betrayed the fact that no work had been done on it in quite some time. An official briefed that all funds for space shuttle work at the institute had been cut off. But he did not say the project was cancelled and there was no indication they were attempting to dismantle anything. Based on this admittedly limited evidence, it would appear to the author that unlike the West, where contractors immediately dismantle a project when funding is cut off, the Russians can simply let a project go into a state of "suspended animation" until the money starts to flow again. This view is supported by a recent interview with two Russian cosmonauts undergoing training for a flight on the U.S. space shuttle. Commenting on the redesign forced upon the space station project by budget cuts, one of them said, "I think our way in this case is better. In case of economic difficulties, we just move the date of a launch, but we do not change the idea. Quoted in William Harwood, "Cosmonauts Tout Strength of Russian Space," *Space News*, 15-21 March 1993, 6.

57. Paraphrased in Andrew Lawler, "Proton Partnership Sparks Political Furor," *Space News*, 4-10 January 1993, 1.

58. K. S. Jayaraman, "US Leans on Russia to Drop Rocket Agreement," *Nature* 36/56 (30 April 1992): 732; Andrew Lawler, "U.S. Pressures Russia to End Deal with India, " *Space News*, 15-21 March 1993, 5; Covault, "Russians Rejuvenate," 59.

59. Vice President's Space Board, 20.

60. Dan Charles, "Bargain Hunters Snap Up Russian Brainpower," *New Scientist*, 14 March 1992, 13; "Iraq Reportedly Hires Rocket Scientists," *Jornal Do Brasil*, 31 July 1990, 3.

61. General Merrill A. McPeak, Chief of Staff, U.S. Air Force, "Does the Air Force Have a Mission?" speech given at Maxwell AFB, AL, 19 June 1992, printed in Reading Selections, 40th Annual National Security Forum, 31 May-4 June 1993 (Maxwell AFB, AL: Air War College, 1993), 6-14 through 6-17.

62. Early observations on the military potential of space, including references to the initial 1946 Rand study on the subject and a 1958 Resolution of the House of Representatives, cited in McLean, 4-6. See also Johnson, 8:423; Colonel Robert B. Giffen, *US Space System Survivability* (Washington, DC: NDU Press, 1982),

2; Patricia Gilmartin, "Gulf War Rekindles U.S. Debate on Protecting Space System Data," *Aviation Week and Space Technology*, 29 April 1991, 55; John M. Collins, *Military Space Forces*, (Washington, DC: Pergamon-Brassey's, 1989), 44; Alasdair McLean, *Western European Military Space Policy* (Brookfield, VT: Dartmouth Publishing Co., Ltd. [Ashgate Publishing Co. in the U.S.], 1992), 145; General Merrill A. McPeak, USAF, "Newsmaker Forum" interview, *Space News*, 15-21 February 1993, 22.

63. Quoted in John Burgess, "Satellites' Gaze Provides New Look at War," *The Washington Post*, 19 February 1991, A13.

64. McLean, *Military Utility of Space*, 22.

65. Johnson, 89.

66. James W. Canan, "A Watershed in Space," *Air Force Magazine*, August 1991, 34; LtGen Thomas S. Moorman, USAF, quoted in Canan, 34; Sheila Galatowitsch, "Squeezing the Most Out of Space," *Defense Electronics*, January 1993, 51; Patrick Seitz, "Short, Sharp Increase in Launch Activity Expected in 1995," *Space News*, 15-21 March 1993, 18.

67. Canan, 35.

68. General Robert T. Herres, USAF, "The Military's Use of Space Based Systems," *Signal*, March 1986, 47.

69. Quoted in Canan, 36.

70. McLean, *Military Utility of Space*, 15, 23; Craig Covault, "USAF Urges Greater Use of SPOT Based on Gulf War Experience," *Aviation Week and Space Technology*, 13 July 1992, 63.

71. Quoted in Covault, "USAF Urges," 63-64.

72. Quoted in Canan, 32.

73. Gilmartin, 55.

74. Quoted in "Mission Control," *Military Space* 8:5 (11 March 1991), 1.

75. Smith, *Space Activities*, 121-126, 141; Thomas G. Mahnken, "Why Third World Space Systems Matter," *Orbis*, Fall 1991, 566, 570-573; Mike Raghuvanshi, "India's Civil Space Budget Gets 14 Percent Increase," *Space News*, 15-21 March 1993, 7; Vice President's Space Board, 21.

76. Vincent Kiernan and Andrew Lawler, "Emirates Want to Buy U.S. Spy Satellites," *Space News*, 16-21 November 1992, 1; Micahel Mecham, "Gulf War Rekindles European Interest in Developing Military Satellites," *Aviation Week and Space*

Technology, 8 April 1991, 59.

77. Mahnken, 568.

78. Smith, *Space Activities*, 119.

79. Mahnken, 577.

80. Burgess, A13; "Iraqis Still Receive Weather Data From U.S. Satellites," *Aviation Week and Space Technology*, 21 January 1991, 26; McLean, *Western European Military*, 101.

81. "Genie" concept taken from Johnson, 16.

82. *National Security Strategy of the United States* (Washington, DC: The White House, 1993), 3.

83. *National Military Strategy 1992* (Washington, DC: Joint Chiefs of Staff, 1992), 4.

84. Jeff Kingwell, "The Militarization of Space," *Space Policy*, May 1990, 11; Marcia S. Smith, *Military Space Programs in a Changing Environment: Issues for the 103rd Congress*, CRS Report 92-879 SPR (Washington, DC: Library of Congress, CRS, 1992), 3.

85. Johnson, 32-33.

86. Ibid., 20-21.

87. Thomas S. Moorman, "Space: A New Strategic Frontier," *Air Power Journal* 6:1 (Spring 1992), reprinted in *Military Studies Course—MS 610*: Book 3 (Maxwell AFB, AL: Air War College, 1992), 211-215.

88. *National Security Strategy*, i.

89. James W. Canan, "Space Gets Down to Earth," *Air Force Magazine*, August 1990, 34, and "Watershed," 37.

90. Carl von Clausewitz, *On War*, ed. and trans. Michael Howard and Peter Paret (Princeton, NJ: Princeton University Press, 1976), 595-596.

91. Smith, *Space Activities*, 85, 86; H. Johnson, 155, 186; the Aspen Strategy Group, *Anti-Satellite Weapons and U.S. Military Space Policy* (Lanham, MD: University Press of America, 1986); McLean, *Military Use of Space*, 43. To get a flavor of some of these arguments, see Raymond L. Garthoff, "ASAT Arms Control: Still Possible," *Bulletin of the Atomic Scientists*, August/September 1984, 29-34; James Oberg, "A Dozen ASAT Fallacies," *Air Force Magazine*, July 1985, 79-81; Paul B. Stares, "Deja vu: The ASAT Debate in Historical Context," *Arms Control Today* 13:11 (December 1983): 2-3; Kosta Tsipis and Eric Raiten, "Antisatellite Weapons: The Present Danger," *Technology Review*,

August/September 1984, 54-63.

92. A particularly succinct and eloquent work is Colonel Robert B. Giffen, USAF, *US Space System Survivability* (Washington, DC: NDU Press, 1982).

93. *National Security Strategy*, 4.

94. John L. Piotrowski, "A Critical Juncture," *The Officer,* September 1989, 24.

95. Report that a hostile Middle East state directed radio interference at a U.S. satellite contained in James T. Hackett and Robin Ranger, "Proliferating Satellites Drive U.S. ASAT Need," *Signal*, May 1990, 156, cited in Thomas G. Mahnken, "Why Third World Space Systems Matter, *Orbis,* Fall, 1991, 576.

96. David J. Lynch, "Toward a New Launcher Lineup," *Air Force Magazine,* January 1993, 48-51; Moorman, 211-215; John M. Logsdon and Ray A. Williams, "U.S. Access to Space," *Scientific American* 260:3 (March 1989): 34-40; Neff Hudson, "Launch Delays Haunt Space Command," *Air Force Times,* 4 January 1993, 38.

97. Moorman, 215.

98. U.S. Department of the Air Force, Office of the General Counsel, letter, 3 February 1992, reprinted in Space and Future Warfare—WS 633 (Maxwell AFB, AL: Air War College, 1992), 59-60; *AU-18, Space Handbook* (Maxwell AFB, AL: Air University Press, 1985), reprinted in course materials for a 1993 Advanced Elective course at Air War College, "Space Issues," 126.

THE EDITOR

Captain John N. Petrie, USN, Director of Research and a Professor of National Security Policy at the National War College, has spent his career in destroyers and is en route to major command at sea. Ashore his assignments have included duty on the Joint Staff and special assignments with State Department and National Security Council teams. Captain Petrie is a Distinguished Graduate of the Naval War College where he served as a Research Associate. He completed Senior Service College at the National War College where he was a Senior Research Fellow. He holds an AB from Villanova University and the MALD and Ph.D. degrees from the Fletcher School of Law and Diplomacy. His previous work has been published by the U.S. Naval Institute, *Naval War College Review*, and *Fletcher Forum*.

☆ U.S. GOVERNMENT PRINTING OFFICE:1994-301-304/00006